MODERNIZING U.S. SECURITIES REGULATION

Economic and Legal Perspectives

MODERNIZING U.S. SECURITIES REGULATION

Economic and Legal Perspectives

Edited by

Kenneth Lehn
and
Robert W. Kamphuis, Jr.

IRWIN
Professional Publishing
Burr Ridge, Illinois
New York, New York

This symbol indicates that the paper in this book is made of recycled paper. Its fiber content exceeds the recommended minimum of 50% waste paper fibers as specified by the EPA.

ISBN: 1-55623-777-4

Printed in the United States of America.

1 2 3 4 5 6 7 8 9 0 DOC 0 9 8 7 6 5 4 3

PREFACE

New developments in securities markets are challenging the Securities and Exchange Commission (SEC) to reconsider some of the basic premises underlying its regulation of these markets. In particular, the growing importance of institutional investors, rapid changes in technology, the proliferation of hybrid financial products, the increased significance of intermarket linkages, and the expanding role of foreign securities markets have created new puzzles and problems for securities regulators. The SEC's policy response to these and other developments has important implications for the cost of raising capital in the United States and, more broadly, for the international competitiveness of U.S. firms.

In addition to creating new challenges for the SEC, the dramatic changes in the operation of U.S. securities markets has spawned a large amount of interrelated scholarly research in economics, finance, accounting, and law. Hundreds of articles have been published in academic journals on a variety of SEC-related topics, including corporate governance, insider trading, the stock market crash of 1987, hostile takeovers and leveraged buyouts, executive compensation, market value accounting, mutual fund performance, and so forth. Unlike the 1930s, when the foundation of U.S. securities law was formed, a large body of empirically oriented scholarship now exists that can assist the SEC in its policy deliberations.

The growth and increasing practical significance of academic research on securities markets can be traced to several major intellectual breakthroughs. Among these are seminal works by several Nobel laureates, including five that are especially prominent.

First, Ronald Coase's pioneering work on transaction costs has inspired bodies of literature on *the modern theory of the firm* and *law and economics*. The modern theory of the firm, which views firms as networks of contracts between different claimants (e.g., stockholders, debtholders, employees, and so forth), is relevant for understanding regulatory issues concerning corporate takeovers, corporate governance, the organization of exchanges, executive compensation, and the economic function of accounting rules. The law and economics literature, which examines how different assignments of property rights and liability rules affect resource allocation, is relevant for issues such as auditor liability, the rights of bondholders versus stockholders in spinoffs and leveraged buyouts, and appropriate liability standards in securities litigation.

Second, George Stigler's seminal work on *the economics of information* has led to a large body of literature on factors that affect the demand for and the supply of information. The literature is germane for understanding the efficacy of SEC disclosure rules, since these rules presuppose that an unregulated securities market results in "too little" and "too fraudulent" corporate disclosure. The information-economics literature recognizes that, although information has attributes of a public good, which strengthens the case for mandated disclosure, it also is costly to produce, which makes it desirable to give producers of information private property rights to their information (in order to encourage the production of information). This literature also provides a framework for understanding the pricing of initial public offerings, the stock price effects of secondary securities offerings, the desirability of transparency in securities markets, and the effects of insider trading on the liquidity of securities markets.

Third, Franco Modigliani and Merton Miller's classic *theory of capital structure* provides the area of corporate finance with a strong theoretical underpinning that had been lacking prior to their work. Modigliani and Miller show the conditions under which capital structure decisions affect the values of firms. This theory provides a framework for understanding a variety of SEC-related issues in the area of corporate finance, including the economics of junk bonds, sources of shareholder gains in leveraged buyouts and leveraged recapitalizations, corporate voting rights and dual-class recapitalizations, and the effects of bankruptcy costs on capital structure.

Fourth, Harry Markowitz's development of *portfolio theory* and William Sharpe's contributions (along with those of Jack Treynor and John Lintner) to the development of the *capital asset pricing model* have revolutionized the field of securities valuation. Markowitz was the first to model explicitly the effect of diversification on portfolio risk, and Sharpe was among the first to develop the implications of portfolio theory for the pricing of securities. An understanding of securities pricing is of obvious importance for most issues in securities regulation. In particular, capital asset pricing models are especially useful for measuring materiality and damages in SEC enforcement cases and mutual fund performance for purposes of investment management regulation. Modern portfolio theory also provides a framework for understanding why portfolio managers value derivative stock indexes, which have been viewed with skepticism by the SEC in recent years.

Fifth, James Buchanan's development of *public choice theory* (with Gordon Tullock) and George Stigler's *economic theory of regulation* show that many public policies can be explained by applying the economic model of rational self-interest to politicians and public sector employees. Rather than viewing agencies like the SEC as promoters of the "public interest," the literature examines the incentives of agencies to redistribute wealth from less organized to more organized political interest groups. The literature recognizes that market failures are not sufficient to rationalize regulation, since regulation also may fail to promote overall welfare.

In addition to the contributions of these Nobel laureates, numerous other scholarly breakthroughs in recent years have important implications for SEC policy. Most prominently, the *efficient markets hypothesis* provides an essential framework for developing sensible securities regulation. The semistrong version of this hypothesis, which is almost universally accepted by scholars in financial economics, states that securities prices reflect all publicly available information and that these prices rapidly absorb new information. This observation has important implications for both optimal disclosure policy and the estimation of disgorgement penalties in securities fraud enforcement cases.

An understanding of *option pricing models* would assist the SEC in its development of broker-dealer capital requirements, its regulation of derivative securities, and its disclosure rules concerning executive stock options. *Agency theory* contains important insights for regulatory issues concerning corporate governance and corporate control. The growing body of literature on the *microstructure of securities markets* provides insights on how rules governing exchanges and NASDAQ affect the liquidity and efficiency of these markets. The *positive theory of accounting* has important implications for understanding the efficiency consequences of alternative accounting standards.

This book contains 39 essays on a variety of SEC-policy issues that illustrate how advances in economics, finance, accounting, and law can be used to analyze the thorny policy issues that will challenge the next SEC. The authors of these essays include leading contributors to the burgeoning body of academic literature on securities markets. Virtually all of the essays reflect the scholarly innovations mentioned above.

The book begins with two essays by former SEC Commissioners that suggest how the SEC could improve its *modus operandi*. These are followed by essays on specific topics in the areas of accounting, disclosure, corporate control and governance, market structure and performance, and mutual funds. Although the essays contain many policy recommendations for the SEC, the primary purpose of this collection is to illustrate how scholarly research can help the SEC frame issues and establish objective criteria for evaluating the efficacy of different policies.

Kenneth Lehn
University of Pittsburgh

Robert W. Kamphuis, Jr.
Virginia Tech

ACKNOWLEDGMENTS

This project was conceived in late September 1992 in conversations with Robert Mackay of Virginia Tech. Mackay and Kamphula had undertaken a similar project focussed on the futures industry, and the core idea was to extend the approach to the broader array of securities market issues.

The editors thank the authors, who worked quickly and efficiently to enable us to move forward on an aggressive timetable. Thanks to their efforts we were able to disseminate a preliminary "working paper" version of the full manuscript already in December 1992. This was done to promote discussion of the issues during the transition from the Bush to the Clinton Administrations. We are grateful for the generous and positive reception accorded to this work.

Maureen Jenkins in the early stages of the project and Helen Breems in the later parts were primarily responsible for keeping things moving. We also thank Audrey Kilmann, Joan Ballas, Barb Turba, and Linda Wilson for their assistance, Bill Johnston who provided the cover for the working version of the manuscript, and Vidhan Goyal who provided valuable editorial assistance.

We wish to thank our publisher, Richard D. Irwin, and especially Ralph Rieves, for interest, support and patience. We are also grateful to Don Chew, editor *The Journal of Applied Corporate Finance*, which published several of these papers in the Winter 1993 issue.

Dean H. J. Zoffer of the Katz Graduate School of Business has been supportive and encouraging at every step in this project and of other projects sponsored by the Center for Research on Contracts and the Structure of Enterprise. We thank him for this support.

And, of course, we wish to thank the donors to the Center for Research on Contracts and the Structure of Enterprise who made this project possible: the Sarah Scaife Foundation and its president, Richard M. Larry; and the Lynde and Harry Bradley Foundation and its president, Michael S. Joyce; and the New York Stock Exchange.

CONTENTS

CONTRIBUTORS

Yakov Amihud, Professor of Finance, Stern School of Business, New York University

Vaughn S. Armstrong, Attorney at Law, and Economist, Economic Analysis Corporation

William J. Baumol, Director, C. F. Starr Center for Applied Economics, New York University

Lawrence E. Benveniste, Associate Professor of Finance, Carroll School of Management, Boston College

Bernard S. Black, Professor of Law, Columbia University School of Law

Michael Bradley, Everett E. Berg Professor of Business Administration, School of Business Administration, University of Michigan

Corinne M. Bronfman, University of Arizona

Andrew A. Christie, Associate Professor, William E. Simon Graduate School of Business Administration, University of Rochester

John C. Coffee, Jr., Adolf A. Berle Professor of Law, Columbia University School of Law

Jeffry Davis, Deputy Chief Economist, Office of Economic Analysis, Securities and Exchange Commission

Franklin R. Edwards, Arthur F. Burns Professor of Economics and Finance, Columbia University Business School

Edward H. Fleischman, Rosenman & Colin

Dean Furbush, Special Consultant, Economists Incorporated

Ronald J. Gilson, Professor of Law, Columbia University Law School

Victor P. Goldberg, Thomas Macioce Professor of Law and Co-Director of the Center for Law & Economic Studies

Joseph A. Grundfest, Associate Professor of Law, Stanford Law School and National Fellow, The Hoover Institution

Lawrence Harris, Professor of Finance and Business Economics, School of Business Administration, University of Southern California

Gregg A. Jarrell, Professor of Finance and Business Administration and Director, Bradley Policy Research Center, William E. Simon Graduate School of Business Administration, University of Rochester

D. Bruce Johnsen, Ken Ruby Term Assistant Professor of Legal Studies, Wharton School of Business, University of Pennsylvania

Yash P. Joshi, Assistant Professor of Finance, School of Business Administration

Robert W. Kamphuis, Jr., Associate Director, Center for the Study of Futures and Options Markets, R. B. Pamplin College of Business, Virginia Tech, and Principal, Financial Markets International, Inc.

Allan W. Kleidon, Professor of Finance, Graduate School of Business, Stanford University

Kenneth Lehn, Professor of Business Administration and Director, Center for Research on Contracts and the Structure of Enterprise, Joseph M. Katz Graduate School of Business, University of Pittsburgh

Anil K. Makhija, Associate Professor of Business Administration, Katz Graduate School of Business, University of Pittsburgh

Burton G. Malkiel, Chemical Bank Chairman's Professor of Economics, Department of Economics, Princeton University

M. Wayne Marr, First Union Professor of Finance, Clemson University

Henry McMillan, Director, Asset/Liability Management, Transamerica Occidental Life Insurance

Haim Mendelson, Professor of Business Administration, Graduate School of Business, Stanford University

J. Harold Mulherin, Visiting Associate Professor, Tuck School of Business, Dartmouth College

Robert Nachtmann, Associate Professor of Business Administration, Joseph M. Katz Graduate School of Business, University of Pittsburgh

Robert Neal, Visiting Economist at the SEC, Assistant Professor of Finance at the University of Washington

Jeffry Netter, Associate Professor of Finance and Adjunct Professor of Law, University of Georgia

Stephen Craig Pirrong, School of Business Administration, University of Michigan

John Pound, Associate Professor of Public Policy and Director of the Corporate Voting Research Project, Kennedy School of Government, Harvard University

Mark J. Roe, Professor of Law, Columbia University Law School

Michael Ryngaert, Assistant Professor of Finance, School of Business, University of Florida

Robert A. Schwartz, Professor of Finance and Economics and Yamaichi Faculty Fellow, Stern School of Business, New York University

James E. Shapiro, Managing Director, Research & Planning Division, New York Stock Exchange

Clifford W. Smith, Jr., Clarey Professor of Finance, William E. Simon Graduate School of Business Administration, University of Rochester

Richard L. Smith, Professor of Finance, Department of Finance, College of Business, Arizona State University

Hans R. Stoll, Anne Marie and Thomas B. Walker Professor of Finance, and Director of the Financial Markets Research Center, Owen School of Management, Vanderbilt University

Ross L. Watts, The Rochester Telephone Corporation Professor and Professor of Accounting and Finance, William E. Simon Graduate School of Business Administration

Lawrence J. White, Arthur E. Imperatore Professor of Economics, Stern School of Business, New York University

I

THE VIEW FROM TWO FORMER COMMISSIONERS

1

Zen and the Art of Securities Regulation

Joseph A. Grundfest
Stanford University

Although the future is impossible to predict, regulations promulgated by the United States Securities and Exchange Commission (SEC) comfort us that corporations can identify "known trends . . . [or] uncertainties" that have material implications for the future of an enterprise.[1] It stands to reason that if the business community can be called upon to discuss the implications of known trends or uncertainties, the same standard might profitably be applied to the work of the Commission itself.

Even a casual review of currently known trends and uncertainties in the world's financial markets reveals a hornet's nest of challenges that have profound implications for the Commission's intellectual "capital resources"[2] and its practical "results of operations."[3] Accordingly, as Administrations change, and as the SEC is about to take a fresh look to the future, it is an opportune time to take stock of these challenges and to consider their implications for the United States' capital markets, as well as for the future of the Commission itself.

The initial temptation is to view these challenges in an issue-specific manner. This approach leads to a rather precise series of concerns. For example: How will the enforcement program adapt to compliance problems raised by the increased volume of international transactions in U.S. markets? How will the agency respond to the burgeoning over-the-counter derivatives market? How will the agency respond to the evolution of proprietary trading mechanisms? The list of questions verges on the infinite and, although each

---

[1] Item 303, Management's Discussion and Analysis of Finanacial Condition and Results of Operations, 17 C.F.R. Section 229.303 (1992).

[2] 17 C.F.R. Section 229.303 (a) (2) (1992).

[3] 17 C.F.R. Section 229.303 (a) (3) (1992).

inquiry may have great merit in its own right, this issue-specific approach masks a far more profound crisis that is certain to challenge the Commission in the coming years.

This more profound crisis is ideological. Known trends and uncertainties already indicate that the agency's traditional approach to promulgating rules and regulations is unlikely to survive in the face of predictable market challenges. For decades, the SEC has publicly based its decisions on an amorphous blend of fairness, efficiency, transparency, and public interest considerations. Moreover, because the Commission has wielded extraordinary market power over U.S.-based issuers and investors as well as over foreigners who wanted access to U.S.-based sources of capital and liquidity, the Commission has had great latitude in exercising its regulatory discretion.

Historically, issuers and investors who objected to SEC regulations could not find non-SEC-regulated substitute markets at reasonable cost. As a result, the Commission was able to fashion regulations without excessive concern for the market's likely response. Regulators were thus largely freed of any market test, and they could seek to implement a wide range of regulatory ideologies without concern that their decisions would diminish the size of the markets under their direct jurisdiction and control.

Put another way, if U.S.-market participants did not like SEC regulations, that was just too bad because there was no other market to which they could practically turn. U.S.-market participants therefore had to play by the SEC's rules or not play at all.

That world no longer exists. Market participants who do not like SEC regulations today have practical substitutes for transactions that would otherwise be subject to SEC jurisdiction. As a result of this new market reality, the agency will be forced to search for novel regulatory paradigms that accommodate rapidly evolving forms of substitution and can pass the market test posed by an ever-changing, technologically sophisticated, highly internationalized, and increasingly institutionalized trading environment. The likely result of these known trends and uncertainties will be the evolution of a new ideology of regulation that is more sensitive to emerging market realities.

Identifying Known Trends and Uncertainties

The known trends and uncertainties that spell doom for the SEC's traditional modes of analysis can be divided into four categories, each of which feeds upon and reinforces the others. The underlying theme connecting these trends is that each promotes a new form of substitution whereby issuers or investors dissatisfied with SEC regulation can exercise a form of self-help to avoid regulatory constraints that would otherwise be imposed by agency action.

The first known trend or uncertainty relates to technological progress in the fields of computer science and telecommunications. Technological progress in this area has already revolutionized the world's financial markets. As the pace of technology speeds up, the implications for capital markets will become even more pronounced. Technology has already made possible computerized markets that instantaneously link traders irrespective of their physical location or institutional affiliation, as in the GLOBEX market.[4] Technology also makes possible the use of novel forms of market-clearing mechanisms, such as the large-scale single price auctions conducted by the new and fully computerized Arizona Stock Exchange.[5] In the future, new market entrants will continue to find ways to leapfrog existing market structures and regulatory constraints by introducing services that take advantage of the latest technological developments. Therefore, unless market systems and regulators alike are willing to reinvent themselves to anticipate and respond to technology's new challenges, the process of technological change will inevitably force a series of regulatory crises in U.S. securities markets. Indeed, the fact that some exchanges have rules specifically designed to impede the flow of technology in order to preserve existing market structures only underscores the markets' and regulators' current vulnerability to technological progress.[6]

---

[4] For a recent description of the GLOBEX market see Division of Trading and Markets, Commodity Futures Trading Commission, *Chicago Mercantile Exchange Proposed GLOBEX Trading System* (1989); Jeffrey Taylor, "Futures Firms Banking on Globex Debut," *Wall Street Journal*, June 24, 1992, C1; Thomas McCarroll, "Futures Shock," *Time*, June 29, 1992, 693.

[5] The Arizona Stock Exchange, which first came into being as a single-price-auction network known as SPAworks, is described in Wunsch Auction System, Inc., SEC No-Action Letter, [1990-1991 Transfer Binder] Fed. Sec. L. Rep. (CCH) Paragraph 79,662 at 78,031 (feb. 28, 1991); Thomas McCarroll, "Bidding Their Brokers Goodbye," *Time*, May 13, 1991, at 46. See generally, Ivy Schnerker, "Wall Street's Quiet Revolution," *Wall Street Technology*, June 1992, 25.

[6] The New York Stock Exchange, for example, prohibits the use of cellular telephones or other wireless devices for communications between NYSE members on the exchange floor and nonmembers located off the floor. New York Stock Exchange Rule 38.20, New York Stock Exchange Guide (CCH) Paragraph 2036.20 (1988). *See also* Order Approving Rule Exchange, Exchange Act Release No. 25842, 53 Fed. Reg. 24539

Closely related to technological progress in its traditional sense is progress in the technology of finance. Market practitioners and scholars continue to develop and refine new financial instruments and trading techniques. These innovations often challenge the legal system's need to pigeonhole instruments into fundamentally empty categories such as "debt" or "equity," or to define an instrument as a "security" or as a "futures contract." Similarly, the evolution of new trading techniques, such as those used in the over-the-counter derivatives markets, can easily frustrate efforts to impose regulatory constraints by opening new channels for capital flows that fail to fit traditional definitions and constraints.[7]

Internationalization presents a third known trend that unsettles assumptions on which much of the SEC's preexisting regulatory structure is based. Issuers and investors who are unhappy with the regulatory environment in their host-country market can often shift their business to foreign jurisdictions at relatively low cost. The ease with which capital now flows across national borders rekindles the debate over regulatory competition and gives new life to the concern regarding an international "race to the bottom" in the market for securities regulation. Whether this concern is warranted or not, it has certainly stimulated interest in the international harmonization of regulatory standards and emphasizes the tenuous grasp that regulators often have over certain market transactions.[8]

The rise of institutional investors presents the fourth known trend certain to challenge the evolution of U.S. securities laws. U.S. securities regulation often rests on the paradigm of a small, individual investor who needs to be protected and informed according to regulatorily prescribed formulas. Indeed, disclosure requirements and trading rules are generally constructed with the interests of the prototypical retail investor in mind, and any deviation from this norm is most often fashioned as an exception to a general rule.

The reality of the matter, however, is that institutions now hold more than half the value of publicly traded U.S. equity and account for more than

---

(1988).

[7] *See,* e.g., Grundfest, "The Limited Future of Unlimited Liability: A Capital Markets Perspective," *Yale Law Journal* 102 (1992), 387.

[8] For a discussion of recent data describing the pace of internationalization and its implications for U.S. securities regulators *see* Grundfest, "Internationalization of the World's Securities Market: Economic Causes and Regulatory Consequences," *Journal of Financial Services Research* 4 (1990), 349.

70 percent of the volume of U.S.-traded equities.[9] Other financial markets, such as those for over-the-counter derivatives, are exclusively or almost entirely institutional. In many situations, the practical significance of the exceptions now overwhelm the market impact of the rules. The Commission must therefore be sensitive to the danger that rules and regulations that might be quite attractive in markets dominated by retail investors can lead to substantial inefficiencies and distortions in markets composed of sophisticated institutional investors.

Needless to say, any suggestion that a regulation might be modified in a way that diminishes the protections afforded to individual investors in order to serve the interests of institutional investors, raises profound political difficulties. On the other hand, any failure to recognize the changing composition of the U.S. investor population provides institutions with a powerful incentive to search for more congenial markets that are not subject to institutionally troublesome constraints. Those markets may well be abroad.

Taken together, technological progress, financial innovation, internationalization, and institutionalization can dramatically reduce the Commission's ability to force issuers and investors to play by the SEC's rules. As a consequence, the agency will be forced to consider more carefully the market implications of new rules that it proposes to adopt, as well as the implications of existing rules that it retains on the books.

Toward a New Ideology

The net result of these known trends and uncertainties will be a Securities and Exchange Commission that is unavoidably more sensitive to the market implications of its regulatory decisions. Decisions that impose private costs in excess of private benefits are more likely to provoke substitution by institutional participants who are able to draw upon the new flexibility provided by the forces of technology and internationalization. Thus, unless the SEC is willing to see markets under its jurisdiction shrink in size and importance, the Commission will have to pay far more attention to economics than ever before—whether it wants to or not.

---

[9] Columbia Institutional Investor Project, Center for Law and Economics Studies, Columbia University School of Law, *Institutional Investors and Capital Markets: 1991 Update* 7 (1991); *The GT Guide to World Equity Markets*, Allen & O'Connor, eds. (1992), 523.

As a consequence of this new market reality, the agency will also find itself constrained in its ability to implement ideological objectives that are inconsistent with least-cost market performance. Therefore, if a rule subsidizes some market participants at the expense of others, the Commission's ability to engage in that cross-subsidization, worthy as it may or may not be, will be limited by market forces. Similarly, if a rule imposes private costs in excesses of its private benefits, market participants will again have an incentive to invoke "known trends and uncertainties" in the market to work around the rule's costs. To some observers this development is cause for celebration because they view the SEC as primarily imposing costs on a market that would function better without the Commission's involvement. To other observers this development is cause for concern because they view the SEC as primarily adopting rules that resolve market failures or that promote socially desirable wealth transfers. But regardless of which camp has the better of the argument, the unavoidable reality is that regulators will not have as much liberty operating in this new environment because they will not be as free to pursue their own visions of the public good. They will, instead, have to spend far more time and energy analyzing the economic realities of the markets they regulate and studying the constraints that those realities place on their regulatory discretion.

Intriguingly, however, as the agency is forced to turn toward economic analysis in its effort to define a new ideology, it will often find that economic analysis yields ambiguous or inconclusive results. The natural temptation under those circumstances will be to resolve the ambiguity by resorting to ideological values of a sort that guided the agency in the past. Though this sort of regulatory response is certainly likely, and perhaps even inevitable, it is important to recognize that there is another path open to the agency that may deserve far more attention than it has received to date.

The Value of Experimentation

Regulations adopted by the SEC are often based on acts of faith more than on the exercise of reason. The cost-benefit analyses included in many adopting releases are, at bottom, nothing more than extended ipse dixits that argue that, if the Commission is willing to adopt a rule, then the rule's benefits must of course exceed the rule's costs because otherwise the Commission would not adopt the rule. But regulations need not be adopted on such slender a reed because, in at least some situations, it is possible for the agency to experiment with various regulatory structures to determine the relative costs and benefits of different regulatory regimes.

Consider, for example, the information that might be gained by an experimentalist approach to the hundreds of disclosure requirements that now inhabit SEC rule books. Suppose some of those requirements were, on a temporary and experimental basis, rescinded for some registrants but not for others. If no adverse consequences are observed, then might it not be prudent to pare down some of these requirements? By the same token, before the agency imposes a new disclosure requirement on all registrants, might it not be prudent to test that requirement on an appropriately selected subsample of registrants? If the rule generates the anticipated benefits, then it might be profitably extended to other registrants. If the rule fails, then perhaps it is time to go back to the drawing board.

Similar experiments can be structured in the area of market regulation: What would happen if payment for order flow was prohibited for some securities but not for others? What if soft dollar arrangements were prohibited for some securities transactions but not others? The list is easily extended to other market practices and to rules governing investment companies, the enforcement program, and other aspects of the agency's work.

The recent decision by the Department of the Treasury to engage in a yearlong experiment with the use of a new auction technique for the sale of U.S. Treasury securities is a notable demonstration of the value of experimentation in financial regulation. Historically, the Treasury awarded securities at auction to bidders who offered to accept the lowest yields and discriminated among bidders by charging the specific price bid by each bidder at the auction—not the single price that cleared the market. Two purchasers of Treasury notes at the same auction might therefore pay different prices for the identical instrument.

In the wake of the Salomon Brothers' scandal, concerns were raised that this bidding mechanism gave rise to incentives for collusion. There were also concerns that, in order to avoid a winner's curse, bidders were not bidding as aggressively as they might in a single-price auction system. If either of these concerns is valid, then the Treasury's current auction system does not help fund the national debt at the lowest possible cost to the taxpayer.

In response to these concerns, the Treasury decided to conduct a yearlong experiment with a single-price auction system for two-year and five-year notes, while selling all other maturities under the preexisting auction rules. At the end of the experiment the Treasury will be able to compare prices bid under the single-price system with those bid under the discriminatory auction rule to determine which system helps fund the deficit at least cost.[10]

The significance of this development for present purposes has nothing to do with the mechanics of funding the national debt. Rather, its import is that it demonstrates the feasibility of an experimentalist approach toward the regulation of financial markets. Indeed, even the most sophisticated and refined scientific minds understand that truth cannot always be revealed through acts of collective introspection. There is a role in life for experimentalists. Physicists slam subatomic particles against each other to learn what happens. Biologists test new substances to learn if they might be cures for diseases. Is there not a sense of regulatory hubris in the suggestion that experimental approaches might be useful for physicists, biologists, and other hard scientists, or for the conduct of Treasury auctions, but that experiments have no role to play in the evolution of securities regulation?

The Value of Regulatory Diversity

As markets become more complex and internationalized the Commission may also recognize that different rules are appropriate for different market participants. The adoption of Rule 144A[11] and of Regulation S[12] already constitute significant steps in this direction because each of those innovations is based on the recognition that not all market participants benefit from the same level of regulatory intervention. Greater progress along this trajectory may, however, be necessary if the Commission is to adapt successfully to emerging market challenges.

To the extent that regulation can add value by resolving collective action problems or by ameliorating the adverse consequences of certain externalities, it does not follow that all market participants suffer from market failures to the same degree or that they benefit equally from the same form of regulatory intervention. To the contrary, as markets become more heterogeneous the optimal quality mix of U.S. regulatory initiatives may also

---

[10] *See* generally, Fuerbringer, "New Process for Auctions to be Tested," *New York Times*, Sept. 4, 1992, D1.

[11] Private Resales of Securities to Institutions, 17 C.F.R. Section 144A (1992).

[12] Regulation S - Rules Governing Offers and Sales Made Outside the United States Without Registration under the Securities Act of 1932, 17 C.F.R. Sections 230.901-230.904 (1992).

become more diverse. The SEC may therefore be better able to promote the public interest by adopting a range of regulatory standards to which different transactions and transactors can be assigned—or, perhaps better yet, from which transactors may choose. Such a "menu" approach to regulatory standards may prove far more robust to the dynamic challenges of the world's evolving securities markets than an inflexible regime that relies more on a "one-size-fits-all" strategy.

How to Decide

Whether the solution to these problems lies in experimentalist approaches or in greater regulatory variation is not, however, the central issue. The central issue is whether the SEC will be able to evolve in its conceptualization of the regulatory process to adjust to inevitable changes in the markets that it is charged to regulate.

Hence the title of this essay. It is almost twenty years since *Zen and the Art of Motorcycle Maintenance* appeared in print.[13] The novel was hailed as a classic tour de force[14] that, by its author's admission, had precious little to do with religion and that "was not very factual on motorcycles either."[15] The book was, instead, about the process of knowledge and the bitter internal battles that might be fought in search of meaning and comprehension.

This essay has nothing to say on Zen. It is also totally devoid of insight about motorcycles. It may not be very factual on securities regulation either. But it is to some extent about the search for knowledge, and it does describe the battles that the SEC is likely to fight as old paradigms fall by the wayside.

This battle over methodology will, in many respects, be the most significant, if subtle, challenge to confront the SEC in the coming years. The extent to which the Commission is willing to embrace new regulatory strategies may be the most important factor in determining its success in confronting inevitable and profound new challenges in U.S. securities markets. Whether the Commission succeeds or fails in this mission may therefore depend much more on how it thinks about markets and on the

---

[13] Pirsig, *Zen and the Art of Motorcycle Maintenance* (1974).

[14] *See*, e.g., Lehmann-Haupt, "The Motorcycles of Your Mind," *New York Times*, Apr. 16, 1974, 37; Lehamon, "A Fine Fiction," *New Republic*, June 29, 1974, 24; Todd, "Praise God From Whom All Ball Bearings Flow," *Atlantic*, Sept. 1974, 92.

[15] Pirsig, supra note 13, Author's Note.

evolution of a new regulatory philosophy than on the resolution of any specific regulatory issues, as important as any of these issues may undoubtedly be.

References and Suggested Readings

Allen, Stuart, and Selina O'Connor, eds. 1992. *The GT Guide to World Equity Markets.*

Columbia Institutional Investor Project. Center for Law and Economic Studies at Columbia University School of Law. 1991. *Institutional Investors and Capital Markets: 1991 Update 7.* New York: Columbia University School of Law.

Fuerbringer, Jonathan. 1992. "New Process for Auctions to Be Tested." *New York Times*, Sept. 4, D1.

Grundfest, Joseph A. 1990. "Internationalization of the World's Securities Market: Economic Causes and Regulatory Consequences." *Journal of Financial Services Research* 4: no. 4 (Dec.): 349.

——. 1992. "The Limited Future of Unlimited Liability: A Capital Markets Perspective." *Yale Law Review* 102:387.

Lehamon, W.T., Jr. 1974. "A Fine Fiction." *New Republic*, June 29, 24.

Lehmann-Haupt, Christopher. 1974. "The Motorcycles of Your Mind." *New York Times*, Apr. 16, 37.

McCarroll, Thomas. 1991. "Bidding Their Brokers Goodbye." *Time*, May 13, 46.

——. 1992. "Futures Shock." *Time*, June 29, 693.

New York Stock Exchange. 1988. *New York Stock Exchange Guide.* (Commerce Clearing House.) New York: New York Stock Exchange.

Pirsig, Robert M. 1974. *Zen and the Art of Motorcycle Maintenance.*

Scherker, Ivy. 1992. "Wall Street's Quiet Revolution. *Wall Street Technology* (June): 25.

Taylor, Jeffrey. 1992. "Futures Firms Banking on GLOBEX Debut." *Wall Street Journal*, June 24, C1.

Todd, Richard. 1974. "Praise God from Whom All Ball Bearings Flow." *Atlantic* (Sept.): 92.

U.S. Commodity Futures Trading Commission. Division of Trading and Markets. 1989. *Chicago Mercantile Exchange Proposed GLOBEX Trading System*. Washington, D.C.: U.S. Government Printing Office.

U.S. Securities and Exchange Commission. 1992a. *Management's Discussion and Analysis of Financial Condition and Results of Operations*. 17. C.F.R., Sect. 229.303.

——. 1992b. *Private Resales of Securities to Institutions*. 17 C.F.R., Sect. 144A.

——. 1992c. *Regulation S: Rules Governing Offers and Sales Made Outside the United States Without Registration Under the Securities Act of 1932*. 17 C.F.R., Sects. 230.901–230.904.

Wunsch Auction System Inc. 1991. SEC No-Action Letter [1990–1991 Transfer Binder] Fed. Sec. L. Rep. (Commerce Clearing House), Feb. 28.

2

Dear Mr. President...

Edward H. Fleischman
Rosenman and Colin

Editors' Note: Mr. Fleischman served as a Commissioner at the SEC during 1986–1992. Before leaving the Commission, Mr. Fleischman wrote a letter to President Bush, which described how the SEC could achieve the president's stated goal of less burdensome regulation. The following essay is excerpted from Mr. Fleischman's letter. With Mr. Fleischman's permission, we modified the letter slightly to conform with the style of this publication.

In January 1992 the president requested that the SEC

> (1) identify each of the agency's regulations and programs that impose a substantial cost on the economy and (2) determine whether each such regulation or program adheres to the following standards:
>
> (a)The expected benefits to society of any regulation should clearly outweigh the expected costs it imposes on society.
>
> (b)Regulations should be fashioned to maximize net benefits to society.
>
> (c)To the maximum extent possible, regulatory agencies should set performance standards instead of prescriptive command-and-control requirements, thereby allowing the regulated community to achieve regulatory goals at the lowest possible cost.
>
> (d)Regulation should incorporate market mechanisms to the maximum extent possible.
>
> (e)Regulations should provide clarity and certainty to the regulated community and should be designed to avoid needless litigation.

A serious and faithful response to this request would turn the course of the SEC's regulatory approach nearly 180 degrees. For example, the Commission regularly describes performance standards as "not consistent" or "inadequate" or "not possible", and therefore regularly imposes command-and-control requirements. Further, the Chairman of the SEC spoke proudly and publicly in December 1991 of the fact that since mid-October 1989 the Commission had approved 57 new rules in either proposed or final form; I have not traced all 57 actions, but I do not believe that more than a small fraction of those new rules were exemptive in substance. Nevertheless, I do believe that, if motivated *toward* compliance with the president's request, analysis of this agency's regulations and programs would in fact demonstrate how the course of the agency's regulatory approach *can* be turned.

For clarity of presentation, I shall divide the remainder of this paper into the following sections:

1. The Commission's "Mission"
2. The Use of Rulemaking for Exemptive Purposes
3. The Consideration of Costs versus Benefits in Rulemaking
4. The Use of Performance Standards in Rulemaking
5. The Use of Market Mechanisms
6. The Concern over Clarity and Certainty
7. Rulemaking by Official and Unofficial Interpretation
8. The Interplay of Rulemaking and Adjudication
9. An Overview of the Commission's Rulebook
10. A List of Additional Proposed Rule Revisions
11. The Balance of Rulemaking and Prosecutorial Enforcement
12. Conclusion

1. The Commission's "Mission"

The Securities and Exchange Commission has historically been understood to be, principally and foremost, an agency directed to the elicitation of disclosure for the benefit of investors. It is true that certain statutes administered by the Commission, particularly the Public Utility Holding Company Act and the Investment Company Act, contemplate a regulatory role for the agency that envelops the regulated entities in substantive federal oversight and review, and it is true that discrete portions of the Securities Exchange Act contemplate a similar role with respect to certain activities of regulated exchanges, securities association, broker-dealers, transfer agents, information processors, and clearing agencies. But the task of "establishing and requiring adherence to standards of business and financial disclosure and procedural standards in the solicitations of proxies" remains the primary task within the Commission's general statutory standard of "the public interest and the protection of investors," only followed by the tasks of regulatory administration over the securities markets and over the more fully regulated entities that I enumerated above.

The emphasis on disclosure even in the realm of investor suffrage is clear from the Commission's own statement of its statutory authority and statutory functions in the first two rules of Subpart A of the very first part of the Commission's chapter in the *Code of Federal Regulations*. For example:

> This [Securities Exchange] Act makes unlawful solicitations of proxies, authorizations or consents from holders of listed securities in contravention of rules prescribed by the Commission. These rules provide for disclosures to securities holders of information relevant to the matters which are the subject of solicitations.

Nowhere in these two rules, except in the context of investment companies, is there any reference—or any inference—to Commission authority over the internal structure of disclosing companies or over the mechanisms for governance of those companies. The notion that the Commission has a broad charter including authority over company governance in a mission "to insure that our private enterprise system serves the welfare of all citizens," may be torn out of context from the preamble to the Commission's Canons of Ethics (Subpart C), but it is a notion that finds no statutory foundation. Rather, appropriate to an agency of specified and limited jurisdiction, those same canons enjoin the Commission to "avoid the adoption of rules which seek to extend the power of the Commission beyond proper statutory limits."

Its mandate to establish and require adherence to standards of disclosure has from time to time tempted the Commission to use that authority for purposes extraneous to the limited jurisdiction conferred upon it by the federal securities laws, and the Commission has periodically had to draw itself back when it has succumbed or was in danger of succumbing to that temptation. Most recently, in 1975, under the universally respected leadership of Ray Garrett, Jr., the Commission stated publicly, after lengthy consideration and discussion:

> The Commission may require disclosure by registrants under the Securities Act and the Securities Exchange Act if it believes that the information would be necessary or appropriate for the protection of investors or for the furtherance of fair, orderly and informed securities markets or for the fair operation of corporate suffrage. Although

> disclosure requirements may have some indirect effect on corporate conduct, the Commission **may not require** disclosure solely for this purpose (emphasis added).

That statement, in Release No. 33-5627, is a pithy and encompassing "mission statement" for the primary activities of this Agency, including all the varied registration and reporting procedures it is mandated to enforce.

The agency's market regulatory function is substantively related to but different from its primary focus on disclosure. The most insightful and inclusive mission statement for performance of the Commission's market regulatory function is not to be found in the mass of securities law literature but rather in a statement made by a professional economist during one of the many Commission meetings held to devise responses to the unprecedented stock market break of October 1987. As close as I can render it, then-Commissioner Cox said:

> There are really only two alternatives for a market regulatory agency. It can seek to promote liquidity in the marketplace, or it can throw sand in the gears. We have spent the last several days mostly trying to devise ways to throw sand in the gears when, as difficult as it may be to accomplish, we *should* be seeking means to *promote* market *liquidity* (emphasis added).

I understand that affirmative promotion of liquidity in the marketplace is for the most part beyond the capability of the SEC, but that does not justify the agency's habitual role of throwing sand in the market's gears. Rather, *removal of barriers* to market liquidity (as the Commission's staff demonstrated in its administration of the "buyback" rule during the 1987 market break) is well within the agency's competence and should be its response of choice.

Therefore, in response to the White House's request, *the Commission could and should* posit as the cornerstones, promoting both the public interest and the protection of investors, on which all its regulations and programs ultimately rest, those two mission statements together with the principle articulated as follows in the president's 1992 Economic Report:

> Regulation can ... play a direct role in improving the performance of the market system. *Any proposal to regulate the market, however, should be tempered by an understanding that regulation can be at least as imperfect*

as the market it is trying to improve. The goal ... is to eliminate or revise those [regulations] that impose costs that exceed their benefits, and insure that other regulations are implemented in a cost-effective manner (emphasis in original).

2. The Use of Rulemaking for Exemptive Purposes

The several statutes administered by the Commission vary in the structure of their delegation of exemptive authority. During its early decades, when the Securities Act was the principal focus of its administration, the Commission compensated for its lack of general exemptive authority under that act by expansive and creative use of its power to "defin[e] ... technical and trade terms used in this title," often in straightforward performance-standard fashion. Somewhere along the way, that approach became unfashionable, giving way (for example) to a style of Securities Act rulemaking that defines technical and trade terms such as *underwriter* or *issue* by affixing paragraph after paragraph of conditions and thereby engenders volume after volume of staff letter interpretations, as command-and-control limitations on the "safe harbor" definitional/exemptive status conferred by the particular rule. That style of rulemaking has also been adopted for rules implementing Exchange Act rulemaking authority, where the exceptions to the general prohibition of the particular rule are, in substance, exemptions hedged about with command-and-control limitations.

The peculiarity of this rulemaking approach is that frequently there is a core element sought to be achieved or avoided by the particular rule, which, in the exemptive arena, is easily susceptible to articulation in performance-standard fashion as an alternative to if not as a substitute for the multiply conditioned safe harbor that in some contexts suits both the regulating and regulated persons. For example, a very important but also very intrusive Commission market regulatory rule (Rule lOb-6), which is four detailed pages long and is said to be "objective" in nature so that no intent is needed to find violation of any of its detailed provisions, contains a proviso permitting transactions that are "not engaged in for the purpose of creating actual, or apparent, active trading in or raising the price of any ... security [covered by the rule].... "

In fact, the underlying objective of the rule, which is to allow the free forces of supply and demand to fix the trading price for securities in distribution, would be achieved so long as persons interested in the distribution did not engage in transactions *for the purpose* (specified in the proviso) of creating actual or apparent active trading or of raising the price of the distributed security. The battalion of conditions that currently surround this core element of the rule addresses the Commission's fear that some day it will be unable to prove, in court, the specified purpose on the part of some malefactor, but that battalion of conditions also carries with it enormous costs to the distributive process and to all the honest companies and all the honest underwriters that participate in that process.

Under those statutes that themselves grant the Commission broad exemptive rulemaking authority, the Commission has been reluctant to exercise that authority except (as phrased in 1941) for "special situations that might have been overlooked or that could not be foreseen at the time the [particular statute] was drafted." However appropriate that attitude may have been in the years shortly after the National Industrial Recovery Act was voided by the Supreme Court, the Commission in 1992 should have no more reluctance to exercise exemptive rulemaking authority conferred by the statutes it administers than to exercise the inclusive or extensive rulemaking authority so conferred. My constant prodding on this issue over the last few years did at least result in a public Commission statement that the source of its exemptive authority under the Investment Company Act

> provides the Commission with standards that, applied with circumspection, allow it to exempt particular vehicles and particular interests from those provisions of the Investment Company Act that inhibit competitive development of new products and new markets offered and sold in or from the United States (Release No. 40-17534).

In response to the president's request, the *Commission could and should* publicly express its receptivity to careful *but flexible* use of its exemptive rulemaking authority, to the extent conferred by the Trust Indenture Act, the Investment Company Act, and the Investment Advisers Act, by a release quoting the several statutory grants of authority—which are very broadly worded—and by utilizing that authority to select appropriate exemptive rule proposals from the inventory of proposals, *including* those passed over in the so-called Small Business Capital Formation Initiative in favor of proposed legislative amendments, that have been considered by or presented to the Commission's staff in recent years.

3. The Consideration of Costs Versus Benefits in Rulemaking

In the commercial sphere regulated by the SEC, the articulation and assessment of benefits implicit in proposed rulemaking is always easier than the articulation and assessment of the related costs. Further, the assurance of achievement of benefits needs no confirmation since the proposed rulemaking is in each case crafted to that end, while in contrast the reliability of estimates of related costs is considered low both because of the wide differences in the range of estimates often presented to the agency and because of the perceived likelihood of exaggeration by the persons presenting those estimates. As a result, evaluations by the agency of benefits in comparison to related costs are frequently superficial and perfunctory. On those occasions on which real consideration is in fact given to that kind of evaluation, the indirect consequences of the prospective rulemaking are usually outside the consideration accorded.

Two important recent examples illustrate this process. In the late 1980s the Commission was faced with an increasingly unacceptable degree of fraudulent and manipulative practices in the off-exchange markets for low-priced stocks, and it responded in 1989 by proposing and adopting a command-and-control rule prescribing in detail a set of highly intrusive sales practice requirements. The Commission knew the benefits it intended to achieve, and assessed the related costs as "minimize[d]" and "justifie[d]"; it did somewhat foresee, but gave only peripheral consideration to, the withdrawal of legitimate dealers from the trading markets in securities of legitimate companies because of the difficulty and resultant cost of establishing and implementing the fulsome procedures necessary to satisfy those requirements. Similarly, in the late 1980s, the Commission also was faced with an increasingly unacceptable rate of noncompliance with its rules for reporting of acquisitions and dispositions of "equity securities" by officers, directors, and 10 percent stockholders of public companies and in this context was faced with the additional possibility that those rules no longer reflected the economic realities of the contemporary marketplace. The Commission responded in the period 1988 through 1991 by proposing and adopting a complete new set of reporting rules directed at allaying its concerns. The Commission again knew the benefits it intended to achieve and assessed the related costs as "some[what] additional" and "outweighed"; it did not foresee, and therefore did not take into consideration, the transition costs in adjusting from one highly complex set of rules to an even more highly complex set of rules that were imposed on ten thousand public companies.

I have not heard a dollar estimate of the indirect costs to legitimate companies whose securities were deprived of much if not most of their liquidity after imposition of the 1989 sales practice requirements and the ensuing proposal of additional requirements pursuant to new legislation directed at the same problems, but the anecdotal reports of loss of market liquidity have come from small broker dealers and small public companies all over the country. I *have* been given a dollar estimate of the transition costs imposed by the 1991 revision of acquisition and disposition reporting rules on companies in the Silicon Valley area alone. That estimate, which was given to me by a former colleague on the Commission who was a participant in the Silicon Valley transition program, is "upwards" of $10 million.

In response to the president's request, *the Commission could and should* resolve that no non-emergency rulemaking be allowed to proceed to adoption without well-considered evaluation of direct costs related to the benefits intended to be achieved or without a fulsome professional effort to evaluate and foresee the indirect consequential costs of that rulemaking proceeding.

4. The Use of Performance Standards in Rulemaking

The agency's single most renowned rule (Rule l0b-5), which has been likened to an acorn from which an entire judicial oak has grown, is a performance-standards rule that was adopted in 1942. As recently as 1990, in its adoption of a general rule governing unregistered securities offerings made outside the United States (Regulation S, Rule 901), the Commission demonstrated that it still knows how to craft performance standards rules. Between those two adoptions, however, and again since the end of April 1990, the Commission has rarely based its rulemaking on performance standards. Earlier in this letter, I listed some of the descriptions the agency applies to the performance-standards alternative in its regulatory flexibility analyses; there certainly must be contexts in which performance standards rules are "not consistent" with the direct mandate of the particular statutory provision, but the assertion that performance standards rules are "inadequate" for the particular rulemaking need is in many cases an admission that the persons engaged in the drafting process have devoted insufficient efforts to the search for an alternative to command-and-control requirements, and the conclusion that performance-standards rules are "not possible" is almost always an admission that no effort at all was devoted to such a search.

Of course performance standards rules are "possible" as long as they are not directly inconsistent with the particular statutory provision. Even when (as was the case with Rule 901, mentioned above) performance standards are used to state the generality and are complemented by intrusive command-and-control requirements affording a "safe harbor" *within* the generality, the very presence of the performance-standards–based general rule affords a safeguard against, and an alternative to, the extremes of intrusiveness of the command-and-control requirements. And there are clearly many instances in which the performance-standards rule can stand alone.

In response to the president's request, *the Commission could and should* insist on whatever effort is necessary to devise performance-standards rules that *are* adequate for the intended rulemaking initiative whenever they *are* in fact possible, standing alone (as does Rule 10b-5) whenever they can do so and providing an alternative to the command-and-control requirements when it is necessary or desirable to proceed in that manner.

5. The Use of Market Mechanisms

Peculiarly for a *market* regulatory agency, the SEC has rarely considered or utilized any natural mechanism of the market as a regulatory device. To the contrary, perhaps owing to the distrust of the market that infused the imperfect but widespread public understanding after the crash of 1929, the very object of Commission rulemaking is frequently to inhibit the operation of naturally occurring market mechanisms. The opportunity to use diverse market mechanisms as regulatory devices is actually afforded to the agency in a variety of contexts (not always recognized for the opportunities they afford), of which I might mention *two* as exemplary.

The most recurrent example is the Commission's reliance on monopoly or near-monopoly exchange market franchises. When standardized and offsettable option contracts were introduced for trading by the Chicago Board Options Exchange, the desire of the exchange for the initial patent-like fruits of its long research and development process coincided with the fear of the Commission that these new instruments would be used for market manipulative purposes. Market surveillance would obviously have been infinitely complicated by multimarket listing and trading of any series of options, so an interexchange options allocation system was sanctioned. Only after years of effort was it decided to allow the options exchanges to list each other's options, and to this day an informal moratorium (via a sequence of letters from our chairman) effectively postpones the time for implementation of that decision while a rivalry between proposals for interexchange information coordination and trade execution capacity preserves the status quo. The real market advantage in this context has lain in the inertia attaching to "first out of the gate" status, but, when presented (by one of its own then members) with the suggestion that that advantage be discarded periodically by means of an auction to reassign trading franchises, the Commission gave that suggestion no consideration at all.

In response to the president's request, *the Commission could and should* implement its own decision on multi-exchange options listing and *could and should* direct its economic and market regulatory staff to recommend criteria (as in evaluation of stock exchange specialist performance) for review and reallocation of options listings.

On the analogous topic of stock exchange limits on member firm trading of listed securities, the ever-expanding development of domestic "third market" and "fourth market" facilities and the everincreasing capability for effecting trades overseas, taken together with the agency's single action in 1979–80 (barring application of those limits to trades in securities listed after April 1979), have brought the pressure of market mechanisms to bear incrementally over this past decade. Mr. William Heyman, director of the agency's Division of Market Regulation, has now taken the initiative to commence a "Market 2000" study that should complete this process. In response to your request, *the Commission could and should* support Mr. Heyman's effort in every possible way.

A different context in which performance of the agency's market regulatory function could benefit from the use of market mechanisms is the context of regulation of short sales. The "bear raids" of the 1920s were manipulative at their core; prevention of such raids is addressed by general antimanipulative rules. By contrast, most short sales are informative of, or responsive to, ordinary market action. Even in 1934 the short sale area was understood to be sufficiently tender and technical, and to have sufficient likelihood of adverse impact on the trading markets, that Congress prohibited only those short sales made "in contravention of such rules and regulations as the Commission may prescribe." The Commission's "uptick rule," applicable to short sales on stock exchanges, was adopted in February 1938. In the intervening fifty years the traditional fear of "the short side" has been diminished by cumulative experience, particularly (during the last fifteen years) experience with risk-shifting instruments (options and futures), the markets for which would not exist without an equal and opposite "short side." It is therefore all the stranger that this agency's "uptick rule" not only persists but is now under consideration for adaptation into the off-exchange market without any serious consideration being given (although a then - majority of Commissioners proposed such consideration only a few years ago) to the market costs and benefits that that rule imports. In fact, studies by the agency's Office of Economic Analysis, made recently in response to market participants' complaints about the absence of an "uptick rule" in a specified segment of the off-exchange market, were unable to find statistically significant support for those complaints.

In response to the president's request the *Commission could and should* direct its economic and regulatory staffs jointly to review and report on the market impact in 1992 of short selling generally and of the agency's short sale regulations in particular (including the separate rule that the Commission designated as "temporary" in response to the studies mentioned immediately above but that the Commission has not since reviewed) and *could and should* revise its short sale regulations in light of the resulting report.

A final context, this time in the arena of disclosure, in which the agency could properly use market mechanisms, is the context of mandated quarterly reports by public companies. It has been thirteen years since Homer Kripke, once a senior staff official of the agency and for decades one of its most constructive critics, concluded as follows in a chapter entitled "Market Forces and Disclosure":

> If we assume an absence of SEC compulsion, those aspects of the SEC system that are considered material to their decisions will be required by lenders and investors without the Commission's prompting, and will be furnished. Other parts will not be demanded.

Professor Kripke buttressed his conclusion with a separate description of the inertial forces that have always held the agency back from serious consideration of the validity and market implications of the position he had reached. The Commission has twice in the recent past heard, from one of its own members, the formal suggestion that in light of the twice-yearly financial reporting provided by public companies through much of the industrialized world, it should consider withdrawing its mandate for quarterly reporting by part or all of the universe of domestic public companies. That suggestion was, of course, based on use of the market mechanisms fundamental to Professor Kripke's position and would have afforded the agency a controlled environment in which to test the functioning of those market mechanisms. Neither that suggestion nor anything similar to it has ever been acceptable to the agency.

In response to the president's request, *the Commission could and should* remove from its mandated periodic disclosures the requirement dictating quarterly reports from domestic public companies for such period of time as it believes is necessary to ascertain whether market mechanisms will elicit substitute information "considered material to their decisions . . . by lenders and investors without the Commission's prompting", and thereafter *could and should* take follow-up measures on the basis of what it has so ascertained.

6. The Concern over Clarity and Certainty

More than twenty years ago I chaired a bar subcommittee that brought to the Commission's staff an alternative version of a proposed rule then under consideration for adoption. We had tried carefully to draw some bright and clear lines in an area that had previously been subject to rather amorphous legal concepts. I remember well the response we received from a then Commissioner who participated in our meeting, to the effect that "uncertainty surrounding the limits of the law is desirable because the 'crooks' can *never* be sure when they have overstepped the bounds." I have always believed that response to be wrong; the honest entrepreneur and the lawyer earnestly trying to give proper legal advice—of whom there are many more than there are "crooks"—are equally hindered by uncertainty from pursuing legitimate transactions. But to this day the Commission follows the tradition of the response that I heard in 1971.

For example, a key item that required disclosure in the takeover battles that characterized the late 1980s was "whether or not any negotiation is being undertaken or is underway by the [target] company in response to the tender offer. . . ." The Commission has initiated several prosecutorial enforcement actions for failure to make prompt disclosure of a "negotiation," as if that word had a clear and generally understood meaning. In connection with one such enforcement matter I collected a group of newspaper articles evidencing that, in diplomacy as in business, what is reported in the press as a "negotiation" can range from face-to-face bargaining to messages conveyed by an intermediary to separate statements separately released to separate audiences. The Commission, even in its quasi-adjudicative decision on this issue, has manifested its own inability to clarify the *meaning* of the term (e.g., "the discussions between and among [the participants] constituted negotiations as of the time period from the evening of September 26 to September 29"—but without specification of precisely when during that time period). Most recently, in June 1991, as has been pointed out in the legal journals, the Commission simply avoided an opportunity to address the issue. As a result, managers of and advisers to target companies are constrained from having any dialogue, however preliminary and nonnegotiatory, with outside parties in response to an unwanted tender offer, unless they are willing either to give the tender offerer the additional advantage of premature information or they are willing to run the risk of prosecution for disclosure law violation. The cost of that constraint is measured in potential profits not realized by target company securityholders.

In response to the president's request, the *Commission could and should* remove that cost by amending its disclosure requirements to clarify those elements (actual or apparent authority, participation of outside persons, discussion of some particulars of price and structure, or whatever the Commission deems appropriate) that, when present together, identify a "negotiation." This very approach to precise identification of the elements sought to be included within the definition of a particular term that imposes substantive obligations, with the same kind of cost-removal effect, has been taken twice in recent years by the Commission in connection with rules turning on the definition of "beneficial ownership" (Rule 13d-3 and Rule 16a-1, which use *different* elements in *different* contexts), and the SEC *could and should* take this same approach with respect (among others) even to definitions of terms as common and as consequential (although undefined) as "tender offer" and "insider trading."

7. Rulemaking by Official and Unofficial Interpretation

The variety and status of Commission Interpretative Releases will be referred to in section 9 of this paper. Those releases themselves divide into statements of Commission positions and statements of staff positions. Their effect, in whichever category, would be beneficent in assisting regulated entities and their professional advisers in complying with the applicable law and rules, were it not for their very profusion (which itself suggests that the rulebook needs rewriting). But behind and beyond those Releases lies a mass of staff interpretive and "no-action" correspondence that traces back to the issuance of opinions of the Commission's General Counsel, initiated in the first months of the Commission's existence nearly sixty years ago as an informal procedure for rendering advice and assistance to affected members of the public.

In earlier years, knowledge of the very existence of that correspondence was a professional advantage limited to a few *cognoscenti*. Once it was made publicly available, however, the self-renewing stream of interpretive and no-action letters was treated by securities lawyers just like other decisional materials: individual letters and groups of letters in particular fields were reviewed and subjected to comparison, to compliment, to criticism, to study for guidance on conduct prohibited, and to analysis for suggestions of activity permissible, for similarly situated persons. For its part the Commission, in rulemaking proceedings, in prosecutorial briefs, in its annual reports to Congress, in its *amicus* program, in settlement orders, and in its adjudicated opinions, has cited these letters for a variety of purposes: to respond to objections, to establish consistency in administrative practice, and sometimes to highlight permissible conduct, but in each case implicitly accepting those letters as statements of the relevant division's view of a generally applicable position. And the staff officially draws attention to "significant" letters, conducts seminars devoted in part to exposing and expounding on recent letters, and from time to time recommends, for publication by the Commission, releases that compile, correct, restate, and cite entire groupings of prior correspondence.

It is very strange, then, to realize that this mass of letters is disavowed by the agency through an official description that they "are not rulings of the Commission or its staff on questions of law or fact." The interpretive and no-action process has far more elasticity and presents far less danger to the Commission's administration of the federal securities laws than that formula recognizes.

In response to the president's request, the *Commission could and should* recognize the realities of contemporary securities law practice, both inside and outside the agency, by officially acknowledging that members of the bar and the public are entitled to rely on staff no-action and interpretive letters as representing the current views of the relevant Division and may in good faith reason from those particular views to derive general propositions concerning both permitted and prohibited conduct, although reiterating that any analysis or extrapolation from particular staff views runs the professional risk of being wrong.

8. The Interplay of Rulemaking and Adjudication

The combination of quasi-judicial work with the work of policy determination, whether in its quasi-executive (prosecutory) or in its quasi-legislative (rulemaking) form, raises recurrent problems for the SEC. The Commission has been vested with the duty to ensure compliance with the federal securities laws. The performance of that duty involves policy determination by implementary rulemaking and by statutory and regulatory interpretation as well as by prosecutorial enforcement. It is undoubtedly true that this power of policy determination "must be exercised consistently and, therefore, by the same body, not only to realize the public purposes which the statutes are designed to further but also to avoid confusion of private interests." It is also true, however, that, as the administrative reach of the federal securities laws has repeatedly been extended in recent decades to include new persons and additional conduct, Commission policy making via interpretation of the successive statutory enactments has necessarily gathered ever-greater scope, and consistency in that policy making has assumed an increasingly self-generative character. As a result, the more consistency the Commission as a body achieves in application of administrative policies, the more committed the Commission as a body becomes to the vindication of the policies thus consistently applied.

While the Supreme Court has concluded that the maintenance by the Commission, in quasi-adjudicative proceedings, of policy positions developed in the performance of administrative responsibilities outside the proceedings themselves contravenes no "constitutional compulsions," nevertheless the shift to the Commission's quasi-adjudicative role ought at least to evoke a clear attitudinal distinction as to the discharge of the two responsibilities—a withdrawal by the Commissioners, in the performance of quasi-adjudicative duties, from those "pressures and influences properly directed toward officers responsible for formulating and administering policy". The fundamental issue here is fairness and the appearance of fairness in the agency's quasi-adjudicative process, both of which are adversely affected by confusion with the forces commanding consistent policy determination in the rulemaking and interpretative process. In response to the president's request *the Commission could and should* invoke upon itself a course of self-restraint, and in appropriate cases even dismissal, in the Commission's quasi-adjudicative proceedings in order to assure that the risk of unfairness to respondents in those proceedings is never allowed to reach a level that is unacceptable as a matter of agency policy even if not yet so "intolerably high" as to be impermissible as a matter of constitutional law.

9. An Overview of the Commission's Rulebook

To effectuate its disclosure mission and to govern the more fully regulated entities, the Commission has a rulebook of more than eleven hundred pages of 8-point and 6-point type in the *Code of Federal Regulations.* (I have omitted from that total the additional one hundred pages that contain only tables of contents or superseded rules.) But that total is misleadingly low, because eight separate parts of the *Code* consist of lists of an aggregate of more than five hundred interpretive releases (perhaps another fifteen hundred pages) that are incorporated by reference into various portions of the formal rules. Six further parts consist of summary descriptions of all the many forms (another few hundred pages) on which filings with the Commission are made, each of which (and the set of instructions to each of which) is formally considered by the Commission to be a Commission rule, since under each act administered by the Commission there is a rule stating generally:

> The term *rules and regulations* refers to all rules and regulations adopted by the Commission pursuant to the act,

> including the forms for registration and reports and the accompanying instructions thereto.

With a rulebook this thick and this diffuse, it is impractical to select more than a few exemplary pieces for comment. I shall mention two, in quite diverse contexts, that fit nowhere else in this paper but merit separate discussion.

The rulebook contains one part (Regulation S-K) that sets forth "Standard Instructions for Filing Forms" under the Securities Act and the Securities Exchange Act. An entrepreneur or a business lawyer seeking guidance from that part is met with the following introductory sentence:

> This Part (together with the General Rules and Regulations under the two Acts, the Interpretative Releases under these Acts . . . and the forms under these Acts ...) states the requirements applicable to the content of the nonfinancial statement portions of [registration statements, reports, and proxy and information statements]. . . .

Perhaps the entrepreneur or lawyer can actually find all those rules, regulations, releases, and forms. Since they would all be applicable even in the absence of that introductory sentence, perhaps the entrepreneur or lawyer is benefited by being put on notice of the necessity to search elsewhere, both inside and outside the rulebook, to find much of what is required by way of disclosure.

In response to the president's request, *the Commission could and should* pare, consolidate, and publish in a single source, this multiplicity of disclosure requirements and *could and should* codify (if worth retaining) or discard this myriad of interpretive glosses.

The rulebook contains a three-page rule (Rule 14a-8), relating to the procedural requirements for inclusion of shareholder proposals in the annual proxy statements of public companies, that includes nearly a full page prescribing the subject matter of proposals that need *not* be so included. The result is to involve the Commission and its staff, annually, in tens upon tens of interpretations and reinterpretations and reversals of prior interpretations of the limits on matters that, except for compliance with disclosure standards and procedural requirements, rest primarily on state law and should be determined by shareholder-management negotiation or by state chancery courts if that process of negotiation fails. In fact, in 1982 the Commission proposed revising the rule so that "all proposals that are proper under state law and that do not involve the election of directors should be included in an issuer's proxy statement, subject to a numerical maximum, but the Commission ultimately preserved the status quo with minor changes.

Now, in response to the president's request, the *Commission could and should* revive that aborted approach in order to withdraw itself from an intrusive regulatory role, revising the rule to prescribe only procedure and disclosure and leaving determinations on the substantive law of shareholder rights to the state courts of equity.

10. A List of Additional Proposed Rule Revisions

Above and beyond the regulatory changes suggested in the preceding parts of this letter, a list of additional proposed rule revisions follows:

(1) The Commission should review and revitalize the responsibilities assigned under its rules to its chief economist and its economic analysis staff. A market regulatory agency that regulates without considering economic analysis and economists' advice as to likely market impact, costs and benefits, is an agency that regulates markets blindly and that has disabled itself from responding to the president's request. The Commission has discouraged and devalued economic analysis and advice.

(2) The Commission *should duplicate* the portions of its organizational rule that enjoin it (a) not to exercise its power beyond proper statutory limits, (b) not to stifle or discourage legitimate business enterprises, and (c) not to interpret its power so as unduly and unnecessarily to burden regulated persons with onerous obligations, so that those injunctions apply not merely to rulemaking but to all its actions.

(3) The Commission *should rewrite* its rule relating to no-action letters to reflect the position that members of the bar and of the public may in good faith reason from the particular views expressed in staff no-action and interpretive letters to derive general propositions, at the risk of being wrong, and may in good faith disagree with staff views so expressed.

(4) The Commission *should review and revise* the portion of its accounting rule that presumes misleading or inaccurate any financial statements not prepared in full accordance with GAAP regardless of accompanying explanatory disclosures.

(5) The Commission *should relinquish* its self-appointed role of designating which organizations qualify as "nationally recognized securities rating organizations." National recognition is determinable in the marketplace according to objective standards, without Commission confirmation.

(6) The Commission *should expand* its reliance on the presentation "in good faith" of disclosure information for which the reporting person has "a reasonable basis" to believe that the information is true and complete. That standard of care, and therefore of liability, should apply to any forward-looking statement, whether or not made in a document filed with the Commission, and to categories of present and historical statements as well.

(7) The Commission *should also expand* its reliance, particularly with respect to small issuers as defined for Regulatory Flexibility Act purposes, on the presentation of disclosure information as to which no material fact known to the reporting person has been omitted, the inclusion of which would reasonably appear necessary, in the circumstances, to make other information not misleading.

(8) The Commission *should utilize* the experience it has gained from the special materiality rule made applicable to its mandated Management Discussion and Analysis to recognize the differences in determination of materiality in different contexts.

(9) The Commission *should amend* its limited offering rule to allow some face-to-face contacts presently prohibited as "general solicitations," for example, presentations by entrepreneurs to venture capital forums regularly sponsored by independent professional firms.

(10) The reasons advanced by the Commission in 1984 for excluding from NASDAQ the securities of foreign issuers that provide home country information in the U.S. no longer support the exclusion. The advantages of on-screen transparency far outweigh the other supposed disadvantages to investors, particularly since the principal price discovery market is overseas.

(11) The Commission *should struggle*, if necessary, to find shorter, more direct, and more comprehensible approaches to the

computation of minimum net capital required of broker dealers. There just must be a better alternative by which to approach this computation than the 41 pages of its incomprehensible rule.

(12) The Commission *should adapt* the approach of its agency cross rule, providing for prospective general written consent, transaction confirmation disclosure, periodic disclosure, and repeated notice of revocability, in other contexts where investors may be presumed to be able to authorize trading activity by means of informed consent.

11. The Balance of Rulemaking and Prosecutorial Enforcement

What always seems most difficult is the balancing of investor protection, on the one hand, and, on the other, removal of cost from the securities offering and securities trading markets in particular and the U.S. economy in general. I see no necessary contradiction between those two. A former Commissioner pointed out, to a group of present and former members and senior staff of the Commission, that reform of the agency's regulatory program has the inevitable concomitant of expansion of the agency's policing and prosecuting program. I **agree** with that analysis, and it leads me to the ultimate conclusion that the Commission's enforcement program *can* fulfill the resulting additional responsibility and can fulfill it well—at a far lesser systemic cost than prevails under the Commission's present regulatory approach. After six and one-quarter years as a Commissioner of the SEC and after the prior twenty six and one-half years of law practice in the field regulated by the Commission, I firmly believe that *the Commission could and should* be willing to rely more heavily on a well-directed policing and prosecuting program to remove a real amount of systemic cost without removing anywhere near an equal extent of direct and indirect benefits to investors.

12. Conclusion

Performance standards, market mechanisms, and clarity in rulemaking all contribute to removal of systemic costs. To the extent that in the securities markets those regulatory methods rely on enforcement by market forces, by self-regulatory organizations and by the SEC, that reliance is both well-founded and well-directed to the maintenance of the fundamental investor protections that have made and have kept the primary and secondary securities markets in the United States (in the words of former Commission

Chairman John Shad), "the deepest, the most liquid, and the fairest securities markets anywhere in the world".

II

ACCOUNTING ISSUES

U.S. GAAP

and the

Listing of Foreign Securities

3

Redundant Regulation of Foreign Security Trading and U.S. Competitiveness

William J. Baumol
New York University

Burton G. Malkiel
Princeton University

1. Introduction and Summary

A major decision facing the Securities and Exchange Commission over the next four years is what information it will require to be provided to investors in foreign securities purchased in markets within the United States. The SEC is charged with the responsibility of ensuring that U.S. investors receive adequate and honest information concerning all securities traded in U.S. markets. Rules that protect investors from inadequate and misleading information can offer significant protection to U.S. investors. If, however, markets in foreign securities are already provided with information sufficient to ensure their efficiency, regulations that require reformulation of foreign earnings data to meet U.S. accounting standards may offer little, if any, protection to U.S. investors. Such regulations can also harm the international competitiveness of the U.S. securities industry if they prevent U.S. exchanges from making markets in many of the largest corporations in the world. This paper concludes that present SEC regulations requiring the restatement of accounting information of major foreign corporations to U.S. standards may, in fact, offer little benefit to U.S. investors while proving potentially detrimental to the U.S. economy. In efficient market, the interactions of buyers and sellers automatically adjust prices so as to eliminate all possibilities of gain derivable from the possession of superior information. In other words, in an efficient market additional information, even if extensive and correct, offers little protection to investors, whose interests are already safeguarded by market forces that fully incorporate all relevant information into securities prices. This paper reviews several studies that have compared the efficiency of stock markets in the United States and those in the major foreign countries and have concluded that the major international markets are as reasonably efficient as those in the U.S. We also report on the results of our own study, which examines the investment performance of professional portfolio managers who invest in European and Pacific Rim securities. These results are compared with the performance of a broad international index of common stocks. If, as we show, indexed funds can perform as well as professionally managed portfolios, there is little reason to believe that investors can gain substantially from the information additional disclosure rules can promise to provide.

The SEC disclosure rules will also be related to the competitive position of the U.S. in the world economy. It will be shown from the most recent data that the overall economic performance of the United States, particularly in manufacturing, is in fact considerably better than is generally recognized. Contrary to what is widely believed, it is in service employment that other countries are threatening to overtake and surpass the U.S. As governments in other countries do what they can to assist their firms and to make it easier for them to compete with those of other nations, it is particularly important that agencies of the U.S. government are careful to avoid needless impediments to the competitive service activities of U.S. firms and markets.

It is ironic that current SEC rules handicap one of the service industries in which the United States is, so far, successfully holding its own against foreign competition. The securities markets of this country clearly continue to hold the lead among international markets. Companies of comparable size in terms of market capitalization tend to enjoy better markets in the United States than they do abroad. Both individual and institutional investors are able to trade at lower bid-ask spreads in the United States' markets. While U.S. and foreign markets may be equally efficient with respect to assimilaton of information, foreign markets tend to be far less efficient in providing transactions ability at low cost. Evidence of the higher costs of dealing in foreign markets is the fact that index funds (those funds that simply buy and hold a broad index of the major companies in each market) charge an extra fee for investing in European and Pacific Rim securities. The added fee is justified because it helps to defray the higher transactions costs involved in purchasing foreign securities. Moreover, the U.S. securities markets have led the world in financial innovation. Extraordinarily liquid markets in financial futures and stock and index options have been developed in the United States. With the national concern over our ability to compete in international markets, it seems ill-advised to restrain one of our service industries that has demonstrated an unparalleled ability as a model of competitiveness and innovation.

2. The SEC Rules: Brief Recapitulation of the Pertinent Facts

Under current SEC regulations, when a foreign company lists its securities on a U.S. exchange or offers its securities for sale to the public, it must provide financial statements entirely reconstituted from the forms called for in the firm's own country, and reconciled with the forms imposed by U.S. generally accepted accounting practices (GAAP). Aside from the expense and time entailed in the translation process, there are difficulties stemming from the fact that the GAAP requirements are often imperfectly adapted to the circumstances of the foreign firm. For example, the rules on corporate taxation vary considerably from country to country, and the GAAP procedures are tailored to fit the tax laws of the United States.[1]

It is not difficult to provide statements by foreign issuers asserting that these rules are burdensome and that they are put off by the tax information requirements. Such statements may perhaps be self-serving. Evidence is, however, provided by their behavior. The London Stock Exchange lists more than five times as many foreign companies as the New York Stock Exchange does. This may, perhaps, reflect a preference by the foreign issuers for the British securities market, but that cannot explain the fact that when, in 1983, foreign firms seeking NASDAQ quotation were for the first time subjected to the more onerous reporting requirements that currently prevail, "the effect . . . was immediate and dramatic" according to former SEC Commissioner Philip Lochner. "After tripling between 1977 and 1983, new foreign participation in NASDAQ was halted when the Commission imposed new reporting requirements."

It should be emphasized that U.S. reporting requirements are probably more demanding than those in most foreign countries. This appears to imply that U.S. investors receive increased protection against incomplete, inaccurate, or misleading information as a result of the SEC rules. But one of the ironies of these regulations is that investors in foreign securities are,

---

[1] An alternative and somewhat less burdensome type of reconciliation is available to foreign issuers of securities under the SEC rules, but the issuers who use this avenue are in most cases still required and in all cases "encouraged ... to provide the [full and fully reconciled] information specified" in the more demanding procedure.

as a result, often forced to turn to foreign markets for their purchases and sales. They are, consequently, effectively denied not only the protection, if any, of the tighter rules, but also the greater liquidity and lower transactions costs that would be available to them if they could carry out their transactions in the U.S. markets.

3. Economic Costs of the SEC Rules

The production of information is a costly activity. However, in the case of the SEC requirements the burden is more than that entailed in a mere requirement of recalculation and translation into the U.S. accounting form. The fact is that much of the requisite information is inherently untranslatable. Foreign firms operate under institutional arrangements and tax regulations different, sometimes very different, from those in the U.S. The information reporting requirements that have evolved in the firms' home countries have been adapted to the special institutional arrangements under which they operate and which determine the structures of those firms. The U.S. reporting structure has simply not been designed to fit these facts.[2] The direct costs to the issuer firm of compliance with the SEC rules are, consequently, considerable. But the difficulties just described lead to three societal costs that, though indirect, are probably also substantial.

First, the required reconciliation of foreign firms' financial information with U.S.-GAAP requirements may actually reduce U.S. investors' mastery of the pertinent facts. Because American investors are not well informed about foreign accounting definitions, the veneer of compatibility conferred by the reconciliation process is likely to lull them into believing that they have command of the reported facts when in fact the data require interpretation very different from what is suggested by their appearance. Thus, far from informing U.S. investors more fully, the GAAP requirements may in fact serve to mislead them.

Second, forcing U.S. investors to buy and sell abroad raises the expenses they incur in the process. Spreads and commissions overseas are usually considerably higher than those in U.S. markets, and, in addition, there are high clearance, settlement, and custody costs.

---

[2] Indeed, because of the heterogeneity of the institutional arrangements in the different countries it is extremely difficult to provide a single form that can encompass them all, though valiant efforts to design such a set of unified accounting standards have been under way for some time.

Third, by forcing investors to trade abroad and to set up custodial and brokerage relations in foreign countries, business is lost to U.S. markets. At a time when the prospects presage rapid growth in international securities trading, the resulting handicap to competitiveness of the U.S. markets and the institutions associated with them may force us to forego an extremely desirable opportunity—an opportunity that foreign financial institutions and their governments will undoubtedly seize if given the chance.

4. The U.S. Economy: Performance and Prospects

There is a widespread impression that the U.S. has lost the battle for retention of the position of the world's economic leader. But careful examination of the facts demonstrates that the dismal scenario described by proponents of the deindustrialization thesis is far from reality. This is not to say that the opposite is true. Our country cannot simply rest assured that it will automatically retain its economic leadership without suitable effort and careful avoidance of measures that impede its economic performance. Ever since World War II other leading industrial nations have converged toward the economic performance of the United States and whittled down our lead in levels of productivity and per capita incomes to the point where our margin of superiority is a small fraction of what it was four decades ago. Yet we remain ahead of all our main industrial rivals in overall productivity level, in our productivity level in manufacturing, in our per capita real GDP, and in a variety of other important areas. In particular, the evidence provides absolutely no support for the contention that the U.S. has lost the manufacturing war. Japanese statistics divide manufacturing into 13 subsectors. In 1950 the U.S. productivity level led the world in all 13 of these subsectors, largely as the result of war damage to so many of the other industrial economies. Today our country's productivity still leads the world in nine of those thirteen subsectors, hardly a despicable performance. Figure 1, only one of many pieces of pertinent evidence, shows that the United States' share of world industrial employment has actually risen persistently throughout the postwar period, at a pace only (barely) exceeded by Japan's.[3] This conclusion appears to be undermined by the growing share of the U.S. labor force that is employed by the services, a trend that the deindustrialization thesis attributes to the success of foreign nations in stealing away our manufacturing markets. Figure 2 indicates, however, that

---

[3] *See* Baumol, Blackman and Wolff (1991) for a full discussion of the evidence on productivity behavior among the major industrialized nations.

every industrialized foreign nation is moving its labor force into the services far more rapidly than we. These data, whose message is generally unknown and whose importance is generally unrecognized, indicate that the battle for competitiveness that is shaping up for the U.S. is likely to be focused upon the services rather than upon manufacturing. The data also show that those services that are and will be the sources of new employment today and tomorrow are not fast food restaurants, but, rather, are made up of the economy's growing sector devoted to the production and use of information. The securities exchanges, clearly, fall within this group.

5. Is Removal of the SEC Information Requirements a Danger to U.S. Investors?

Thus, there is a strong case, in terms of contribution to U.S. competitiveness, for removal of the SEC reconciliation rules for the information provided by (at least the major) issuers of foreign securities who want their securities to be traded in U.S. markets. The question that remains can not, however, be dismissed lightly. Is there a dangerous trade-off? Will elimination of these rules subject U.S. investors to risks significantly greater than those that they currently face?

Clearly, if the unreconciled accounting information released by major international corporations not currently traded in the United States is inadequate for investors to make informed judgments about the worth of their securities, then investors may be protected by making it more difficult for them to purchase these issues. Moreover, if foreign firms are not presently providing full and fair disclosure of their operating results, then their stock prices may fail to reflect their true economic situation. U.S. investors may therefore be harmed by inability to value the pertinent securities reliably, as well as by deliberate manipulation of stock prices. By requiring full and fair reporting, the SEC's traditional and proper historical role is to ensure that the accounting information provided by foreign issuers is sufficient to permit prices to reflect true economic values.

The issue then becomes an empirical one. For at least the major international corporations, does the evidence suggest that accounting information released in accordance with local standards is adequate to ensure that those securities are efficiently priced? Is there any evidence that lax accounting standards in foreign countries may put investors at a disadvantage? If it can be shown that inadequate accounting information does not permit investors to price those securities efficiently, then it may be appropriate for the SEC to insist that more adequate disclosure (perhaps in accord with GAAP) is necessary to protect investors. If, however, it can be shown that foreign stock markets (at least for the major corporations' common stocks) appear to be as efficient as U.S. stock markets, then it must be presumed that the benefits of additional reporting requirements may be illusory.

In section 7 of this paper we review the evidence on the efficiency of the major foreign stock markets. Before presenting that analysis, however, we show in section 6 how investors can benefit from international diversification. Since there are major advantages to investors who diversify their portfolios among countries, it will be shown that regulations that restrict or make more costly the access of U.S. investors to foreign securities will tend to worsen their investment performance.

6. The Benefits of International Diversification

One of the time-honored investment maxims is that risk can be reduced by diversification. The Nobel Prize in economics was awarded to Harry Markowitz in 1990 for a rigorous explanation of this phenomenon. It is important to have in one's portfolio stocks that do not all depend on the same economic variables, such as consumer spending, business investment, housing construction, and so forth. As long as stocks in the portfolio do not move completely in parallel, fluctuations in the fortunes of individual stocks will at least partially offset one another, and the resulting portfolio performance will be more stable than the fluctuations of the individual components.

Figure 3 illustrates the point. Looking first at the top curve in the figure, labeled "U.S. Stocks," we see that, as the number of securities in the portfolio increases, total portfolio risk is reduced. By the time the portfolio contains close to 20 equal-sized and well-diversified issues, the total risk (the variance of returns) of the portfolio is reduced by more than 60 percent. Of course, the stocks in the portfolio must be widely diversified. Clearly, a portfolio composed only of 20 oil stocks would not produce an equivalent amount of risk reduction. Since the movements of foreign economies and foreign stock markets are not always synchronous with those of the U.S. economy and stock market, additional benefits are obtained by including foreign companies in the portfolio, as is illustrated in the bottom line of the figure. Here the stocks are drawn not simply from the U.S. stock market but also from Europe and the Pacific Rim countries. As is to be expected, the internationally diversified portfolio tends to be less risky than the one of corresponding size drawn purely from U.S. stocks. Thus, investors would improve their performance by diversifying internationally and, to the extent that we can encourage more international stocks to be traded on organized exchanges in the United States, international diversification will be facilitated. As was indicated above, it is generally quite expensive for individuals to trade abroad. Thus, allowing more foreign firms to trade on organized U.S. exchanges is likely to improve the investment options open to U.S. investors. Equivalently, regulations that make it more difficult and costly for U.S. investors to buy foreign securities will impose substantial costs in terms of investment performance.

7. On The Efficiency of Stock Markets, Domestic and Foreign

Here we turn to the remaining central question—whether SEC regulations on accounting disclosure are necessary to improve the efficiency of the markets in foreign securities. A stock market is considered reasonably efficient if full information about individual companies is readily available and if the information is very rapidly incorporated into market prices. In an efficient market no above average gains can possibly be obtained by analyzing either past stock price patterns or any publicly available accounting or other fundamental information. In the strongest form of efficient market, not even the possession of private (nonpublic) information allows a stock trader to earn extraordinary returns.

Most studies of the U.S. market appear to be broadly consistent with the efficient market theory. While the strongest form of efficiency is not found in reality, and thus the SEC must be extremely diligent to ensure that no investor profits from private information at the expense of other investors, the evidence shows fairly clearly that efficiency of the narrower form prevails.

Studies of market efficiency have also been conducted for the major foreign markets. The remarkable conclusion of this research is that foreign markets, despite the differences in their accounting information and in disclosure requirements, appear to be as efficient as U.S. markets. Hawawini (1984) surveyed more than 280 studies of European stock-price data and concluded that "the random walk models cannot be rejected and there is no evidence that mechanical trading rules can be applied to earn abnormal returns net of transactions costs". While in foreign markets one finds some anomalies, such as "January effects" and "day-of-week effects," similar patterns occur in the U.S. market, and it is not clear that they are large enough to represent unexploited arbitrage opportunities.

Studies have also been performed to evaluate the impact of accounting information on the determination of stock prices. One popular test of whether markets are efficient involves the speed at which new accounting information is reflected in stock prices. Following the seminal work of Ball and Brown (1968), studies in the U.S. have found that earnings announcements had considerable information content and that markets are efficient in adjusting extremely rapidly (indeed almost instantaneously) to such accounting news. A number of similar studies (summarized by Hawawini 1984), found there is important content in foreign accounting information prepared in accord with home country accounting practices. Foreign stock prices also appear to adjust extremely rapidly to such accounting announcements.[4]

Lessard (1990) reviews a number of studies that have attempted to measure the effects on stock prices of potentially misleading changes in accounting practice. He concludes that there is no association between purely cosmetic earning changes and market values. While poorly performing companies may be more likely to inflate reported earnings through accounting changes, the market does not appear to be fooled by such manipulations. Lessard concludes that "the evidence is overwhelmingly in favor of the view that price setting investors in the marketplace are not misled by accounting policies.: The conclusion holds not only for the United States but also for major foreign markets.

Further analyses have been conducted to address the question of whether the efficiency of foreign markets would be improved if investors had access to earnings data prepared on the basis of U.S. accounting conventions. Chen (1992) reports on two studies that analyzed the potential benefits of restating foreign accounting numbers in terms of U.S. GAAP. In general, these studies have found that accounting numbers prepared in conformity with accepted home-country accounting conventions contained more information than those restated in accord with U.S. GAAP.

Meek (1983) studied the response of stock prices of non-U.S. multinational corporations to earnings announcements prepared on the basis of home-country conventions and later announcements of earnings reconciled with U.S. GAAP. While the subsequent release of U.S. GAAP data does not appear to possess any additional information, home-country earnings announcements do have considerable information value for investors. Moreover, utilizing a sample of matched pair U.S. and non-U.S. firms, Meek concluded that there is no appreciable difference in the stock market's

---

[4] The same sorts of event studies have investigated how rapidly foreign markets adjust to other announcements such as dividend changes, announcements of mergers and acquisitions, and so forth. Again, the results suggest that both in the United States and in the major foreign markets adjustment to such information is extremely rapid.

response to earnings announcements, whether presented on the basis of U.S. or home-country standards.

Pope and Rees (1991) studied the effect of earnings announcements for United Kingdom firms, where earnings were alternatively presented in conformity with U.K. standards and then reconciled in terms of U.S. GAAP. They concluded that U.K. accounting numbers may contain more information than U.S. GAAP reconciled figures. Chen concludes that while both studies have certain limitations, and may not be considered conclusive, there is certainly no evidence that requiring foreign issuers to rereport their earnings in accord with U.S. accounting numbers would improve the protection of U.S. investors.

An overall test of market efficiency asks whether professional investors have any advantage over smaller individual market participants. In effect, these analyses test market efficiency by asking whether prices so well reflect everything that is known about a company that uninformed investors buying at the current tableau of market prices can do as well as the experts. Hawawini (1984) reviews approximately a dozen studies comparing the risk-adjusted performance of foreign institutional investors with market averages. He concludes that there is substantial evidence of efficiency in European markets. Professionally managed portfolios in various countries do not appear to outperform country market averages on a consistent basis.

8. An Updated Test of the Efficiency of Foreign Markets

Using more recent data, we have examined whether globally diversified funds have been able to outperform broad stock market indices over the period 1982 through December 31, 1991. Table 1 presents the results for a number of leading global funds, that is, funds investing in both U.S. and foreign securities. The results are shown for the 10 years 1982–1991. The S&P 500 Index is used as the appropriate market portfolio because 10-year data for global indices were not available. The table shows that the average global fund underperformed the S&P 500 over the period. A similar conclusion holds if the returns are recalculated on a risk-adjusted basis using beta (measured against the S&P Index) as the appropriate measure of risk.

TABLE 1
Analysis of Global Funds, 1982–1991

Fund Name	Average Annual Return
First Investors Global	15.3%
New Perspective	17.2
Oppenheimer Global	17.4
Putnam Global Growth	17.5
Templeton World	15.7
Templeton Growth	15.8
Templeton Small Company Growth	16.6
Average of Funds Listed Above	16.5%
S&P 500 (1982–1991)	17.6%

Table 2 presents an analysis of mutual funds investing in non-U.S. securities for the period 1984 through 1991. This period was chosen because it is the period for which the Morgan Stanley non-U.S. Index was available. It is shown that the average mutual fund investing in non-U.S. stocks has underperformed the Morgan Stanley non-U.S. Index of European and Pacific Rim securities. Again we adjusted the returns for risk, using beta measures calculated against the international index, and found once more that the funds underperformed on a risk adjusted basis. Of course, it is possible that the underperformance was attributable to heavier investment by the mutual funds in those markets that underperformed the non-U.S. average. There appears to be no evidence, however, that, even within a single market, the stock selection of individual managers has consistently exceeded that of the specific country index. Similar conclusions have been reached by Cumby and Glen (1990). The Cumby and Glen paper also uses a variety of benchmarks and different performance measures. They conclude, "We find no evidence that the funds, either individually or as a whole, provide investors with performance that surpasses that of a broad, international equity index."

TABLE 2

Analysis of Funds Investing in Non-U.S. Securities: 1984-1991

Fund Name	Average Annual Return
Kemper International	15.0%
Kleinwort Benson International Equity	15.3
T. Rowe Price International	17.6
Scudder International	16.7
Trustees International	18.5
Average of Funds Listed Above	16.6%
Lipper Index of All International Funds	16.0%
Morgan Stanley Non-U.S. Index	18.8%

Taken as a whole, the evidence supports the view that markets for the shares of non-U.S. companies appear to be as efficient as those for U.S. firms. Publicly available information seems to be incorporated quite rapidly into share prices in all markets. Thus, uninformed investors can expect that the shares of non-U.S. companies are reasonably priced in relation to those of other firms. If this is the case, there is good reason to doubt that investors would benefit at all from any additional disclosure.

It can even be argued, as Lessard has persuasively stated (1990), that presentation of foreign accounting statements adjusted to U.S. GAAP would contribute a false sense of comparability that could even mislead individual investors. GAAP-adjusted earnings do not indicate the significant effect of corporate cross-holdings of securities, which are considerably more important in foreign countries than in the United States. Moreover, GAAP accounting numbers do not adjust for inflation nor do they capture regulatory or institutional differences such as the implicit obligation of companies to provide continued employment in many foreign countries. Given the kind of differences that exist, it is highly unlikely that U.S. investors would find GAAP-reconciled accounting statements useful in making cross-company comparisons.

Finally, it is important to reemphasize that it is not necessary for all investors to be able to follow and interpret all relevant accounting statements. As long as some sophisticated investors are able to take the trouble to collect the relevant data and capture the facts about cash flows for companies in different countries (which local accounting standards allow them to do), then even uninformed investors buying at current prices will suffer no disadvantage.

9. Concluding Comment

Current SEC rules require that the information supplied on foreign securities be reconciled with U.S. accounting standards before those securities can be traded on U.S. exchanges. We have shown that these rules promise little benefit and can be costly to our economy. This conclusion follows particularly from the evidence showing that the markets for foreign securities are efficient. The implication is that further information will not yield much benefit to U.S. investors. Moreover, reconciliation may distort some of the data, which are, naturally, not adapted to U.S. tax laws and U.S. regulations. As a consequence, reconciled information may even prove to be misleading to U.S. investors who may regard it as more informative than it really is. In short, the benefits promised by the required reconciliation are questionable, at best.

On the other hand, the resulting impediment to trading of foreign companies in U.S. markets is a critical disadvantage to individual U.S. investors for whom the transactions costs of dealing in these issues is much higher if they are not traded on organized U.S. exchanges. There is also a serious disadvantage to the exchanges themselves. Our financial industry leads the world in its competitiveness and ability to innovate. It is difficult to defend a regulatory policy that prevents it from competing effectively in making markets in foreign securities.

Figure 1
Shares of World Industrial Employment
Four Countries, 1962 - 85

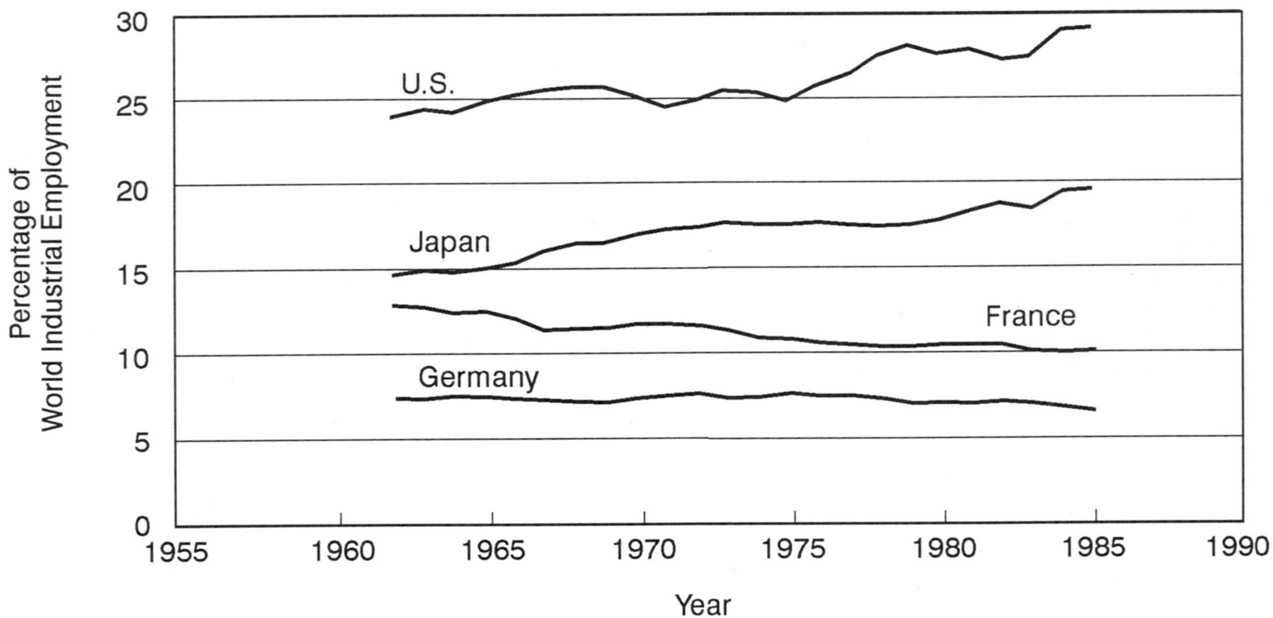

Figure 2
Growth in Share of Service Jobs

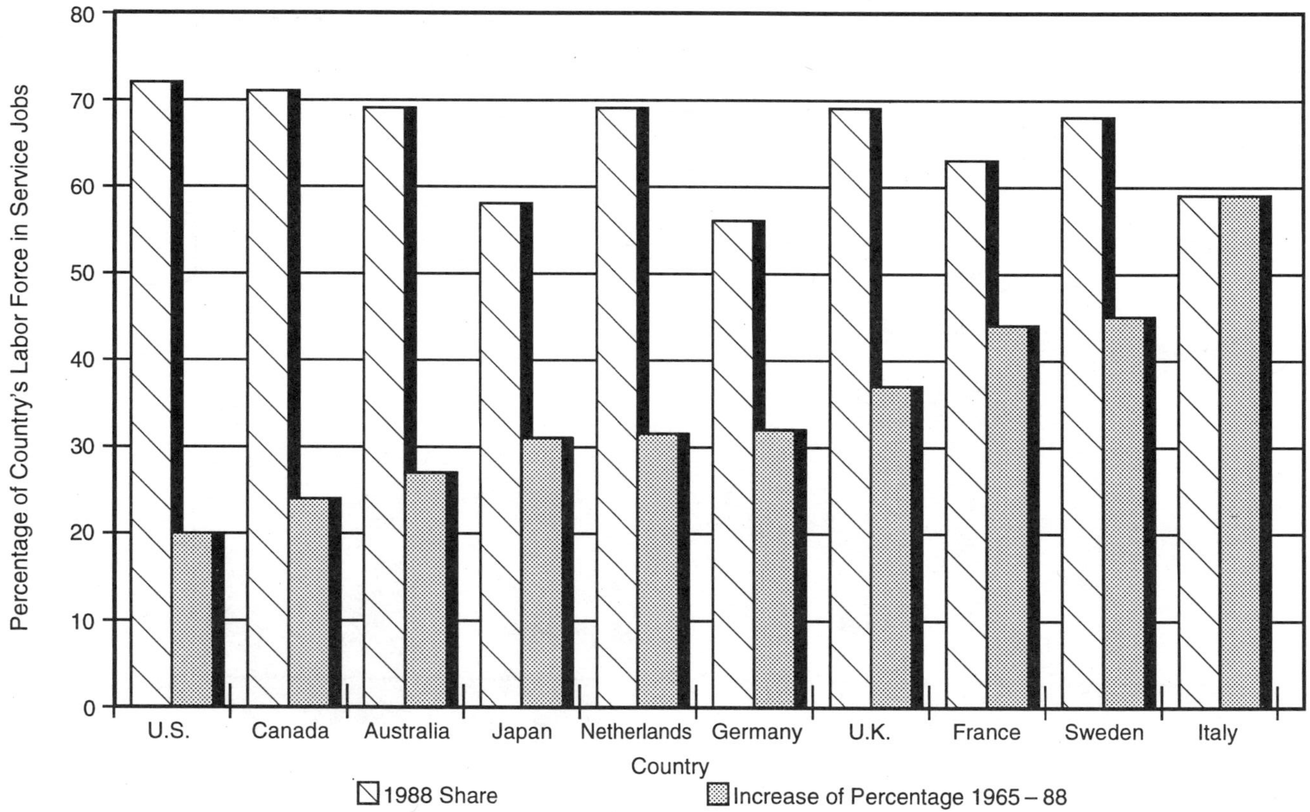

Figure 3
The Benefits of Diversification

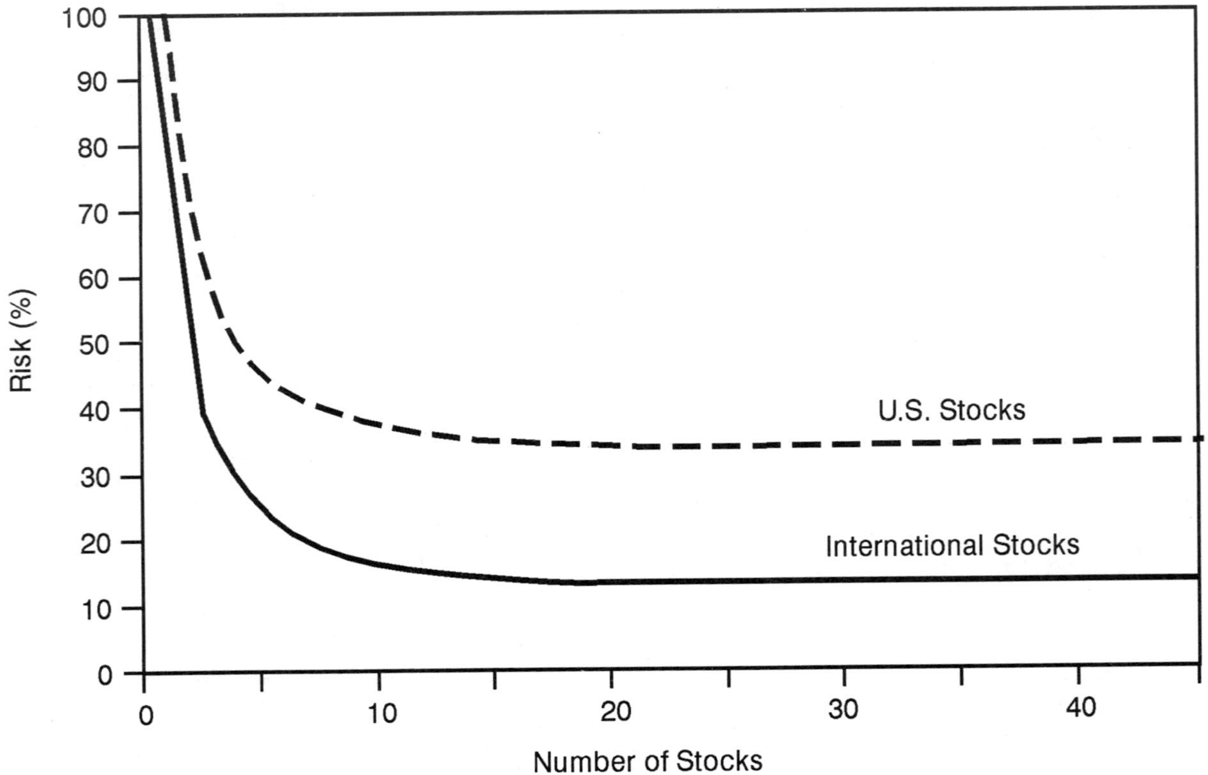

References and Suggested Readings

Ball, Ray, and P. Brown. 1968. "An Empirical Evaluation of Accounting Income Numbers." *Journal of Accounting Research* 6 (Autumn): 159-77.

Baumol, William J., Sue Anne Batey Blackman, and Edward N. Wolff. 1991. *Productivity and American Leadership: The Long View.* Cambridge: MIT Press.

Chen, Show-Mao. 1992. "U.S. Financial Reporting Requirements for Private Foreign Issuers: Policy Implications of Recent Empirical Studies." Unpublished manuscript.

Cumby, Robert E. and Jack D. Glen. 1990. "Evaluating the Performance of International Mutual Funds." *The Journal of Finance* (June): 497-522.

Hawawini, Gabriel. 1984. "European Equity Markets: A Review of the Evidence on Price Behavior and Efficiency." In *European Equity Markets.* New York: Garland.

Lessard, Donald R. 1990. "The Implications of Market Efficiency for U.S. Disclosure by Non-U.S. World-Class Issuers." Working paper, Massachusetts Institute of Technology, Cambridge (Sept. 24).

Meek, Gary K. 1983. "U.S. Securities Market Responses to Alternate Earnings Disclosures of Non-U.S. Multinational Corporations." *The Accounting Review* 58 (Apr.): 394-402.

Pope, Peter F., and William P. Rees. 1991. "International Differences in GAAP and the Pricing of Earnings." Paper presented at the 1991 Annual Meeting of the American Accounting Association, Nashville (Aug.).

4

SEC Requirements For Trading of Foreign Securities on U.S. Exchanges[1]

Franklin R. Edwards
Columbia University

A controversy has arisen between U.S. exchanges and the Securities and Exchange Commission (SEC) over the listing and trading of foreign securities on U.S. exchanges. A foreign company's securities cannot be listed on a U.S. exchange unless that company registers with the SEC in accordance with the Securities Exchange Act of 1934.[2] Among other things, registration requires that a company disclose certain information about itself in a format that conforms to Generally Accepted Accounting Principles in the United States (U.S. GAAP). Although many foreign companies meet all of the listing requirements of U.S. exchanges, most have chosen not to register with the SEC, making their securities ineligible for trading on U.S. exchanges.

Foreign issuers contend that the reporting required by SEC registration is costly for them, unnecessary to protect stockholders, and in

[1] I wish to thank Gur Huberman for helpful comments on an earlier draft of this paper and Trevor Harris for useful discussions at an earlier stage of this project.

[2] Sections 12, 13, 14, and 16 of the Act impose registration, reporting, proxy, and insider-trading requirements on issuers whose securities are traded on a national securities exchange. In 1964 section 12(g) and Rule 12g-1 extended in 1964 registration requirements to all companies "engaged in a business affecting interstate commerce, or whose securities are traded by use of the mails or any means or instrumentality of interstate commerce," and that have (1) total assets exceeding $5 million and (2) a class of equity security (other than an exempted security) held of record by 500 or more persons.

some cases may even mislead their stockholders. They argue that the information they already provide to stockholders, which is in accordance with their own country's disclosure requirements and accounting principles, is sufficient for stockholders. In particular, the requirement that foreign firms reconcile their financial statements to U.S. GAAP often provides no new information to stockholders but simply imposes on them the additional cost of having to compile and restate information in a different format. Further, although in some cases reconciliation would require firms to disclose additional information, foreign firms generally consider such information to be of little value and may even be detrimental to stockholders' interests by disclosing important information to competitors.

The Growth of Foreign Securities Trading and Worldwide Competition

Why has the controversy over foreign securities trading and worldwide competition arisen now? The SEC requirement that firms be registered in order to qualify for listing on U.S. exchanges is, after all, not new: it has applied to foreign issuers for decades, and in 1983 the requirement was extended to the listing and trading of foreign shares on NASDAQ as well. The issue has taken on new importance in the last few years because of the rapid growth of trading in foreign shares and because of the development and growth of foreign securities exchanges, which are now providing intense competition for U.S. exchanges. Further, as capital markets in foreign countries continue to grow, the trading of foreign companies' shares promises to become a huge market. Thus, the SEC's registration requirement, and more particularly its requirement of reconciliation to U.S. GAAP, stands as an insurmountable competitive barrier for U.S. exchanges in their quest to capture a significant share of the growing foreign equities market.

While it is difficult to measure the growth of trading in foreign equities worldwide, we do know that U.S. investors have become much more active in this market. Ownership of foreign equities by U.S. investors has more than doubled over the last four years. (See Figure 1.) By the end of 1991, U.S. investors held $148.8 billion in foreign equities, up from only $58.8 billion in early 1988. Most of these shares are held by institutional investors: approximately 80 percent by ERISA pension funds and 13 percent by global and international mutual funds or closed-end country funds.[3]

---

[3] Estimates of Salomon Brothers.

There has also been a significant increase in the trading of foreign securities by U.S. investors in foreign equity markets. This trading has expanded at a cumulative annual growth rate of 32.8 percent during the 1980s: U.S. purchases and sales of securities abroad grew from $17.9 billion in 1980 to 230.3 billion in 1989.[4] (See Table 1 and Figure 2.) Japanese and British markets were the big winners in attracting U.S. investors. Although foreign purchases and sales in U.S. equity markets have also grown during the 1980s, they have grown at a slower pace (at a compound annual growth rate of 21.0 percent).[5]

U.S. exchanges fear that by not being able to list the securities of large and actively traded foreign firms, they will lose out in the competitive struggle with foreign exchanges. Since the application of the SEC's registration requirement to NASDAQ in 1983, there has been no growth in the number of foreign listings on U.S. exchanges and NASDAQ, despite the rapid expansion that has taken place in the trading of foreign securities. (There are currently a total of 399 foreign listings on the NYSE, AMEX, and NASDAQ.[6]) Further, improved technology and the expansion of trading on foreign securities exchanges threatens to make foreign exchanges even more effective competitors in the future. If U.S. exchanges continue to be unable to compete with foreign exchanges, in the next few years foreign exchanges could gain an irrevocable advantage in the trading of foreign shares that U.S. exchanges may never be able to overcome. London, in particular, is racing ahead in an effort to capture this market: nearly two thousand foreign issues are already traded in London, many on an unlisted basis.

In an effort to alter the competitive imbalance, the New York Stock Exchange has proposed that two hundred world-class issuers— issuers that have stock market capitalizations in excess of $1 billion, have substantial foreign share ownership, and are listed on at least one major world exchange in addition to a home country exchange—be permitted to have their shares listed and traded on U.S. exchanges without having to reconcile their financial statements to U.S. GAAP. Instead, these companies would be allowed to file their own, independently audited, home-country financial

---

[4] Grundfest, "Internationalization of the World's Securities Markets: Economic Causes and Regulatory Consequences," *Journal of Financial Services Research* 4, no. 4 (Dec. 1990): 99–100.

[5] Ibid., 352–53.

[6] *See* no. 9 below for a more complete breakdown of this number.

statements, together with a written explanation of the material differences between home-country accounting practices and U.S. GAAP.

The SEC's Opposition to Foreign Listings

The SEC has rejected this proposal. The long-standing SEC position has been that foreign issuers should be subject to the same rules and requirements that apply to U.S. (or domestic) issuers—in other words, to national or host-country treatment. The NYSE's proposal opens the door to at least the partial application of a home-country policy, since foreign firms would need to disclose only in accordance with their home countries' requirements. As a consequence, the present situation is in stalemate: U.S. exchanges are unable to compete for a large and growing segment of foreign securities trading, and the SEC is standing firm on its contention that it is unnecessary to alter its present disclosure requirements vis-à-vis foreign issuers.

The SEC bases its unwillingness to alter its requirements on two primary policy considerations: investor protection and the need to avoid a disclosure system that would discriminate against U.S. issuers.[7] We can surmise from various statements issued by representatives of the SEC that the SEC fears that any change in the disclosure requirements applicable to foreign issuers may undermine the protection of U.S. investors for two reasons. First, if foreign firms do not make public the same information that is currently provided by U.S. issuers to stockholders, U.S. investors will not be able to evaluate as accurately the value of foreign companies. As a consequence, there will be more mispricing of foreign shares and therefore will be less price efficiency. Some investors may pay too much, and others too little. This argument, obviously, is based on the implicit assumption that the information disclosed by foreign firms under home-country standards is inferior to the information disclosed by U.S. firms. Second, the SEC fears that, in the absence of equivalent disclosure, U.S. markets will become less fair: U.S. investors in foreign companies will be subject to more insider

---

[7] *See*, for example, the statement by former SEC Commissioner Philip R. Lochner, Jr., "The Effect of the S.E.C.'s Foreign Company Reporting Requirements on the U.S. Equity Markets," Remarks before the 11th Annual Ray Garrett Jr. Corporate and Securities Law Institute Conference, Chicago, Ill., (May 1991). *See also*, Securities Act Release No. 33-6437 (Nov. 19, 1982), "Adoption of Foreign Issuer Integrated Disclosure System," 26 S.E.C. Docket (CCH) 964; and Securities Act Release 6360, 24 SEC Dock. 3, 6 (1981).

trading, since there will be more scope for insiders in these companies to possess superior knowledge about the company.[8]

The SEC's second policy concern is that to adopt different disclosure requirements for foreign issuers would establish a two-tier disclosure system: one for foreign firms and a more onerous one for U.S. firms. This would arguably put U.S. firms at a competitive disadvantage, since it would impose greater disclosure costs on them. Further, the eventual result of unequal disclosure standards might be the complete unraveling of the current SEC disclosure standards, since U.S. firms may then also seek to avoid the more onerous U.S. regulations. (The implicit assumption that would seem to underlie this scenario is that investors do not place a value on the additional information disclosed by U.S. firms equal to the cost of producing it. Otherwise, the additional disclosure requirements imposed on U.S. firms would not be a competitive disadvantage.)

SEC Protection of U.S. Investors: Who and How?

SEC mandatory disclosure requirements arguably protect investors principally by requiring firms to disclose information that investors need to value a firm or its stock. In addition, the Securities Exchange Act establishes penalties for improper or fraudulent disclosure and has the subsidiary benefit of imposing uniformity on the way that firms report information. Uniformity of accounting and reporting should reduce the transactions costs experienced by investors in collecting and deciphering information.

The public interest rationale for mandatory disclosure, therefore, contains the obvious presumption that, left unregulated, firms in a free-market setting will fail to report sufficient information for shareholders to be able to accurately value their shares or, alternatively, that unregulated firms will disclose misleading or fraudulent information with the intention of deceiving shareholders. Further, if these practices were widespread, equity markets would be less fair and investors might abandon them, resulting in less liquid and less price-efficient markets.

These presumptions are not accepted by everyone. Critics of SEC disclosure requirements argue that, even in the absence of requirements, firms would voluntarily provide investors with sufficient information. They

---

[8] *See*, for example, Richard C. Breeden, Chairman, Securities and Exchange Commission, "Remarks at the American Stock Exchange Perspectives Conference," Washington, D. C., Nov. 4, 1992.

point, for example, to the voluntary disclosure that now takes place in the private placement market, which is exempt from SEC requirements, as well as to the disclosures that firms commonly made prior to enactment of the SEA in 1933. Further, although SEC requirements may result in firms disclosing more information than they otherwise would, it is not self-evident that the additional information is either useful or cost-effective. Even assuming that the additional information has value, at least for some firms, the costs borne by all firms in having to report this information may exceed its societal benefits. The SEC, it is contended, does not properly weigh the costs associated with greater disclosure. In addition, experience shows that SEC requirements are not an effective deterrent to fraud, nor are they needed to give defrauded investors legal recourse. Finally, while uniformity of reporting can be beneficial, it also limits the flexibility that firms have in how and what they report and as a consequence may result in less useful disclosures.

These contentious issues are unlikely to be resolved in the near future. In the meantime, the application of SEC disclosure requirements to foreign firms is an effective deterrent to U.S. exchanges competing in world securities markets and could eventually lead to the erosion of our preeminent position in world markets. Only a short time ago many of us believed that the United State's dominant positions in automobiles, electronics, computers, and other industries were impregnable. We do not want to make the same mistake again about our financial industries.

How does the SEC's requirement that foreign firms whose shares are traded on a U.S. exchange register under the SEA protect U.S. investors? More particularly, how does the requirement that foreign firms reconcile to U.S. GAAP protect U.S. investors? U.S investors already hold and trade the shares of unregistered foreign firms in large volume. As already shown in Table 1, the aggregate purchases and sales of U.S. investors in foreign equity markets amounted to $230.3 billion in 1989, and this trading is growing rapidly. In addition, it is not necessary for foreign firms to register with the SEC to have their shares traded in the United States—this requirement *applies only to trading on U.S. exchanges and NASDAQ.* As a consequence, unregistered shares of foreign firms are increasingly being traded in the United States in the over-the-counter market, either through the Electronic Bulletin Board (EBB) or the pink sheets. In these over-the-counter markets there is no last-sale reporting, no volume reporting, no real-time price quotes, and little readily available financial information about the companies traded. In a word, these markets are lightly regulated, in comparison to that of exchange-traded securities. During the last decade, SEC requirements have continued to push more and more trading of foreign shares into these less-regulated markets. Currently, there are 722 unregistered American Depository Receipts (ADRs) traded over-the-counter in the United States, compared with 492 foreign reporting (or registered) companies.[9] But the more telling statistic is what has happened since October 6, 1983. On that date the SEC amended Rule 12g3-2 to provide that both securities traded on a national exchange and those traded in the NASDAQ over-the-counter quotation system must be registered.[10] Prior to that time, the securities of foreign firms could be traded on NASDAQ without Section 12 registration by availing themselves of the information-supplying exemption of Rule 12g3-2(b).[11] In the seven years preceding the elimination of this exemption, from 1977 to 1983, the number of foreign securities traded on NASDAQ tripled, growing from 85 to 294. Since the exemption was eliminated in 1983, the number of foreign securities traded on NASDAQ has declined to 213 (as of the end of 1991). In contrast, since 1983 the number of foreign securities traded in the Electronic Bulletin Board or pink sheets, where the SEC exemption still applies, has grown noticeably. As of the end of 1991, 376 foreign, unregistered companies were traded in the over-the-counter EBB or pink sheets.[12]

Clearly, U.S. investors are already trading unregistered foreign securities both in the United States and in foreign countries in markets in which there is less regulatory oversight and where transactions costs are considerably higher. Figure 3 shows the average transactions costs for an institutional investor in 1989, for four different size transactions and for three

---

[9] Of the 492 reporting foreign issuers, 119 are listed on the NYSE, 67 on AMEX, and 213 are quoted through NASDAQ. In addition, 107 companies are traded in over-the-counter markets. I am indebted to James Shapiro of the NYSE for providing these figures.

[10] *See* Securities Act Release 6493, 28 SEC Dock. 1263 (1983).

[11] Exempted foreign companies still had to provide specified information to the SEC. The required information was limited to whatever during the last fiscal year had been made public by the issuer pursuant to the law of the country of its domicile or in which it is organized or by a stock exchange on which its securities are traded or has been distributed to its securities holders. Issuers were required to furnish whatever information was deemed material to an investor's decision to purchase the company's securities.

[12] For estimates of the foreign stocks traded in the United States prior to 1983, see "New Disclosure Requirements for Foreign Issuers," *Financial Analysts Journal*, Nov.-Dec., 1983.

major foreign markets versus the United States. Transactions costs are significantly lower in the United States than in either the United Kingdom or Japan, where most of the trading of foreign securities by U.S. investors occurs. Figure 3 also does not reflect the higher bid-ask spreads and execution costs that are characteristic of both foreign markets and the over-the-counter markets in the United States on which unregistered foreign securities are traded. The SEC registration requirement, therefore, does not protect U.S. investors by preventing them from trading foreign securities, but rather forces this trading to take place in more costly and less regulated markets.

Nor can we take much solace from the contention that the SEC requirements protect small U.S. investors. Although these requirements may make it more difficult for small, unsophisticated investors to find out how to trade foreign securities and to learn about the business activities and financials of foreign companies, small investors are nevertheless harmed by the inability of U.S. investors to trade foreign stocks on U.S. exchanges. The U.S. investors now trading foreign securities are largely pension funds and mutual funds, so that the higher costs of trading in foreign markets, as well as in the over-the-counter markets, are passed through to fund beneficiaries and shareholders, most of whom are the very same small investors that the SEC seeks to protect.

The Efficiency of Foreign Stock Prices and Investor Protection

The SEC's refusal to accept home-country reporting as a basis for permitting foreign firms to be traded on U.S. exchanges is premised on the implicit assumption that foreign securities markets are less price efficient than U.S. markets because of poorer reporting standards in foreign countries. Stated in another way, the SEC's implicit view is that the prices of foreign securities are unlikely to reflect the future prospects of firms as accurately as do security prices in the United States because SEC disclosure requirements result in more information being available about U.S. firms.

This view is difficult to verify. Even accepting the argument that more information is always better than less, there is no evidence to suggest that foreign stock markets are not price efficient in the sense that resources are not allocated efficiently among firms. Empirical studies, for example, generally show that accounting information disclosed by foreign firms is used by foreign investors to value stocks in foreign markets in the same manner as U.S. investors use the information disclosed by U.S. companies to value shares in U.S. markets.[13] Whether the resulting stock values are as macroefficient (or are efficient in an absolute sense), we do not know.[14] Even if more information is disclosed by firms in the United States, it is possible that at least some of this information is without value—in other words, that there is too much information disclosed by U.S. firms.

Or, alternatively, since in many foreign countries the structure of firm ownership is characterized by a greater role for large owners, information asymmetries between managers and stockholders may be less, and, as a consequence, stocks may be even more efficiently priced in those countries. Further, this could be true even if less information were disclosed by foreign firms than American firms. Different industrial and corporate structures, therefore, can influence the efficiency of equity prices in different countries.

Although it is clearly very difficult to determine the relative accuracy of U.S. versus foreign equity markets in a macro or absolute efficiency context, several studies of the relative or micro efficiency of foreign equity markets suggest that these markets are as efficient as U.S. equity markets. By relative efficiency I mean the extent to which security prices are efficient *relative* to each other, or to previous securities prices. Academic studies of relative efficiency can be grouped into four types: (1) studies of security price behavior—tests of serial correlation, price randomness, and so forth; (2) studies of the effects of public announcements—tests of the reactions of securities prices to the disclosure of accounting information, such as SEC reports; (3) studies of investment performance—whether professional investment managers make money using publicly available information; and (4) studies of whether private information has value.[15] Over the past 10 years hundreds of these studies have been done on foreign securities markets (mostly European), with the

---

[13] *See*, for example, Harris and Lang, "Relations Between Security Market Prices, Returns and Accounting Measures in Germany," Working paper, Columbia University, August, 1992. For a contrary view, *see* Hall, Hamao, and Harris, "A Comparison of Relations Between Security Market Prices, Returns and Accounting Measures in Japan and the United States," Working paper, Columbia University, September 30, 1992.

[14] For a discussion of the alternative concepts of price efficiency *see* Myers, "Fuzzy Efficiency," *Institutional Investor*, Dec., 1988.

[15] *See* Gordon and Kornhauser, "Efficient Markets, Costly Information, and Securities Research," *New York University Law Review* 60:761–833, 775.

general finding that foreign markets are as efficient as U.S markets, especially in the case of large firms.[16]

There have, in addition, been a few studies on the specific question of whether the restating of the earnings of foreign firms in accordance with U.S. GAAP provides useful information to investors. Specifically, if accounting data stated according to U.S. GAAP were more informative than data commonly disclosed by foreign firms, we would expect to observe a closer association between the stock prices of foreign firms and their disclosures according to U.S. GAAP.[17] While the results of these studies are subject to alternative interpretation, the general finding is that the SEC's current U.S. GAAP reconciliation requirement may not provide investors with useful information (even though it may result in the disclosure of different information). More studies, however, must be done before we can draw definitive conclusions.

In summary, most of the evidence on the relative efficiency of foreign equity markets suggests that the efficiency of these markets is quite similar to that of U.S. markets. Further, as foreign trading volume expands in the future relative to U.S. markets, both the liquidity and efficiency of foreign markets is likely to increase. It is still possible, of course, that the SEC may be right—that foreign markets are not as efficient in an absolute value sense as are U.S. markets, but at present there is little evidence in support this view.

---

[16] For surveys of these studies, *see* Lessard, "The Implications of Market Efficiency for U.S. Disclosure by Non-U.S. World-Class Issuers," Working paper, Massachusetts Institute of Technology, Sept. 24, 1990; and Hawawini, *European Equity Markets: Price Behavior and Efficiency*, Monograph Series in Finance and Economics, Salomon Brothers Center for the Study of Financial Institutions, Graduate School of Business, New York University, 1984.

[17] *See*, for example, Meek, "U.S. Securities Market Responses to Alternate Earnings Disclosures of Non-U.S. Multinational Corporations," 58 *The Accounting Review*, 394–402 (1983); Pope and Rees, "International Differences in GAAP and the Pricing of Earnings," paper presented at the 1991 Annual Meeting of the American Accounting Association, Nashville, Tenn., Aug., 1991; and Choi and Hong, "The Decision Utility of Restating Accounting Information Sets: Korea," in 4B *Advances in Financial Planning and Forecasting*, 123–42, Aggarwal and Lee, eds. 1990.

Insider Trading and Investor Protection: A Bogus Issue

Another SEC concern is that poorer disclosure policies in foreign countries may result in more insider trading in foreign stocks, to the detriment of U.S. investors in these stocks. Even if foreign markets were price efficient, greater insider trading would, arguably, result in greater market unfairness—U.S. investors would be at a disadvantage vis-à-vis insiders.

It is important to recognize, however, that there are insiders in all countries and in all markets—investors, and other "tippees," who at times possess information that public stockholders do not have. In the United States the ability of insiders to disadvantage other investors is controlled by various laws. Specifically, insiders are prohibited from trading on, or otherwise taking advantage of, their superior information under penalty of both substantial fines and prison terms. These laws apply equally to foreign companies whose shares are traded in the United States.

Further, to the extent that insiders in foreign companies now take advantage of public stockholders in foreign equity markets, requiring foreign companies to reconcile to U.S. GAAP will in no way curb this activity. Even with the disclosure of more or better information, U.S. investors, as well as foreign public investors, will still be subject to trading-ahead by insiders.

Thus, insider trading is a separate issue, independent of the question of what the proper level of disclosure is for foreign firms. Further, if foreign stocks were traded on U.S. exchanges, the SEC would be in a better position to monitor and restrict insider trading in these stocks.

Do U.S. Investors Need to Be Protected against Foreign Issuers?

If the securities of foreign companies were permitted to be traded on U.S. exchanges without having to meet the current SEC registration requirements (as is now the case in the EBB and pink-sheet over-the-counter markets), how might we expect U.S. investors to react? Further, suppose that foreign firms did not provide information to investors that was as complete or as good as that provided by U.S. firms. Under these conditions it is unlikely that U.S. investors would be willing to value foreign stocks on the same basis as the shares of U.S. firms. With less information, foreign stocks would undoubtedly be viewed as more risky and therefore subject to a higher discount rate. This is especially likely in today's markets, where the dominant U.S. stockholders in foreign firms are sophisticated institutional investors. Stated another way, U.S. investors would demand a higher risk premium for holding foreign stocks or a higher rate of return in compensation for not being kept as well informed.

The effect of this investor reaction will be to impose a higher cost of capital on foreign firms. To prevent this from happening, of course, foreign firms can voluntarily disclose more information—they can disclose fundamentally the same information that U.S. firms provide. They would then no longer be penalized by investors. There is some evidence that this in fact happens. In particular, in the private-placement market, foreign firms provide investors with information comparable to that disclosed by U.S. firms. Similarly, they frequently provide rating agencies with more complete information. Thus, foreign firms can be expected to respond voluntarily to the needs of U.S. investors for more information if by supplying that information they can reduce their cost of capital. Whether the equilibrium level of information that is ultimately provided by foreign firms will be optimal in a welfare sense is difficult to determine. But it must be recognized as well that there also is no way of determining whether the SEC's current disclosure requirements provide the optimal amount of information. Since SEC requirements are not subject to a market-based, cost-benefit evaluation, it is not unreasonable to think that they may result in firms having to produce too much information.

In addition, the U.S. exchanges on which foreign shares are listed have a direct interest in requiring adequate disclosure. The more trading of foreign securities that takes place on an exchange, the better for exchange members. If, because of inadequate disclosure, an embarrassing episode were to occur with respect to the foreign securities traded on that exchange, customers might be driven away from the exchange, and the exchange's trading volume reduced. The result could be lost revenues for the exchange for many years into the future. Major U.S. exchanges have been in business for many years and can be expected to protect their long-term interests.[18]

Finally, suppose that foreign firms did not disclose adequate information and that as a result some U.S. investors suffered losses—perhaps there might even be a scandal involving a foreign company. Would this event significantly harm the market for U.S. securities in the United States? Would U.S. investors stop trading the securities of U.S. companies because

---

[18] The New York Stock Exchange, for example, had disclosure standards for firms long before they were required by federal legislation in 1933 and 1934. For a description and analysis of the information reported by firms prior to the SEA, *see* Benston, "Required Disclosure and the Stock Market: An Evaluation of the Securities Exchange Act of 1934," *American Economic Review*.

of inadequate disclosure by foreign firms? It seems doubtful. A more likely response is for U.S. investors to stop trading the securities of foreign firms. Thus, the fear that inadequate disclosure by foreign firms could somehow undermine U.S. equity markets seems unwarranted.

A Two-Tiered Disclosure Policy and Competitive Equality

The final SEC argument is that to accept different disclosure standards for foreign issuers would be to establish a two-tiered reporting system that may favor foreign firms. With less onerous disclosure requirements, the SEC argues, foreign firms will have lower costs than U.S. firms and will therefore have a competitive advantage. Further, if this cost advantage proves to be significant, it will not be long before U.S. firms agitate for less burdensome disclosure standards for themselves, which could lead to the wholesale undermining of the SEC's current disclosure standards.

Several points seem worth noting in response to this argument. First, to the extent that foreign countries now impose less burdensome reporting standards on firms, U.S. firms already operate at a competitive disadvantage. U.S. investors already trade the securities of unregistered foreign firms in volume in foreign markets. Second, the argument implicitly assumes that the present SEC disclosure requirements are not optimal: that investors are not willing to pay for the additional information that U.S. firms are required to disclose. Stated another way, if a foreign firm reports less information and investors recognize this as a deficiency, the firm's cost of capital will be higher than for a similar U.S. firm. Alternatively, if by providing the information required by the SEC a U.S. firm's cost of capital is lower, there will be no incentive for U.S. firms to abandon the current disclosure standards. Third, to the extent that neither U.S. firms nor U.S. investors value the greater information required by the SEC, and prefer to relax disclosure standards to make them more compatible with those of foreign countries, this suggests that current SEC requirements may in fact be too burdensome.

If our current disclosure policies are superior to those of foreign countries, therefore, it is not clear why either U.S. investors or firms would want to abandon these policies in favor of inferior disclosure standards. It is clearly in the interests of investors to have securities accurately priced, and, as a general proposition, having accurately priced shares is also in the interests of firms. To contend otherwise is to assume that U.S. investors and firms behave irrationally, or that there are significant externalities that are not being internalized. It is difficult to see what these externalities might be. If, on the other hand, our current disclosure policies are not superior, or are more costly than the provision of the additional information warrants, we should be happy to abandon them in favor of a better policy. Thus, at least in the case of reporting standards, worldwide competition among exchanges, as well as among alternative government disclosure policies, may result in the establishment of optimal global disclosure standards.

Policy Choices

The feasible policy choices now facing the United States are (1) to require foreign companies to adhere to current U.S. disclosure and registration requirements; (2) to accept home-country reporting by foreign companies from some or all foreign countries; or (3) to attempt to harmonize accounting standards and disclosure requirements across all major countries, perhaps under the auspices of the International Organization of Securities Commissions (IOSCO). A variation on these is for the SEC to relax its registration requirements for only a certain class of foreign firms—such as to no longer require reconciliation to U.S. GAAP for foreign world-class issuers.[19]

The analysis in this paper suggests that there is little danger to U.S. investors in the SEC relaxing its reporting requirements for foreign companies. A continuation of the present SEC policy threatens to jeopardize the long-term competitiveness of U.S. exchanges and possibly their long-term viability as well. Simply dropping the requirement that foreign firms reconcile their financial statements to U.S. GAAP may be sufficient to ameliorate the competitive problem in the short run. In the long run, however, we must squarely face the question of what our disclosure policies should be in a world of competitive and global capital markets in which a firm's securities can be traded anywhere in the world.

---

[19] The NYSE's proposal, for example, would relax these standards for only world-class issuers: those with capitalizations in excess of $1 billion, substantial foreign share ownership, and a listing on at least one major world exchange in addition to a home-country exchange.

Figure 1
Holdings of Foreign Equities by U.S. Residents
1988–1991

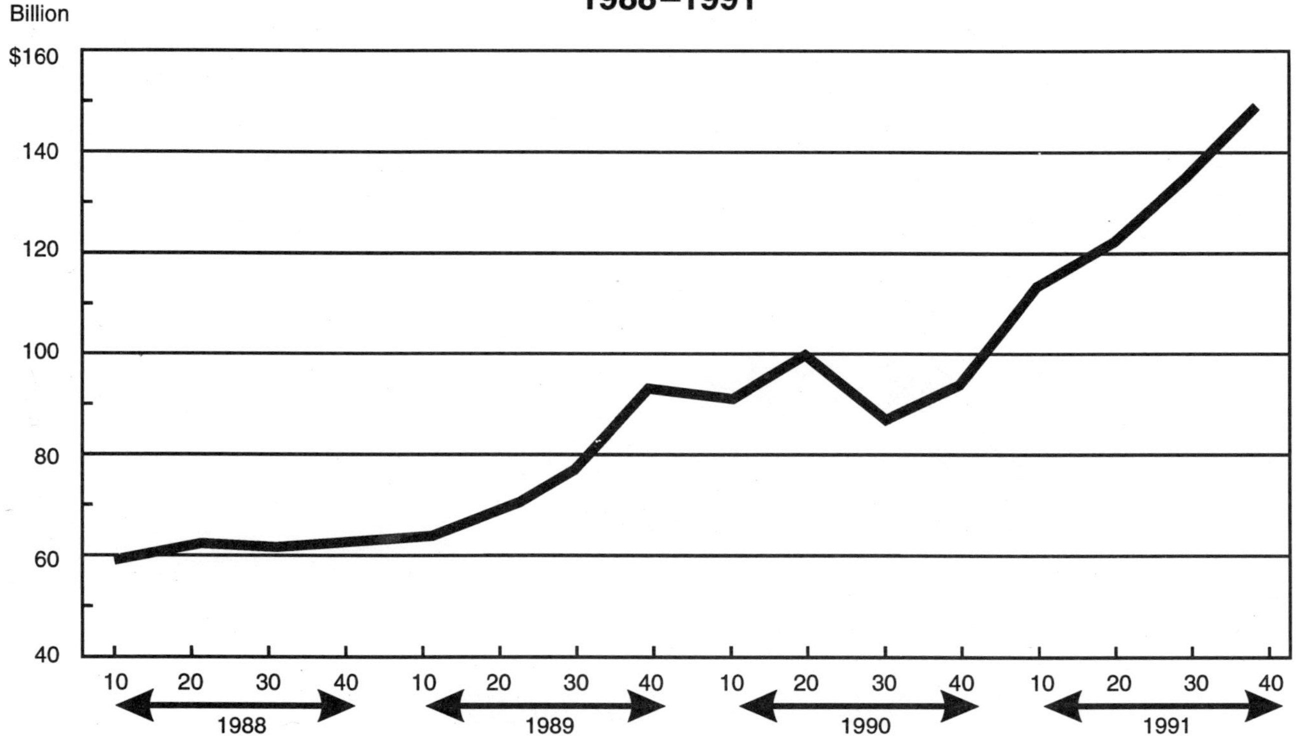

Source: Federal Reserve Board view of Funs.

Figure 2
Aggregate U.S. Transactions in Foreign Equities Markets, by Geographic Region, 1980–1989

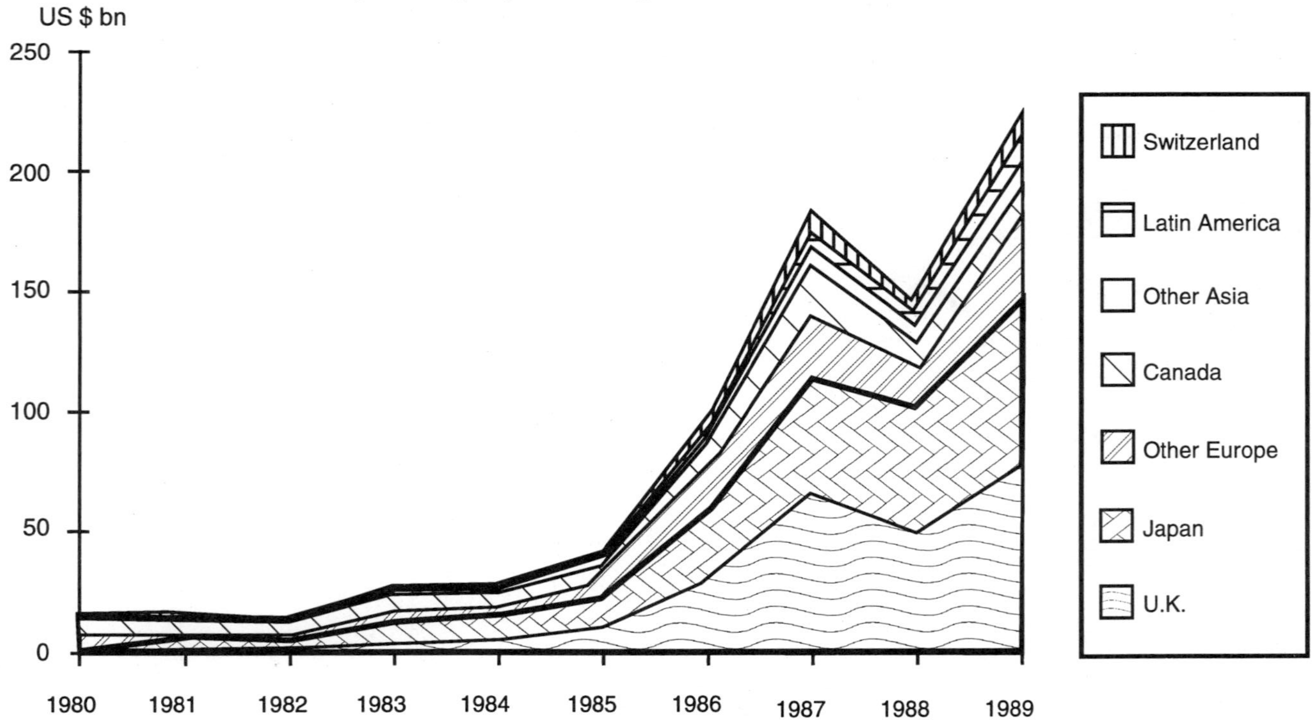

Note: Aggregate U.S. Transactions is the sum of purchases and sales.
Source: *U.S. Treasury Bulletin,* various issues.

Current Institutional Equity Transaction Costs

(by trade size)

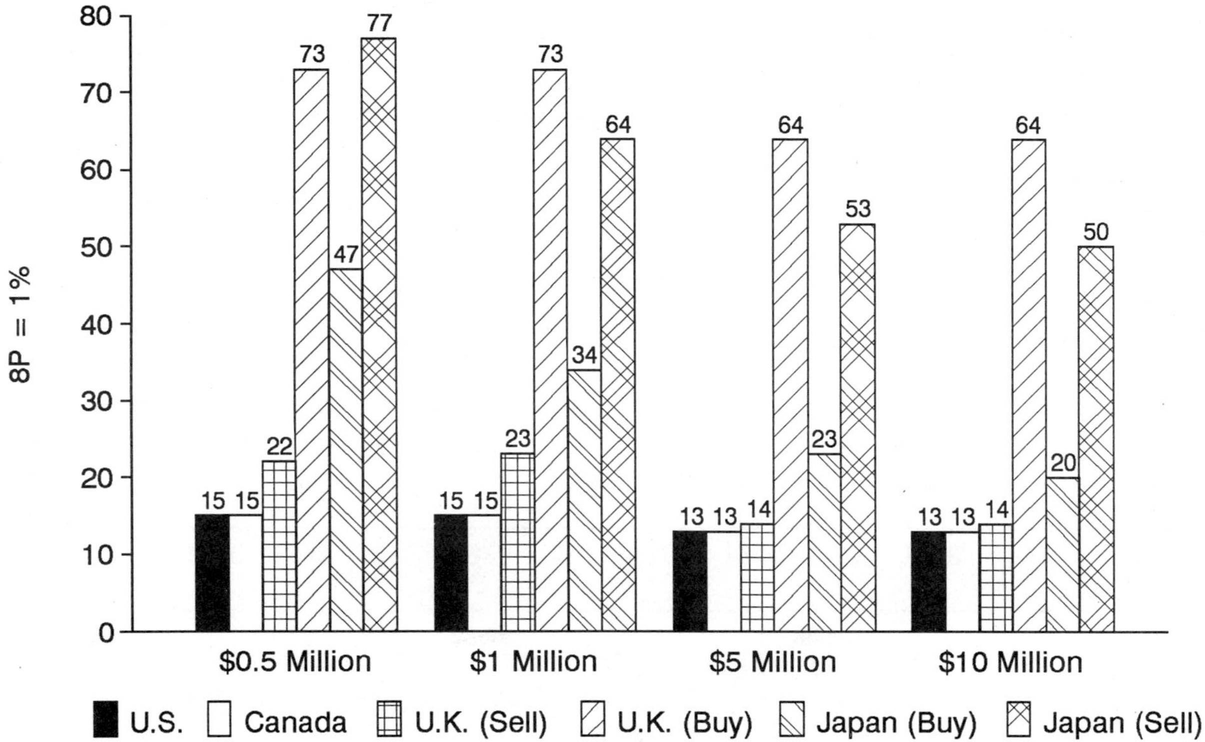

Source: Securities Industry Association, "Institutional Equity Transaction Costs," August 8, 1990 p 8.

Table 1
Aggregate U.S. Purchases and Sales of Foreign Securities, by Geographic Region, 1980–1989 (in U.S. $ billions)

	1980	1981	1982	1983	1984	1985	1986	1987	1988	1989	1980-1989 CAGR	1989 Mkt shr
Canada	6.7	4.9	2.9	5.0	4.4	6.8	9.8	18.9	9.7	10.9	5.5%	4.7%
Total Europe	6.9	5.7	6.5	13.6	13.3	21.5	55.3	101.4	75.6	128.9	38.5%	56.0%
United Kingdom	2.8	2.9	3.6	6.5	7.8	13.3	32.6	67.9	51.2	80.1	45.3%	34.8%
Switzerland	1.6	0.9	0.7	1.8	1.3	1.6	3.2	6.3	5.3	8.5	20.8%	3.7%
Other Europe	2.5	1.9	2.2	5.4	4.2	6.6	19.5	27.2	19.1	40.3	36.0%	17.5%
Total Asia	3.3	6.5	5.1	9.4	10.7	14.0	30.1	56.7	56.2	75.8	41.8%	32.9%
Japan	2.7	5.4	4.3	8.0	9.0	11.6	25.6	47.8	50.4	65.8	42.4%	28.6%
Other Asia	0.6	1.1	0.8	1.4	1.6	2.5	4.5	8.9	5.8	10.1	38.0%	4.3%
Latin America	0.7	1.1	0.8	1.6	0.9	1.2	3.6	7.1	5.3	9.3	33.3%	4.0%
All other	0.3	0.4	0.3	0.8	1.1	2.0	2.7	5.8	4.8	5.4	36.4%	2.3%
Total	17.9	18.6	15.7	30.3	30.4	45.6	101.5	189.8	151.4	230.3	32.8%	100.0%

Source: Office of the Secretary, U.S. Department of Treasury, *Treasury Bulletin,* table CM-V-5, Spring issues.

[a] CARG is the cumulative annual growth rate.

References and Suggested Readings

Benston, George J. "Required Disclosure and the Stock Market: An Evaluation of the Securities Exchange Act of 1934." *American Economic Review.*

Breeden, Richard C. 1992. "Remarks at the American Stock Exchange Perspectives Conference." Washington, D.C. (Nov. 4).

Choi, Frederick D.S. and S.B. Hong. 1990. "The Decision Utility of Restating Accounting Information Sets: Korea." In *Advances in Financial Planning and Forecasting*, Raj Aggarwal and Cheng-Few Lee, eds., 123–42.

Gordon, Jeffrey N., and Lewis A. Kornhauser. "Efficient Markets, Costly Information, and Securities Research." *New York University Law Review* 60:761–833.

Grundfest, Joseph A. 1990. "Internationalization of the World's Securities Markets: Economic Causes and Regulatory Consequence." *Journal of Financial Services Research* 4, No. 4 (Dec.): 99–100.

Hall, Charles, Yasushi Hamao, and Trevor S. Harris. 1992. "A Comparison of Relations Between Security Market Prices, Returns and Accounting Measures in Japan and the United States." (Working paper, Columbia University, New York) (Sept. 30).

Harris, Trevor S., and Mark Lang. 1992. "Relations Between Security Market Prices, Returns and Accounting Measures in Germany." Working paper, Columbia University, New York, (Aug.).

Hawawini, Gabriel. 1984. *European Equity Markets: Price Behavior and Efficiency*. Monograph Series in Finance and Economics, Salomon Brothers Center for the Study of Financial Institutions, Graduate School of Business, New York University.

Lessard, Donald R. 1990. "The Implications of Market Efficiency for U.S. Disclosure by Non-U.S. World-Class Issuers." Working paper, Massachusetts Institute of Technology, Cambridge (Sept. 24).

Lochner, Philip R., Jr. 1991. "The Effect of the S.E.C.'s Foreign Company Reporting Requirements on the U.S. Equity Markets." Remarks before the 11th Annual Ray Garrett, Jr., Corporate and Securities Law Institute Conference, Chicago (May).

Meek, Gary K. 1983. "U.S. Securities Market Responses to Alternate Earnings Disclosures of Non-U.S. Multinational Corporations." *The Accounting Review* 58 (Apr.): 394–402.

Myers, Stewart. 1988. "Fuzzy Efficiency." *Institutional Investor* (Dec.).

"New Disclosure Requirements for Foreign Issuers." 1983. *Financial Analysts Journal* (Nov./Dec.).

Pope, Peter F., and William P. Rees. 1991. "International Differences in GAAP and the Pricing of Earnings." Paper presented at the 1991 Annual Meeting of the American Accounting Association, Nashville (Aug.).

5

On Trading Foreign Securities in U.S. Markets[1]

Clifford W. Smith, Jr.
University of Rochester

The New York Stock Exchange has requested permission from the Securities and Exchange Commission to list foreign stocks for trading without meeting U.S. disclosure requirements. The SEC appears cool to the proposal. Chairman Breeden has been particularly negative in his reaction to what he has called the "Teutonic issue" (a reference to the NYSE's specific interest in listing certain German securities).

In this paper I will examine the implications of permitting such foreign stock listing on domestic exchanges. I focus on three primary questions: (1) Why would U.S. investors want to acquire foreign securities? (2) Why would the SEC reject the exchange's request? (3) What difference does it make if it does reject the NYSE's request?

Why Invest in Foreign Securities?

The basic motive for U.S. investors to acquire foreign stocks is to achieve additional diversification. In the 1950s Nobel laureate Harry Markowitz recognized that the risk of a portfolio of securities can be lower than the risk of every security in the portfolio. This is because idiosyncratic sources of risk are spread and thereby reduced as an investor's portfolio is distributed among more securities. These diversification benefits are least when security returns are highly correlated. Investors thus find foreign securities particularly useful in reducing portfolio risk because the returns to foreign securities typically have relatively low correlation with the returns of domestic securities.

---

[1] This work has been supported by the Bradley Policy Research Center, William E. Simon Graduate School of Business, University of Rochester.

At this point, it is critical to note that rejecting the NYSE proposal does not prohibit U.S. citizens from investing in foreign securities. U.S. investors currently face several quite legal alternatives for foreign investing. First, one can purchase foreign shares on a foreign exchange—frequently employing a U.S. brokerage firm.

Second, one can purchase American Depository Receipts. (ADRs are financial assets issued by U.S. banks that represent indirect ownership of a specified number of shares of a foreign firm; the underlying shares are held on deposit in a bank in the firm's home country.) Third, one can invest in mutual funds that hold foreign shares. Moreover, these alternatives all provide U.S. investors with only the level of disclosure mandated by the foreign companies' local exchanges and regulations.

The New York Stock Exchange has made large investments in the development of sophisticated systems to supply transactions services at low cost. Therefore, allowing foreign firms to list on the NYSE would provide U.S. investors with lower cost access to securities that offer particularly attractive diversification opportunities. Moreover, with U.S. listing, the U.S. financial press would have stronger incentives to cover those listed foreign firms more extensively. This would lower the information costs investors incur in global investing.

Why Reject the Request?

Why would the SEC reject a proposal that would benefit U.S. investors by lowering their costs? The logical place to search for an answer is to look for groups that would be harmed by approval. For example, one might reason that giving foreign companies access to U.S. capital markets lowers their costs of capital and makes them more competitive in world product markets. Therefore one potential class of damaged parties are U.S. firms. But this reasoning is too narrow; it focuses on only one aspect of foreign listing. Allowing foreign listing will attract not just foreign issuers but also foreign investors to U.S. capital markets, increasing the demand for domestic securities. Moreover expanding the alternatives faced by investors in U.S. capital markets could lower the cost of capital for U.S. firms as well. Thus, it is difficult to argue that U.S. businesses would be hurt by this proposal.

However, a powerful interest group that I believe would be damaged by foreign listing is the SEC itself. Allowing foreign firms to trade on U.S. exchanges would force the Securities and Exchange Commission to face a difficult set of questions. SEC rules mandate more extensive disclosure than most other countries. If the Commission were to allow foreign firms to be traded on U.S. exchanges without meeting U.S. disclosure requirements, it would inevitably receive requests from domestic firms to allow them to be traded on similar terms. I do not believe that the SEC wants to reopen this debate.

In making private disclosure decisions corporate managers have incentives to maximize the value of the firm. Disclosing an item like manufacturing costs might be informative (and thus valuable) to owners and creditors, but such numbers also might be valuable to the firm's competitors. So long as the managers' forecast of the value of the information to potential securityholders exceeds their forecast of the reduction in firm value resulting from the release of the information to competitors, they have strong private incentives to release the information publicly. (Note, however, that some of the favorable financing effects of the provision of such information still could be obtained by privately contracting with a lender such as a bank or a private equity supplier and supplying the information in confidence under the contract.)

Foreign-security regulators have been more sensitive to potential adverse disclosure impacts of proprietary information than has the SEC. By mandating disclosure of valuable proprietary information, the SEC imposes a regulatory tax on U.S. corporations. Such mandated disclosure transforms private information into a public good, reduces the value of this valuable corporate asset, and thereby reduces the competitiveness of U.S. businesses in global markets. This disclosure regulation thus can harm investors.

Obviously, the costs of this regulation vary across firms as the value of information varies. But even if reducing mandated disclosures would benefit all investors by increasing the value of U.S. corporations, this regulatory change would reduce the Commission's leverage over the business community and thus reduce the political power of the SEC. In such circumstances, the Commission's reticence is not surprising.

What Difference Does It Make?

Given the current structure of world securities markets, costs associated with the rejection of foreign listing take on the two major forms that I have already discussed: (1) the incremental costs imposed on U.S. investors from more expensive access to foreign securities and (2) the higher regulatory tax imposed on U.S. business because of the SEC's disclosure rules. But incentives exist for the ongoing evolution of global securities markets. To understand these evolutionary pressures, it is useful to review the history of U.S. stock exchanges. The exchange industry of the 1880s was quite different from today's. Then, virtually every major city had a stock exchange; today, there are only seven regional exchanges left (and much of their continued viability depends on trading options or their access to the national exchanges resulting from the SEC's central market regulation, which grew out of the Securities Acts Amendments of 1975).

At least two things have occurred over the last century to reduce the importance of the regional exchanges: technological changes and the institutionalization of investing. Institutionalization has increased the frequency of large block trades; this increases the demand for the additional liquidity provided by a national exchange like the NYSE. Through investments in technology, the NYSE has increased its capacity to supply trading services at lower cost. Increased volume has been handled by the expanded use of computers to process the administrative and operational aspects of securities trading. Changes in the communications technology also increase the incentives for market centralization as the financial community has more rapid access to relevant information about companies' fortunes and the costs of clearing orders at a distant location fall.

Some of the incentives that led to the centralization of trading within the U.S. apply to global financial markets today. Thus, there are incentives that could lead to the centralization of securities trading on a global basis in ways that mirror the centralization that occurred within the U.S. over the last century.

If such global market centralization occurs, the NYSE will face new competition for dominance in trading from foreign exchanges like those in London and Tokyo. The battle will first be fought over making the market in shares of large multinational firms, the firms that currently are among the more profitable listings of the respective national exchanges. In this competition for dominance of global securities trading, the regulatory climate in each of these markets will be an important determinant of the respective exchanges' success. Thus the SEC faces constraints not unlike those faced by state security regulators a century ago. If it imposes too many costs, listed firms will migrate to other exchanges. Firms that are first to migrate are likely to be among the higher volume firms. Such migration changes the payoffs to continuing technological investment across the exchanges. The exchange that is growing has higher returns to capacity-increasing investments. The additional exchange capacity lowers costs, thus attracting more listings and higher trading volume. The other exchange is left with lower volume securities and with more firms having more geographically concentrated ownership.

I believe that securing the title of "global financial capital" is valuable. Along with the title would go complementary investment banking activities, employment of some of the most talented (and highly paid) individuals in the global business community, and substantial international influence.

In the evolution of global securities markets, it is unlikely that the transition will be a smooth process. In fact, we have already observed initiatives that have failed. For example, the number of foreign companies listed on the Tokyo Stock Exchange grew from 11 in 1985 to 125 in 1990. However, over the past year a number have delisted. The major explanation offered for the decision was cost. For example, GM suggested that it cost $160,000 per year to maintain its Tokyo listing. Only $3,000 was for listing fees, the rest was for lawyers' fees and the cost of meeting regulations that require foreign companies to translate and print annual reports in Japanese.

More effective global competition among exchanges is likely to increase regulatory focus on global competitiveness. For example, a recent commodity swap ruling by the Commodities Futures Trading Commission (the futures market equivalent of the SEC) reflects these concerns. Commodity swaps employ the basic contract structure developed for currency swaps. An oil swap, for instance, allows an airline to hedge its exposure to jet fuel price changes. Although U.S. firms represented the majority of user firms for commodity swaps and U.S. multinational banks were the leaders in creating the market, virtually all the business was booked in London. The enabling legislation that established the CFTC required all commodity futures contracts to be traded on an exchange regulated by the Commission; the basic commodity-swap structure made it fall within the general definition of a futures contract. To remove this regulatory impediment to the development of an oil-swap market in the U.S., the CFTC announced that it would exempt commodity swaps from Commission oversight if the commodity swaps are arranged by a U.S. financial institution regulated by another major government regulatory agency.

The benefits of competition in the private sector have been widely acknowledged for decades. Although similar benefits of competition among regulatory bodies are feasible, they are less frequently discussed. More regulatory focus on global competition thus could produce more efficient regulation.

References and Suggested Readings

Harris, Trevor S., and Mark Lang. 1992. "Relations Between Security Market Prices, Returns and Accounting Measures in Germany." Unpublished manuscript, Stanford University.

Smith, Clifford, W. 1991. "Globalization of Financial Markets." *Carnegie--Rochester Conference Series on Public Policy* 34:77–96.

FASB Issues

6

An Analysis of the Properties of Fair (Market) Value Accounting

Andrew A. Christie
University of Rochester

1. Introduction

In September 1990 the Securities and Exchange Commission (SEC) involved itself in longstanding discussions about revisions in accounting methods for banks being conducted by the Accounting Standards Executive Committee (AcSEC) of the American Institute for Certified Public Accountants (AICPA).[1] The heart of the issue before AcSEC was whether to move banks from predominantly cost-based accounting to a (perhaps limited) form of market-value-based accounting. The interest of both AcSEC and the SEC stems from alleged gains trading by banks. Gains trading is the sale of securities on which profits have accrued while continuing to hold securities with unrealized losses. The unrealized losses are not recognized for accounting purposes.[2]

The SEC's initial position was that all bank assets were to be "marked to market," irrespective of whether the assets were traded in liquid markets or not. In a letter to AcSEC, the SEC stated that current accounting methods have "repeatedly proven to be irrelevant to valuing investment portfolios of financial institutions." SEC Chairman Richard Breeden reinforced this view in his remarks to the Senate Banking Committee, where

---

[1] In this paper, the term "bank" includes commercial and savings banks as well as other financial institutions.

[2] There is an exception to this treatment under Financial Accounting Standard (FAS) 12. Unrealized losses on short-term marketable equity securities and permanent impairments of long-term marketable equity securities are recognized for accounting purposes. There is no corresponding requirement for marketable debt securities.

he cautioned that some bank financial statements should be captioned "once upon a time." In contrast to the proposals to mark assets to market, liabilities would remain at historical carrying values.

The scope of the proposal has widened considerably since the initial exchange between the SEC and AcSEC. The Financial Accounting Standards Board (FASB) currently controls the agenda, and on September 9, 1992, it issued an exposure draft (No. 119-A) titled "Accounting for Certain Investments in Debt and Equity Securities." This proposal is intended to supersede FAS 12, which covers accounting for marketable equity securities. The essential features of the exposure draft are as follows:

1. It applies to all firms, not just banks.

2. Both debt and equity securities held as assets are affected. As with the original SEC proposal, there is asymmetric treatment of assets and liabilities. The liability side of the balance sheet is not marked to market, even when those liabilities are actively traded.

3. Any debt securities that managers intend to hold to maturity are to be accounted for at amortized cost, not market value. Managerial intent determines which debt securities are marked to market and which are to be accounted for at amortized cost. Changes in intent should be rare.

4. Unrealized gains and losses on securities held for trading, including mortgage-backed securities, are included in net income.

5. Unrealized gains and losses on securities classified as available for sale, but not actively traded, will not flow through the income statement. Instead, these losses and gains will be reported in a separate component of owners' equity. Classification of securities into traded and tradable groups requires the exercise of judgment.

6. The proposed accounting treatment does *not* apply to trade receivables, commercial loans, or real estate loans unless they are securitized. It also does not apply to derivative securities and lease contracts. That is, the definition of the term *securities* excludes these instruments.

Loosely, these provisions amount to the elimination of most of the lower-of-cost or market rules in FAS 12 and an extension of FAS 12 to debt securities.

This paper examines the merits of these various proposals. It is concluded that when active trading in securities is an integral part of a firm's operations, it is useful to include both realized and unrealized gains and losses in the measure of managerial performance: net income. In cases where holding or trading securities is tangential to a firm's primary operations, the case for recording securities at market is weak, provided there is adequate footnote disclosure of market values. In particular, when the holding period of securities is long relative to the accounting period, there is a strong case against recording unrealized gains and losses in net income.

There are multiple reasons for the foregoing conclusions, but three are fundamental to accounting. First, net income serves both a performance evaluation and a valuation function, and these two functions can conflict. Second, use of net income as an input for valuation of a firm as a going concern conflicts with including changes in liquidation values in net income. When the holding periods for assets are long relative to the length of the reporting period, including changes in liquidation values of assets in net income effectively adds a random variable to net income. This reduces the usefulness of net income for valuing a firm as a going concern and results in the volatility of reported net income being greater than the true volatility of the underlying assets. Third, uniformity, which is imposition of the same accounting method on all firms independent of circumstances, is not a desirable aim in accounting, since it prevents firms from optimally tailoring their internal and external accounting methods to their particular circumstances.

Some constraints on managers' ability to choose accounting methods are necessary to make net income a useful performance measure. In determining such constraints, it is crucial to distinguish uniformity from comparability. Comparability requires use of the same accounting procedures by different firms when they are in the same circumstances and consistent application of accounting procedures through time. Imposition of a common standard on *all* firms makes net income a less useful performance measure for some firms and stifles innovation. One of the reasons managers are hired is that they have a comparative advantage at making the accounting choices necessary to maximize value. Uniformity of accounting methods interferes with this process.

The following analysis includes discussion of the conflicting uses of accounting numbers, both inside and outside firms. The proposals are also placed in historical perspective, since they are variations of prior debates about alternatives to historical cost accounting. The historical perspective permits the inclusion of evidence derived from prior experiments with non—historical-cost accounting in the U.S., as well as the evaluation of experiences in other countries. More detailed conclusions are in the final section.

2. Accounting and the Firm

Evaluation of competing accounting techniques cannot be separated from the issue of why firms exist. Firms exist because they have a comparative advantage over markets at some forms of contracting. By their very nature, firms' internal transactions do not take place at market prices (See Coase 1937 and Ball 1989.) Accounting provides substitutes for market prices and is the glue that holds the firm together. The accounting substitutes for prices include product and service costs, budgets, standards and transfer prices. Not only are accounting numbers not values, they cannot be values, since valuation is a function of markets. Without accounting, firms could not exist. Accounting facilitates internal decision making and internal performance evaluation, external performance evaluation, valuation and regulation. The demands of each of these for accounting numbers is discussed below. The relation between internal and external reports and the relation between the income statement and balance sheet are also discussed.

Throughout the paper it is assumed that firms produce only one set of financial statements,which is used for multiple purposes. This could occur either because it is too costly to prepare multiple specialized sets of financial statements or because using one set for multiple purposes increases the credibility of the statements for each purpose. Whatever the cause, this assumption is consistent with practice and in particular is consistent with most bond covenants being written in terms of generally accepted accounting procedures (GAAP), rather than in terms of accounting methods specific to a particular bond issue.

2.1 Internal Decision Making and Internal Performance Evaluation

In an unregulated, all-equity, owner-managed firm there is a demand for accounting numbers. Accounting facilitates measurement of long-run marginal costs, opportunity costs, product and service pricing, and make-or-buy decisions. Accounting also provides internal control and performance appraisal mechanisms, including budgeting, transfer pricing, and income measures for profit centers. The optimal form and combination of these depends on the firm's decision-right allocations, which in turn depend on the nature of the firm's activities (see Christie, Joye, and Watts (1991), Jensen and Meckling (1991) and Christie and Zimmerman (1992). Accruals and cost allocations including depreciation are central to all these functions.

The owner/manager chooses accounting methods that facilitate decision making and the monitoring of subordinates. However, the owner/manager must also evaluate his own performance; he must determine whether his actions this period increased or decreased value. Current accruals such as receivables, inventory, payables, prepayments, and accrued expenses aid such evaluations, since they correct for some timing discrepancies between managerial actions and the outcomes of those actions. Dechow (1991) presents evidence that current accruals are associated with value changes.[3] In evaluating his own performance, the owner/manager will focus on firm-specific events. Events, such as marketwide shocks, that change value but do not stem from the owner/manager's actions are irrelevant for performance evaluation purposes; when the objective is performance evaluation, such events are noise.

The owner/manager chooses accounting procedures to maximize the value of the firm. The form of optimal accounting procedures varies with the type of business, that is, with the characteristics of the firm's investment opportunity set. For example, revenue-recognition rules vary with the length of the production process, the ease with which output can be sold, and the type of customer. Further, accounting procedures are judged *not* by whether they increase or decrease income but by whether they better approximate opportunity costs, provide more efficient monitoring, or better adjust for timing differences between actions and their outcomes. Christie and Zimmerman (1992) use the term *efficient choice* to describe such value maximizing accounting choices.

2.2 External Performance Evaluation

Managers are hired because they have a comparative advantage at the contracting, both internal and external, valued by firms. In particular, managers have a comparative advantage at choosing accounting methods for both internal and external contracting. This comparative advantage leads shareholders to delegate the choice of accounting methods to managers, *despite* the result that managers thereby partly determine their own performance measures.

---

[3] All accruals have the additional property that they facilitate the tracking and control of assets and the recording of liabilities.

Delegating the choice of accounting methods to managers creates a demand for constraints on allowable accounting procedures and a demand for delineation of the circumstances in which particular methods are allowed. That is, there is a private (i.e. market) demand for accounting procedures that are comparable. Accounting methods that meet these standards become generally accepted. Shareholders trade off the benefits of using managers' knowledge to maximize value via internal decision making and performance evaluation against the possibility of a less useful performance measure for external reporting. The practical trade-off is between the relevance and the verifiability of alternative procedures and this results, for example, in recording of known unrealized losses but not unrealized gains. This constraint ensures that the performance measure—net income—is biased against the manager.

It is argued above that current accruals help an owner/manager evaluate his own performance by correcting for timing differences between his actions and the actions' effects on value. When there is a separation of ownership and control, these accruals also have the useful property that they provide managers with incentives to undertake policies that lead to value maximization. For example, owners want managers to choose an optimal credit-granting policy. Including credit sales and bad debts in net income, the performance measure, rewards managers for making good credit sales and penalizes them for making bad ones. In a similar vein, owners want managers to choose an optimal inventory-holding policy. This involves a trade-off between stock-out costs and inventory-holding costs. Evaluating managers based on operating cash flow would give them an incentive to defer inventory acquisition and would lead to unnecessary stock-out costs. Accrual of inventories and write-off of obsolete and damaged items, that is, recognition of known losses, mitigates this problem. All the current accruals, which an owner/manager implements to evaluate his own performance, encourage implementation of such value-maximizing strategies by managers. Current accruals are, hence, incentive compatible when there is a separation of ownership and control.[4]

The evolution of constraints on accounting procedures predates the Securities Acts and parallels the growth of the modern corporation, with the attendant separation of ownership and control. As early as 1915, concern

---

[4] The discussion here focuses on manager-stockholder relations, but the analysis applies also to manager-debtholder relations. While the interests of stockholders and debtholders often diverge, they have similar interests in evaluating managerial performance and determining value.

was expressed about different firms using different accounting procedures to record (ostensibly) similar transactions. Together with concern about changes in procedures through time for a given firm, this later became known as the comparability issue. While the Committee on Accounting Procedure (CAP) did not begin operations until 1938, precursors to it had existed in various forms since 1918. The New York Stock Exchange (NYSE) and the accounting profession cooperated to develop an acceptable set of accounting procedures between 1926 and 1932, prior to the passage of the Securities Acts. In 1933, these discussions resulted in the AICPA publication "Audits of Corporate Accounts," which introduced GAAP and the standard audit report. In a letter to the NYSE in 1932, the AICPA observed that measurement of firm performance by annual valuation had become impracticable and recommended the earning capacity of a firm as an alternative. The committee also recommended that no attempt should be made to restrict firms' rights to choose accounting procedures within the general principles. The evolution of the modern audit firm also parallels the evolution of the modern corporation. By 1933 over 90 per cent of NYSE-listed firms were voluntarily audited.

The necessity for some constraints on managers' choice of accounting procedures does not imply that uniformity in accounting methods is optimal. Uniformity assumes that the circumstances of all firms are the same and results in net-income numbers that are less useful performance measures for some firms. Alchian (1950) points out the importance of economic Darwinism, which also plays a crucial role here. Variation in accounting methods that allows managers to make better decisions or that leads to better performance measures will survive and be adopted by other firms. Managers and firms that systematically choose value-decreasing accounting methods will not survive. Uniformity not only forces suboptimal accounting methods on some firms, it also prevents innovation. There is a private demand for comparability because it increases value. There is no corresponding private demand for uniformity.

2.3 Valuation Demand, Rational Expectations and Disclosure

There is also a demand for information for valuation purposes. For traded securities, this demand is continuous, and with nontraded securities it is sporadic. Unlike the performance evaluation demand, for which only firm-specific events are relevant, valuation demand is for information about *all* sources of value change, including those beyond the control of the manager. In particular, interest rate and other marketwide shocks affect value but are noise for performance-evaluation purposes. Gjesdal (1981) and

Paul (1992) analyze this point at length, and it is also broadly consistent with the notion of relative performance measurement in Holmstrom (1982). Sloan (1992) provides evidence that accounting-earnings numbers predominantly reflect firm-specific, not marketwide, events.

When investors have rational expectations and market prices of traded securities reflect all publicly available information (that is, when the market is semistrong efficient), the central issue for valuation purposes is disclosure.[5] Footnote disclosure is sufficient. Value-relevant information need not be embedded in income statements or balance sheets to be useful. Valuation demand is primarily for valuation as a going concern rather than liquidation values. This assertion is consistent with the longstanding emphasis in accounting on the going concern (continuity) assumption. Continuity is necessary to justify many standard accounting methods, including allocation of costs to time periods and classification of the balance sheet into current and long-term components. Going concern and liquidation values are discussed further below. It is shown that inclusion of changes in liquidation values in net income reduces the usefulness of net income as an input to valuation of a going concern.

Costs of disclosure are also relevant. Costs of mandatory disclosure include compliance, enforcement, and opportunity costs associated with the disclosure of proprietary information. Compliance costs include preparation costs by firms, costs imposed on firms when mandatory disclosures effectively modify existing contracts or increase the probability of the firm or managers being sued, and the effect on competitiveness of U.S. firms compared with foreign firms that face lower disclosure costs. Contracts potentially affected by changes in mandatory disclosures include debt covenants, compensation contracts, and other contracts such as joint ventures and collective bargaining agreements.

With rational principals, agents have an incentive to offer cost-effective monitoring mechanisms and disclosures that mitigate these costs.[6]

---

[5] Market efficiency implies that all price changes are permanent. That is, temporary price changes can exist only when today's price does not reflect all publicly available information. Therefore, the distinction between temporary and permanent price changes that is in both FAS 12 and the FASB's mark-to-market exposure draft, "Accounting for Certain Investments in Debt and Equity Securities" (No. 119-A), is ill-founded.

[6] Whether agents or principals or both bear agency costs depends on the structure of labor and asset markets. In competitive securities markets, rational principals can price protect themselves. They pay a price for the security that reflects expected

Justification of any mandatory disclosure requires both that *private* incentives to disclose lead to a *socially* suboptimal amount of disclosure *and* that benefits of the disclosures outweigh the compliance, opportunity, and regulatory costs. See Watts and Zimmerman (1986, ch. 7) for an expanded discussion.[7]

2.4 Effect of Regulation

In some industries, including banking, insurance, transportation, and utilities, accounting statements are also used for regulatory purposes. Other things being equal, any accounting procedures required for regulatory purposes that differ from those that are optimal for internal decision making and performance evaluation, or external performance evaluation, lower firm value.[8] While it is possible to completely separate accounting for regulatory purposes from other reporting functions, regulators have an incentive not to do this. Managers have a comparative advantage in choice of accounting procedures. It is probably easier to blame the regulators for a crisis when the accounting methods used for regulation differ from the methods chosen by those with a comparative advantage at making such decisions, the managers.

To justify their salaries, regulators must appear to be solving perceived problems. Crises generate demands for both scapegoats and solutions. This paper is not intended as an analysis of the cause of bank and bank regulatory failures. But it is important not to blame accountants for failures of Congress and regulators. Ill-conceived laws, perhaps combined with under- or overzealous regulation, are *not* reasons to mandate change in accounting methods. First, concern about bank regulation should not influence accounting for nonfinancial corporations. Second, accounting is only one component of bank regulation. If there are flaws in existing laws

---

agency costs. The principal earns a normal return, and the agent bears the agency costs.

[7] An alternative view of regulation in accounting is that it is endogenous. Changes in economic conditions generate changes in optimal accounting procedures. The FASB's due-process provisions are the institutional mechanism by which agreement is obtained on general acceptance. Apparent mandatory changes then simply reflect private demands for agreement on revised, optimal GAAP.

[8] Accounting methods in regulated firms can aid earning of monopoly profits and hence generate wealth transfers from consumers to firms; *see* Jarrell 1978; 1979.

and regulation, it is hard to conceive that the solution to these regulatory problems lies in changing accounting requirements without evaluating other components of the regulation such as capital requirements, restrictions on diversification, and the evolving role of banks in capital markets.[9]

2.5 The Relation between Internal and External Accounting Reports

Financial accounting has traditionally been viewed as an end in itself that largely determines internal management and cost accounting procedures. Extensive efforts have been devoted to understanding the form of external reporting in isolation from the structure of the firm and internal uses of accounting. For instance, it is often asserted that depreciation is a mere cosmetic adjustment to financial statements that has no real effects. However, a change in estimated lives of depreciable assets or a change in depreciation method affects product costs, transfer prices, budgets, and divisional and firm performance measures. If, for instance, such changes occur following technological or demand shifts to better measure long-run marginal costs or opportunity costs, trying to explain them with reference to external reporting is futile. Financial accounting is substantially determined by internal revenue recognition and cost allocations for decision making and monitoring. If accounting choices are made for internal efficiency reasons, judging them as external reporting and signaling mechanisms is inappropriate (Christie and Zimmerman 1992).

---

[9] Regulated solutions often have unintended effects. In an editorial page article in the *Wall Street Journal* on Nov. 13, 1992, Timothy Ryan, retiring director of the Office of Thrift Supervision, laments the difficulties of finding qualified persons for bank directorates since the explosion in litigation against bank officers. A related *Wall Street Journal* article on Nov. 16, 1992, cites new capital rules for banks and insurance firms as an impediment to midsized firms obtaining loans. The press tends to compound these problems, since they have an incentive to create or compound perceived crises in order to sell newspapers. The oil "crisis" comes to mind. This situation was caused by government intervention, price controls, and compounded by more intervention: the windfall profits tax. But the press contributed to this problem in the way in which they reported changes in oil company profits.

2.6 Going Concerns, the Income Statement and Balance Sheet

Consider the objectives of preparing the income statement and balance sheet. If the primary function of financial statements is performance evaluation, and valuation is secondary, then the emphasis is on obtaining the optimal measure of net income. The balance sheet merely connects consecutive income statements and is not intended to reflect values. Under this view, balance sheets need not reflect any standard definition of assets and liabilities.

Contrast the foregoing situation with one in which valuation is more important than performance evaluation. Net income is useful in projecting future cash flows and valuing the firm as a going concern (Ball and Brown 1968). Producing a balance sheet that shows values of individual assets and liabilities provides information about the liquidation value of the firm but may produce an income statement that is less useful both for valuation of the firm as a going concern and for performance evaluation. If the valuation demand for information is primarily for value as a going concern, then the primary emphasis should again be on the income statement rather than the balance sheet. Except for cases in which the holding period of assets is short relative to the accounting period, including changes in liquidation values in the income statement impairs the income statement for performance evaluation and valuation as a going concern. This is discussed in section 4, below. Only when liquidation value is most important does the balance sheet become primary.

Under current GAAP, there is a fundamental conflict between the objectives of the income statement and balance sheet. The conflict occurs because a change in either the income statement or balance sheet implies a change in the other. The linkage among the income statement and consecutive balance sheets is known as articulation and is easy to see with inventories. Independent of whether input prices are increasing or decreasing, LIFO matches current costs against current revenues and results in the oldest costs being passed through to the balance sheet. If the objective of inventory method choice is to obtain a performance measure that induces managers to respond to opportunity (current) costs, then LIFO is the optimal choice. This conflicts with the objective of having the balance sheet reflect current value (net realizable value or replacement cost). If disclosure of current value is useful for valuation purposes, this can be accomplished either by footnote or by showing inventories at, say, FIFO cost less a LIFO reserve to bring them to the net LIFO number.[10]

Articulation stems from the restriction in Accounting Principles Board Opinion No. 30 (APB 30) that all gains and losses must flow through the income statement and ensures that similar conflicts occur between all related income statement and balance sheet components. APB 30 eliminates managers' discretion to book gains and losses directly to retained earnings when those items are not useful for performance evaluation or valuation of the firm as a going concern, notwithstanding the fact that managers have a comparative advantage at making these judgments. This is often referred to as the clean surplus or all inclusive approach to income determination. There is a longstanding exception for corrections of errors in the financial statements of prior years. These are known as prior-period adjustments and are made directly to retained earnings.[11] Presumably this exception is justified because corrections to prior periods have no implications for either managerial performance this period or for future cash flows. With adequate disclosure and rational investors it is not clear what the benefit of the articulation requirement is. Dechow (1991, supplementary table) provides evidence consistent with the conjecture that APB 30 simply adds noise to earnings, thereby making earnings less useful for valuation.

3. Historical and International Perspectives

It is useful to put the current controversy over market-value accounting in perspective, since this is not a new debate. Arguments about the merits of alternatives to historical cost accounting have been ongoing most of this century. The common alternatives are replacement cost (entry price), selling price (exit price, current cash equivalent, or fair market value) and price-level adjusted numbers. The debate intensifies every time there is

---

[10] This discussion abstracts from tax-motivated inventory method choices that follow from the LIFO conformity rule and from limitations on the carry forward of net operating losses. IRS rules at one point prohibited firms from disclosing FIFO or weighted average cost when using LIFO for tax purposes. This is no longer the case.

[11] Additional recent exceptions to clean surplus are in translation of the results of foreign operations (FAS 52), and in accounting for pensions and other postretirement benefits by employers (FAS 87 and FAS 106). If it survives, the FASB's mark-to-market exposure draft (No.119-A) provides another exception.

a perceived crisis. The current crisis is bank failures; the crisis of the 1970s was inflation.

One benefit of examining the outcome of prior debates is that they resulted in accumulation of evidence that is useful in assessing the merits of recent proposals. Such debates are also not unique to the United States and have taken place in most English-speaking countries. Since other countries have less restrictive GAAP than the U.S., evidence from these countries is also germane; they are useful laboratories.

3.1 Relevant U.S. and Foreign GAAP

Prior to the Securities Acts of 1933 and 1934 the accounting profession exhibited a preference for cost-based accounting on the grounds of verifiability. SEC administrative rules prohibiting asset write-ups above cost reinforced this attitude. This restriction was later incorporated in GAAP and now appears in APB 6. This provision states that property, plant, and equipment cannot be written up to appraisal, market, or current values that are above cost to the enterprise, except in a reorganization or quasi-reorganization. When appreciation is recorded under a reorganization or quasi reorganization, depreciation must be based on the written-up amounts. In the Netherlands and the British Commonwealth countries except Canada, which follows U.S. practice in this regard, write-ups of assets above cost are common. The gains are credited directly to separate components of owners' equity known as capital reserves, and depreciation is based on the written-up amounts.

3.2 Evidence from the Replacement Cost Experiment

Following several years of above-average inflation, in 1975 the SEC issued Accounting Series Release (ASR) No. 190. ASR 190 required that roughly the largest one thousand non-financial firms report supplemental data about the replacement cost of depreciable assets and inventories. These were footnote disclosures and did not affect the income statement or balance sheet. ASR 190 preempted an FASB exposure draft on price-level–adjusted accounting and became effective for fiscal years ending after December 24, 1976. ASR 190 was eventually withdrawn and superseded by FAS 33. The chairman of the SEC at the time of passage of ASR 190, Harold Williams, described historical-cost accounting as "The `Alice in Wonderland' accounting of cost and profits that now passes for orthodoxy...." (Williams 1977). Chairman Williams went on to say "...in my judgment the issue of the need for disclosure of the impact of inflation on corporate performance is simply no longer open to serious debate; the question is not whether it should be disclosed, but how" (Williams 1977.) ASR 190 included the statement "The data are of such importance that the benefits of disclosure clearly outweigh the costs."

Beginning with Beaver, Christie, and Griffin (1980), numerous studies examine the effect of the replacement-cost disclosures on stock prices. A consistent finding across all the studies is that the disclosures had no effect on stock prices, despite the claimed benefits.[12] In December 1986, FAS 89 reduced compliance with FAS 33 from mandatory to voluntary. The SEC's recent claims about the merits of market-value accounting are reminiscent of the rhetoric that surrounded ASR 190. Yet that rhetoric proved to be ill-founded. ASR 190 led to the imposition of substantial compliance costs on U.S. firms, with no discernible benefits.

3.3 Asset Writeups and Market-value Accounting in Other Countries

In the absence of government interference, asset writeups above cost have persisted for a long time in the U.K., Australia, New Zealand, and the Netherlands. Whittred and Chan (1992) investigate why Australian firms periodically voluntarily write up assets to a valuation of either the directors or an independent appraiser. Their explanation and evidence are consistent with valuation maximization. These revaluations are conducted by firms with insufficient internally generated funds to finance growth opportunities and with borrowing limitations in their debt covenants that preclude financing the growth opportunities with debt. There is no evidence in bond covenants of attempts to restrict these write-ups, which suggests that relaxing existing borrowing constraints is in both the stockholders' and bondholders' interests or at least that the bondholders are adequately compensated for this

---

[12] A minor exception is some weak evidence in Bernard and Ruland (1987) that replacement-cost data affected stock prices in a few industries, although the authors downplay these results and largely treat them as a statistical artifact. Even if we do not discount the Bernard and Ruland findings, this is a meager output from approximately 20 studies spread over nearly ten years. For the purposes of this study, the cause of the empirical findings is largely irrelevant. The results could occur either because investors already understood these effects and the effects were reflected in prices or because the data are irrelevant. Given the variety of research methods employed and the long time period involved, two alternative explanations are implausible. It is unlikely that the results are caused by either lack of statistical power or a flat learning curve for investors.

option via higher yields at issue of the debt. The write-ups are efficient (value maximizing).

An alternative explanation for asset write-ups is that they lead to better measures of long-run marginal cost and opportunity cost for internal decision making and performance evaluation. A third motivation for write-ups is that the resultant capital reserves can sometimes be used as a source of tax-free capital dividends. Whittred and Chan (1992) do not consider either of these explanations, both of which are consistent with value maximization.

Bernard, Merton, and Palepu (1992) investigate the use of market-value accounting by Danish banks. They conclude that market-value accounting, together with rigid intervention policies, is associated with effective regulation, as judged by small losses to taxpayers. They do not analyze the effect of market-value accounting on internal decision making, internal and external performance evaluation, or going-concern valuation of these banks. More specifically, first, they do not address the effect on managerial behavior of including losses and gains that are not firm-specific in net income. Second, they do not assess the effect of rigid intervention policies on the investment strategies of Danish banks. Third, their evaluation does not account for the relative complexity and different institutional and regulatory arrangements of the U.S. and Danish economies. In is unclear how one would perform such analyses. But, given that minimizing default costs to taxpayers is peculiar to the banking industry and that it ignores other important aspects of value creation, it is unclear that minimizing losses to taxpayers is a useful objective function for judging the merits of alternative accounting procedures.

3.4 Lessons from History and Foreign Experience

When firms write up assets above cost, unrealized gains are credited directly to equity accounts and future depreciation expense increases. Write-ups are income decreasing with no direct benefits to managers. There is no evidence that write-ups hurt bondholders. When government fiat does not prohibit them from doing so, managers exercise the option to write up assets above cost when it increases value. They do this *despite* the reduction in future net income (their performance measure) that results. In contrast, the evidence from the U.S. replacement-cost experiment suggests that requiring disclosure of current value for all firms is of no value. Given that the Bernard, Merton, and Palepu (1992) evaluation of the Danish experience with mark-to-market accounting in banks ignores the activities of managers that increase value, it is not clear how it contributes to this debate.

4. Application to Market-Value Accounting

The preceding sections argue that the information requirements of internal and external managerial performance evaluation and those of valuation are not the same. To the extent that improving the usefulness of financial statements for valuation or regulatory purposes involves incorporating the effect of events, such as economywide shocks, that would not be included to satisfy the decision-making and performance-evaluation demands, the financial statements are less useful for these purposes. If, for liquidation valuation or regulatory purposes, the emphasis is shifted from the income statement (the performance measure) to the balance sheet, then a less useful performance measure results. This analysis is now applied to the issue of market-value accounting. Some issues that are particular to the FASB and SEC proposals are also discussed.

4.1 Internal and External Performance Evaluation

For debt and equity securities traded in liquid markets, there is no difficulty verifying market values. Ignoring the form of disclosure, disclosure of the values of traded assets should be low cost, since this does not lead to disclosure of proprietary information and the data are readily available and verifiable. However, low disclosure cost does not imply anything about the optimal *form* of disclosure. For valuation purposes, footnote disclosure is sufficient. Disclosure by marking traded securities to market on the balance sheet suffers from the disadvantage that any increase in the volatility of book equity increases the probability of violation of existing debt covenants. Even with the changes in value flowing directly to equity, working capital, net equity and book leverage are affected. Sweeney (1992) provides evidence that debt covenant violations are costly and that working capital and book equity constraints are often the first debt covenants violated when firms perform poorly.

The situation is aggravated when value changes affect earnings. First, there is an increased probability that firms will violate interest coverage constraints in existing debt covenants. Second, since sources of value change that are not firm-specific are included in net income, net income is less useful as a measure of managerial performance in the firm's primary operations. Third, because net income largely reflects firm-specific events (Sloan 1992), managerial compensation often depends, in part, on some function of earnings. Increased volatility of earnings increases the volatility of managers' compensation streams and this risk is nondiversifiable. Since managers are risk averse, owners either must compensate managers for the increased risk or change the form of managements' compensation. Otherwise, managers have an incentive to change real investment decisions to adjust for the increased risk. Without knowing whether firms allocate the effect of firm-level accounting effects to divisions, it is difficult to know whether new reporting requirements for traded securities have any effect on internal performance evaluation and lower-level managerial behavior.

Any changes in accounting rules that lead to changes in investment and financing decisions or lead firms to renegotiate explicit or implicit contracts decrease value. Since debt covenants and compensation contracts are private contracts, firms have always had the alternative of using market-value accounting in debt contracts. Yet they choose not to do this. The opposition of the Federal Reserve Board to the mark-to-market proposals, which Chairman Greenspan expressed in a letter to Chairman Breeden of the SEC, is in part founded on an argument that banks are likely to change their investment strategies as a response to the accounting changes. Similar statements were made by Comptroller of the Currency Robert L. Clarke in an address to the AICPA National Conference on Banking on November 8, 1990. The essence of these arguments is that firms are being forced away from an optimum; this cannot increase value.

4.2 Value Changes, Net Income and Volatility of Net Income

When *active* trading of securities is an integral part of a firm's operations, marking assets to market enhances performance evaluation, since it links managers' actions with reporting the results of those actions. However, when either holding securities is a peripheral activity for the firm or when the holding period for the securities is long relative to the accounting reporting period, market-value accounting has three important deficiencies. First, net income is less useful for valuing a firm as a going concern. Second, net income becomes less useful as a measure of managerial performance, since marketwide shocks to cash flows and discount rates over which the managers have no control are incorporated in net income. Third, net income is more volatile than the flows from the underlying assets. To simplify the discussion, assume that the current period cash flow is the best predictor of all future cash flows.[13] This also implies that, over time, the change in value has a mean of zero.

When net income is the current cash flow from the security, a firm is valued as a going concern by discounting a perpetual flow equal to net income. Including current value changes in net income inhibits this process, since net income is no longer the best predictor of future cash flows. To see the nature of the problem, recognize that value changes are the present value of changes in expectations of future cash flows caused by new information (Christie 1987). Net income now includes both current flows and the present value of changes in expectations of future flows. A zero mean random variable has been added to net income. Net income is now a noisy predictor of future cash flows. Since volatility is additive, the volatility of net income exceeds the volatility of the flows from the security. The firm appears riskier than it really is. It is not that the volatility increases but that it is overstated.

The objective of holding any asset long-term is to earn the flows it produces. The flows are evidence of managers' abilities and accountants create better ways to measure those flows.[14] As discussed earlier, evidence suggests that accounting earnings numbers largely filter out marketwide effects and thereby facilitate evaluation of managers' actions. Value changes partly reflect marketwide changes in expectations of future cash flows and marketwide changes in discount rates. Including these effects in net income lessens its usefulness for performance evaluation of managers and for valuation as a going concern.

4.3 Asymmetric Treatment of Assets and Liabilities

Even if one concluded that accounting for traded securities at market were desirable, focusing only on traded assets and ignoring traded liabilities generates undesirable results. Consider a bank whose assets and liabilities have the same duration. The bank is largely hedged against changes in interest rates. The hedge may not be perfect because the equity may not have the same duration as the assets, but for most banks equity is less than

---

[13] This assumption can be relaxed without changing the basic tenor of the analysis.

[14] An obvious example is the use of equity accounting for long-term investments in equity securities when the firm can exercise significant influence over a security's management.

10 percent of assets. Under the current FASB exposure draft, and under all proposals to date from the SEC, fluctuation of the value of the liabilities with interest rates is ignored. Fluctuations in the value of the assets caused by interest-rate changes would cause fluctuation in accounting earnings that does not stem from economic effects. While this example is a polar case, to some degree it is characteristic of *all* proposals that ignore variation in the value of liabilities. Such policies lead to fluctuation in accounting income that does not reflect the underlying economics.

Accounting for only one side of an economic hedge is not unique to the fair-market-value proposal. It also appears in foreign currency translation under FAS 52 and in the accounting for futures contracts under FAS 80. Firms can have economic hedges that do not qualify as accounting hedges. Banks could be perfectly hedged against interest-rate risk yet still report substantial accounting gains or losses under the proposals.

4.4 The Special Case of Banking

An additional difficulty arises in evaluating the effect of the current proposals on banks, since existing bank accounting rules may not be efficient. This precludes an appeal to economic Darwinism to justify existing choices. Use of historical cost in bank accounting dates to the 1938 Agreement on Uniform Examination Procedure. Prior to that time, the industry norm was to account for investment-grade securities at market. These were primarily U.S. Treasury securities and constituted roughly 90 percent of bank securities and approximately 40 percent of total bank assets (Simonson and Hempel 1990). Since there was no default risk associated with these securities, for practical purposes the move from market- to cost-based accounting eliminated the effect of market interest rate changes from banks' income statements. It is unclear whether bank accounting methods were chosen efficiently before 1938, after 1938, neither, or both. Whether marking some bank assets to market increases or decreases value depends on whether the current rules are efficient.

Volatility of reported net income and equity is especially important for banks, since they are subject to minimum capital constraints. Increasing the volatility of book equity increases the probability of violation of the constraints. For this purpose, it is irrelevant whether the value changes causing an increase in volatility also affect net income. Volatility of reported income does affect existing debt and compensation contracts. There are two important issues with volatility. First, because of the effect on contracts and capital regulation, it is important that volatility of reported equity does not overstate the true volatility of the underlying assets. Tailoring the accounting method to the relative lengths of the reporting period and holding period for securities is crucial to achieving this. Second, accounting methods and regulatory methods cannot be chosen in isolation from each other. The accounting methods are so important to a bank's internal and unregulated external operations that determining accounting methods first and then reconsidering bank capital regulation is less likely to generate dysfunctional regulation.

5. Summary and Conclusions

The uses of accounting in firms and markets for internal decision making, internal and external performance evaluation, valuation as a going concern, valuation for liquidation, and regulation are analyzed. In general it is not possible for any particular accounting method to simultaneously be optimal for all these uses. Any one accounting method is a compromise. The recent FASB exposure draft (No. 119-A) titled "Accounting for Certain Investments in Debt and Equity Securities" implicitly makes the distinctions that are central to striking a balance among the competing demands for accounting. The key distinctions are whether trading is an integral part of a firm's activities and the relative length of the reporting and holding periods. Detailed conclusions follow.

1. Managers use net income to evaluate their own actions and shareholders and debtholders use it to evaluate the managers. Use of net income for valuation purposes can conflict with the performance-evaluation objective. When holding securities is tangential to the firms primary operations, inclusion in net income of value changes caused by marketwide changes in values and interest rates is counterproductive. Such rules make it more difficult for managers, shareholders, and debtholders to determine whether managers' actions in a given period have increased or decreased value.

2. For traded securities, both verification costs and disclosure costs of market values, gains, and losses are low. Subject to point 3, below, when trading in securities or holding traded securities is an integral part of a firm's operations, it is appropriate to treat both realized and unrealized gains and losses as part of net income. These gains or losses are an integral part of managers' performance.

3. Valuation as a going concern and valuation for liquidation purposes also conflict. For valuing a firm as a going concern, the flows

from ownership of assets is key. Incorporating changes in liquidation values of assets in net income results in overstatement of the volatility of the assets when the holding period for the assets exceeds the length of the reporting period. Clearly, the holding period depends on managers' intent and the FASB exposure draft recognizes this. The SEC chooses to call accounting based on managerial intent "psychoanalytic accounting."[15] But this intent is crucial to obtaining net-income numbers that reflect firm-specific events and are not more volatile than the flows from the underlying assets.

4. By focusing on traded assets and ignoring traded liabilities, the proposals can induce accounting gains and losses when there are no economic gains or losses. Essentially, only one side of a (partial) hedge is accounted for and the volatility of reported net income is greater than the economic volatility.

5. Changes in accounting are proposed to correct broader failures in bank regulation that have little to do with accounting. The proposals impose accounting rules on all firms that are motivated by troubles in the banking industry. The rhetoric emanating from the SEC about the benefits of recording some assets at realizable values is reminiscent of SEC statements about the importance of replacement costs in the mid-1970s. The evidence accumulated subsequently did not support the SEC's claims about the merits of mandating disclosure of replacement costs. Forcing all firms to mark all traded assets to market also is inappropriate.

6. The FASB exposure draft (No. 119-A) wisely excludes assets that do not meet the definition of a security. This is contrary to the spirit of the SEC's proposals but consistent with the nature of firms. Valuation is a function of markets. Most of a firm's internal transactions do not take place at market prices. If firms did nothing more than transact at market prices, they would not exist.

The apparent drive for uniformity in accounting is counterproductive, since it assumes that the circumstances of all firms are the same. Two important constraints in GAAP inhibit managers' ability to choose value-maximizing accounting methods. These constraints are the provisions in APB 6 that prevent write-ups of depreciable assets above cost and the

---

[15] Letter dated Sept. 13, 1990, from Edmund Coulson and Robert A. Bayless of the SEC to Jack Kreischer, chairman of the AcSEC.

provisions in APB 30 that eliminate managers' discretion to charge losses and gains directly to retained earnings. These constraints promote uniformity that results in net-income numbers that are less useful internal and external performance evaluation and going-concern valuation measures.

References and Suggested Readings

Alchian, A. 1950. "Uncertainty, Evolution and Economic Theory." *Journal of Political Economy* 58 (June): 211–221.

Alchian, A., and H. Demsetz. 1972. "Production, Information Costs and Economic Organization." *American Economic Review* (Dec.): 777–795.

Ball, R. 1989. "The Firm as a Specialist Contracting Intermediary: Application to Accounting and Auditing." Working paper, University of Rochester.

Ball, R., and P. Brown. 1968. "An Empirical Evaluation of Accounting Income Numbers." *Journal of Accounting Research* 6 (Autumn): 159–178.

Beaver, W. H. 1979. "Accounting for Inflation in an Efficient Market." *International Journal of Accounting*: 21–42.

Beaver, W. H., A. A. Christie, and P. A. Griffin. 1980. "The Information Content of SEC Accounting Series Release No. 190." *Journal of Accounting and Economics* 2:127–57.

Bernard, V. L., R. C. Merton, and K. G. Palepu. 1992. "Mark to Market Accounting for U.S. Banks and Thrifts: Lessons from the Danish Experience." Working paper, University of Michigan, Ann Arbor.

Bernard, V. L., and R. G. Ruland. 1987. "The Incremental Information Content of Historical Cost and Current Cost Income Numbers: Time-Series Analysis for 1962–1980." *The Accounting Review* 62, no. 4:707–22.

Christie, A. A. 1987. "On Cross-Sectional Analysis in Accounting Research." *Journal of Accounting and Economics* 9:231–58.

——. 1990. "Aggregation of Test Statistics: An Evaluation of the Evidence on Contracting and Size Hypotheses." *Journal of Accounting and Economics*: 15–36.

Christie, A. A., M. Joye, and R. L. Watts. 1991. "Decentralization of the Firm: Theory and Evidence." Working paper, University of Rochester.

Christie, A. A., and J. L. Zimmerman. 1992. "Efficient and Opportunistic Choice of Accounting Procedures: Corporate Control Contests." Working paper, University of Rochester.

Coase, R. H. 1937. "The Nature of the Firm." *Economica*, New Series: 386–405.

Dechow, P. 1991. "Accounting Earnings and Cash Flows as Measures of Firm Performance: The Role of Accounting Accruals." Working paper, University of Pennsylvania, Philadelphia.

Gjesdal, F. 1981. "Accounting for Stewardship." *Journal of Accounting Research* (Spring).

Holmstrom, B. 1979. "Moral Hazard and Observability." *Bell Journal of Economics* (Spring): 74–91.

——. 1982. "Moral Hazard in Teams." *Bell Journal of Economics* (Autumn): 324–40.

Jarrell, G. A. 1978. "The Demand for State Regulation of the Electric Utility Industry." *Journal of Law and Economics* 21:269–95.

——. 1979. "Pro-Producer Regulation and Accounting for Assets: The Case of Electric Utilities." *Journal of Accounting and Economics* 1:93–116.

Jensen, M., and W. Meckling. 1991. "Specific and General Knowledge, and Organizational Structure." In *Main Currents in Contract Economics*, L. Werin and H. Wijkander, eds. London: Blackwell.

Kirk, D. J. 1991. "Competitive Disadvantage and Mark-to-Market Accounting." *Accounting Horizons* 5, no. 2:98–106.

Klein, B., R. Crawford, and A. Alchian. 1978. "Vertical Integration, Appropriable Rents, and the Competitive Contracting Process." *Journal of Law & Economics* (Oct.): 297–326.

Mian, S. L. and C. W. Smith, Jr. 1990a. "Incentives for Unconsolidated Financial Reporting." *Journal of Accounting and Economics* 12:141–71.

——. 1990b. "Incentives Associated with Changes in Consolidated Reporting Requirements." *Journal of Accounting and Economics* 13:249–66.

Paul, J. M. 1992. "On the Efficiency of Stock Based Compensation." *Review of Financial Studies.*

Simonson, D. G. and G. Hempel. 1990. "Running on Empty: Accounting Strategies to Clarify Capital Value." *Stanford Law and Policy Review* (Spring).

Sloan, R. J. 1992. "Accounting Earnings and Top Executive Compensation." Working paper, University of Pennsylvania, Philadelphia.

Snavely, H. J. 1967. "Accounting Information Criteria." *Accounting Review* (Apr.).

Sweeney, A. 1992. "Debt Covenant Violations and Managers' Accounting-Choice and Production-Investment Decisions." Ph.D. diss., University of Rochester.

Watts, R. L., and J. L. Zimmerman. 1986. *Positive Accounting Theory.* Englewood Ciffs, N. J.: Prentice Hall.

——. 1990. "Positive Accounting Theory: A Ten-Year Perspective." *Accounting Review* 65 (Jan.): 131–56.

Whittred, G. P. and Y. K. Chang. 1992. "Asset Revaluations and the Mitigation of Under Investment." *Abacus* (Mar.).

Williams, H. 1977. Keynote Address, Seaview Symposium on the Conceptual Framework for Financial Reporting, Seaview, N. J.

7

Accounting for Executive Compensation

Ross L. Watts
University of Rochester

1. Introduction

The current political debate over the level of senior corporate executive compensation is likely to affect accounting for executive compensation. Currently, executive stock options are not required to be valued or expensed in the corporation's financial statements if the option plan is fixed and the exercise price is greater than or equal to the stock's market price at grant.[1] A congressional bill earlier this year proposed requiring executive stock options to be valued in corporate disclosures as a step toward expensing those values against revenues in corporate financial statements. Reducing the bottom-line earnings number by the additional expense was apparently intended to constrain executive compensation ("American Accounting: Optional" 1992, 88, 90).

In response to the congressional pressure, the Securities and Exchange Commission recently issued new rules for proxy statement disclosure of senior executive compensation (U.S. SEC 1992). Those rules do not require the valuation of executive stock options in proxy statement disclosures, but they are likely to induce firms to supply that valuation data.[2] In addition, the Financial Accounting Standards Board recently revived its longstanding project on stock compensation plans. The FASB intends to issue an exposure draft in the first quarter of 1993 (see Financial Accounting

[1] An option plan is fixed if the number of shares that can be granted under the option is fixed at the time the option is granted.

[2] The new rules require either the listing of future values of options assuming annual rates of stock price appreciation of 5 and 10 percent or a current valuation of the options at the date of grant. Given that future values will be much larger than the current valuation, corporate management will almost certainly choose the current valuation.

Foundation, 1992). That draft is expected to propose that stock options that currently do not generate expense be valued at the time of grant and that value be expensed over a service period that runs from the time of the grant to the first date the options can be exercised ("American Accounting: Optional" 1992, 90).

Corporate executives, as represented by the conference board, are opposed to the FASB proposal (see, for example, *Fortune*, November 30, 1992, 17). This opposition is at least partially motivated by fear of the proposal's effect on compensation expense relative to earnings (see also "American Accounting: Optional" 1992, 88, 90). I expect this fear will prove baseless. For most public corporations the FASB proposal is unlikely to generate compensation numbers that are large relative to earnings. Further, for corporations employing variable stock-price-based incentive-compensation plans such as stock appreciation rights (SAR) plans, I expect the FASB proposal to reduce the likelihood of reporting relatively large compensation expense. Under present accounting requirements, variable stock-price-based plans can generate compensation expense that is large relative to earnings. The reason is that for these plans compensation expense is recorded as a function of stock-price movements *after the date of grant* of the option, SAR, or other instrument, but expected future cash flow changes that generate those stock price movements (and thus the compensation expense) are not recognized and included in current earnings. The consequence is a mismatching of costs and benefits in the earnings calculation and the possibility of large compensation expense relative to earnings. I expect the FASB proposal to fix total compensation expense at the value of the option *at the date of grant* for both fixed and variable stock-price-based plans. This will eliminate the variance in the compensation expense-earnings relation generated by the current mismatching of revenue and expense. An important consequence is likely to be earnings numbers that are better measures of management's performance.

To demonstrate the effects of the expected FASB proposal on compensation and earnings, this paper applies three alternate accounting methods for incentive compensation plans to the case of a simple stock option or SAR whose exercise price is equal to the stock price at grant. In section 2, the paper describes the existing accounting method for the option if it qualifies as fixed (*fixed method)*, the alternate method expected to be proposed by the FASB (*proposed method*), and the accounting method that is currently applied to SARs (*variable method*). Section 3 describes a criterion for choosing among the alternative accounting methods, and section 4 evaluates the methods using that criterion. The conclusions and policy recommendations are given in section 5.

2. Alternative Accounting Methods

Before describing the alternative accounting methods, it is useful to review the nature of stock options and SARs (for a detailed review of executive stock options and other incentive plans and their accounting see Arthur Andersen & Co. 1991).

Stock options give the executive the right to purchase a given quantity of the corporation's stock any time within a given period (the exercise period) at a prescribed price (the exercise price). The exercise period typically expires five to ten years from the grant of the option and often begins some time after the grant. For example, Gerber Products' proxy statement dated June 23, 1992, indicates Gerber's executive stock options have an exercise period that begins one year after the date of the grant and ends ten years after the date of the grant. The exercise price is typically set at the market price of the stock at the time of the grant. The option typically terminates if the executive leaves the corporation.

Stock appreciation rights provide the executive with a cash payment and/or stock in an amount equal to the difference between the stock price at a future date and a stated price (the appreciation) multiplied by a given quantity of stock. SARs are often issued in tandem with stock options to allow the executive to reduce transactions costs. When issued in tandem with stock options, the SARs have a stated price equal to the options' exercise price and the same exercise period as the options. Since the payoff distribution of an SAR is equivalent to that of its tandem stock option, the value of the two is the same at grant.

The fixed method is the existing accounting for stock options that have an exercise price equal to the market price at grant date and whose plan qualifies as fixed and involves no accounting entry when the options are granted. The only entry occurs if and when the options are exercised. At that time, the exercise price is credited to paid-in capital. No compensation expense is recognized at any time. The existing method of accounting for SARs with the same essential terms does recognize compensation expense and is described below as the variable method.

The proposed method of accounting would involve an entry at the time of the grant. It is expected that the value of the option at that time would be credited to paid-in capital and debited to deferred compensation. The deferred compensation would be amortized to compensation expense over a service period extending from the date of the options grant to the first date on which the options could be exercised. It is expected that the FASB will allow some flexibility in the choice of option valuation method including the use of the popular Black-Scholes model.

The variable method recognizes compensation expense if and when, following the grant date, the stock price rises above the exercise price for SARs with a stated (or exercise) price equal to market price at grant. The amount of compensation recognized is a function of that appreciation and the period until the SARs are vested. If in the first year following the grant the stock price has risen above the exercise price, that appreciation, multiplied by the given quantity of stock and divided by the number of years in the vesting period, is recognized as compensation expense. In the second year, the cumulative appreciation for the given quantity of stock is multiplied by two and divided by the number of years in the vesting period to give the cumulative compensation expense for the two years. The compensation expense for the first year is deducted to determine the compensation expense for the second year. If the stock price has declined, the compensation expense for the second year could be negative (i.e., earnings increasing). However, that negative amount can be no more than the cumulative compensation expense already recognized. Compensation expense continues to be recognized in this fashion until the end of the vesting period. After the SARs are vested, the full cumulative appreciation is compared to the cumulative amount of compensation expense previously recognized to determine the current charge to compensation expense. This process continues until the SARs are exercised. If the SARs are expected to be paid in cash, the accrued compensation is reported as a liability. If the SARs are expected to be paid out in stock, the accrued compensation is reported as paid-in capital.

It is important to note that at the time of the grant total compensation expense is fixed under the fixed method (at zero) and the proposed method (at the option's estimated value) but is not determined until exercise under the variable method. This differential treatment is due to a rule originally developed by the FASB's predecessor, the Accounting Principles Board, that separated incentive plans into those for which the number of shares granted under the option is fixed at the time of grant (as in the stock options considered in this paper) and those for which the number of shares is variable at the time of grant (as in SARs). This distinction between variable and fixed plans will be less important if, as expected, the FASB fixes compensation at the time of grant for both types of plan.

3. Criterion for Choice among Methods

Accounting earnings serve as performance measures, both formally (for example, in accounting-based incentive compensation and debt contracts) and informally (for example, when investors are considering investing in a corporation). The more effectively accounting earnings measure performance, the better the decisions based on them and the better corporate management's performance.

Absent regulation, or income taxes, accounting methods evolve to provide cost-effective measures of managerial performance (Watts and Zimmerman 1986). Accounting starts with the firm's current cash flows and modifies them with accruals to produce accounting earnings that measure performance (Dechow 1992). Current management actions have an impact on both current and future cash flows, so in order to make earnings a more timely performance measure, the accounting accrual process incorporates some future cash flows into earnings. An example is the accrual for accounts receivable, which represent cash expected to be received in the future. However, some other future cash flows are excluded from the accrual process because estimates of them are unreliable. An example is the future cash flows that will be generated from a manager's investment in a new plant. Managers have the best information about those future cash flows, but their estimates are likely to be noisy and, because they are being evaluated on the estimates, biased. Verifying those estimates or generating reliable alternative estimates is not cost-effective, so those cash flows are excluded. The result of private incentives is an accounting process that trades off reliability and timeliness to produce a cost-effective measure of management performance.

When the future cash flows generated by an expenditure are too unreliable to include in earnings, accountants also tend to exclude that expenditure from earnings. For example, the expenditure incurred to build the plant in the above example is excluded from earnings. It is capitalized so that the expenditure can be included in earnings as the cash flows from operating the plant are realized.

Using the rate of return on the stock price (adjusted and unadjusted for marketwide movements) as a measure of performance, Dechow (1992) finds that accruals that existed prior to disclosure regulation and income tax (primarily working capital accruals) significantly improve earnings' ability to measure performance. Further, consistent with the theory, Dechow finds that the extent to which working capital accruals improve the ability to measure performance is a function of the corporation's operating cycle.

The above arguments provide a basis for evaluating the alternate methods of accounting for executive stock options: their effect on the ability of accounting earnings to measure managerial performance. That basis underlies many of the rules the FASB codifies, but the FASB necessarily has to generate heuristics (such as the distinction between fixed and variable incentive-compensation plans) to provide guidance to practitioners. Unfortunately, those heuristics do not always improve earnings' ability to measure performance.

4. Evaluation of Alternative Methods

A specific example will help to illustrate the alternative methods' effects on earnings and so help evaluate the methods. Assume an option gives the right to buy 100 shares at an exercise price equal to the current market price of $10 and has an exercise period that stretches from the end of the third year to the end of the fifth year. To apply the variable method, make the preceding assumptions except assume an SAR with a stated price of $10 rather than an option with an exercise price of $10. Assume that the stock prices for the five years from the grant to the end of the exercise period (year 5) are as given in the assumptions in Table 1 and that the stock option or SAR is exercised at the end of year five. There are one thousand shares outstanding when the stock option or SAR is granted. Finally, the corporate income tax rate is 50 percent.

Table 1 gives compensation expense, accounting earnings, and primary earnings per share for each year under the three methods. The option valuation method used for the proposed method is one recommended by Smith and Zimmerman (1976). That method values options as the difference between the stock price at grant and the discounted value of the exercise price. An annual discount rate of 10 percent is used in the example and the exercise price is discounted from the first date that the option can be exercised. The method is simple, is easily applied, and is conservative.

The fixed method generates no compensation expense and so shows zero compensation expense each year in Table 1. The cost of the option to existing stockholders never finds its way into earnings. The benefits from the stock option (the cash flows generated by the manager's decisions) do find their way into current and future earnings, thus current and future earnings are positively biased measures of performance. If the cost of the options at grant is relatively constant over time, however, investors can easily estimate that bias.

The proposed method yields a total five-year compensation expense in Table 1 of $249. That amount is amortized equally over the three years between the grant year and the first year the option could be exercised (years one through three). This method fixes compensation expense at the time of the grant and that compensation expense is a function of the normal expected rate of return rather than of unexpected shocks to stock prices following grant of the option. Compensation expense is essentially expected compensation expense, so earnings should on average be a less biased measure of performance than under the existing rules. Further, given stability in compensation plans, I expect compensation expense under this proposal to be relatively stable (as under the existing rules) and to have a trivial effect on the variability of earnings (compare the existing and proposed methods' earnings in Table 1, for example). For most public firms, earnings generated under the expected FASB proposal should have at least the same association with management performance as earnings generated under the existing methods.

Indeed, for most public corporations, the effect of the proposed method on the bottom line is likely to be trivial. For example, using the popular Black-Scholes model, Gerber Products valued stock options granted to executive officers in 1991 and 1992 at $112,000 and $350,000, respectively. Using the larger of these numbers as an estimate of the effect on annual compensation expense, the percentage reduction in Gerber's 1992 net earnings ($94 million) would be only .37 of one percentage point.

The variable method generates much larger compensation expense than the proposed method in the example in Table 1. The variable method's total compensation expense is $1,000 versus $249 for the proposed method. The $1,000 is the $10 appreciation on each share ($20 stock price at the end of five years minus the exercise price of $10) multiplied by 100 shares. The reason the compensation expense is much larger under the variable method is that it incorporates stock price movements after the grant date (the $10 appreciation). As a consequence, the variable method can generate extreme compensation expense and for small growth corporations could have a significant effect on earnings and earnings per share. In the example in Table 1, if the stock price were $40 at the end of year five, the total compensation expense for the five years would be $3,000, 40 percent of earnings before impact of the plan.

An example of a significant effect of the variable method on earnings occurred in the early 1980s. At that time, a large increase in oil prices caused a substantial increase in the stock price of Quanex Corp., an oil fields service company. The stock price appreciation so increased compensation expense on the corporation's SARs that earnings were reduced by 40 percent.[3]

Note that not only does the variable method increase the level of compensation expense, it increases the variance of compensation expense from year to year. The proposed method fixes compensation expense for the first three years in Table 1 at $83 per year, but the variable method has before-tax compensation expense varying from $467 in year three to -$100 in year four.

Now consider the effect of using the variable method on the ability of accounting earnings to measure managerial performance. In particular, consider the case in which compensation expense increases significantly *after* grant because of large increases in stock prices. Changes in stock prices in a given year reflect changes in cash flows that appear in current and future earnings (see Kothari and Sloan 1992). A large increase in stock price relative to current earnings is likely due to increases in the corporation's prospects, that is, in expected future cash flows, more than to increases in current cash flows. If so, the increased expected cash flows that cause the stock price increase do not appear in earnings until future years, but the full compensation cost associated with the stock price change appears in current earnings. This would appear to be the situation in the Quanex Corp. example given above. In this case then, and probably in most cases,[4] the variable method provides a less effective match between cash inflows and outflows than the fixed method; it introduces more noise into accounting earnings and reduces earnings' ability to measure performance.

Also, if the variable method of accounting for options makes options less attractive, they will be used less, weakening the ability of corporations to align managers and shareholders' interests. Consistent with this observation, Scholes and Wolfson (1992, 191) suggest the variable method currently causes corporations to avoid SARs even when they are tax

---

[3] This example was supplied by Don Chew, the editor of the *Journal of Applied Corporate Finance.*

[4] Most stock price changes are likely to be primarily due to changes in expected future cash flows. Even when stock-price changes are associated with current operating cash flow and earnings changes, those operating cash flow changes are permanent, implying higher future operating cash flows. The value of the increase in expected future operating cash flows is likely to be much higher than the value of the increase in current cash flows. Hence, applying all the associated compensation expense to the current period is likely to provide a worse mismatch than using the existing method.

advantageous. There is formal evidence consistent with this observation. Smith and Watts (1992) find that over the period 1965–1985 larger corporations were more likely to use stock option plans. Smith and Watts also investigate (but do not report on) the use of SARs for the period 1977–1985. They find corporate size has a much larger effect on SAR use than on stock option use: small corporations are much less likely to use SARs. Since small corporations' stock-price rate of returns have higher variances, the variable method induces a larger variance in SAR compensation relative to earnings in small corporations than in large corporations.

5. Conclusions and Policy Recommendations

There are good reasons for leaving the determination of executive compensation to the marketplace rather than to government regulation. Therefore, my assessment of the alternative methods of accounting for executive compensation is based on their effects on the effectiveness of corporate accounting in measuring management performance and providing that information to investors.

The preceding analysis suggests that the expected FASB proposal for accounting for executive stock options at a minimum will not harm accounting earnings' ability to measure performance and may improve it. If, as expected, the proposal modifies the accounting for SARs so that, like stock option compensation expense, SAR compensation expense is fixed at grant, the proposal will avoid large swings in compensation expense and significantly improve earnings' ability to measure performance. The improvement comes from a better matching of cash flows inflows and outflows.

For the preceding reason, I endorse the determination and fixation of compensation expense under stock option plans and SAR and similar stock-price-based incentive plans using value at grant. This endorsement does not extend to variable incentive compensation plans that are accounting-number based, such as book-value formula plans (see Arthur Andersen & Co. 1991, 36–37). The accounting numbers are a function of current and past cash flows and so recognizing compensation expense as those numbers change does not generate a problem in matching cash flows and measuring performance.

The negative impact of the variable method on matching of cash flows and therefore on the ability of earnings to measure performance raises questions about the process by which the FASB and its predecessor bodies set accounting standards. Requirement of the variable method for stock-price-based plans was the result of concentration on measurement and development of heuristics (e.g., definitions of fixed and variable plans) for individual plans without adequate consideration of the matching notion that accountants have long used to help earnings measure performance. One could argue that the FASB's recent standards on liabilities reflect a similar myopic concentration on measurement of individual liabilities with insufficient concern for matching revenue and expense.

Table 1
An Example
Comparing Compesation Expense and Accounting Earnings under Three Accounting Methods

Assumptions of the Example

	1	2	3	4	5
Stock price					
Average during year	$11	$12	$17	$18	$19
At year-end	$11	$15	$18	$17	$20
After tax corporate earnings before	$1,000	$1,400	$1,700	$1,600	$1,800
Number of shares outstanding (year end)					
Excluding option exercise	1,000	1,000	1,000	1,000	1,000
Corporate income tax rate	0.50	0.50	0.50	0.50	0.50
Stock option					
Exercise price	$10	$10	$10	$10	$10
Number of shares	100	100	100	100	100

Table 1 (cont.)

Compensation Expense under the Three Methods

	Year					
Accounting method	1	2	3	4	5	Total
Fixed method	$0	$0	$0	$0	$0	$0
Proposed method	$83 [1]	$83	$83	$0	$0	$249
Variable method	$33 [2]	$300 [3]	$467 [4]	$(100)	$300 [6]	$1,000

Accounting Earnings under the Three Methods

	Year					
Accounting method	1	2	3	4	5	Total
Fixed method	$1,000	$1,400	$1,700	$1,600	$1,800	$7,500
Proposed method	$959	$1,359	$1,659	$1,600	$1,800	$7,376
Variable method	$983	$1,250	$1,467	$1,650	$1,650	$7,000

Primary Earnings per Share under the Three Methods

	Year					
Accounting method	1	2	3	4	5	Total
Fixed method	$1.00	$1.39	$1.67	$1.57	$1.71	$1.47
Proposed method [7]	$0.96	$1.36	$1.66	$1.60	$1.71	$1.46
Variable method	$0.98	$1.25	$1.47	$1.65	$1.65	$1.40

Notes to Table 1

[1] The $83 expense is calculated as follows: 100 shares x $\dfrac{[\$10 - \dfrac{\$10}{(1.10)^3}]}{3 \text{ years}}$

[2] The $33 year 1 expense is calculated as one third the cumulative stock price appreciation: $\dfrac{[\$11 - \$10] \times 100}{3}$

[3] The $300 year 2 expense is calculated as two-thirds the cumulative stock price appreciation minus previously recognized expense:

$\dfrac{[\$15 - \$10] \times 100 \times 2}{3} - \$33$

[4] The $467 year 3 expense is calculated as the cumulative stock price appreciation minus previously recognized expense: [$18–$10] x 100 - $333

[5] The -$100 year 4 expense is calculated as the cumulative stock price appreciation minus previously recognized expense: [$17–$10] x 100 - $800

[6] The $300 year 5 expense is calculated as the cumulative stock price appreciation minus previously recognized expense: [$20–$10] x 100 - $700

[7] Under the proposed method, primary earnings per share is simply earnings divided by the average number of shares outstanding. No allowance has been made for dilution due to the outstanding option since that involves double counting. Nor has any allowance been made for the difference between tax and accounting treatments. The Smith and Zimmerman valuation method is used to value the option.

References and Suggested Readings

Arthur Andersen & Co. 1991. *Accounting for Compensation Arrangements in the United States,* second edition. Chicago: Arthur Andersen & Co.

Dechow, P. 1992. "Accounting Earnings and Cash Flows as Measures of Firm Performance: The Role of Accounting Accruals." Ph.D. dissertation, University of Rochester.

The Economist. 1992. "American Accounting: Optional." Oct.: 88–90.

Financial Accounting Foundation. 1992. *Financial Accounting Series*, No. 120-A. Norwalk, Connecticut: Financial Accounting Foundation.

Kothari, S. P. and R. G. Sloan. 1992. "Information About Prices in Future Earnings." *Journal of Accounting & Economics* 15:143–71.

Scholes, M. S. and M. A. Wolfson. 1992. *Taxes and Business Strategy.* Englewood Cliffs, N. J.: Prentice Hall.

Smith, C. W. and R. L. Watts. 1992. "The Investment Opportunity Set and Corporate Financing, Dividend, and Compensation Policies." *Journal of Financial Economics* 32.

Smith, C. W. and J. L. Zimmerman. 1976. "Valuing Employee Stock Option Plans Using Stock Option Pricing Models." *Journal of Accounting Research* 14:357–64.

U.S. Securities and Exchange Commission. 1992. *Final Rules, Reform of Executive Compensation Disclosure Rules.* Washington, D.C.: U.S. Government Printing Office.

Watts, R. L. and J. L. Zimmerman. 1986. *Positive Accounting Theory.* Englewood Cliffs, N. J.: Prentice Hall.

Auditor Liability

8

Restoring the Privity Barrier for Negligent Accounting

Victor P. Goldberg
Columbia University

A few years ago I wrote a paper in which I argued that accountants should not be held liable to third parties for conducting an audit in a negligent manner.[1] Since then the world has not been kind to accountants. They have become favorite targets in the litigation following the savings and loan debacle.[2] Huge verdicts, notably an Arizona jury's holding Price Waterhouse responsible for losses of $338 million arising from a negligent bank audit,[3] have shaken the industry. Perhaps worse, punitive damages and RICO liability are now real possibilities—a Texas jury awarded disgruntled investors over $200 million in punitive damages following the failure of Miniscribe, a computer disk drive manufacturer,[4] and the question of the accountant's vulnerability to civil RICO claims is before the Supreme Court

---

[1] Goldberg, "Accountable Accountants: Is Third-Party Liability Necessary?" *Journal of Legal Studies* 295 (1988).

[2] For example, Ernst and Young recently settled all the government's claims against it for $400 million. *See* Berton, "Ernst Accord May Give FDIC Leverage," *Wall Street Journal* (Dec. 3, 1992).

[3] The case is described in Lochner, "Black Days for Accounting Firms," *Wall Street Journal*, Sec. A, 10 (May 22, 1992).

[4] The judgment was set aside when the judge found the verdict not supported by sufficient evidence. *U.S. National Bank of Galveston v. Coopers & Lybrand*, No. 89-CV-1081-A-212 (Texas D. Ct. 1992). The defendants then settled for an undisclosed amount.

this term.[5]

Not all the news is bad for the accountants. A $590 million suit by the FDIC against Ernst & Young did not survive summary judgment.[6] New York, which has not permitted third party suits against accountants (save for a narrow exception), reasserted its position;[7] indeed, the dissent even accused the majority of further narrowing the exception.[8] And California, which had been one of the major movers in expanding the scope of the accountant's liability, made a dramatic about-face, adopting a position much closer to the New York rule.[9]

I want to argue that, while the news from the California and New York courts is encouraging, they did not go far enough. The privity requirement makes good sense in the context of accountant negligence. Liability to third parties need not be determined by tort law, but should instead be resolved by contract. The argument has three strands. First, contract dominates tort; anything tort can do, contract can do better. Contract provides the flexibility to tailor rules in a way that tort does not. The other two strands concern the usual arguments in favor of extending liability: deterring careless behavior and efficient spreading of losses. While it is true that the accountant who performs negligently faces no legal penalty, there remains an incentive to audit with care; the consequence of poor performance is a decline in the value of the accountant's "brand name." As

---

[5] The Supreme Court heard oral argument in *Reves v. Ernst & Young*, No. 91-886, Oct. 1992.

[6] *Federal Deposit Insurance Corporation v. Ernst & Young, et al.*, 967 F.2d 166 (5th Cir. 1992). However, in its settlement with the FDIC of all claims against it (see note 2), Ernst & Young agreed that it would not object to the FDIC's efforts to vacate that decision; see Berton (1992).

[7] *Security Pacific Business Credit, Inc. v. Peat Marwick Main & Co.*, 79 N.Y.2d 695, 586 N.Y.S.2d 87, 597 N.E.2d 1080 (1992).

[8] 79 N.Y.2d 695, 718.

[9] *Bily v. Arthur Young & Co.*, 3 Cal. 4th 370, 11 Cal. Rptr. 2d 51. The court noted that U.S. courts have followed three basic patterns: the New York privity (or "akin to privity") rule; the "reasonable foreseeability" rule from which California has now retreated; and the rule suggested in the Restatement Second of Torts Sect. 552, which makes the accountant liable only to a narrow class of third parties (the new rule in California). The decision provides an excellent summary of the different rules, a good summary of their relative popularity, and a thoughtful analysis of the issues.

for loss spreading, the accountant's comparative advantage vis-à-vis the usual victims (banks, insurance companies, and other financial intermediaries) is not readily apparent.

There is no question that third parties would often want (and be willing to pay for) some form of assurance when entering into financial transactions. There exists a wide range of options from which they might choose as to how much assurance should be provided by whom, to whom, and with respect to which contingencies. The assurance could take the form of security interests in specific assets; or some party could guarantee payment of certain obligations in the event that the firm were unable to pay. Guarantees could include ceilings, deductibles, copayments, liquidated damages, exclusions, disclaimers, or other qualifications. The guarantees could be conditional on specific events (say, fire, theft, or negligence by accountants) and could be fine-tuned to fit the needs of different third parties. There might well be a demand for some form of guarantee regarding losses arising from an accountant's negligence. But there is no need for the law to guess as to whether the demand exists or the shape the guarantee should take. The terms of the guarantee can be worked out by contract.

One might object that it would be impractical for an accountant to enter into contracts with dozens, or perhaps thousands, of people who might want to rely in some way on an audited statement. But, in fact, it would not be at all difficult. For example, the accountant's client could post a bond assuring particular classes of third parties (say lenders) that they would be compensated for losses suffered because an outside observer (an arbitrator or jury) concluded that the accountant's audit was negligent. If the client were to contract for indemnification by the accountant, then this essentially reproduces via contract what some courts have been imposing via tort. True, contract might not allow for much fine-tuning of the assurance, but it certainly provides more flexibility than would imposition of a nonwaivable legal duty under tort or securities law.

If the efficient contractual solution is other than "the accountant is never liable," then there will be some administrative problems. It could be very hard to write unambiguous rules defining the conditions under which the accountant must pay and to whom. There will inevitably be boundary problems that will be similar to the questions that arise under the present rules. However, contract will continue to maintain two significant advantages vis-à-vis tort. The boundaries, fuzzy as they might be, will at least be established by parties with the incentive to economize on litigation costs. Further, contract permits the accountant (and clients and third parties) to decide *ex ante* whether the decision should be taken out of the hands of a jury by substituting arbitration. Given the juror's questionable ability to understand complex financial matters, this can be a considerable advantage.[10]

Perhaps the contract solution would become less attractive as the scope of the class of victims increases. But, conversely, when the scope of the victim class is small and well defined, contracting should be easy. Ironically, it is in precisely those situations that the courts have been most inclined to fall back on tort. When the third party is in a relationship with the accountant that is "akin to privity," the New York court, which has taken the most restrictive position, will recognize an exception. In denying recovery to a lender just on the far side of this boundary the court recognized that ruling otherwise would mean that the lender would acquire at almost no cost "deep pocket surety coverage, with no opportunity for actuarial assessment and self-protection, by the party sought to be charged."[11] Yet, it somehow failed to perceive that such coverage was being extended at a price of zero to those firms that fell within the exception and that were ideally situated to bargain for that "surety coverage."

Even if accountants were never held liable to third parties for negligence, they would have ample incentives to audit with care. The accounting firm, in effect, engages in activities that enhance the value of its brand name and then rents that name to clients. Clients then use that name as one element of a strategy to enter into financial arrangements with others on favorable terms. The client's willingness to pay depends, in the long run, on the quality of the accountant's work. Poor performance by the accountant today means lower fees tomorrow. This brand-name mechanism is not, of course, perfect. If prospective third parties have difficulty in ascertaining the quality of individual accounting firms, as opposed to a broader class of firms, then firms might have an incentive to fudge on their quality. Part of the reputation loss would be externalized to other members of the class so that each accounting firm would have an incentive to free ride on the reputation of the group. The net result of such a process could be an inefficiently low level of quality. Moreover, since clients hire the accountants, there are constant pressures on the accountants to bias their findings in favor of the clients. It is plausible, therefore, that accountants might want to supplement the reputation bond with a more tangible financial bond.

Nonetheless, the lack of any such guarantee in the half-century in

---

[10] As Lochner (1992) sardonically points out, there is some cause for concern when the lawyers feel compelled to explain to the jurors what the initials CEO stand for.

[11] 79 N.Y.2d 695, 706.

which accountants were largely sheltered from tort liability suggests that there was not sufficient demand for such assurance.[12] But if it had been necessary to supplement the reputation bond, the blunt instrument of tort liability is inappropriate given the more nuanced contract alternative.

Imposing liability on accountants has been justified in terms of the accountant's superior ability to spread risks. As the California court said when it broke from the *Ultramares* rule: "The risk of such loss is more appropriately placed on the accounting profession which is better able to pass such risk to its customers and the ultimate consuming public."[13] This argument is a careless extension of the enterprise liability catechism: injurers are better insurers than their victims. Victims in, say, a product liability suit might find it extremely difficult to spread certain risks by diversification or contract. But that is not a serious problem where the potential losses are financial and the potential victims are typically financial professionals. It is hard to imagine that accounting firms and their professional liability insurers (to the extent that accountants can still get coverage) would be the best providers of risk-spreading services for banks, mortgage companies, insurance companies, and other financial professionals who rely upon the audit statements produced by accountants. It is even harder to imagine that accountants would offer such an open-ended guarantee in a context in which most of the other defendants are insolvent and the accountant is one of the few available deep pockets to be saddled with joint and several liability.

In the long run the accountants must cover their costs, and that includes the costs of defending and settling lawsuits, costs that must ultimately be covered by the clients. If clients (and third parties) believe that accountant liability provides them additional assurance, then the demand for auditing services increases beyond the no-liability baseline; with the appropriate assumptions, clients end up buying the same amount of auditing services at a price that reflects the additional value of the assurance. (That

---

[12] The rule that shielded accountants from liability in most instances was enunciated in *Ultramares Corp. v. Touche, Niven & Co.*, 255 N.Y. 170, 174 N.E. 441 (1931). While there were some modest extensions of liability in the intervening years, the major innovation came in 1983, when New Jersey and Wisconsin both extended the accountant's liability to persons whose reliance on the audit was reasonably foreeable. *See H. Rosenblum, Inc. v. Adler*, 93 N.J. 324, 461 A. 2D 138 (1983), and *Citizens State Bank v. Timm, Schmidt & Co.*, 113 Wis. 2d 376, 335 N.W. 2d 361 (1983).

[13] *International Mortgage Co. v. John P. Butler Acct. Corp.*, 177 Cal. App. 3d 806, 820, 227 Cal. Rptr. 218, 227 (1986).

is a manifestation of the Coase Theorem.)[14] It is likely, however, that these assumptions are not met and that users of auditing services end up being harmed by an expansive liability rule. Litigation is expensive, and these costs, too, must be borne by clients. A 1991 survey of securities fraud claims against the Big Six found the average settlement to be $2.7 million while the average legal cost per claim was $3.5 million.[15] Moreover, accountants have learned that while one way to reduce the likelihood of an adverse judgment is to conduct an audit with greater care, another is to be more careful in choosing audit clients. There is some anecdotal evidence that clients posing a higher risk of liability are having difficulties finding accountants.[16] Liability brings with it not deterrence, but avoidance. That is, tort liability requires users of accounting services to bear the high costs of administering the tort system and to risk the consequences that accountants will shy away from certain types of engagements. If, for example, the profits in certain activities have a high variance and accountants are likely to be sued when things go wrong for the client, then accountants would be more likely to steer clear of such business.

The preceding suggests that third party liability is unwise as a purely prospective standard. Accountants charge clients a fee which reflects their potential liability, and rational clients (and third parties) conclude that the cost is not worth bearing. The picture is muddied by the existence of a large number of claims arising from past audits. Accountants cannot pass on the costs of settling past claims; they can only charge clients for bearing the *future expected costs* of claims that will arise out of present engagements. Thus, even if users of accounting services as a class might prefer a prospective rule holding that accountants never compensate, they could still sensibly argue in favor of holding accountants liable for past transgressions. The liability overhang is substantial. Indeed, the Big Six have argued that litigation costs currently are 9 percent of gross revenues,[17] and assertions that

---

[14] *See* Goldberg, n. 1, 300.

[15] "Campaign for Tort Reform," *The Financial Times Limited, World Insurance Report*, Sept. 11, 1992. The accountants presented these data as part of a campaign to reform tort law. I confess to being wary of data that are presented selectively by parties with a political axe to grind.

[16] Id.

[17] "Campaign for Tort Reform," note 15.

accountants current liability exposure exceeds $10 billion are common.[18] It is not, therefore, terribly surprising that third parties (and their lawyers) might be unwilling to give up their retrospective claims in pursuit of the prospective gains in a new world in which accountants are liable for negligence only to the extent that they assume liability by contract.

---

[18] *See*, for example, Lochner, (1992); and Berton and Lublin, "Seeking Shelter: Partnership Structure is Called into Question as Liability Risk Rises," *Wall Street Journal*, Sect. A, 1 (June 10, 1992).

References and Suggested Readings

Berton, Lee. 1992. "Ernst Accord May Give FDIC Leverage." *Wall Street Journal*, Dec. 3.

Berton, Lee, and Joann S. Lublin. 1992. "Seeking Shelter: Partnership Structure Is Called into Question as Liability Risk Rises." *Wall Street Journal*, June 10, A1.

Bily v. Arthur Young & Co., 3 Cal 4th 370, 11 Cal. Rptr. 2d 51.

"Campaign for Tort Reform." 1992. *The Financial Times Limited, World Insurance Report*, Sept. 11.

Goldberg, Victor P. 1988. "Accountable Accountants: Is Third-Party Liability Necessary?" *Journal of Legal Studies* 17:295.

Lochner, Philip. 1992. "Black Days for Accounting Firms." *Wall Street Journal*, May 22, A10.

Siliciano, John A. 1988. "Negligent Accounting and the Limits of Instrumental Tort Reform." *Michigan Law Review* 86:1929.

III

DISCLOSURE ISSUES

Insider Trading

9

Insider Trading versus Selective Disclosure: Distinguishing Fraud from Favoritism

John C. Coffee, Jr.
Columbia University

Introduction

The debate over insider trading has long had an overbroad, all-or-nothing character. On one side are those (mainly economists) who defend the practice, based largely on the claim that it enhances market efficiency.[1] On the other side stand those (mainly lawyers) who insist that fundamental fairness requires a level playing field in which no one can exploit improperly obtained informational advantages.[2] The problem with this polarized way of framing the issue is that it ignores an intermediate category: namely, informational advantages that are properly obtained (i.e., informational advantages that are intentionally conferred by the issuer and are not the result of any side payment to, or fiduciary breach by, a corporate official).

The importance of this intermediate category stems from two facts: (1) this zone is chiefly inhabited by the securities analyst, who is the professional typically viewed as the key force in keeping the market

---

[1] *See*, e.g., Manne, *Insider Trading and the Stock Market* (1966); Wu, "An Economist Looks at Section 16(b) of the Securities Exchange Act of 1934," 68 *Columbia Law Review* 260 (1968); Carlton & Fischel, *The Regulation of Insider Trading*, 35 *Stanford Law Review* 857 (1983).

[2] For a strong statement of this position that considerations of distributive fairness outweigh those of allocative efficiency, *see* Stout, "The Unimportance of Being Efficient: An Economic Analysis of Stock Market Pricing and Securities Regulation," 87 *Michigan Law Review* 613 (1988).

efficient,[3] and (2) recent SEC enforcement policy has tended to view corporate disclosures that are narrowly targeted to a limited group of securities analysts as a form of insider trading.[4] Nonetheless, this brief comment will argue that the two contexts of insider trading and selective disclosure should be sharply distinguished and separately addressed by the law. Unquestionably, *insider trading* should be criminalized, but it should also be narrowly defined as conduct that in essence amounts to a form of embezzlement (namely, the wrongful conversion of confidential business information) from a party entitled to maintain the confidentiality of that information. In contrast, selective disclosure applies to the dissemination of material, nonpublic information by the corporation for an arguably legitimate corporate purpose to a limited class of recipients. To be sure, selective disclosure presents troubling policy issues, but these should be addressed on the merits and not obscured by pejoratively characterizing such practices as insider trading. At bottom, the difference is between a form of theft and a form of favoritism. For the law to ignore that difference would not only render it morally myopic but also would subject securities analysts to a level of legal uncertainty that could prove injurious to the interests of all investors.

To approach this topic of how the law should regulate selective disclosure, Section 1 of this paper will first survey the rationales for the prohibition on insider trading; Section 2 will examine the current state of the law, and Section 3 will then assess the special status of the securities analyst. Finally, Section 4 will argue that, to the extent that regulation is necessary, less drastic means than criminal sanctions are available by which to address the problems associated with selective disclosure. In particular, the self-regulatory rules of the stock exchanges and the National Association of Securities Dealers, are superior because their burden chiefly falls on the corporate official as "tipper," not on the securities analyst as "tippee."

1. Why Is Insider Trading Illegal?

Without resort to intuitive claims of unfairness or vague references to a level playing field, specific coherent reasons can be given why insider

---

[3] *See*, e.g., *Dirks v. United States*, 463 U.S. 646, 658-59 (1983).

[4] *See SEC v. Stevens* (1991) SEC LEXIS 451 (S.D.N.Y. March 19, 1991); *see also* Note, "Rule 10b-5 and Voluntary Corporate Disclosures to Securities Analysts," 92 *Columumbia Law Review* 1517 (1992); Phillips & Nojeim, "Disclosures to Securities Analysts: The Drafty Exposure of the Open-Door Policy," *Prentice Hall Law & Business Insights*, (May 3, 1990).

trading results in unjustifiable injury and should be prohibited. These include the following:

1.1. The Injury to Corporate Property and Privacy

Corporations have reason to guard the confidentiality of much of the information they possess. For example, if a corporation engages in test drilling for oil or minerals, it may want to keep the results of this program secret. Premature revelation of those results could impair its ability to exploit its discovery (for example, by denying it the ability to acquire the surrounding land or drilling rights).[5] Similarly, a takeover bidder's acquisition program could be frustrated if trading by insiders in the target's stock drove up the price of the target's stock.[6] For injury to result, it is not necessary that either the insider or a tippee actually reveal the information to others, because often the market can decode the trades and infer that favorable undisclosed information has motivated the insider's transactions. From this perspective, the prohibition on insider trading chiefly protects the corporation's property right in its confidential business information.

1.2. The Principal's Need to Control the Agent's Compensation

Insider trading can be viewed as a system of executive compensation. But, if so, it is a notoriously inefficient system, because the profits received by the agent are secret, highly speculative, unrelated to the agent's own contribution to the firm, and beyond the knowledge or control of the principal. As a system of compensation, insider trading resembles paying managers with lottery tickets, instead of cash. More importantly, unless the employer can control the agent's profits from the employment relationship and keep them a function of the firm's profitability, perverse

---

[5] For such a fact pattern, *see SEC v. Texas Gulf Sulphur Co.*, 401 F.2d 833 (2d Cir. 1968) (en banc); *see also*, Scott, "Insider Trading: Rule 10b-5, Disclosure and Corporate Privacy," 9 *Journal of Legal Studies* 801 (1980); Macey, "From Fairness to Contract: The New Direction of the Rules Against Insider Trading," 13 *Hofstra Law Review* 9 (1984).

[6] For this fact pattern, *see United States v. Newman,* 664 F. 2d 12 (2d Cir. 1981).

incentives are created, and the agent has less reason to be loyal to the interests of the principal.[7]

1.3. The Adverse Impact on Disclosure Timing

Another consequence of insider trading can be to delay the release of material information that otherwise would have been released if insider trading were effectively banned. Although individual items of information may have a limited impact on the market price, corporate managers might learn to bunch up the disclosure of multiple items of information that, if delayed and released together, would have a measurable impact on stock prices. Put simply, if insider trading were legalized, it could give corporate managers an incentive to magnify the volatility of their firm's stock by manipulating the timing and content of their disclosures.[8]

Other sensible reasons can also be given for the prohibition against insider trading.[9] What none of these justifications do, however, is make the case for a universal rule precluding all use of material, nonpublic information. Such a broader rule would eliminate the incentive to search for new information and thereby reduce market efficiency. Rather, the common denominator of these rationales is their focus on the improper acquisition of information in a manner that either infringes upon the corporation's legitimate property rights or that permits agents to earn secret profits from their employment. So viewed, the prohibition on insider trading need not necessarily reach every form of selective disclosure of nonpublic information by the corporation, at least if the disclosure to the tippee does not jeopardize a legitimate corporate interest in confidentiality or otherwise result in secret profits to a corporate agent.

---

[7] *See* Clark, *Corporate Law*, 274-76 (1986); Easterbrook, "Insider Trading, Secret Agents, Evidentiary Privileges, and the Production of Information," 1981 *Supreme Court Review* 309; Levmore, "Securities and Secrets: Trading and the Law of Contracts," 68 *Virginia Law Review* 117 (1982).

[8] *See* Choper, Coffee, and Morris, *Cases and Materials on Corporations,* 463 (1989); Haft, "The Effect of Insider Trading Rules on the Internal Efficiency of the Large Corporation," 80 *Michigan Law Review* 1051 (1982).

[9] *See*, e.g., Wang, "Trading on Material Nonpublic Information on Impersonal Stock Markets: Who is Harmed, and Who Can Sue Whom Under SEC Rule 10b-5?," 54 *Southern California Law Review* 121 (1981) (insider trading inevitably preempts transaction by a person on same side of transaction as the insider).

2. The Scope of the Prohibition

Where the reason for the rule stops, a well-known legal maxim says, there too should stop the rule. Not infrequently, however, this principle is honored more in the breach than in the observance. Three principal legal theories are recognized today under which insider trading can be punished (both civilly and criminally), and each is surrounded by a penumbra of uncertainty.

2.1. The Fiduciary Breach Theory

In *Dirks v. U.S. SEC*,[10] the Supreme Court found that the mere receipt by a tippee of confidential information from an insider did not preclude the tippee from trading. Rather, it said, liability arose for the tippee only if the insider/tipper breached a fiduciary duty by passing on the information and the tippee knew (or should have known) that the insider would receive a personal benefit from the tip.[11] This focus on the relationship between the tipper and the corporation (rather than between the trading parties) explains why selective disclosure can be distinguished from insider trading. Clearly, the Court's requirement in *Dirks* that the tipper receive a personal benefit known to the tippee was motivated by the Court's concern that, absent an objective, bright-line standard, securities analysts would be exposed to criminal liability in connection with the everyday pursuit of their business. Implicit in *Dirks* is the view that the injury to the market's allocative efficiency from chilling securities analysts was greater than the cost to distributive fairness from permitting analysts to trade on information received from a corporate source and not available to all. Nonetheless, some ambiguous language in *Dirks* left open the question of what could constitute the illicit "personal benefit" to the insider/tipper.[12]

2.2. Misappropriation Theory

Although not yet endorsed by the Supreme Court, most federal circuits have agreed that an agent (whether or not an insider to the

---

[10] 463 U.S. 646 (1983).

[11] Id., 663.

[12] Id., 658-59; discussed *infra* in text and notes *infra* at n. 22.

corporation) violates Rule 10b-5 when the agent converts information received from the principal by trading on it (or passing it on to others who trade), in violation of a duty owed to the principal.[13] The crux of this idea is the traditional notion of embezzlement: when information is entrusted by the principal to the agent in connection with the former's business, its use by the agent for personal benefit amounts under common law to an unlawful conversion of the information.[14]

Ultimately, misappropriation theory has the potential to criminalize virtually any form of misbehavior or breach of professional ethics involving an agent who trades on confidential information acquired from a client. For example, a recent case shows the outer reach of this theory: a psychiatrist was criminally convicted under Rule 10b-5 for using information obtained from a patient (who was the wife of a CEO) to make a trading profit.[15] No one doubts that such behavior is highly culpable, but the duty here breached was owed not to the investors that the defendant traded with (to whom he owed no legal duty), but to his non-trading patient. Obviously, it can be debated whether the protection of patients and newspaper editors from disloyal agents were among the purposes that Rule 10b-5 was intended to address. Perhaps little harm will come if both these professions are subjected to some threat of criminal liability, but the simpler, clearer theory of Rule 10b-5's scope is that it protects market participants from persons trading contemporaneously with them who have failed to disclose information that they are under a duty to disclose.

2.3. Rule 14e-3

Today, to prove an insider trading violation under Rule 10b-5, the government must show a fiduciary breach in which the defendant participated. Precisely to avoid this requirement, the SEC adopted Rule 14e-3 in 1980. Although Rule 14e-3 applies only to tender offers, a defendant can be convicted under this rule for trading on a prospective tender offer, even though there was neither a fiduciary breach nor any other misappropriation of information, so long as the information so acquired can be traced back to either the bidder, the target, or professionals associated

---

[13] *See*, e.g., *United States v. Newman*, supra note 6; *Rothberg v. Rosenbloom*, 771 F.2d 818, 822 (3d Cir. 1985).

[14] *See Carpenter v. United States*, 484 U.S. 19 (1987).

[15] *See United States v. Willis*, 778 F. Supp. 205 (S.D.N.Y. 1991).

with either.[16] As a result, persons who would search out prospective tender offers are to a degree chilled. Although they can still seek to identify possible takeover targets based on publicly available information, any tip from either the bidder or target carries criminal liability, if used.

Arguably, Rule 14e-3's harsher standard is justified by the greater incentive within its limited context to trade based on inside information and by the lesser frequency of such information. Thus, any chill that it creates for those seeking to discover such information about takeovers seems unlikely to create any significant mispricing in the securities markets or otherwise to interfere with allocative efficiency. Tender offers are too brief (and today too rare) an epiphenomenon for the market's delayed recognition of their approach to have much macroeconomic impact. Indeed, the probable net result of Rule 14e-3 is to assist bidders to economize on takeover costs by keeping the pre-takeover price of the target lower than it otherwise would be in the absence of the Rule.

3. The Uncertain Legal Status of the Securities Analyst

Most of the reported decisions dealing with insider trading have involved idiosyncratic facts: remote tippees, unusual forms of misappropriation, or other exotic circumstances. As such, these cases may present fascinating vignettes of corporate life, but their public policy significance is limited. Only in its Dirks decision has the Supreme Court considered a case involving a securities analyst,[17] and that special circumstance appears to have motivated the Court to alter preexisting law in order to fashion a protective safe harbor for the analyst. In *Dirks*, the Court wrote what has been described as a "paean to the analyst" [18] as it justified why the securities laws should not prohibit the analyst from using material, nonpublic information that the analyst uncovered in the ordinary course of business:

> Imposing a duty to disclose or abstain solely because a person knowingly receives material nonpublic information from an insider and trades on it could have an inhibiting

---

[16] *See United States v. Chestman*, 947 F.2d 551 (2d Cir., 1991), which upheld Rule 14e-3.

[17] *Dirks v. SEC*, 463 U.S. 646 U.S. (1983).

[18] *See* Loss, *Fundamentals of Securities Regulation* 769 (2d ed. 1988).

> influence on the role of market analysts, which the SEC itself recognizes is necessary to the preservation of a healthy market. It is a commonplace for analysts to "ferret out and analyze information," and this often is done by meeting with and questioning corporate officers and others who are insiders. . . . It is the nature of this type of information, and indeed of the markets themselves, that such information cannot be made simultaneously available to all of the corporation's stockholders or the public generally.[19]

Read broadly, this language in *Dirks* seemingly established a safe harbor for selective disclosure by corporate officials to analysts of material, nonpublic information.

Never happy with *Dirks*, the SEC's staff has, however, increasingly read this language narrowly. Just how narrowly *Dirks* can be interpreted is shown by a recent SEC enforcement action, *U.S. SEC v. Stevens.*[20] In *Stevens*, the SEC brought an injunctive action, charging violations of Rule 10b-5, against the CEO of a small over-the-counter company, Ultrasystems, Inc. The CEO had telephoned several of the principal securities analysts following his company's stock to inform them that Ultrasystems would shortly announce an unexpected decline in quarterly earnings. The CEO received no pecuniary or other direct personal benefit for tipping these analysts, and his motive seems to have stemmed from the fact that on a prior occasion when the company had surprised the analyst community with an unanticipated decline in earnings, some analysts had publicly attacked the company's credibility. To avoid a similar controversy, the CEO appears to have been trying to justify to the analysts why the decline was unexpected and thus did not imply that previous predictions of earnings by the company had been exaggerated. So viewed, the CEO was protecting the corporation's reputation and market credibility.

In any event, this fact pattern seems a paradigmatic case of selective disclosure—exactly the kind of situation in which *Dirks* implied that the securities analyst was protected. Predictably, the SEC's staff saw it

---

[19] 463 U.S., 658-59.

[20] *See SEC v. Stevens*, supra note 4. For recent commentary on this case, *see* Coffee, "The SEC and the Securities Analyst," *New York Law Journal*, May 30, 1991, 5; Hiler, "The SEC and the Insider/Tipper," *New York Law Journal*, Aug. 29, 1991, 5; Note, supra note 4.

differently and alleged in its complaint that defendant Stevens placed the calls to the analysts "in order to protect and enhance his reputation."[21] This characterization of the facts represented an attempt to shoehorn the defendant's conduct within *Dirks's* somewhat ambiguous description of what constituted an illicit personal benefit. In *Dirks*, the Court had instructed

> courts to focus on objective criteria, i.e., whether the insider receives a direct or indirect personal benefit from the disclosure, such as a pecuniary gain or *a reputational benefit that will translate into future earnings*[22] [emphasis added].

In addition, the Court also suggested that a "gift of confidential information to a trading relative or friend" could also supply the requisite personal benefit.[23] Thus, if defendant Stevens was viewed either as seeking to protect his own personal reputation (as opposed to pursuing a legitimate corporate purpose) or as making a gift to a favored analyst, *Dirks's* safe harbor would be unavailable.

Although the *Stevens* case was settled without any judicial decision, several subsequent pronouncements by SEC officials suggest that the *Stevens* theory will be used again by the Commission.[24] One SEC enforcement official has even suggested that a personal reputational interest is present in virtually every case of selective disclosure, regardless of whether there is also a legitimate corporate purpose.[25] Even if this universal a theory of reputational benefit is rejected, the SEC could focus on a variety of other easily manipulated and subjective factors that will arguably be present in most cases: Was the disclosing officer new to the job (and so desirous of acquiring a reputation with the analyst community)? Was the official already subject to criticism for poor performance (and so eager to curry favor with

---

21 *SEC v. Stevens*, 1991 SEC LEXIS 451, 2 (S.D.N.Y. Mar. 19, 1991).

22 463 U.S., 663.

23 Id., 664.

24 *See* Schneider, "Fencing on the Electrified Tightrope: Shocking Executives Who Value Reputation," *Insights* (July, 1991): 2.

25 *See* Hiler, supra note 20.

analysts to protect and entrench him- or herself)?[26] Whatever the specific theory advanced in any individual case, this approach can quickly trivialize *Dirks's* attempt to protect the securities analyst. The Second Circuit once described the encounter between the securities analyst and corporate management as "a fencing match conducted on a tightrope."[27] With *Stevens*, the Commission has, in the words of one former commissioner, sought to "electrify the tightrope."[28]

4. Selective Disclosure: A Policy Analysis

Although the seeming ease with which the SEC staff has disregarded *Dirks* may offend purists, the doctrinal issues are less interesting than the broader policy issue of how the law should deal with selective disclosure. A variety of responses are possible, ranging from the SEC staff's attempt to assimilate selective disclosure under the rubric of insider trading to *Dirks's* casual acceptance of the practice as inevitable. From a public policy perspective, the appropriate legal response to selective disclosure requires a preliminary evaluation of two subsidiary issues: (1) the claimed efficiency justifications for the practice, and (2) the practical costs and difficulties of implementing an effective prohibition (including the error costs of penalizing false positives).

4.1. Is Selective Disclosure Efficient?

The distributive consequences of permitting selective disclosure are obvious: some investors are given informational advantages over others; wealth transfers in favor of the beneficiaries of these informational asymmetries are therefore predictable. Only slightly less obvious is the impact on dealers, market makers and specialists: knowing that some sophisticated traders may be able to obtain an informational advantage over them through selective disclosure, these professional market makers may be

---

[26] These examples were posed by former SEC Commissioner Edward Fleischman in his critique of the *Stevens* decision. *See* Commissioner Edward H. Fleischman, "Ferreting in the Interstices of SEC Attitudes to Securities Analysts," Presented to Eighteenth Annual Securities Regulation Institute, University of California, San Diego (Jan. 24, 1991).

[27] *SEC v. Bausch & Lomb, Inc.*, 565 F.2d 8, 9 (2d Cir. 1977).

[28] *See* Fleischman, supra note 26 (quoted also in Schneider, supra note 24).

forced to widen their bid-asked spreads, thereby making the market less efficient.

Against these social costs, there are, however, possible efficiency gains. First, some commentators have noted a recent tendency for the stock prices of large publicly traded companies to collapse precipitously when the company's reported earnings failed to meet analysts' predictions.[29] For example, Hewlett-Packard's stock fell 18 percent in one day on August 7, 1992 when it reported flat earnings, in the face of earlier predictions by analysts that its earnings would surge.[30] Other examples can easily be given,[31] and the basic pattern is one of high stock volatility in the face of unexpected earnings announcements. To the academic, such discontinuous price movements show the value of asymmetric information and the greater plausibility of the semi-strong theory of the efficient market over the strong form. To the realist, the more important implication is that such price volatility triggers securities litigation, costly lawsuits, large settlements, and the distraction of executives away from running the business. Both would agree, however, that it is desirable and efficient to reduce the frequency of such sudden price movements based on unanticipated earnings changes.

What is the answer? Some suggest that the best way to curb both the overreaction to earnings announcements and unnecessary litigation in the wake of these surprises is "continuous communication of relevant forward-looking information to the investment community."[32] Yet, according to a study by Professor Baruch Lev at the University of California at Berkeley, only one firm in fifteen today precedes its earnings announcements with a "quantitative, prospective disclosure concerning earnings or sales."[33] Clearly, there is little consistency among firms today in the way adverse developments and earnings estimates are communicated to the market: some firms regularly communicate revised earnings forecasts to analysts; others

---

[29] *See* Lev, "The Curse of Great Expectations," *Wall Street Journal* (Nov. 30, 1992), A-12.

[30] Id.

[31] Harley Davidson lost 31 percent of its market value on October 23 and 24, 1991, when it announced a 36 percent increase in quarterly earnings, although this was less than analysts had anticipated. Id.

[32] Id.

[33] Id.

avoid analysts. Predictably, those that avoid analysts experience sharp stock price declines when earnings announcements fall below the market's expectations (while those that do communicate forecast revisions experience more gradually sloping declines).

Why is there such variation and why do so few firms make forward-looking disclosures? A likely partial answer may be the SEC's policy against selective disclosure and the fear of private class-action litigation based on it. Continuous communication between the corporation and its analysts necessarily requires private contacts and a steady flow of information on a nearly daily basis. As I will argue in the next section, some selectivity is inherent in any program of continuous disclosure. Today, such private contacts invite both SEC attack and class-action litigation; thus, many firms avoid analysts (while others may cautiously disguise their contacts).[34] Yet, in the absence of a smooth flow of information to analysts, sharp, discontinuous price movements surrounding quarterly earnings announcements become predictable.

A second possible virtue of selective disclosure is that it may permit the securities analyst to be a more aggressive interrogator and to verify or discredit publicly available information more effectively. Although the paradigmatic example of selective disclosure is that in the *Stevens* case where management gratuitously made information available to analysts, it is equally possible that the selective revelation could follow a period of close questioning of management by the analyst.[35] Suppose this questioning results in a concession by management that reveals material, nonpublic information to the analyst. Here, the analyst would be fulfilling the private investigatory role that *Dirks* envisioned, and the market would be receiving information that might otherwise remain hidden for an indeterminate (but likely extended) period. Yet, to encourage the analyst to elicit such information, it is necessary that the analyst be allowed to use it by trading

---

[34] Some companies now refuse to discuss forward-looking information with analysts because they have been frequently sued in the past based on such voluntary disclosures. *See* "Vengeance or Growth?," *Wall Street Journal*, Nov. 16, 1991, A-14, which discusses Oracle Systems, a company that was sued 19 times in 1990 based on disclosure issues.

[35] Such inadvertent or unplanned disclosures do occur and also produce litigation. For a recent example, *see* Eichenwald, "Belmac Told Brokers of Deal Before Disclosure to Public," *New York Times*, Nov. 18, 1992, D-1, which discusses a corporate issuer who made inadvertent disclosure of pending acquisition before a meeting of analysts and brokers.

on it—before the corporation issues a corrective press release. Put simply, the price of costly research and verification efforts by analysts is the freedom to use the information developed.

Balanced against these possible benefits from selective disclosure, there is an even more likely cost: selective disclosure can potentially be used as a form of polite bribery by which a management coaxes and seduces securities analysts into favorable recommendations. That is, managements could reward analysts who make favorable recommendations of their stock with more precise estimates of the next quarter's earnings. True, this danger exists, but there are inherent limits on this practice: because analysts compete for clients in a world of near perfect competition, they cannot afford to bias their recommendations to please corporate managements if doing so would injure their clients. Possibly, a polite equilibrium may be achieved: because managements care (deeply) about how their own performance is evaluated, analysts may accurately predict a decline in earnings, but still imply in diplomatic ways that management is doing its best under difficult circumstances. Orally, the analyst might indicate otherwise to favored clients, but management will still find the favorable evaluation helpful in dealing with its own board and other shareholders. The overall market distortion from such an exchange of information for favorable evaluations is difficult to assess, but the distortion may involve more form than substance.

In contrast, another characteristic of selective disclosure is more troubling. Much selective disclosure to analysts may occur only days or hours before the public release of information (either in a press release or an SEC filing). In such a context, the gain in terms of increased market efficiency seems minimal when measured against the cost in terms of distributive fairness. This suggests a possible compromise: permit corporations to revise earnings forecasts and communicate these revisions freely to analysts up to the eve of (or until some reasonable interval before) earnings announcements are made to the public or the SEC.

4.2. Is a Rule against Selective Disclosure Feasible?

Proponents of the SEC's position will argue that disclosure to analysts is fine, but it should be accompanied by simultaneous disclosure to the public. This is ideal, but infeasible. Some selectivity in disclosure and timing advantages are inherent in any system that seriously seeks to update and keep current corporate earnings forecasts. First, smaller companies tend to be followed by relatively few analysts. Even in the case of larger companies, only institutional investors will be in contact with securities analysts, and public shareholders will rarely read SEC filings or press releases. Thus, except in the case of the largest companies where the market price will almost instantaneously absorb and reflect new public information, trading gains will be possible to shareholders who are aware that new information is about to reach the market. Even if selective disclosure were wholly forbidden, it would probably remain possible for corporate managements (particularly in companies with smaller capitalizations and a lesser market following) to alert favored analysts that a press release of interest to them would be released later that day or the next day. Because few would learn of the release (which the major media regularly are unable to run), selective disclosure following the press release would still remain possible. At most, the time period within which the information could be exploited would be shortened.

Some will argue that the corporation could issue an immediate press release at the time it makes any disclosure to analysts. True, it could, but few would see it. What this compromise overlooks is that the media does not have unlimited resources to publish constantly updated earnings estimates for several thousand publicly held companies. Ultimately, scarce media resources must be rationed and allocated to larger, more important companies and transactions.

What kinds of reform are possible? The most feasible system might be to link companies with analysts through computerized e-mail networks, so that once an update was given to any single analyst, it would be made available to all. But even this system (which could be implemented by allowing all recognized securities analysts access to an SEC or exchange supervised computer network system) would still leave public investors behind for a few critical hours. Realistically, some timing advantages are the cost of any system for continuous updating of corporate earnings estimates to prevent sudden market surprises.

4.3. What Would Be the Impact on Analysts?

Suppose selective disclosure were deemed a form of insider trading and analysts who used such information therefore faced a prison sentence of up to ten years.[36] A predictable result would be to chill the dialogue between individual analysts and corporate managements. Analysts who obtained new information from outside sources such as, customers, suppliers or industry rivals, might hesitate to confirm or verify that information with

---

[36] Criminal sentences of up to ten years are authorized by Sect. 32(a) of the Securities Exchange Act of 1934.

management. Analysts would still attend sizable group presentations made by corporate managements (because there would be legal "safety in numbers"), but individual interviews would be more risky. With a diminished capacity to show their analyses to management, analysts would at the margin make more errors than otherwise would have occurred if they could safely check their analyses with management.

4.4. Less Drastic Alternatives

Selective disclosure is obviously troubling and may offer only minimal efficiency gains, which do not justify any substantial deviation from a rule of equal treatment of all shareholders. But, even if true, this conclusion still does not imply that it must be equated with "hard-core" insider trading in which information is misappropriated from the corporation. Nothing suggests that the Draconian penalties now authorized for insider trading need to be focused on the analyst community. Thus, other means of regulation need to be considered as alternatives to extending the definition of insider trading to reach selective disclosure. Among the obvious possibilities are: (1) stock exchange rules, (2) the Investment Advisers Act of 1940 (which applies to most securities analysts), and (3) Sect. 15 of the Securities Exchange Act of 1934 (which gives the SEC broad regulatory authority over broker dealers, with whom most analysts are employed). The advantages of these less drastic alternatives are (1) that they do not invoke the pejorative word *fraud* to establish the Commission's jurisdiction and (2) that as nonfraud rules, they permit more precise line drawing and do not threaten massive class-action litigation.

In particular, stock exchange rules (which the SEC probably has authority to amend)[37] provide an attractive vehicle for any necessary degree of regulation because they apply chiefly to the corporate issuer, not the securities analyst. At most, the analyst is an aider and abetter of corporate management's tipping, and, thus, rules that establish specific guidelines for management seem preferable to fraud rules that potentially apply as much to the analyst, as the alleged tippee, as to the company.

Such rules could insist not only on an open door policy, but also on prompt dissemination of earnings estimates through real-time computerized

---

[37] Under Sect. 19(c) of the Securities Exchange Act of 1934, the SEC can "abrogate, add to, and delete from" the rules of any stock exchange as it deems "necessary or appropriate to insure the fair administration of the self-regulatory organization." The extent of this power is beyond the scope of this paper.

information systems. They could also distinguish various categories of selective disclosure. For example, there is a significant difference between nonpublic, material information reaching the analyst as the result of the analyst's vigorous cross-examination of management and the simple release of a quarterly earnings statement to an analyst one day before its release to the public. In particular, stock exchange rules could create a prophylactic rule against selective contact with analysts on the eve of a quarterly or annual filing. They could also establish rules requiring some forms of information to be released only at sizable group sessions with analysts—thus precluding favoritism and most forms of analyst bribery.

Conclusion

One need not endorse selective disclosure as efficient to recognize that the *in terrorem* threat of insider trading liability is not the best means by which to regulate it. Yet, the *Stevens* case and subsequent SEC staff pronouncements suggest that this may unfortunately be the direction in which at least the SEC's staff is currently headed.

Ultimately, the Commission must choose the pattern of market responses it wants to encourage: sharp, discontinuous price swings when the market is surprised by an earnings announcement or constant and less volatile price adjustments as the market responds to a steady free flow of information between corporations and analysts. If one is seeking to maximize investor welfare (and not bureaucratic power), the choice seems easy.

References and Suggested Readings

Carlton, Dennis, and Daniel Fischel. 1983. "The Regulation of Insider Trading." *Stanford Law Review* 35:857.

Carlton v. United States. 1987. 484 U.S. 19.

Choper, J., J. Coffee, and R. Morris. 1989. *Cases and Materials on Corporations*.

Clarke, R. 1986. *Corporate Law*.

Dirks v. United States Securities and Exchange Commission. 1983. 463 U.S.

Easterbrook, Frank. 1981. "Insider Trading, Secret Agents, Evideniary Privileges and the Production of Information." *Supreme Court Review* 1981:309.

Eichenwald. 1992. "Belmac Told Brokers of Deal Before Disclosure to Public." *New York Times*, Nov. 18, D1.

Fleischman, Edward. 1991. "Ferreting in the Interstices of SEC Attitudes to Securities Analysts." Paper presented to the Eighteenth Annual Securities Regulation Institute, University of California, San Diego (Jan.24).

Haft. 1982. "The Effect of Insider Trading Rules on the Internal Efficiency of the Large Corporation." *Michigan Law Review* 80:1051.

Hiler. 1991. "The SEC and the Insider/Tipper." *New York Law Journal* (Aug. 29):5.

Lev, Baruch. 1992. "The Curse of Great Expectations." *Wall Street Journal*, Nov. 30, A12.

Levmore. 1982. "Securities and Secrets: Trading and the Law of Contracts." *Virginia Law Review* 68:117.

Loss, L. 1988. *Fundamentals of Securities Regulation*. 2nd edition.

Macey, Jonathan. 1984. "From Fairness to Contract: The New Direction of the Rules Against Insider Trading." *Hofstra Law Review* 13:9.

Manne, H. 1966. *Insider Trading and the Stock Market.*

Note. 1992. "Rule 10b-5 and voluntary Corporate Disclosures to Securities Analysts." *Columbia Law Review* 92:1517.

Phillips, R., and G. Nojeim. 1990. "Disclosure to Securities Analysts: The Drafty Exposure of the Open-Door Policy." *Prentice Hall Law & Business Insights* (May):3.

Rothberg v. Rosenbloom. 1985. 771 F.2d 818, 822 (3d Cir.).

Schneider, Carl W. 1991. "Fencing on the Electrified Tightrope: Shocking Executives Who Value Reputation." *Insights* (July):2.

Scott, Kenneth E. "Insider Trading: Rule 10b-5, Disclosure and Corporate Privacy." *Journal of Legal Studies* 9:801.

Stout. 1988. "The Unimportance of Being Efficient: An Economic Analysis of Stock Market Pricing and Securities Regulation." *Michigan Law Review* 87:613.

United States v. Chestman. 1991. 947 F.2d 551 (2d Cir.).

United States v. Newman. 1981. F.2d 12 (2d Cir.).

United States v. Willis. 1991. 778 F. Supp. 205 (S.D.N.Y.).

U.S. SEC v. Bausch & Lomb, Inc. 1977. 565 F2d 8,9 (2d Cir.).

U.S. SEC v. Stevens. 1991. SEC LEXIS 451 (S.D.N.Y. March 19).

U.S. SEC v. Texas Gulf Sulphur Co. 1968. 401 F. 2d 833 (2d Cir.).

"Vengeance or Growth?" *Wall Street Journal*, Nov. 16, A14.

Wang. 1981. "Trading on Material Nonpublic Information on Impersonal Stock Markets: Who is Harmed, and Who Can Sue Whom Under SEC Rule 10b-5?" *Southern California Law Review* 54:121.

Wu. 1968. "An Economist Looks at Section 16(b) of the Securities Exchange Act of 1934." *Columbia Law Review* 68:260.

Securities Fraud Litigation

10

Using Financial Economics in Securities Fraud Litigation

Jeffry Netter
University of Georgia

Financial economics is playing an increasingly important role in securities fraud litigation. In this paper, I review several of the areas of securities fraud law in which the principles of financial economics have had the greatest impact. I also provide an overview of one methodological technique developed by academic financial economists that is used in litigation—the event study. An event study is a method of determining whether and by how much security prices react to new information. In securities fraud litigation, event studies can be used to discover whether information that was used in securities fraud is important enough to be the basis of a fraud suit. Additionally, event studies can be used to estimate damages in a fraud action.

The best evidence that the courts have recognized the importance of financial economics comes from the 1988 Supreme Court decision *Basic v. Levinson.*[1] The Court held in *Basic* that investors are presumed to rely on the integrity of security market prices. This presumption is explicitly based on the efficient market hypothesis (EMH). Later in this paper I discuss the reasoning in *Basic.*

Financial economics is also becoming more important in litigation because the number of securities fraud suits has grown dramatically over the past decade. As a crude measure of the number of fraud cases, I searched *LEXIS* for the number of reported federal cases that mentioned the phrase *Rule 10b-5*, the regulation on which most securities fraud litigation is based. In the 1970s, the number of cases averaged 205 per year. From 1980 through 1984, the average number of cases per year was 245 and from 1985 through 1989 the average number was 352. For the first two years of the 1990s, this

[1] 485 U.S. 224 (1988).

number had increased to 404 per year. If we assume the number of security fraud suits will continue to increase, there will be more opportunities for the use of financial economics in litigation.[2]

In Section 1, I outline event-study methodology. In Section 2 I discuss the usefulness of the technique in securities fraud litigation.

1. Event Study Methodology

An event study is a technique for estimating whether and by how much a stock price has reacted to news.[3] Specifically, in an event study we compare how a stock price moves in the period when the market receives the news of the event (the actual return) with how the price would have moved without the news of the event (the predicted return).[4] This difference, called the abnormal return, indicates the impact of the news on the stock price. There are four steps in an event study: (1) defining an event period, (2) computing daily abnormal returns, (3) computing cumulative abnormal returns, and (4) testing statistically the likelihood that any abnormal return we find occurred by chance.[5]

Defining an Event Period

The first step in conducting an event study is to select an event period, which is the period during which news about the event under study might have had an impact on the stock price of the affected company or companies. There is a trade-off in defining the length of an event window. The longer the event window, the more likely that the window includes all

---

[2] Interestingly, the increase in security fraud suits is highly correlated with the increase in the volume of shares traded (from 1970 to 1991 the correlation coefficient between the yearly number of cases mentioning the term *10b-5* and the yearly volume of shares traded on the NYSE is .816).

[3] Most event studies examine changes in stock prices although the methodology is similar for prices of other types of securities. *See* Macey, Miller, Mitchell, and Netter (1991) and Cornell and Morgan (1990) for more thorough discussions of how to perform event studies in securities fraud litigation.

[4] Stock returns are calculated as $(P_{new} - P_{old})/P_{old}$.

[5] I am outlining how to perform a basic event study. For a more sophisticated analysis, including discussions of problems that can arise in event studies see Brown and Warner (1985) and Henderson (1990).

dates on which new information about the event became available to traders. But the longer the window, the greater the possibility that the company's stock return was affected by news of other events (confounding events) making it difficult to isolate the impact of the relevant event.

The difficulty in defining the event window depends on the type of event. If the relevant information was unanticipated, it is relatively easy to establish the beginning of the event period—when the market first receives the information. It is more difficult to define the beginning of the event period for events that are at least partially anticipated. Thus, in event studies the event windows frequently start before the public announcement date, because information about corporate events may leak to the market before the formal announcement of the event.[6] In contrast, it is usually easier to choose the end date of an event window, because a large amount of empirical evidence shows that the market absorbs and processes information rapidly. Financial economists frequently end the event window at the close of trading on the day the market can first trade on the information.

Computing Daily Abnormal Returns

The next step in an event study is to calculate the abnormal return associated with the event. Assuming the event window is properly specified and that there are no confounding events, the abnormal return indicates the impact of the news on the firm's stock return. The method used to calculate the abnormal return varies. For instance, in specifying the normal or predicted return, a simple approach involves comparing the actual return with the firm's average return during a control period. I use this approach in the next section where I outline a simple statistical test to use in litigation.

A problem with using an event study to determine the impact of the news of an event on a stock price is that other new (confounding) information may impact the stock price during the event window. One of the most important sources of confounding information is news that affects the market as a whole. Thus, in calculating abnormal returns, most event studies account for marketwide news. The simplest method of correcting for marketwide influences computes abnormal returns as the difference between the actual returns on a stock and the returns on a market index. The difference is typically referred to as a net-of-market return. More

---

[6] In many security fraud cases, defining the event window is straightforward because we generally know precisely when the misstatement (and/or the revelation of the misstatement) became known to the market.

sophisticated techniques account for the fact that individual stocks react differently to changes in overall economic conditions, usually using the firm's beta (sensitivity of the firm's stock price to changes in the market) to make this adjustment.

As a practical matter the method used to estimate abnormal returns makes little difference when the stock's return is large relative to the market return and the event period is short. Fama (1991, 1607) summarizes this conclusion:

> When an information event can be dated precisely and the event has a large effect on prices, the way one abstracts from expected returns to measure abnormal daily returns is a second-order consideration.

This is true in many situations in securities fraud litigation, especially in determining materiality, when the alleged fraud involves important information released over a short period. More sophisticated analyses that account for market effects are more important in damage calculation, when the stock has been held for a long period of time.

Computing Cumulative Abnormal Returns

When the event window extends for more than one day, we sum the abnormal returns to obtain the cumulative abnormal return:

$$CAR_{iT} = \sum_{t=1}^{T} AR_{it},$$

where T is the length of the event window. CAR_{iT} measures the total impact of the event on the stock return. Generally, event studies report both the daily AR_{it}s and the CAR_{iT} over the event window.

Statistically Testing Whether Abnormal Returns Occurred by Chance

We may be interested in determining the statistical significance of the abnormal returns (or cumulative abnormal returns) we have identified—that is, is the abnormal return significantly different from zero? If, under normal circumstances, it is unlikely that a certain size abnormal return would occur by chance, the occurrence of that size abnormal return suggests that firm-specific news reached the market at that time. A common method of assessing the statistical significance of an abnormal stock return around an event is to compare the return during the event period to returns during a control period different from the event period. The control period is used to determine both the normal return and volatility of the security.

Statistical tests are useful in proving materiality and reliance since the tests indicate the likelihood that information was important enough to affect the stock price. Further, statistical tests can be used to indicate how confident we are of damage estimates based on event study evidence. In the next section I provide simple guidelines for determining materiality and reliance based on a statistical test.

2. Potential Uses for Event Study Analysis in Securities Fraud Litigation

I have outlined above a procedure for determining the response of a firm's stock price to the release of new information. In this section I suggest several areas in securities fraud law where financial economics and event studies can play a role. I concentrate on Rule 10b-5 cases although I discuss one other area of securities fraud where event studies can be useful.

SEC Rule 10b-5 is the most important of the antifraud provisions in the federal securities laws. Rule 10b-5 states that it is unlawful:[7]

> (1) to employ any device, scheme, or artifice to defraud,
>
> (2) to make any untrue statement of a material fact, or to omit to state a material fact necessary in order to make the statements made, in the light of the circumstances under which they were made, not misleading, or
>
> (3) to engage in any act, practice, or course of business which operates or would operate as a fraud or deceit upon any person, in connection with the purchase or sale of any security.

Rule 10b-5 is the basis for many securities fraud actions including insider trading and suits based on fraudulent disclosure. Both the SEC and private plaintiffs can bring a Rule 10b-5 suit. Since Rule 10b-5 does not explicitly say what is illegal, the interpretation of the rule comes from court decisions. In a typical case, the plaintiff must show (1) a misstatement or

---

[7] [17 C.F.R. 240.10b-5]

omission of (2) a material fact (3) made with intent (4) that the plaintiff justifiably relied on (the SEC need not show reliance) (5) causing injury in connection with the purchase or sale of a security (see Carney 1989).

Financial economics can be useful in several elements of a 10B-5 case—justifying reliance, determining materiality, and calculating damages or disgorgement. Event studies are useful for materiality and reliance because they show whether certain information affected a stock price. In the case of damages and disgorgement, event studies can help establish what the value of information used in alleged fraudulent activity is. I discuss each in turn.

Reliance

The importance of financial economics in litigation is best illustrated by the Supreme Court decision in *Basic v. Levinson*. In *Basic*, the Court adopted the fraud-on-the-market theory, a legal theory based on the efficient markets hypothesis. The Court stated:

> Recent empirical studies have tended to confirm Congress' premise that the market price of shares traded on well-developed markets reflects all publicly available information, and, hence, any material misrepresentations. (*Basic v. Levinson* 1988, 246)

The fraud-on-the-market theory allows a plaintiff who has not actually seen a misleading statement to still satisfy the reliance requirement in 10b-5 suit if the misleading statement distorted the market price and the security traded in an efficient market. That is, investors rely on the integrity of a market price and they are defrauded by misleading statements that affect the market price. The fraud-on-the-market theory is especially useful in class action suits where it would be difficult to prove each plaintiff individually relied on the allegedly fraudulent statement.

Materiality

Another element of a Rule 10b-5 case is materiality—to be actionable a fraudulent statement must be material. Material means important. For example, in an insider trading case, was the information the insider used in trading material? Alternatively, in a suit based on false disclosure, was the allegedly misleading information material? The Supreme Court in *Basic* adopted the reasonable-investor standard for materiality: "[an] omitted fact is material if there is a substantial likelihood that a reasonable shareholder would consider it important."

Event studies can be useful both in proving reliance under the fraud-on-the-market theory and in demonstrating materiality.[8]

Since event studies illustrate the impact of the release of information on stock prices, their use in showing reliance under the fraud-on-the market theory is straightforward—if stock prices are affected by the fraud, then there is a presumption of reliance. Similarily, one method of demonstrating materiality under the reasonable-investor standard is by demonstrating that the information affected stock prices when released (the so-called market-impact test). That is, reasonable shareholders in their investment decision would use information important enough to affect stock prices.

Statistical Guidelines

In Table 1, I provide general guidelines for determining materiality and reliance in cases where the information allegedly used in securities fraud is released to the public over a short time period of one day.[9] I noted above that the method of calculating abnormal returns is relatively unimportant for events in which the information reaches the market over a short period of time. Therefore, assume for the moment that a normal daily return for a stock is zero. Thus, the abnormal return on the day the information in question was released is simply the actual return. In demonstrating materiality and reliance with event studies, we have to determine how large the abnormal return must be to suggest that some important firm-specific news reached the market on that day. Put another way, how large must an abnormal return be to suggest that the stock-price movement on that day was unlikely to have occurred by chance (assuming a normal daily return of zero)?

To calculate this number it is necessary to take account of the individual stock's return volatility. Table 1 presents estimates of the size of daily abnormal returns that are unlikely to have occurred by chance, taken

---

[8] This argument is based on what plaintiffs must prove. Defendants can also use event studies to show that information did not affect stock prices and thus was not material or reliance should not be presumed.

[9] This is a condensed version of the approach presented in Macey, Miller, Mitchell and Netter (1991).

from the average volatilities of daily stock returns for every stock listed on the NYSE, AMEX, and NASDAQ each trading day in 1989.[10]

The stocks in each of these markets are divided into quartiles based on the value of the outstanding equity, because empirical evidence suggests that, on average, the larger the firm the less volatile the firm's stock returns.

Table 1 is easy to use. For example, a firm in the top quartile of NYSE stocks (average equity value of $6.44 billion) must have a daily return of 2.86 percent to suggest that some important firm-specific news reached the market on that day. In contrast, for the bottom quartile of NASDAQ stocks, the necessary price change is 10 percent. If the news is the public announcement of the information used in the alleged securities fraud, the abnormal return must be greater than the relevant number in Table 1 to suggest the information was material (or that there is a presumption of reliance). The numbers are only a guideline, however. In an actual securities fraud case, it is necessary to examine the volatility of the returns of the firm in question.

Disgorgement and Damages

The other major potential use of event studies in securities fraud litigation is in the calculation of penalties—usually disgorgement or damages.[11] Disgorgement requires defendants to give up the profits they made from securities fraud and is frequently the basis for SEC remedies in securities fraud suits. Damages are the usual remedy in private suits and are usually based on the plaintiff's losses. In both cases, event study evidence can provide important assistance in determining the value of information.

The theoretical basis for the use of event studies in disgorgement calculation is illustrated in an influential 1983 U.S. Appeals Court decision (*SEC v. MacDonald*).[12] In *MacDonald*, the court said that disgorgement should be based on the amount of profit attributable to the information used in the fraud, calculated as the difference between the purchase price and a price a reasonable time after the release of the information. The court rejected the argument that disgorgement should be based on the defendant's

---

[10] The statistical-test is at the 5 percent level of significance.

[11] For greater detail on the use of event studies in disgorgement *see* Mitchell and Netter (1992) and in private damage suits see Cornell and Morgan (1990).

[12] 699 F.2d. 47 (1st Cir. 1983).

actual profit from the investment. Event studies are well suited to estimate the value of information to a defendant.

The use of event studies in damage calculations based on a plaintiff's losses is less straightforward because courts in Rule 10b-5 cases sometimes award all losses suffered by plaintiffs (actual losses) whether or not the losses are directly attributable to the fraud. However, event studies can be useful in damage calculation especially when the plaintiff has held the security for a long time and the information used in the alleged fraud was revealed over time. In those cases, some courts adjust for market movements (either in reducing or increasing estimated damages). Using event studies to account for market movements can be especially useful in cases arising from Section 11 of the Securities Act of 1933, which deals with civil liabilities for false and misleading registration statements.[13] Generally, the Securities Act provides that plaintiffs may recover the difference between the amount paid for the security and the value at the time the suit was brought. If a share price fell for reasons other than or in addition to defendant's fraud (for example marketwide factors) damages are offset accordingly.

Summary

In this paper, I present several areas in which financial economics has been usefully applied in securities fraud litigation. A common methodological technique developed in financial economics, the event study, provides the means to isolate the impact of new information on stock prices. The technique can be valuable in determining whether information used in securities fraud is material and whether investors relied on a piece of information in making an investment decision. Additionally, event studies can be used in the calculation of damages caused by securities fraud.

---

[13] 15 U.S.C. Sects. 77a, 77k (1988).

Table 1
Guidelines for Determining Whether an Abnormal Return is Large Enough that it is Unlikely to Have Occurred by Chance (in percent)

	NYSE	AMEX	NASDAQ
All Firms	4.10	6.12	7.29
(Mean size firm in millions of $)	($1907)	($145)	($98)
1st Quartile	2.86	3.88	4.47
	($6440)	($494)	($338)
2nd Quartile	3.12	4.76	6.45
	($893)	($57)	($37)
3rd Quartile	3.84	5.80	8.29
	($243)	($21)	($12)
4th Quartile	6.55	10.02	10.00
	($57)	($6)	($3)

Source: Macey, Jonathan, Geoffrey Miller, Mark Mitchell and Jeffry Netter, 1991, "Lessons from Financial Economics: Materiality Reliance and Extending the Reach of *Basic v. Levinson," Virginia Law Review 77, 1017–49.*

References and Suggested Readings

Basic v. Levinson. 1988. 485 U.S. 224

Brown, Stephen, and Jerold Warner. 1985. "Using Daily Stock Returns: The Case of Event Studies." *Journal of Financial Economics* 14:3–32.

Carney, William. 1989. "Limits of the Fraud on the Market Doctrine." *The Business Lawyer* 44:1259–92.

Cornell, Bradford, and R. Gregory Morgan. 1990. "Using Finance Theory to Measure Damages in Fraud on the Market Cases." *UCLA Law Review* 37:883–924.

Fama, Eugene. 1991. "Efficient Capital Markets: II." *Journal of Finance* 46:1575–1617.

Gilson, Ronald J. 1986. *The Law and Finance of Corporate Acquisitions*. Mineola, New York: Foundation Press.

Henderson, Glenn. 1990. "Problems and Solutions in Conducting Event Studies." *Journal of Risk and Insurance* 57:282–306.

Macey, Jonathan, Geoffrey Miller, Mark Mitchell, and Jeffry Netter. 1991. "Lessons from Financial Economics: Materiality Reliance and Extending the Reach of *Basic v. Levinson*." *Virginia Law Review* 77:1017–49.

Mitchell, Mark, and Jeffry Netter. 1992. "The Role of the Efficient Markets Hypothesis in Insider Trading and Other Security Fraud Cases at the Securities and Exchange Commission." Working paper, University of Chicago and University of Georgia.

SEC v. MacDonald. 1983. 699 F.2d 47 (1st Cir.).

Rule 144A

11

Misperceptions About Private Placement Discounts: Why Market Reaction to Rule 144A Has Been Lukewarm[1]

Richard L. Smith and Vaughn S. Armstrong
Arizona State University

In April 1990 the SEC adopted Rule 144A and amended Rule 144, in part to address concerns that the secondary market for privately placed securities was unnecessarily illiquid. It was believed that once unnecessary restraints on reselling were removed, private placement activity would increase and the cost of funds would decrease for firms placing securities privately.[2] The rule changes, however, have had less impact on the market than was hoped.[3] Rule 144A governs resales directly and only indirectly affects initial placements. We define a 144A placement as a placement initially sold with a view to making the securities immediately resalable

[1] We wish to thank Stephen Axilrod, vice-chairman, Nikko Securities; Stephen Glover of Fried, Frank, Harris, Shriver and Jacobs; Gregg Jarrell, University of Rochester; and our colleagues Mike Hertzel and Janet Smith for useful comments on prior drafts.

[2] It was also argued that the rule changes would foster development of an international debt market in the U.S. similar to the Eurodollar market.

[3] *See*, e.g., "SEC Approves Rule Changes on QIBs, Shelf Registration," *Securities Regulation and Law Reporter*, 24 (Oct. 23, 1992), 1631. "Rule 144A Deemed Disappointing One Year After Implementation," *International Finance Daily* (BNA)(July 25, 1991), notes that in the 14 months after its adoption there had been 65 deals worth $6 billion and that the NASD's PORTAL system for secondary trades had proven to be a failure.

under the 144A safe harbor.[4] Although 144A placements have increased, the overall level of private placement activity has been declining both absolutely and relative to public issue activity.

We demonstrate that expectations about the impact of the rule changes are based on misperceptions about the reasons for the observed discounts of privately placed securities. In part, what has been widely characterized as an illiquidity discount, actually reflects compensation to private placement investors for the costs of becoming informed about the value of the securities and, in some cases, compensation for a monitoring function expected to be performed by the investors. Although the changes have reduced legal constraints on resale, the private investors' demands for information about the securities still must be satisfied. In this paper we describe the rule changes and their impact and cite evidence that demonstrates that the actual discount for illiquidity per se is only a fraction of the total discount. Since the rule changes only affect this piece of the total, it is not surprising that the market response has been slight.

1. Background: Motivations for the Rule Changes

The registration and ongoing reporting requirements of the Securities Act of 1933 and the Securities Exchange Act of 1934[5] were intended to protect investors in distributions and resales of securities *to the public*.[6] The laws assure availability of financial and other information about issuers and promote a liquid secondary market for the securities. In recognition that access to capital markets would be restrained unnecessarily if registration were required for all securities, the 1933 Act excludes private placements and secondary sales that are not related to original issues. Thus, the act exempts transactions by sellers other than issuers or underwriters, and by dealers when they are not participating in a distribution (i.e., a sale to the public).

---

[4] Normally such securities will contractually obligate the issuer to provide basic financial information to investors who purchase in the secondary market.

[5] 73rd Cong., Sess. I, Ch. 38, 48 Stat. 74—95 (1933)(current version codified at 15 U.S.C. Sects. 77a—77mm) and 73rd Cong., Sess. II, Ch. 404, 48 Stat. 881—909 (1934)(current version codified at Sect. 78a—78ll).

[6] *See*, e.g., H. R. Rep. No. 85, 73rd Cong. 1st Sess., 5—6 (1933) concerning intent.

The act defines an underwriter as any person who has purchased from an issuer with a view to distribution of the security. Because distribution is defined broadly, investors in restricted securities face the risk that a resale could be viewed as a distribution and, therefore, subject to the registration requirements of the 1933 Act, potentially invalidating the sale. Until recently, private investors could protect themselves by structuring a resale as a private placement or by reselling in compliance with Rule 144.[7] The rule created a safe harbor, that is, if the reseller had been the beneficial owner of the securities for at least two years, the securities were deemed to have been purchased with investment intent rather than a view to distribution. Thus, a nonaffiliated reseller who held the securities for at least two years would not be an underwriter as defined by the 1933 Act. Prior to the recent amendment of Rule 144, a separate two-year holding period was required for each subsequent purchaser.[8]

It was widely believed that the ambiguity of the 1933 Act, together with the limited safe harbor for resellers under Rule 144, made the private placement market unnecessarily illiquid. Lack of a liquid secondary market is claimed to have significantly reduced the prices of unregistered securities, increasing the cost of capital for firms raising funds via private placement.[9] Hence, in October 1988 the SEC issued a proposed Rule 144A and proposed

---

[7] 17 C.F.R. Sect. 230.144 (1991).

[8] If the 144 criteria are not met, a transaction may still be exempt under case law, depending on "whether the particular class of persons affected needs the protection of the [Securities] Act. An offering to those who are shown to be able to fend for themselves is a transaction `not involving any public offering.'" Investors not needing protection are those "who have access to the kind of information which registration would disclose." *U.S. SEC v. Ralston Purina Co.*, 346 U.S. 119, 125-127 (1953). The *Ralston Purina* case dealt with an offering by an issuer, but subsequent cases have applied the same standard to resales. *See*, e.g., *Ackerberg v. Johnson*, 892 F. 2d 1328, 1334-1337 (8th Cir. 1989); *Gilligan, Will and Co. v. U.S. SEC*, 267 F. 2d 461, 466 (2d Cir. 1959); *The Value Line Fund, Inc. v. Marcus*, [1964-66 Transfer Sec. L. Rep.] (CCH) ¶ 91,523 (Mar. 31, 1965).

[9] *See*, e.g. "SEC Rule Could Give Small Firms New Way to Raise Money," *Wall Street Journal*, June 22, 1990; Seidman, "SEC Rule 144A: The Rule Heard Round the Globe - Or the Sounds of Silence?" *The Business Lawyer*, Nov, 1991, 333—54; Glover, "Good Intentions in a Bad Economy," *Legal Times*, Dec. 31, 1990, 20.

to amend the holding period requirements of Rule 144.[10,11] In reviewing anticipated costs and benefits of the proposed rule changes, the Commission noted that increased marketability of unregistered securities was expected to reduce capital-raising costs of issuers and enable them to issue at more favorable prices.[12] Buyers and sellers were also expected to benefit from increased liquidity in the secondary market. While the proposed Rule 144A was broader than the version adopted in April 1990, the Commission continues to view the rule as a first step toward a more liquid and efficient resale market that will benefit both issuers and investors.[13] The amendment to 144 was enacted without substantial modification to the initial proposal.

---

[10] In part the proposed changes were motivated by rapid growth of the private placement market. The reported dollar volume of private placements increased from $20 billion in 1985 to $202 billion in 1988 and accounted for 43 percent of total corporate financing. *See* Maher, "Boom! A Year of Explosive Growth," *Investment Dealers' Digest*, Mar. 27, 1989, 14-15.

[11] Securities Act Release No. 6806 (Oct. 25, 1988) 53 FR 44016.

[12] The 1933 and 1934 acts have been criticized in the past for raising unnecessary barriers to the capital markets. George Stigler, for example, examined the effect of the 1933 Act on returns to investors in new issues and found that during the first year after public sale, new issues underperformed the market by similar magnitudes before, as compared to after, the act. He concluded that "grave doubts exist whether, if account is taken of costs of regulation, the SEC has saved the purchasers of new issues one dollar." (Stigler, "Public Regulation of Securities Markets," 37, *Journal of Business* (1964).) Stigler, however, did not fully examine whether risk-adjusted returns were enhanced or whether the Act increased or reduced the size of the new issue market. Gregg Jarrell updated the analysis to focus on risk-adjusted returns. Jarrell found that new issues after the Act were less risky and that risk adjusted returns during the first year were superior to those for new issues done prior to the act, but that performance over a five year period was comparable to the pre-act period. Jarrell also examined differences between private placements and public issues to test the hypothesis that SEC regulation (including ongoing reporting requirements) discriminates against high risk issuers causing their issues to be placed privately. He found support for this hypothesis in the sense that riskier issues tended to be sold privately. Jarrell tentatively concluded that his findings are "supportive of the view that SEC regulation imposes higher registration costs on relatively risky new issues." (Jarrell, "The Economic Effects of Federal Regulation of the Market for New Security Issues," *Journal of Law and Economics* 24 (Dec. 1981).)

[13] Securities Act Release No. 6862 (Apr. 23, 1990) 55 F.R. 17933 (Codified at 17 C.F.R. Sect. 230.144A [1991]).

Rule 144A provides an additional safe harbor from the 1933 Act registration requirements for resales of restricted securities to Qualified Institutional Buyers (QIBs) regardless of the seller's holding period. To limit ambiguity, the rule states a precise formula for identifying QIBs. Generally, the list includes any corporation or partnership with discretionary ownership of at least $100 million in securities of nonaffiliated issuers. The discretionary investment requirement is reduced to $10 million for securities dealers acting as principals. An additional net worth requirement is imposed on banks and savings and loan associations or equivalent institutions.

The rule applies only to securities that are not of the same class as securities listed on a national exchange or an automated quotation system such as NASDAQ.[14] Thus, equivalent securities cannot trade in a public market and be eligible for the 144A safe harbor.[15] The limitation extends to American Depository Receipts and to securities of substantially similar character that afford the holder substantially similar rights and privileges.

The amendment of 144 was intended as a companion to 144A, however, the class of affected securities is broader. The original Rule 144 specified a two-year holding period from acquisition of the restricted securities without regard to date of the original sale by the issuer. This was viewed by the Commission as unnecessarily restrictive and was replaced by a single period beginning from the date of the original sale. Thus, any privately placed security of a reporting company under the 1934 Act could be sold publicly after two years.[16] In effect, the amended Rule 144 creates a mechanism for bypassing the registration requirements for a public issue under the 1933 Act.

2. The Impact of the Changes Has Been Slight

---

[14] The original proposed Rule 144A contemplated exempting resales of privately placed securities that were fungible with publicly traded securities provided the seller made an effort to prevent a purchaser from reselling in an unregistered, non-exempt distribution. *See* Securities Act Release No. 6806 supra note 11, at Sect. VB.

[15] While the final Rule 144A enacted only one of three tiers initially proposed, extension of the safe harbor to securities fungible with publicly traded securities is still being debated. *See* Securities Act Release No. 6862, supra note 13, Sect. I.

[16] A reporting company is any firm with publicly traded securities outstanding that is not exempt from the reporting requirements of the 1934 Act.

Since Rule 144A was enacted, the numbers and dollar volumes of 144A placements have grown steadily. Placements of debt under 144A totaled $12 billion during 1990, $23 billion during 1991 and approximately $20 billion during the first half of 1992.[17] By that time 144A financing represented 38 percent of overall private-placement volume. However, the rule has not contributed substantially to growth of the private-placement market. In fact, for various reasons unrelated to the rule, private-placement volume has declined. In 1989 private placements totaled 38 percent of the $479.5 billion U.S. securities market but declined 32 percent during the first half of 1990. Volume declined an additional 13 percent in 1991 and 10 percent more in the first half of 1992.[18] In contrast, from the date of the Rule 144A enactment through July 1991, $433.9 billion of securities were registered for public sale.[19] To a degree 144A has simply caused a shift away from sales with 144 limitations.

The increase in 144A issues has been facilitated by strategic moves of the various exchanges and rating services to position themselves in the private placement market. Concurrently with enacting the rule, the SEC approved a proposal by the National Association of Securities Dealers to create a computerized, screen-based quotation, trading, and settlement system called PORTAL, which was designed to facilitate secondary-market trades of 144A securities by QIBs.[20] Subsequently the American Stock Exchange and Reuters Holdings PLC announced a letter of intent to develop a similar system called SITUS.[21] Almost concurrently the New York Stock Exchange

---

[17] "Moody's Says Rule 144A Debt Placements Rose To $23 B In 1991" Dow Jones News Wire, Mar. 4, 1992; "Private Placement Volume Fell 10 percent In The First Half" *Wall Street Journal*, Sept. 2, 1992, 16.

[18] "IDD Says Private Placement Volume - 32 percent in '90 1st Half" *Wall Street Journal*, Sept. 4, 1990; "Private Placements of Securities Off 13 percent in 1991" *Wall Street Journal*, Feb. 28, 1992; supra note 16. *See also* Swimmer, "U.S. Private Placement Market Outlook Strong," *Reuters*, Oct. 30, 1991, available in LEXIS/NEXUS Library, OMNI file.

[19] "The SEC Reviews Rule 144A and the Secondary Market" *Private Placement Reporter*, Feb. 24, 1992. Public new-issue activity declined somewhat over the period, but not to the extent of decline in the private placement market.

[20] Securities Exchange Act Release No. 27956 (Apr. 27, 1990) 55 F.R. 18781.

[21] "AMEX, Reuters Sign Pact to Create Trading System," Dow Jones News Wire, Sept. 5, 1990.

announced approval of a system for conducting primary- and secondary-market trades of 144A securities either by electronic billboard or on the exchange floor.[22]

Believing that lack of bond ratings was a factor contributing to the illiquidity of the market for privately placed securities, both Moody's Investors Service and Standard & Poors Corp. have become active in rating 144A debt securities.[23] Moody's reports that approximately 90 percent of 144A volume during the first two years involved transactions rated by Moody's.[24] S&P rates 144A securities on request of the issuer or the buyer, and Moody's tries to rate all 144A compatible private placements even if ratings have not been requested.[25]

Despite these efforts, not much has changed in the wake of 144A enactment. While the volume of 144A debt placements has been increasing, it has not displaced either the public-issue market or the more traditional private-placement market. And despite the efforts to add liquidity to the secondary market for 144A securities, not much is going on in the secondary market among QIBs. It now appears that both the AMEX and NYSE systems for trading 144A securities have been abandoned.[26] Further, trading on PORTAL by QIBs, as yet, is extremely limited and the NASD has sought approval to expand the scope of PORTAL and to make trading easier.[27]

In summary, investor and issuer reactions to Rule 144A have fallen well short of many people's expectations. Supporters argue that the benefits of added liquidity will take more time to be realized. Careful analysis, however, suggests that even if many issuers elect to place securities under 144A, the benefits will remain limited.

---

[22] "NYSE Board Backs Formation of Unregistered Securities Market," *Wall Street Journal*, Sept. 11, 1990.

[23] "The SEC Reviews Rule 144A and The Secondary Market," *Private Placement Reporter*, Mar. 2, 1992.

[24] "Industry Notes 144A Trends," *Private Placement Reporter*, Mar. 16, 1992.

[25] Supra note 23.

[26] "NASD Is Trying to Revive System For Foreign Stocks," *Wall Street Journal*, May 8, 1992, C11; Sommar, "American Stock Exchange May Have Killed SITUS," *Investment Dealers' Digest*, May 6, 1991.

[27] Id.

3. The Reasons for Issuer and Investor Ambivalence to the Rule Changes

Issuing firms can choose from among three alternatives: traditional private placement, 144A eligible placement, and public issue. The perceived benefits of Rule 144A derive from two sources. First, issuers may save registration and reporting costs that would be required if securities were sold publicly. Second, increased liquidity in the secondary market may motivate investors to pay more than for identical securities placed privately outside the rule.[28] Our analysis indicates that these perceived benefits are of limited value. Registration cost savings are small and only foreign companies and possibly companies with no other public securities outstanding can save costs related to periodic reporting under the 1934 Act. Perhaps more important, secondary market liquidity is not likely to be significantly enhanced by the Rule.[29]

Proposition 1: Registration Cost Savings under Rule 144A Are Small

While private placement can save the cost of registering securities, most of the costs of public issue are not registration costs, but costs of underwriting and issuing the securities. In public sales the investment banker is involved in preparing the prospectus, securing credit ratings, advising on issue structure, preselling, pricing, and effectively certifying the value of the issue.[30] Out-of-pocket expenses of the issuer include legal and accounting fees, trustee fees, printing and engraving costs, and fees for registering with the SEC.

---

[28] It is also argued that the rule changes can open up a new market for foreign issuers, potentially lowering their overall cost of funds.

[29] To a degree, the amendment to 144 should have reduced interest in 144A, since the amendment enhances the liquidity of all securities placed privately by reporting companies. Our reasoning and evidence, however, imply that this is not an important reason for lack of interest in the 144A option.

[30] A general discussion of the certification role of investment bankers appears in Smith, "Underwriting of New Issues," *The New Palgrave Dictionary of Money and Finance*, 1992. Booth and Smith, "Capital Raising, Underwriting, and the Certification Hypothesis," *Journal of Financial Economics* 15 (1986) provides a formal model of the certification function. Tinic, "Anatomy of Initial Public Offerings of Common Stock," *Journal of Finance* 43 (1988) explains how the threat of lawsuit for shortcomings of due diligence reviews contributes to the certification role of investment bankers.

Although public-issue underwriting costs, some out-of-pocket costs, and SEC fees for registration of the securities are avoided by private placement, the private investors' demands for information about the issue still must be satisfied. Thus, even though SEC registration, certified financial statements, bond counsel opinions, and so forth, are not required by the SEC for securities that are placed privately, the investors' willingness to pay for the issue depends on availability of equivalent or similar information. Only if public issuance causes the information needs of investors to be met inefficiently can private placement reduce the cost of informing investors. Similarly, while the issuing costs of public sales are avoided, they are partly offset by the costs of finding private investors. Evidence comparing the costs of public issues and private placements is limited. Blackwell and Kidwell (1988) compare the average underwriter spread for public issues with the average fees paid to agents in private placements of debt by public utilities from 1979 through 1983. They report an average underwriter spread of .806 percent and an average agent fee of .364 percent.[31] The difference appears to reflect primarily the additional services performed by investment bankers for public issues. Thus, even though agent fees for private placements are less than underwriter spreads for public issues, the difference is offset by other costs of valuing the securities, which costs are either borne directly by the issuer or indirectly reflected in the interest rate differential between public and private sales.

While data for Rule 144A sales have not been subject to rigorous analysis, it now appears that some of the placements resemble public offerings. The securities are purchased by investment bankers who then resell to QIBs.[32] This practice of mimicking the public issue process attests to the limited savings of issuing costs likely to be realized under the rule.

Proposition 2: Reporting Cost Savings under Rule 144A Are Large for Some Firms and Negligible for Others

Savings of the reporting costs required under the 1934 Act can be substantial. However, such savings are nonexistent for companies that are

---

[31] Blackwell and Kidwell, "An Investigation of Cost Differences Between Public Sales and Private Placements of Debt," *Journal of Financial Economics* 22 (1988) 253-78.

[32] "Underwritten Offerings Gaining Under Rule 144A," *Private Placement Reporter*, Jan. 13, 1992; Cooper, "Private Placement Under Rule 144A: A Rose By Another Name," *New York Law Journal*, Jan. 27, 1992, 1.

already reporting companies. For nonpublic companies, even the limited ongoing information needs of investors may be sufficient to discourage private issue under 144A.[33]

For the purpose of assessing potential reporting cost savings we distinguish among domestic reporting companies, foreign firms with publicly traded securities outside the U.S., and firms without publicly traded securities. If a firm issues privately with 144A eligibility, the rule requires that limited financial information be made available on an ongoing basis. Since reporting companies already are committed to incurring the costs of public financial reporting, the limited information requirements of the rule do not afford any savings. As long as public issue registration costs are low, the rule provides no benefit to such firms for issuing privately relative to issuing publicly. In contrast, foreign issuers with public securities are the primary beneficiaries of the Rule since they generally can satisfy the 144A reporting requirements with existing published reports that do not conform to the specific requirements of the 1934 Act. Provided the existing reports satisfy the information demands of QIBs, the rule can facilitate sales of foreign securities in the U.S. This has been the primary effect of the rule and was always expected to be an important effect. Finally, firms without publicly traded securities may reduce ongoing information costs by issuing under 144A as compared to issuing publicly. However, if information demands of private investors are similar to those of public investors, the

---

[33] For a corporate issuer that is neither a reporting company nor a foreign public company that is exempt under Rule 12g 3-2(b) from 1934 Act reporting availability of the rule is conditioned upon, "the holder and a prospective purchaser designated by the holder having the right to obtain from the issuer, upon request of the holder . . . a very brief statement of the nature of the business of the issuer and the products and services it offers . . . and the issuer's most recent balance sheet and profit and loss and retained earnings statements, and similar financial statements for such part of the two preceding fiscal years as the issuer has been in operation (the financial statements should be audited to the extent reasonably available)" (17 C.F.R. Sect. 230.144A [d][4][i]). In recognition that the ongoing information requirements of paragraph (d)(4) could be burdensome, Commissioner Fleischman dissented from adopting that paragraph, stating that "the adverse impact of its inclusion falls principally upon the class of business enterprises most needy of the benefits promised by the Rule and most capable of magnifying those benefits to the advantage of the entire American economy, namely the smaller domestic privately-owned issuers" (separate statement of Commissioner Fleischman, Securities Act Release No. 6862, supra note 13). Though we agree that the ongoing information costs may be substantial for such firms, our analysis suggests that striking the paragraph would not materially benefit this group of issuers, since the information demands of investors would not be affected.

actual cost savings will be small. By traditional private placement such an issuer can avoid any SEC requirement for ongoing reporting and can expand the potential market to include buyers other than QIBs who are interested in privately placed securities. The disadvantage of the traditional approach is the sacrifice of liquidity during the first two years after the sale.[34] Whether this is sufficient to tip the balance in favor of Rule 144A depends on the size of the return premium investors require for investing in illiquid securities.

Proposition 3: Private Placement Discounts Reflect Information and Monitoring Costs Borne by Private Investors

When securities are sold without registration, private investors must incur costs to inform themselves about the value of the securities and to monitor the firm's performance after the sale. For public sales, costs of information disclosure at issue and on an ongoing basis are, for the most part, *explicitly borne* by the issuer. In contrast, the costs that investors in privately placed securities incur for information and monitoring are *implicitly* borne by the issuer and are reflected in the price discount for privately placed securities.

Evidence of the relation between private-placement discounts and information and monitoring costs is provided by Hertzel and Smith (1993) in a study of private placements of common stock by firms with publicly traded stock outstanding.[35] For a sample that includes both restricted shares and shares registered at or shortly after the time of issue, the average private placement discount is 20 percent, relative to the public market price after the issue. The size of the discount is strongly related to the cost of becoming informed about the value of the securities. For example, discounts are larger for firms that are difficult to value, such as firms involved in speculative new product development and firms with high risk of financial distress. There is a significantly larger discount for restricted shares, but rather than reflecting a cost of illiquidity, this component of the discount appears to reflect anticipated monitoring costs.

The Hertzel and Smith study also addresses the choice between placing securities privately and issuing publicly. Issuers tend to prefer public

---

[34] Securities originally sold privately in the traditional way can be made 144A eligible if the issuer is willing to commit to the ongoing information requirements of paragraph (d)(4).

[35] Hertzel and Smith, "Market Discounts and Shareholder Gains for Placing Equity Privately," *Journal of Finance* 48, 1993, 459-485.

issue when they believe their securities are overvalued by the market and prefer private placement when they believe the market has undervalued their securities. Private placement provides a mechanism for issuers to reveal their information to private investors, which mechanism is not as readily available for public issues. Private sales of shares to informed investors, even at discounted prices, can convey good news about the firm, partly because they can signal commitments by the purchasers to invest for the long term and to monitor future performance of the firm.[36]

The analysis of discounts can be generalized to any security where riskiness of the issuer affects value. Thus, discounts for private placements of risky debt are expected also to reflect information and monitoring costs. Corroboration that the analysis applies to other securities is provided by Fields and Mais (1991), who find that stock prices react positively to private placements of convertible debt.[37]

Proposition 4: The Discount for Privately Placed Securities Reflects Illiquidity but Is Not Materially Caused by Restrictions on Trading

To evaluate the illiquidity issue, it is useful to distinguish between illiquidity that results from regulatory impediments to trading and a broader concept of illiquidity that results from informational asymmetries between buyers and sellers as discussed above. Rule 144A addresses the narrower concept but cannot deal with the more important cause of illiquidity: informational asymmetry. The presumption that a QIB is capable of protecting itself from trading with an information disadvantage merely shifts the burden of due diligence to the QIB.

Illiquidity that derives from regulatory impediments to resale is not necessarily costly to issuers since it does not necessarily result in discounting the issue price. If enough capital is available from investors who do not

---

[36] A similar positive stock price reaction is found by Wruck who suggests that the reaction is due to ownership structure effects including changes in monitoring efforts and that the private placement discount may reflect monitoring costs. *See* Wruck, "Equity Ownership Concentration and Firm Value: Evidence from Private Equity Financing," *Journal of Financial Economics* 23 (1989) 3-28. For a summary discussion of the Hertzel and Smith and Wruck studies, *see* Hertzel, "Private Equity Issues," *The New Palgrave Dictionary of Money and Finance*, 1992.

[37] Fields and Mais, "The Valuation Effects of Private Placements of Convertible Debt," *Journal of Financial Economics* 46 (Dec. 1991), 1925-32.

regard illiquidity as costly, then the market will assess no penalty to issuers for selling illiquid securities. The private-placement market is dominated by such investors. Shapiro and Wolf (1972) indicate that life insurance companies are the most active and consistent participants in the market.[38]

Based on interviews with market participants during 1988, the SEC staff concluded that insurance company acquisitions of securities account for "the vast majority of total private placement offerings."[39] Former SEC Chief Economist Gregg Jarrell, cites a 1963 study indicating that 97 percent of private bond placements listed life insurance companies as the principal purchasers.[40] Investors such as life insurance companies, as well as some investment companies and pension funds, have developed investment policies around the need to meet cash flow requirements in the future. If there is a potential discount for illiquidity then investors who do not anticipate much trading are the natural clientele for illiquid securities so that the illiquidity discount per se would be small. They are also the natural clientele if reselling is costly because of concerns about informational asymmetries between buyers and sellers, since such concerns impede the resale market.

Regulatory impediments to reselling can only cause illiquidity discounts if there is excess supply of restricted securities at a price consistent with the public-issue price. The supply of such securities would have to be so large that investors who desired liquidity were induced to forego it by the opportunity to earn a higher return than for investing in liquid securities. Market evidence, however, suggests that illiquidity discounts deriving from regulatory impediments to resale are small or nonexistent. If such discounts were material, then large reporting companies with investment-grade securities could save money by issuing debt publicly rather than privately. Since such firms can shift easily between the public and private debt markets, the costs of public issue are not likely to be much different than the costs of private placements.[41]

---

[38] Shapiro and Wolf, *The Role of Private Placements in Corporate Finance* (1972).

[39] Supra note 11, Sect. IIC.

[40] Jarrell, supra note 12.

[41] Thus the public and private debt markets are connected. Since, to firms that contribute substantially to the volume of both private and public debt, the markets are good substitutes for each other (effectively a single market) the price of regulation induced illiquidity is near zero. Hawkins examines a sample of large firms listed in the

Evidence is provided by Blackwell and Kidwell (1988), who analyze the effective interest cost of publicly and privately placed debt for a sample of public utility firms that have demonstrated the ability to substitute between the two markets. They find that the difference in effective interest cost between public and private issues is not statistically significant after controlling for characteristics of the security and market volatility.[42] For those issuers the private debt market was less costly during periods of high interest rate volatility, suggesting that investors in privately placed debt are less concerned with short-term variability of bond values than public investors.[43] The choices by these firms of whether to issue publicly or privately depend heavily on factors such as the ability to design tailor-made securities with special monitoring arrangements, which is less possible for public issues.[44] Smith and Warner (1979) report that restrictive covenants of privately placed debt tend to be more extensive and detailed. They also indicate that renegotiation provisions are more frequently included and exercised.[45]

Thus, in economic terms, large reporting companies are the marginal demanders of funds in both the public and private debt markets. Their ability to move between private and public debt markets at low cost guarantees that illiquidity discounts due to regulatory impediments on reselling will be small. Since the market for investment funds is competitive, it does not matter that some demanders of funds in the private-placement market would face substantially higher costs of public issues.

1977 *Moody's Industrial Manual* and reports that 80 percent of firms that had done public issues also borrowed privately. Hawkins in Brealy & Myers, *Principles of Corporate Finance* 4 ed., 355.

[42] The reduced interest cost spread between 144A debt issues and public issues that some claim to have observed is more likely due to the sacrificing of some of the flexibility of traditional private placements and to the fact that 144A eligible securities generally receive credit ratings than to enhanced secondary market liquidity. In effect, at this time, 144A placements are being subsidized by the willingness of Moody's to rate the issues at no cost to the issuers or investors.

[43] Supra note 31.

[44] Supra note 12.

[45] Smith and Warner, "On Financial Contracting: An Analysis of Bond Covenants," *Journal of Financial Economics* 7 (1979), 117-61.

Those issuers still benefit from competition on the margin between the private and public markets.

In summary, although observed yields for privately placed securities tend to be higher than the yields for comparable publicly traded securities, the difference appears to be due more to information costs than to regulatory illiquidity. For Rule 144A securities that have been rated it is reported that the discounts are virtually nonexistent—this despite the fact than an active secondary market has not emerged. The explanation appears to be, that for Rule 144A eligible securities, the discounts reflect the costs private investors would have to incur to assess the quality of the securities. Once Moody's and S&P began rating 144A securities, those costs were shifted to the rating services and the discounts disappeared.[46] Some traditional investors in private placements view this change negatively, apparently preferring to make their own assessments of risk and to capture the returns for doing so.[47]

4. Conclusion

Since registration cost savings are negligible and savings of reporting costs can be substantial only for foreign firms with publicly traded securities in foreign markets, Rule 144A should not be expected to markedly impact the activities of domestic firms unless it leads to smaller discounts for privately placed securities. These discounts arise from informational asymmetries between sellers and buyers. For public issues the information disparity is reduced by SEC reporting requirements and by the ability of investors to rely on the reputations of investment bankers as certifiers of the fairness of issue prices.[48] For private placements the investor must expend resources analyzing the issuer and the value of the securities. The private-placement discount includes compensation to the investor for performing this evaluation. Thus, in part, the discount substitutes for explicit compensation to investment bankers for their due diligence and certification services. Regulatory impediments to reselling securities in the secondary market do not appear to significantly affect the discounts for privately placed securities.

---

[46] Sommar & Maker, "Morgan Stanley Underwrites United Biscuits 144A Deal," *Investment Dealers' Digest*, May 6, 1991, 16.

[47] *See*, e.g., Connolly, "144A Piques Mild Insurer Interest," *National Underwriter-Life & Health*, June 29, 1992, 45; Crosson, "Reaction Mixed to New Private Placement Rule," *National Underwriter-Life & Health*, Oct. 1, 1990, 9.

[48] Supra note 30.

Neither Rule 144A nor the amendment to Rule 144 can remove informational asymmetry as a cause of illiquidity or private placement discounts. Although Rule 144A permits secondary market trades among QIBs, it does not remove the concern that insider selling could be motivated by private information that would affect the value of the securities negatively. Secondary market discounts of this type could only be reduced if the seller was known not to have an information advantage or if repeat trading among QIBs was important enough to cause sellers to invest in reputations for fair pricing in their dealings with other QIBs. Such mechanisms, however, are independent of Rule 144A and the amendment to Rule 144.

Similarly, although the amendment to Rule 144 allows public trading of reporting company securities after a two year holding period from the issue date, it can only have an impact if the seller is known not to be an insider. For non-reporting companies the amendment allows more frequent resale after the first two years, but the buyer still faces the concern that the seller is attempting to exploit an information advantage.

5. Implications for Issuers, Investors, and Policy Makers

Issuers

Issuers of more risky or speculative securities are attracted to the private-placement market because that is where they find investors who can accurately assess the risks and who do not demand large return premiums for investing in securities that are innately illiquid. Reducing regulatory impediments to reselling cannot make the securities of such firms liquid or materially reduce their cost of funds.

Investors

The distinction between an illiquidity discount due to regulatory impediments to trading and a discount due to asymmetric information is an important one. In large part the discount for privately placed securities is compensation for the expected costs private investors incur to value the securities in which they invest and to monitor the firm's performance after the investment. Thus, investors who assume the discount is a return for accepting illiquidity and who fail to analyze their investments in privately placed securities carefully may be acting imprudently. Whether discounts for resales in the secondary market will be smaller under 144A depends on whether the ongoing disclosure requirements under the rule are adequate for

QIBs. At this point there is little reason to expect that an active secondary market will develop for such securities.

Policy Makers

In the private sector, sellers of new products naturally are disappointed when the products do not attract much interest from consumers. To a degree the SEC seems to be acting like a disappointed seller. Since Rule 144A was enacted, the Commission has continued to broaden the definition of a QIB as if expanding the definition would eventually bring enough players into the picture so that a liquid secondary market would develop.[49] The analysis presented here suggests that, even if the definition were substantially broadened, not much would change.

Rather than being disappointed about the limited interest in the 144A market, a better focus would be on what the experiment is telling us about the efficiency of the public and private markets as they existed prior to the rule. Market reaction to Rule 144A is a new piece of evidence that conflicts with the view that SEC regulations unnecessarily penalize risky issuers. Even though the rule would allow risky issuers to avoid SEC registration and reporting costs and still promote a liquid market for their securities among QIBs, the rule cannot overcome the basic problem of informational asymmetry between issuers and investors. The fact that the rule has attracted little interest suggests that it is not the regulations that have caused risky issuers to select private placements. In effect, the regulations appear to function as a quality screen enabling low risk issuers to signal their quality level and causing high risk issuers to reveal themselves. While the sorting may reduce the cost of funds for low-risk issuers and increase it for high-risk issuers, such a result cannot be characterized as discrimination against high-risk issuers. The market response to Rule 144A is, therefore, testimony to the efficiency of securities regulation in the U.S.

---

[49] Securities Act Release No. 6963, (Oct. 28, 1992) 57 F.R. 48721.

12

Rule 415, Rule 144A, and Regulation A[1]

M. Wayne Marr
Clemson University

In this paper I trace the easing in regulation (or changes in regulation) of the capital markets brought about by the Securities and Exchange Commission over the last 10 years. More specifically, we examine Rule 415, Rule 144A, and proposed changes in Regulation A as examples of loosening of the SEC's hold over the nation's capital markets.

Rule 415 allows firms to register securities only once, and sell them at convenient times over a period of two years. Rule 144A allows foreign issuers to make private placements with minimal SEC disclosure and registration. Proposed changes in Regulation A aim to reduce the cost of accessing the capital markets for small businesses by reducing the registration and disclosure requirement for eligible firms. In all three cases, reduced SEC regulation has resulted (or will likely result) in lower issuance costs and, except for Regulation 144A deals, the changes make the nation's capital markets more accessible to issuing companies.

Rule 415 or Shelf Registration

With shelf registration, the SEC allows continuous and delayed offering of conventional underwritten public offerings and other securities that may be registered on Form S-3 (or Form F-4 for foreigners); securities are put "on the shelf" for a period of two years for subsequent use. In the SEC's view, integrated disclosure is a particularly valuable ingredient in achieving market efficiency; the SEC said in connection with its adoption of Rule 415 that companies for which Form S-3 is available "provide a steady stream of high quality information to the marketplace [which] is constantly

[1] I thank Pawan Bareja for excellent research assistance.

digested and synthesized by financial analysts, who act as essential conduits and is broadly disseminated on a timely basis".

In the late 1970s, Euromarket financing, in either dollars or foreign currencies, interest rate, and currency-swaps were successfully competing with conventional U.S. debt placements. U.S. issuers increasingly opted for these offshore financing and swap arrangements. Not only did these financing arrangements provide funds at low costs[2], but speedy execution of private or offshore transactions outside the requirements of the 1933 Act has enabled the issuer to make use of temporary windows of opportunity in the world's capital markets. To retain the large and frequent capital raisers in the United States, the SEC had to reduce its bureaucratic delays; thus, the adoption of shelf registration.

The popularity of shelf registration can best be understood by observing the tangible savings accruing to the issuers. Under the shelf method, an eligible issuer can file registration documents specifying that the firm intends to sell a certain amount of a particular class of securities at some unspecified points within the succeeding two years. Thus the firm does not incur repeated costs of registration. Not only does the firm save the monetary costs of registration and time costs of SEC bureaucratic delays, but it is likely that the firm will also save on the fees the firm would pay to the investment bankers underwriting their issue.

Once the registration statement has been filed the issuer can receive bids from various investment bankers offering to buy the securities at a given set of terms and price. Many studies document that Rule 415 has increased the competitive vigor among investment banks in the securities market and has reduced the issuer net borrowing cost.[3] The studies suggest that industrial

---

[2] For evidence concerning lower borrowing costs *see* Kidwell, Marr, and Thompson, "Eurodollar Bonds: Alternative Financing for U.S. Companies," Vol. 15 *Financial Management* 18 (1985) (correction in following volume); Marr and Trimble, "Eurobond Financing Bargains: Evidence Supporting the Clientele Hypothesis," *Journal of Business Research* (1992), forthcoming; Marr and Trimble, "The Persistent Borrowing Advantage in Eurodollar Bonds: A Plausible Explanation," Vol. 1 *The Journal of Applied Corporate Finance* (1988); Marr, Trimble, and Varma, "The Integration of International Capital Markets: Evidence From Euroequity Offerings," Vol. 20 *Financial Management* (1991); and Marr, Trimble, and Varma, "Innovation in Global Financing: An Investigation of Euroequity Offerings," Vol. 5 *Journal of Applied Corporate Finance* (1992).

[3] For documentation of these savings *see* Kidwell, Marr, and Thompson, "SEC Rule 415—The Ultimate Competitive Bid," Vol. 19 *Journal of Financial and Quantitative Analysis* (1984); Kidwell, Marr, and Thompson, "Shelf registration: Competition and Market Flexibility," Vol. 30 *Journal of Law and Economics* (1987); Bhagat, Marr, and

bond issues sold by shelf registration incur an all-in cost of funds between 20 and 30 basis points lower than the all-in cost of funds for comparable non—shelf offerings. Apparently, the cost savings are achieved through intense bidding by the competing underwriting firms. It is also likely that the shelf procedure provides cost savings to the issuer because of the shorter time lag between registration and sale of the debt. This shorter time lag gives finer estimates of the true market conditions.

The banking firm that is ultimately successful in purchasing the securities for resale also has access to future business opportunities with the same client and a larger market share. This cross-selling of services is sufficient motivation for the underwriters to compete vigorously, accept smaller underwriting spreads, and form smaller syndicates (or go solo in case of "bought" deals). One study suggests that larger investment banks tend to increase their commitments in a given deal and thus make good profits even with slimmer spreads.[4]

Shelf registration remains an innovative tool for bankers. For example, in 1990, J. P. Morgan & Co. debt-underwriting electronic system CapitaLink entertained the possibility of rendering underwriters redundant for high-quality issuers. Its electronic link-up permits an issuing corporation to bypass underwriters and receive direct bids from institutional investors. Without Rule 415, such a new electronic bidding system would not have been possible.

Rule 144A

Securities regulators around the world are increasingly preoccupied with the globalization of capital markets. Both lenders and borrowers are finding it easier than ever to move from one capital market to another capital

---

Thompson, "The Rule 415 Experiment: Equity Markets," Vol. 40 *Journal of Finance* (1985); Foster, "Syndicate Size, Spreads, and Market Power During the Introduction of Shelf Registration," Vol 44 *Journal of Finance* (1989); and Denis, "Shelf Registration and the Market for Seasoned Equity Offerings," Vol 64 *Journal of Business* (1991).

[4] *See* Marr, Poulsen and Netter, "Effects on Securities Deregulation in Underwriting: An Analysis of Intra-Industry Changes Caused by Shelf Registration," University of Georgia Working paper, 1992.

market to find the best pricing for their securities.[5] On April 19, 1990, the SEC approved Rule 144A. The rule establishes requirements covering the purchase and resale of so-called restricted securities. Restricted securities are exempt from SEC registration and cannot, therefore, be released to the public trading markets. Rule 144A permits Qualified Institutional Buyers (QIBs) to trade privately placed securities without the current two-year holding restriction on privately placed securities.

The SEC's principal objective in adopting Rule 144A was to increase the efficiency and liquidity of the U.S. market for privately placed debt and equity securities by allowing large institutional investors to trade restricted securities more freely with each other. Rule 144A also provides safe-harbor relief from the registration requirements of the 1933 Act for resale of certain unregistered securities to QIBs.

A QIB is defined as an institution that owns and manages $100 million ($10 million in case of a registered broker-dealer) or more in qualifying securities.[6] With Rule 144A the SEC wants institutional investors to bring their millions (or billions) of dollars and become active players in the private placement market. The increased liquidity will supposedly open up the private placement market to a wide range of domestic and foreign buyers and investors.

In contrast to the approach adopted by the SEC (adopting new rules within the existing law), Mahoney argues that there is a better way to react to the increasing globalization of the markets.[7] He writes:

> National securities authorities should construct a multinational regulatory system based on the mutual recognition of regulatory standards. Such a system should

---

[5] *See* Kim and Stulz, "The Eurobond Market and Corporate Financial Policy: A Test of the Clientele Hypothesis," *Journal of Financial Economics*, Vol. 22 and Marr and Trimble, "Eurobond Financing Bargains: Evidence Supporting the Clientele Hypothesis," *Journal of Business Research* (1992).

[6] For banks and savings and loans to qualify as institutional buyers in the private-placement market, the firms must have at least $100 million in assets invested in securities and have a net worth of at least $25 million. According to federal banking agencies, about 500 banks and 210 savings and loans meet these criteria.

[7] Mahoney, "Regulation of International Securities Issues," *Regulation*, Spring 1991.

> be based on the proposition that the rules of the market having the closest connection to a transaction will govern that transaction, and other affected markets will recognize and give effect to those rules instead of asserting concurrent regulatory jurisdiction.

I agree with Mahoney, but I also do not feel that the SEC will move in this direction any time in the near future. Unfortunately, the SEC's new rules such as Rule 144A are consistent with Mahoney conclusion that "to date [new regulations] have been a series of ad hoc responses to pressing problems of overlapping or overreaching regulation rather than a comprehensive framework for avoiding such problems." (p. 62)

The obvious reason for the enactment of Rule 144A is that securities regulators have become increasingly preoccupied with the internationalization of capital markets. Lenders and borrowers are finding it easier than ever before to move from one capital market to another in search of the lowest cost for credit. Regulators should encourage this trend for two reasons: first, internationalization of credit sources typically lowers a firm's cost of capital and, second, lenders (for example, U.S. based commercial banks) reduce their risk because of increased diversification opportunities for their corporate clients.

Additionally, securities regulation is a negative sum game. Both issuers and investors suffer as regulatory costs (from their home market and the SEC) are passed on to investors. Marginal investors drop out, and the remaining investors suffer a reduction in yields from their investments because of duplicate regulatory compliance.

Rule 144A has had its fair share of problems since it was approved by the SEC. The rule was intended to increase liquidity in the declining private placement market. The private placement market had ballooned during the 1980s—increasing from $18 billion (22 percent of all 1980 corporate financings) at the beginning of the decade to $201 billion (43 percent of all corporate financings) by close of the decade. The fall-off in employee stock-ownership plans (ESOPs), privately placed junk paper, and takeover activity during the 1990s seem to be the main factors dampening the private-placement market. Rule 144A was supposed to invigorate the private-placement market by allowing privately placed securities to be traded more actively among sophisticated investors.

Rule 144A was based on an argument that foreign companies seeking debt and equity funding in the United States were discouraged by the

SEC registration process.[8] Potential issuers especially disliked converting accounts to conform with U.S. accounting procedures, disclosing sensitive business information, and reporting the compensation of senior executives. Registration also made it difficult to time issues to coincide with windows of opportunity and for the separate tranche of multijurisdictional offerings to be synchronized. Consequently, these companies turned either to their domestic markets or to the Euromarkets for funds.

Rule 144A removes the hurdle of registration, allowing issuers easy and efficient access to the US capital markets; but foreign issuers are still elusive. Foreigners appear skittish about the close and sometimes time consuming scrutiny of 144A deals by the SEC. The SEC can invoke Rule 10b-6, which forbids U.S. underwriters in all issue tranches from dealing in the shares. But problems of a larger dimension than the SEC evidently confront foreign issuers. The large U.S. institutional investor does not seem to accept a stingy disclosure of information, perhaps for fiduciary reasons.

One of the great half-truths about Rule 144A is that it reduces disclosure. Privately placed securities are not subject to SEC registration. They are, however, subject to liability under Section 12(2) of the Securities Act of 1933, which allows a purchaser to sue for material misrepresentation and omissions in connection with the sale of a security.[9] Therefore, despite the absence of an SEC registration requirement, the prudent issuer (and the party assisting in the private placement, whether as agent or principal) will prepare a private placement memorandum to protect themselves against Section 12(2) liability. The effort required to put together such a memorandum is similar to that required for a registration statement for a public offering. The major distinction is that the issuer makes its own judgments as to the materiality of information, rather than being guided by specific SEC rules.

In a private financing such as financing in an overseas market, confidentiality, speed, and lower issuance expense are attractive features.

---

[8] The first non-U.S. 144a equity deal was brought to the market in May 1990 by First Boston. The deal was a $49 million American depository-receipt offering Stockholm-based Atlas Copco, part of a $214 million global offering coordinated by Enskilda Securities. This was the first time Atlas Copco. issued securities in the U.S. market ("Two Cheers for 144a" *Institutional Investor*, July 1990, 119).

[9] For example, SEC standards of accounting, auditor independence, and general disclosure are sufficiently different, and usually more stringent than those applicable to most foreign companies, that compliance with U.S. law is a costly process that could require the keeping of two separate sets of accounting records.

Moreover, private issues are not registered with the SEC and do not require a rating. In case of foreign issuers, provision of all relevant information does not lower issuance cost unless they have been in the U.S. market before and have registered with the SEC. In the latter case, they have no incentive to do a private placement since they no longer require the confidentiality. A foreign issuer who chooses a private placement so as not to disclose sensitive information to the SEC is unlikely to disclose the same information to a rating agency. Without a rating (whether public or private), institutions do not seem comfortable investing in the company. Given these circumstances, the foreign investors have chosen to tap European capital markets.

Rule 144A will be revolutionary when the market evolves over time and develops some standardized documentation that will make private securities easily transferable from one holder to another, increase knowledge among the potential buyers of the issuers credit worthiness, and increase the extent of knowledge among buyers about the specific terms of the security (for example, through a standardized prospectus). Until some efficient mechanism for communicating essential information has evolved, the buyers will not flock to this market. My prediction is simple, the 144a market will remain small. Unfortunately, Rule 144A was not another Rule 415 success story.

Regulation A

Regulation A exempts a public offer of securities from registering with the SEC. The issuer can offer unregistered securities up to $1.5 million within a 12-month period. This regulation aims to reduce the cost of acquiring new capital for small businesses. Most small businesses find it difficult to put together three years of audited financial statements to qualify for entering into the capital markets. Taking this requirement into account, the SEC has permitted qualified issuers to file one year of unaudited financial statements under Regulation A. Also the reporting obligations for qualified issuers have been bent for their benefit, though not broken. Qualified issuers are not subject to reporting obligations under section 15(d) of the Exchange Act nor to the liability provisions of Section 11 of the Securities Act. However, the antifraud provisions are still applicable to the offer and sale of securities under Regulation A. The entrepreneur is required to submit a mandated disclosure document subject to SEC review.

With shelf registration and (possibly) Rule 144A, the SEC has made the access to the capital markets easy for large corporate issuers. But the 20 million small businesses in the U.S., who employ more than half of the domestic labor force and produce nearly half of the gross domestic product were unable to access the capital markets.[10] Small businesses frequently use high technology, and produce new technology, products, and services. These firms are the innovators and the true entrepreneurs in the economy. But raising capital is a difficult task. At present these entrepreneurs raise capital from their kith and kin.

Since the 1987 stock market crash, U.S. based commercial banks have been increasingly shy of lending capital to these small businesses for lack of established track record. The decline of the junk bond market has not helped small businesses either. Accessing the capital markets through public offerings also became difficult after the 1987 market crash, because the regional firms, the traditional underwriters of the small businesses, fared badly in the aftermath of the crash. Engaging large underwriters is expensive for small businesses.

The consequent decline in small business offers is expected. While initial public offerings of equity rose to $16 billion in 1991, a fourfold increase over the 1990 levels, Regulation A financing have declined from $408 million in 1981 to a trickle of $41.5 million in 1991. The number of start-up businesses decreased in 1991, with more than 50,000 fewer businesses founded in 1991 than 1990. With proposed modifications to Regulation A, the SEC is trying to rectify the environment faced by small businesses.

To an entrepreneur the cost of tapping the securities market today, whether in a limited private offering or in a widespread public offering, is about $200,000. All the SEC-mandated disclosures, financial statements, and investment banker fees become a hefty burden for the start-up business. Aside from these costs, the entrepreneur also bears the risk of a disinterested public. Instead of risking the premature demise of the venture, the SEC is permitting small businesses to "test the waters" to see whether potential investors will bite their bait. For a start-up company or a developing business it is essential to know whether the potential investors are interested in the issue before making an offer and conforming to all the regulatory prescriptions of the SEC. Regulation A permits an issuer to solicit indications of interest prior to filing the mandated offering statement. Thus the eligible issuer can use a factual statement to gauge investor receptiveness to a possible offering and determine whether to proceed with the offering or raise capital from alternative sources.

---

[10] U.S. Small Business Administration, *Annual Report on Small Business and Competition*, 125 (1990).

To ensure the success of the test-the-waters proposal, the proposal is accompanied with simple and user-friendly disclosure forms. By lowering the disclosure costs, the SEC is trying to encourage small issuers to exploit the capital markets and still provide investors with the benefit of continuous reporting. The SEC is simplifying the disclosure forms and reducing the nonmonetary filing costs for the small companies.

With reduced costs of filing for a new public issue, it remains to be seen whether small companies use the opportunities provided by the Regulation A or abuse them. Regulation A has rarely been used by reporting issuers. Of the 177 Regulation A filings made with the SEC in the past three years, only 30 were made by reporting companies. Hence, the current simplified disclosure requirement can only increase the information received by the investors and encourage them to consider small companies as a serious investment alternative. For small businesses a chance to test potential investor interest accompanied with lower issuance and disclosure costs is a window to a potential vast avenue of raising capital. The SEC is also proposing to raise the dollar ceiling for a Regulation A offering to a statutory limit of $5 million, up from its current $1.5 million and make small businesses' dream a reality. At the present we can only hope the SEC continues to lessen the regulatory burden on raising capital for small business so that these businesses have the incentive to directly tap the nation's capital markets.

Conclusion

The SEC has been liberalizing the capital markets in the past decade with the introduction of shelf registration, Rule 144A, and recently with proposed changes to Regulation A. Shelf registration allowed an issuer to make delayed or continuous offering of issues over a period of two years. The firm must register these issues but once with the SEC and avoid reregistration costs for the succeeding two years. Under Rule 144A, large institutional investors are encouraged to invest in private-placement issues. The SEC seeks to enhance liquidity and efficiency of the market so that foreign issuers will use the U.S. capital markets more often. On both counts the SEC has been unsuccessful. Once the market streamlines the documentation and disclosure requirement to the satisfaction of both the issuer and the buyer, Rule 144A has the potential of being another success story. With the proposed changes to Regulation A, the SEC is making capital markets more accessible to small businesses.

References and Suggested Readings

Bhagat, Sanjai, M. Wayne Marr, and G. Rodney Thompson. 1985. "The Rule 415 Experiment: Equity Markets." *Journal of Finance* 40.

Denis, David J. 1991. "Shelf Registration and the Market for Seasoned Equity Offerings." *Journal of Business* 64.

Foster, Douglas. 1989. "Syndicate Size, Spreads, and Market Power During the Introduction of Shelf Registration." *Journal of Finance* 44.

Kidwell, David S., M. Wayne Marr, and G. Rodney Thompson. 1984. "SEC Rule 415: The Ultimate Competitive Bid." *Journal of Financial and Quantitative Analysis* 19.

——. 1985. "Eurodollar Bonds: Alternative Financing for U.S. Companies." *Financial Management* 15:18.

——. 1987. "Shelf Registration: Competition and Market Flexibility." *Journal of Law and Economics* 30.

Kim, Yong-cheol, and Rene M. Stulz. "The Eurobond Market and Corporate Financial Policy: A Test of the Clientele Hypothesis." *Journal of Financial Economics* 22.

Mahoney, Paul G. 1991. "Regulation of International Securities Issues." *Regulation* (Spring).

Marr, M. Wayne, Annette B. Poulsen, and Jeffry M. Netter. 1992. "Effects on Securities Deregulation in Underwriting: An Analysis of Intra-industry Changes Caused by Shelf Registration." Working paper, University of Georgia, Athens.

Marr, M. Wayne, and John L. Trimble. 1988. "The Persistent Borrowing Advantage in Eurodollar Bonds: A Plausible Explanation." *The Journal of Applied Corporate Finance* 1.

——. 1992. "Eurobond Financing Bargains: Evidence Supporting the Clientele Hypothesis." *Journal of Business Research.*

Marr, M. Wayne, John L. Trimble, and Raj Varma. 1991. "The Integration of International Capital Markets: Evidence from Euroequity Offerings." *Financial Management* 20.

——. 1992. "Innovation in Global Financing: An Investigation of Euroequity Offerings." *Journal of Applied Corporate Finance* 5.

"Two Cheers for 144a." 1990. *Institutional Investor* (July):119.

U.S. Small Business Administration. 1990. *Annual Report on Small Business and Competition.* Washington, D. C.: U.S. Government Printing Office.

Small Business

Registration Requirements

13

The SEC's Proposed Small Business Capital Formation Initiative (A Separate Statement of Commissioner Fleischman)

Edward H. Fleischman
Rosenman and Colin

[Editors' Note: On March 11, 1992, the SEC released "Proposed Small Business Capital Formation Initiative" (see Securities Act of 1933 Release No. 33-6924). Mr. Fleischman, who was an SEC Commissioner at the time, issued a separate statement on this proposal, which is presented here. We edited and cut this statement, with Mr. Fleischman's approval, in order to conform with the publication style of this book.]

For the Commission's Small Business Capital Formation Initiative (proposed) my fundamental premises are those that I apply to every exercise in regulatory review. As most recently stated by an author far more articulate than I:

> Regulation can . . . play a direct role in improving the performance of the market system. *Any proposal to regulate the market, however, should be tempered by an understanding that regulation can be at least as imperfect as the market it is trying to improve.* The goal . . . is to eliminate or revise those [regulations] that impose costs that exceed their benefits, and insure that other regulations are implemented in a cost-effective manner (emphasis in original).[1]

[1] *Economic Report of the President*, transmitted to the Congress February 1992, 191.

> During the past two decades, *the Federal Government has significantly widened the scope of regulatory activity in [areas such as market regulation], generally using a command-and-control approach. As a result, costs to the economy have increased substantially*, because legislation in these areas has rarely required legislators to balance the costs and benefits of their actions. Recent initiatives have attempted to improve on traditional regulation by allowing more flexibility and by balancing benefits and costs (emphasis in original).[2]

From those premises, I conclude that the objective of the Commission's initiative should be, plainly and simply, to eliminate those regulations that impose costs on small business exceeding their benefits to investors.

Achievement of that objective requires a twofold effort: (1) understanding, and wherever possible removal, of costs of the investment offering process, without correlative reduction in the benefits enjoyed by investors; and, equally, (2) understanding, and wherever possible removal, of barriers to liquidity in the after-market where the fruits of those investments can be realized, again without correlative reduction of the benefits enjoyed by investors. (I should note that the first is much easier to achieve than the second—but only because the second requires more attention and effort.) What is key here, to me, is not acceptance but rather the initiation of constructive discussion and debate.

Proposal 1

One of the two largest costs of the investment-offering process is auditing expense. For all exempt offerings (whether under Regulation A, Regulation D, or otherwise), the best balance of costs and benefits that I have seen is achieved in Part F/S of the proposed Form 1-A:

> Such financial statements shall be prepared in accordance with generally accepted accounting principles (GAAP) in the United States.

---

[2] Id., 182-183.

> Issuers which have audited financial statements because they prepare them for other purposes, shall provide them.
>
> The Commission's Regulation S-X . . . relating to the form, content of and requirements for financial statements shall not apply to the financial statements required by this part, except that if audited financial statements are filed, the qualifications and reports of an independent auditor shall comply with the requirements of Article 2 of Regulation S-X.

I propose that the above-quoted paragraphs of Part F/S of proposed Form 1-A, appropriately adapted in context, be substituted with respect to small business issuers into each subparagraph of Rule 502(b)(2) and be made part of each other rule affording an exemption for small business issuers from the registration requirements of the Securities Act.

I also propose that the Commission require certification of unaudited statements by the chief financial officer of each small business issuer, at least with respect to compliance with GAAP.

Proposal 2

The other major cost of the investment offering process is legal fees. The effort to prevent misleading statements (i.e., statements that require amplification in order not to be incomplete or inaccurate) is a prime example of similar costs falling unequally on large and small issuers. For a major industrial company, an omission to find and describe a $50 million contingency is not likely to be material but, for a small business issuer, the failure to catch a $25,000 contingency may well be material.

I propose that a special materiality rule (akin to the present MD&A materiality rule[3]) be added to Rule 405 and Rule 12b-2, for small business issuers, applicable not to misstatements but to omissions only:

> The term "material", when used with respect to facts or information necessary in order to make other statements not misleading, shall be limited to facts or information concerning acts, events, or contingencies *reasonably likely*

[3] *See* fn. 27 to Release No. 33-6835 (May 18, 1989) and accompanying text.

> to alter significantly the total mix of information made available about a small business issuer.

Proposal 3

For the same reasons, a standard for care, and therefore for liability (akin to Rule 175 and Rule 3b-6), should be separately specified for small business issuers.

I propose that the following be adopted as Rule 177 and Rule 3b-10:

> Any statement that is made by or on behalf of a small business issuer or by an outside reviewer retained by a small business issuer shall be deemed not to be a fraudulent statement (as defined in paragraph (d) of Rule 175 and paragraph (d) of Rule 3b-6), unless it is shown that such statement was made or reaffirmed without a reasonable basis or was disclosed other than in good faith.

By so doing, the reasonable-basis-and-good-faith liability standard for "forward-looking statements" made in documents filed with the Commission would be broadened to apply to all underlying statements, whether they are in filed documents or not, made by small-business issuers.

Proposal 4

Professional broker-dealers, acting as underwriters or otherwise in exempt offerings, do not have available the protection afforded by Section ll(b)(3) for audited and otherwise expertised statements. The absence of that protection discourages many broker dealers from acting in exempt offerings. I propose that a new Rule 178, affecting exempt offerings by small business issuers, be adopted as follows:

> With respect to a broker or dealer registered under Section 15(a) of the Securities Exchange Act, a statement in a prospectus[4] published by or on behalf of a small business issuer other than as part of a registration statement filed under the act, which statement purports to be made on the

---

[4] Prospectus would have the normal Section 2(10) meaning of any written or broadcast offering of a security for sale.

> authority of an expert (other than the broker or dealer itself) or purports to be a copy of or extract from a report or valuation of an expert (other than the broker or dealer itself), shall be deemed not to be a fraudulent statement (as defined in paragraph (d) of Rule 175) if the broker or dealer had no reasonable ground to believe, and did not believe, that the statement was untrue or that there was an omission of a material fact required to be stated therein or necessary to make the statement not misleading or that such prospectus did not fairly represent the statement of the expert or was not a fair copy of or extract from the report or valuation of the expert.

Proposal 5

The Regulation A exemption has long struggled under the uncertainty of whether a suspension order results in a retroactive violation of Section 5. Professor Loss pointed out (as long ago as the 1962 edition of his treatise) that a posteffective stop order to a registration statement does not destroy the effectiveness of that registration statement *ab initio*. It is important to specify, and to limit, those provisions of the regulation that *do* result in retroactive violation. It should be remembered that almost every other failure to comply with the conditions of the exemption will be subject to prosecution on antifraud grounds.

Proposal 6

The purpose of the test-the-waters feature has, since its first presentation to the staff by a small group of very thoughtful lawyers,[5] been clear and salutary: to allow entrepreneurs who are contemplating small business issuer financing to ascertain whether there is in fact any receptivity for their offerings *before* they incur the thousands of dollars of expense for an offering document. It would be totally counterproductive to construct a test-the-waters feature based on the assumption that the entrepreneur will have consulted with a lawyer *in advance* so as to know the detailed requirements for testing the waters.

---

[5] *See* Memorandum from Richard S. Morse, Jr., and Richard M. Leisner to Mary E. T. Beach and Barry Guthary (August 22, 1990).

I propose that:

(1) the statements *required* to be included in the test-the-waters document (paragraph [b] of proposed Rule 254) be deleted and

(2) the requirement for *prior* filing of *each* test-the-waters document (paragraph [d] of proposed Rule 254) be replaced by a requirement for filing of *all* test-the-waters documentary material along with and at the same time as the preliminary offering circular.

In this way, all the antifraud, anticommitment and antibroadcast provisions of proposed Rule 254 would be maintained, the staff would be able to review all the prior written material, and the entrepreneur would not risk the likelihood of losing the exemption before it starts.

Proposal 7

The staff and the Commissioners have received, from a blue-ribbon American Bar Association task force,[6] a detailed proposal for a local-transaction exemption directed at transactions limited geographically to standard metropolitan statistical areas that cross state lines. If implemented under Section 3(b), that kind of exemption could greatly multiply the utility of the local-transaction exemption that has always been particularly suited to the needs of small business issuers but has always been limited to individual states under Section 3(a)(11).

Without repeating here the full text of the ABA proposal, I propose that the Commission adopt such a metropolitan-area exemption for small business issuers.

Proposal 8

The prohibition of general solicitation applicable to offerings under Rule 505 and Rule 506, as presently interpreted, inhibits and derails many offerings by small business issuers. Obviously, a truly *general* solicitation would turn a limited offering into a public offering, but some face-to-face contacts presently prohibited could be allowed: for example, presentations by entrepreneurs to venture capital forums regularly sponsored (akin to Rule

---

[6] *See* Letter from Mark H. Morgenstern, Carl W. Schneider, and Stanley Keller to Linda C. Quinn and Mary E. T. Beach (August 9, 1991).

139) by independent professional firms. I propose that there be added to the end of paragraph (c)(2) of Rule 502 the following:

> except that a presentation made at any seminar or meeting that is held with reasonable regularity under the sponsorship of a service enterprise no partner or officer of which is a promoter or affiliate of the issuer, and at which several nonaffiliated issuers also make presentations, shall not be deemed to constitute general solicitation or general advertisement.

Proposal 9

The Commission historically has had various rules affording exemption for *de minimis* offerings. Prior to Regulation D, for example, Rule 240 allowed sales of up to $100,000 within a twelve-month period. I propose that the Commission adopt what would in essence be a performance-standard rule for *de minimis* transactions by small business issuers as follows:

> Offers, offers to sell, offers for sale, and sales by a small-business issuer of up to $250,000 in value of its securities within any twelve-month period shall be exempt from the provisions of Section 5 of the act under the authority of Section 3(b) of the act; provided only that the issuer may not sell more than $5,000 in value of such securities to any single person. Such transactions are not, however, exempt from the antifraud, civil liability, or other provisions of the federal securities laws.

Proposal 10

The single most complained-about problem for small-business issuers is the multiple overlay of federal *and* state securities regulation. The Commission is apparently unwilling to request any kind of legislative preemption, but that still leaves to the Commission the possibility of taking away the federal layer of regulation (as in present Rule 504) where the state registration procedures apply and *are* satisfied.

I propose that, in addition to the proposed revision of Rule 504 included in the release, a new Rule 504A be added to Regulation D preserving the present Rule 504 but with a dollar limit raised to the maximum allowable under Section 3(b) ($5 million now and $10 million under the Commission's proposed legislative amendments).

Proposal 11

The Commission has previously (most recently in Release No. 34-23407 [July 8, 1986]) considered proposals to increase the threshold for registration and reporting under the Exchange Act. A May 1990 study entitled "Reporting Requirements under the Securities Exchange Act of 1934 as They Affect Small Businesses: Defining the `Small Public Company'" was undertaken at the request of the director of the Commission's Division of Corporation Finance and published by that division. The very purpose of the study was to address the question of which publicly held businesses should be subject to the reporting requirements of the Exchange Act. "In particular, [the study] is concerned with the affect (sic) of 1934 Act reporting requirements on small businesses." The study concluded that, "from the perspective of the size of the entity itself, total assets, net sales and number of employees provide appropriate size criteria [for defining small business issuers]. Total assets provides an indicator of financial resources primarily on an historical basis, whereas net sales and number of employees provide an indication of size based on current operations."

I propose that, consonant with the recommendations of that study and in keeping with the statistics reflected at the opening of the Release, Rule 12g-1 be amended to exempt any issuer that, at the end of its last fiscal year, had assets of not more than $5 million or an employment roll of not more than 500 persons.

Proposal 12

Another example of similar costs falling unequally on large and small issuers is the cost of quarterly reporting. The direct costs of quarterly reporting are multiplied by the indirect costs of diversion of management attention, in a small-business organizational context in which all management personnel must fulfill multiple roles. Outside the U.S., semi-annual reporting is the norm even for larger issuers.

I propose that proposed Form 10-QSB be changed into a new Form 10-SSB, due sixty days after the end of the first half of each fiscal year and reporting with respect to that semi-annual period. For this purpose, I propose that old Rules 13a-13 and 15d-13 (relating to old semi-annual Report Form 9-K) be revived and adapted for small business issuers.

Proposal 13

The second major thrust of the Commission's small business initiative should be to remove barriers to liquidity in the after-market.

The efficiency of secondary markets is always impeded by lack of information concerning the securities traded in those markets. Issuers are sometimes motivated to discontinue the flow of information about themselves and their securities in circumstances that gradually sap liquidity and ultimately terminate all but isolated trading in the after-market. Investors are thereby left without a means to realize on their investment. Representatives of both professional traders (STA) and professional analysts (AIMR) have often complained about this practice, as it affects both the debt and equity markets.

I propose that there be added to Item 512 of Regulation S-B an additional undertaking by which each small-business issuer would assure those who purchase its securities that, so long as it remains in existence, whether or not it may be obligated to file reports under the Exchange Act, it will, no less than annually, provide every securityholder of record the opportunity to receive certain core financial and descriptive information about the issuer, its management, its financial condition, and the results of its operations.

I also propose that a similar provision be added as a condition to Regulation D and to each other rule affording an exemption for small-business issuers from the registration requirements of the Securities Act.

Proposal 14

The impact of the penny-stock rules (Rule 15c2-6 and the rules proposed under the recent Penny Stock Reform Act) has been very strongly felt by legitimate small business issuers. Broker-dealers have shied away from offering, underwriting, and making markets in the securities of small business issuers as a result of the present and proposed requirements, including written preapproval by investors, relating to trades in designated securities. Section 15(g)(4) gives the Commission power to exempt persons and transactions from the provisions of the Penny Stock Reform Act, "as it determines consistent with the public interest and the protection of investors." In an analogous context (agency cross transactions by investment advisers) the Commission has devised a pattern of consent and disclosure, that could be adapted as the basis for exempting certain broker-dealers from the requirements of the Penny Stock Reform Act to the extent that those broker-dealers purchase or sell the securities of small business issuers for their customers.

Disclosure always having been the principal tool for investor protection, I propose that the Commission adopt a rule (akin to Rule 206[3]-2) providing in substance that a broker-dealer would be exempt from Rule 15c2-6 and from the rules under Section 15(g) if

(1) the customer for whom it executes a purchase or sale transaction in the securities of a small business issuer has executed a written consent prospectively authorizing the broker dealer to effect transactions in the securities of small business issuers for such customer, after full written disclosure of the generic risks of investing in the securities of small business issuers;

(2) the broker-dealer includes on each confirmation of such a transaction a statement that the securities purchased or sold are in fact the securities of a small business issuer;

(3) the broker-dealer sends to each such customer, at least semi-annually, a written disclosure statement identifying all the transactions in the securities of small-business issuers since the date of the last such statement; and

(4) each written disclosure statement and confirmation includes a conspicuous statement that the written consent initially given by the customer may be revoked at any time by written notice to the broker-dealer from the customer.

Proposal 15

The development of liability theory for insider trading under Rule 10b-5 has to a very large extent replaced the function intended by the Congress in 1934 to be performed by the shortswing reporting and recapture provisions of Section 16. In view of the costs of complying with the Commission's new and highly intricate rules under Section 16 (which again fall disproportionately on small business issuers) and in view of the analogous benefits afforded by Rule l0b-5, I propose that the Commission exercise its exemptive power under Section 12(h) to exempt the directors, officers, and 10 percent beneficial owners of equity securities of small business issuers from the reporting requirements of Section 16(a) and the profit-recapture provisions of Section 16(b).

Item 405 would then be removed from Regulation S-B, and the references to Item 405 would be removed from various of the proposed new forms.

Proposal 16

On a prior occasion I pointed out that, in my opinion,[7] paragraph (d)(4) of Rule 144A should have been stricken from that Rule as contrary to longtime Commission policies affecting small business issuers. At the time, I said that "[these] are the start-up and the smaller private ventures that have historically been, and still are believed to be, a prime source of innovation and competitiveness in the American economy." The Commission then was unwilling to listen; rather, it singled out the group of what we are now calling, respectfully, "small business issuers" for exclusionary treatment. Perhaps the Commission will listen now.

I propose that the introductory clause of paragraph (d)(4) of Rule 144A be amended to read as follows:

> In the case of securities of an issuer that is neither subject to Section 13 or 15(d) of the Exchange Act nor exempt from reporting pursuant to Rule 12g3-2(b) under the Exchange Act nor a foreign government as defined in Rule 405 under the Securities Act eligible to register securities under Schedule B of the act *nor a small business issuer as defined in Rule 405 under the act....*

Proposal 17

There was lengthy discussion of whether there is, and if so what is, the economic or legal grounding for the particular definition of small business issuer proposed in the Commission's release. (Reference is made, on the public meeting tape, to the several colloquies on that subject between Divisional Director Quinn and each of the several Commissioners.) That is a subject to which much public commenter attention *should* be paid. But, whatever the ultimate definition, it certainly stands to reason that, having gone to all the effort of crafting a definition of small-business issuer, the Commission would use that definition for purposes of the Regulatory Flexibility Act, so that future consideration of the dissimilar impact of rule

---

[7] *See* Separate Statement attached to Release No. 33-6862 (April 23, 1990).

proposals on small entities will carry forward and not detract from the Commission's small business capital formation initiative.

I therefore propose that each of the several RegFlex rules (Rule 157 under the 1933 Act, Rule 0-10 under the 1934 Act, Rule 110 under the 1935 Act, Rule 0-7 under the 1939 Act, Rule 0-10 under the Investment Company Act and Rule 0-7 under the Investment Advisers Act) be amended to reflect the new "small-business issuer" definition.

* * * * *

The foregoing proposals comprise *my* response to the opportunity to respond substantively to recent and current presidential policies concerning small business capital formation, to the congressional directive on that subject in Section 506(a) of the Small Business Investment Incentive Act of 1980, and to the needs of the public that the Commission is mandated to serve. My response is weakest in its address to barriers to after-market liquidity; the substantive provisions of the rule proposals under the Penny Stock Reform Act are the subject of a separate rulemaking proceeding, and it would take a Section 19(c) proceeding to undo the NASD's exclusion of between 400 and 1000 small companies from NASDAQ (see my dissenting statement attached to Release No. 34-29638, dated August 30, 1991) or to require the NASD to upgrade its bulletin board to replace the exposure (and resulting liquidity) thereby lost to those companies and their securityholders.

What elicits these proposals from me—what underscores the extent of the opportunity presented to and foregone by the Commission today—is that the release, for all its length and for all the number of its proposed changes, touches only the topmost crust of an inordinately complex and multilayered disclosure regulatory scheme.

To me at least, the Commission's action in raising dollar limits, renumbering forms and rules, restating detailed regulatory requirements in more comprehensible language, and relieving small business issuers from the necessity of complying with that topmost crust of regulation without examining the continuing need for the layer-upon-layer that lies beneath, singly and collectively falls far short of constituting any real effort to balance costs and benefits, not to speak of any real effort to eliminate regulations that impose costs exceeding their related benefits—which are the goals set forth in the *Economic Report of the President* quoted at the beginning of this statement. *The Commission could do so much toward those goals!!* The several rather simple and straightforward proposals I have presented above evidence how easy it would be to make real progress in removing costs from the securities offering and after-market processes without depriving investors of substantial protections.

IV

CORPORATE CONTROL AND GOVERNANCE

Corporate Governance

14

Next Steps in Corporate Governance Reform: 13(d) Rules and Control-Person Liability

Bernard S. Black
Columbia Law School[1]

Abstract

The Securities and Exchange Commission (SEC) has just finished reform of its proxy rules, with the express goal of reducing regulatory obstacles to shareholder oversight of corporate managers. The proxy rules, though, are only a small part of a complex web of securities, corporate, antitrust, banking, insurance, tax, bankruptcy, environmental, and other rules that, taken together, make it difficult and legally risky for institutional investors to own large percentage stakes in particular companies or to play an active role in corporate governance.

This article discusses next steps that the SEC could take, to encourage shareholder oversight of the managers of our large public companies, especially indirect oversight through boards of directors. The 13(d) disclosure rules and the control person liability rules are the most important obstructive laws within the SEC's jurisdiction. Both are amenable to regulatory change that would significantly enhance the prospects for

[1] This article draws on several longer articles that address the role of institutional investors in corporate governance. See Black, "Shareholder Passivity Reexamined," 89 *Michigan Law Review* 520 (1990); Black, "Agents Watching Agents: The Promise of Institutional Investor Voice," 39 *UCLA Law Review* 811 (1992); Black, "The Value of Institutional Investor Monitoring: The Empirical Evidence," 39 *UCLA Law Review* 895 (1992); and Black, "Securities Regulation and Corporate Governance: Adapting Old Rules to a New Paradigm" (forthcoming). Citations below are highly selective; full citations to the academic literature can be found in my prior work.

oversight and might thereby improve long-term corporate performance. I suggest specific deregulatory steps that the next SEC ought to consider.

Introduction

U.S. productivity growth has been dismal for two decades, especially in the service sector where most U.S. citizens work. As productivity goes, so goes our standard of living. The average worker's take-home pay has dropped over 15 percent in the last 20 years. Could the U.S. corporate governance system be part of the problem?

Scholars increasingly recognize that the large U.S. firm, with its strong shareholders and relatively weak, dispersed shareholders, may have evolved not because it is efficient, but in response to a complex web of state and federal rules that make it difficult and sometimes illegal for institutional shareholders to monitor corporate managers. In other countries, institutional investors face fewer obstacles to oversight and are far more active than they are here. Different rules might foster greater oversight in the U.S. as well.[2]

More oversight does not guarantee better performance, but the potential gains are large. Strong shareholders might, for example, have installed a more vigorous board of directors at General Motors. A strong board might have forced change in *1982*, when GM's problems were already obvious to outsiders, instead of *1992*, after $100 billion or so had been wasted. Stronger shareholders might be forcing more rapid change today at IBM, our other stumbling behemoth, or at misshapen conglomerates like ITT. Some of this oversight might come directly, but much would be indirect, as shareholders elect truly independent directors, who would then be able to fix problems before they become obvious to the outside world and engage in company-specific oversight more easily than institutional investors.[3]

---

[2] *See* Roe, "A Political Theory of American Corporate Finance," 91 *Columbia Law Review* 1 (1991); Roe, "Some Differences in Corporate Structure in Germany, Japan, and America," 102 *Yale Law Journal* 1927 (1993); Gilson & Roe, "Understanding the Japanese Keiretsu: Overlaps Between Corporate Governance and Industrial Organization," 102 *Yale Law Journal 871* (1993); and Kester, *Japanese Takeovers: The Global Contest for Corporate Control* (1991).

[3] Others who stress the central role of the board of directors as a focal point for institutional activism include Gilson & Kraakman, "Reinventing the Outside Director: An Agenda for Institutional Investors," 43 *Stanford Law Review* 863 (1991); and Millstein, "The Evolving Role of Institutional Investors in Corporate Governance" (unpublished manuscript, June 1992).

The SEC recently responded to institutional complaints and to the new political explanation for shareholder passivity by loosening its proxy rules, with the avowed goal of encouraging shareholder oversight of corporate managers. The reforms were modest, and further steps are needed if the proxy rules are to be truly shareholder friendly. But more centrally, reform limited to the proxy rules is unlikely to have a major impact on institutional investor behavior—and it is from institutional investors that oversight must come, if at all. To invigorate shareholder oversight, the Commission must also revisit other rules, notably the 13(d) rules and the expansive definition of *control* for purposes of control-person liability, both of which have a far greater chilling effect on shareholder oversight than the proxy rules ever had.

The Central Role of Large Shareholders

Basic to understanding the potential for shareholder oversight of corporate managers is the simple fact that a large shareholder will do more than a small shareholder. Similarly, a group of large shareholders will do more than one shareholder acting alone. This is because all shareholders, large or small, face collective action problems in monitoring corporate managers, which arise because each shareholder owns a small fraction of a company's stock. A shareholder who chooses to monitor bears all of the cost of that effort, yet receives only a prorata share of the benefits. Meanwhile, other shareholders can freeride on the monitoring shareholder's efforts. A shareholder who owns 1 percent of a company's stock must believe that the expected benefits are more than 100 times the cost, before monitoring is worthwhile! Since success is uncertain, the expected benefit *if the monitoring effort succeeds* must be greater still. That will often be enough to discourage monitoring.

There is no complete solution to collective-action disincentives to monitor, but size helps. For a 10-percent shareholder, monitoring will seem worthwhile if the ratio between expected benefit and cost is only 10:1. Moreover, if other shareholders also hold substantial stakes, the cost of persuading other shareholders of the merits of a particular action—say an effort to elect a few new directors to the board of a poorly performing company—will decline, while the odds of success grow, because large shareholders have greater incentive to join a monitoring effort begun by

---

(unpublished manuscript, June 1992).

Yet few take this course. Instead, the large institutions take diversification to ridiculous extremes, far beyond the point where more diversification offers meaningful reduction in risk. Most limit their percentage ownership of any one company. Most are passive.[4]

The SEC's proxy reforms reduce the cost of monitoring efforts made through the proxy process. But the Commission has left in place rules that discourage large holdings, especially if those holdings are coupled with active oversight. I consider below the most important of these obstructive rules—the 13(d) rules, and the SEC's expansive view of control-person liability.[5]

The 13(d) Rules

Section 13(d) of the Securities Exchange Act and related SEC rules require any person or group that beneficially owns 5 percent or more of a public company's stock to file a Schedule 13D, disclosing information about the person or group, how much stock it owns, and its plans with respect to the company, including plans for a proxy campaign. In contrast, a purely passive 5-percent shareholder can file a much simpler Schedule 13G. The 13(d) rules discourage shareholders from owning over 5 percent of a company's stock, discourage 5-percent shareholders from becoming active on corporate governance issues, and discourage shareholders with smaller holdings from acting jointly.

The 13D filing is not complex, but it involves substantial litigation risk, which means heavy legal bills, win or lose. Proponents are commonly

---

[4] To put the risk reduction from diversification in context, the base level of risk from owning the entire U.S. stock market is a standard deviation of about 20 percent per year. That is, in a typical year, the market is likely to do about 20 percent better or worse than one expected when the year began. An institution that owns 50 suitably chosen stocks will face annual risk, measured by standard deviation, of about 20.2 percent. Owning 500 stocks reduces this risk to 20.02 percent. The same roughly 0.2 percent reduction in risk can be obtained by putting 1 percent of one's total assets into Treasury bills. Treasury bills have a lower expected return than common stocks, but the cost in expected portfolio return is only about .05 percent per year—a mere 5 basis points. If the potential gains from monitoring exceed 5 basis points a year, there would be net gains from holding only 50 stocks and using one's larger stakes to engage in more monitoring. Monitoring gains of half this amount—2.5 basis points per year— would justify reducing one's portfolio to 100 stocks.

[5] *See also* Conard, "Control, Responsibility and Abdication: A Dilemma of Securities Regulation," 17 *Journal of Corporation Law* 539 (1992).

corporate governance issues, and discourage shareholders with smaller holdings from acting jointly.

The 13D filing is not complex, but it involves substantial litigation risk, which means heavy legal bills, win or lose. Proponents are commonly sued by the SEC or the company's managers for various real or imagined misdisclosures. For example, plans for a proxy campaign must be disclosed *when formed*, even if the campaign has not yet begun. In one recent case, the SEC sued a proxy contestant—unsuccessfully, it turns out—for (1) disclosing on February 18, 1985, instead of February 10, that it was considering a proxy contest and (2) not disclosing that its plans for a contest were firm until February 28, 1985, when the SEC believed those plans had become firm on an earlier date.[6] Shareholders, of course, learned of the proxy contest in ample time to decide how to vote. The proxy rules ensured that.

SEC rules treat a shareholder consortium formed to influence company policy through the voting process as a 13(d) group. Congress defined a group as "two or more persons [who] act as a . . . group for the purpose of *acquiring, holding, or disposing* of securities of an issuer."[7] This language needs stretching to reach a consortium formed solely to solicit votes, but the SEC has so stretched it. The Commission defines a group to include "two or more persons who agree to act together for the purpose of acquiring, holding, *voting*, or disposing of equity securities."[8] The courts have allowed the stretch and have also construed the group concept broadly. A group can be formed informally, without written documentation, and its existence can be proven by circumstantial evidence.

The 13(d) rules thus create a double bind for shareholders who own modest individual stakes. If they do not organize, collective-action problems are severe. If they do organize, they have formed a group, with attendant reporting requirements and litigation risk. The larger and thus potentially more effective the group is, the more burdensome the reporting requirements will be. Each member can file its own Schedule 13D, but each filing must

---

[6] *SEC v. Amster & Co.*, 762 F. Supp. 604 (S.D.N.Y. May 20, 1991).

[7] Securities Exchange Act Sect. 13[d][3]; emphasis added.

[8] Exchange Act Rule 13d-5(b)(1); emphasis added.

identify all other group members and disclose all information about other filers whom "the filing person knows or has reason to know."[9]

Shareholders who stop short of cosponsorship must still be wary of the 13(d) rules. If a proponent seeks indications of support from a few other shareholders before beginning a proxy campaign, has he or she unwittingly formed a group? The only sensible answer legal counsel could give is "maybe," which means "do not risk it." A proponent who can safely contact other shareholders under the proxy rules *cannot* do so under the 13(d) rules.

Institutions that acquire a 5-percent stake without the purpose or effect of "changing or influencing the control of the issuer" can file a simpler, less risky Schedule 13G instead of Schedule 13D.[10] The Schedule 13G option offers scant comfort, however. The SEC has offered no guidance on what the the elastic concept of "influencing control" means. Much of what shareholders might want to do, especially any effort to nominate and elect directors, thus creates litigation risk if one tries to use Schedule 13G. The net effect is that no active 5-percent shareholder even tries to use Schedule 13G, and its availability merely provides an incentive to stay passive.

The SEC can reduce the obstacles to shareholder voting created by the 13(d) rules by taking several modest steps. First, the Commission can cut back its broad definition of group, so that the definition, *like the underlying statute*, only covers acquiring, holding, and disposing of shares, not voting them. Proxy campaigns were around long before the 13(d) rules, without any apparent need for the additional disclosure that the 13(d) rules currently require. At a minimum, the Commission should exempt voting groups whose actions are not intended to change control.[11]

If the SEC wants to require disclosure of the existence of a voting group that exceeds a threshold size, such as 30 percent, before a proxy campaign begins, that can be handled under the proxy rules. The Commission could require a short notice filing that would carry less litigation risk than a Schedule 13D filing, perhaps patterned on the notice filing recently adopted under the proxy rules for certain solicitations that are

---

[9] Exchange Act Rule 13d-1(f)(2).

[10] See Securities Exchange Act Sects. 13(d)(5), 13(g); Exchange Act Rule 13d-1(b)(1), 17 C.F.R. Sect. 240.13d-1(b)(1); Schedule 13G.

[11] Fidelity Investments has proposed such an exemption. Letter from Fidelity General Counsel Arthur Loring to Linda Quinn, Director, SEC Division of Corporation Finance (July 18, 1990).

exempt from the need to prepare a full proxy statement. The notice filing would still have some chilling effect, but might be a reasonable compromise between the current system and no disclosure at all.

Second, the Commission can make Schedule 13G more available to institutions that want to be active in corporate governance, in several ways. The statute permits reduced disclosure if the securities were not acquired with the purpose or effect of changing or influencing *control.* Presumably Congress did not mean to cast a net so broad that it would catch all attempts to influence corporate *policy.* The Commission can seek to draw a regulatory line between attempts to influence policy and attempts to influence control. Any such line will be imperfect but will provide greater comfort than no line.

The Commission can also clarify that what matters, for the availability of Schedule 13G, is the purpose or effect *of the acquisition of shares,* not voting actions that a shareholder may thereafter take while holding stock that was bought for investment purposes. This is the most natural interpretation of § 13(d)(5), but SEC silence creates risk that *any* action to influence corporate policy, even if unrelated to the acquisition of stock, might bar use of Schedule 13G.[12]

To reduce legal risk, the SEC can also create a safe harbor under Schedule 13G for shareholders who are legally barred from exercising control or who disclaim a control intent. To give shareholders some freedom to nominate and elect directors, the safe harbor ought to include efforts to nominate and elect a minority of board members—say up to one-third of the board.

---

[12] Exchange Act Sect. 13(d)(5) allows the Commission to exempt shareholders from the Schedule-13D-filing requirements if "such securities . . . were not *acquired* by such person for the purpose of and do not have the effect of changing or influencing the control of the issuer" (emphasis added). Schedule 13G is the SEC's implementation of this exemptive power. The relevant purpose in Sect. 13(d)(5) is the purpose *of the acquisition of shares.* Similarly, the words *do not have the effect of* modify *such securities,* and thus appear to refer to circumstances inherent in the ownership of securities, rather than governance-related action after the securities are acquired. This interpretation, which treats the *purchase and ownership of securities,* rather than the governance actions taken by the owner, as the principal trigger for a 13(d) filing obligation, is consistent with the reference in Sect. 13(d)(3), discussed in the text, to a group formed for the purpose of "acquiring, holding, or disposing" of securities and is consistent with the general history of Sect. 13(d), which is part of the Williams Act, passed to regulate the acquisition of shares by tender offer. There is no evidence that Congress expected a 13(d) filing, directed toward a shareholder vote, to be triggered by actions by *existing* shareholders.

Finally, the SEC should revisit the expansive and litigation-prone disclosure requirements of Schedule 13D. For example, the Commission could narrow Item 4(d), which requires disclosure of plans or purposes relating to *any* change in the present board of directors, to require disclosure only if the plans involve more than one-third of the board. This would distinguish control contests from campaigns for minority representation. And the SEC could delete altogether Item 4(g), which requires disclosure of plans for *any* change in an issuer's charter or by-laws.

Control-Person Liability

The liability and legal risks facing control persons under the securities laws, coupled with the Commission's extraordinarily expansive and vague definition of control, are a further important obstacle to a shareholder or group owning more than 10 percent of a company's stock. The disincentive is especially great if the shareholders seek to select even a minority of directors.

A controlling shareholder is liable for the company's securities-law violations. There is an exemption from liability under the Securities Act if the shareholder "had no knowledge of or reasonable ground to believe in the existence of the facts [which create liability]" and an exemption under the Exchange Act if the shareholder "acted in good faith and did not directly or indirectly induce the . . . violation," but these exemptions offer scant comfort. Both are highly context specific, and the shareholder's knowledge or good faith will always be judged in hindsight, after a violation has taken place.[13]

A shareholder proponent must already bear the full cost of monitoring for only a prorata share of the expected company benefits. A proponent or group that might be deemed a control person must add to the expected cost the risk of liability for company actions that the proponent or group supposedly influenced, caused, or even just failed to prevent. This radically raises the ante for holding a large stake and using that stake to influence corporate policy or for forming a shareholder group that might overcome the collective-action problems that plague individual shareholders. The disincentive is especially great for a financially troubled company, because the corporate deep pocket may be unavailable in case of need, even though troubled companies may most need shareholder intervention.

---

[13] Securities Act Sect. 15; Exchange Act Sect. 20(a), 15 U.S.C. Sect. 78t(a) (1988).

Limited liability is a central feature of corporate law. Shareholders are at risk only for the amount invested. Control-person liability, in contrast, can far exceed the amount one invests, with the perverse feature that the *smaller* one's percentage stake, the greater the potential loss, as a multiple of the amount invested.[14]

In addition to this huge liability, a controlling shareholder loses much of his or her liquidity. A shareholder or group which controls a public company can sell its shares only through a registered offering or the dribble-out provisions of Securities Act Rule 144. Registration involves delay, expense, strict liability for material misstatements, and no assurance that registration is possible, since the company's assistance is needed and may not be forthcoming.

Some disincentive to institutional investors exercising actual control might be desirable. I have argued elsewhere that legal rules should encourage *institutional voice*, by which I mean a world where institutions can easily own 5 to 10-percent stakes in particular companies, but find it more difficult to own much more than 10 percent; in which institutions can easily talk to each other and select a minority of a company's board of directors, but can not easily exercise day-to-day control or select a majority of the board; in which a half-dozen institutions can collectively influence major corporate actions, often indirectly through the board of directors, but any one institution can not do much on its own.

Institutional voice can be seen as occupying a middle range along a continuum with passivity at one extreme and *institutional control*—control of particular firms by particular institutions—at the other extreme. Institutional voice has value in large part because it involves *sharing* of power, both between managers and institutional shareholders and among institutional shareholders. Money managers can watch each other at the same time that they are watching corporate managers and corporate managers

---

[14] Recent scholarship questions whether liability limited to the amount invested is always good policy for tort claims. *See* Hansmann & Kraakman, "Toward Unlimited Shareholder Liability for Corporate Torts," 100 *Yale Law Journal* 1879 (1991); Leebron, "Limited Liability, Tort Victims, and Creditors," 91 *Columbia Law Review* 1565 (1991). But the strongest liability that anyone seriously defends is *prorata* liability of shareholders to tort claimants, perhaps limited to some multiple of the original investment. Control-person liability has no prorata feature and no such limit. Moreover, control-person liability runs predominantly to other capital providers. For capital providers and other contractual creditors, the standard arguments against unlimited liability remain strong. Capital providers can determine by contract whether liability should be limited to the amount invested, and there is no compelling case for overriding their choices.

are watching them. In contrast, the case for encouraging institutional *control* is weaker, because institutional control poses greater risks of institutional abuse of power. A properly crafted definition of control might help to police the fuzzy line between voice and control; it might help to encourage the former and discourage the latter.

Unfortunately, the SEC does not give control its customary meaning. Instead, the Commission defines control as the "*power* to direct . . . the management and policies of a person, *whether through the ownership of voting securities . . . or otherwise*."[15] This definition goes well beyond actual control to reach *potential control* as well. The standard practitioner's advice is that a 10-percent holding "should create caution" and may even "creat[e] a rebuttable presumption of control, expecially if such holdings are combined with . . . membership on the board, or wide dispersion of the remainder of the stock."[16] Why the mere *power* to control, not in fact exercised, should trigger such enormous liability, the Commission has never explained.

The broad definition of control is especially troubling for shareholder efforts to nominate and elect directors. Success in that endeavor can show *power* to direct the company's management and policies and thus lead to liability. Frequent contact between directors and the shareholders who selected them enhances that risk, because it offers evidence that the shareholders are exercising, or at least *could* exercise, that power. One finds bizarre cases such as Tiger Management running a proxy contest to elect a minority of independent directors to the board of Cleveland-Cliffs, *and then refusing to talk to the directors*, for fear of legal liability!

The SEC's broad definition discourages almost any exercise of voice by a shareholder or group large enough to be in the suspect range. Anything one does becomes evidence of *power* to control.[17] We need a new definition

---

[15] Securities Act Rule 405; Exchange Act Rule 12b-2 (emphasis added).

[16] Sommer, "Who's "in Control"?—S.E.C.", 21 *Business Lawyer* 559, 568 (1966).

[17] Suits claiming that a control person is liable for the securities law violations of a company look, apart from the additional claim that a control person exists, much like other securities fraud cases. In securities-fraud cases generally, some suits surely have merit, but many are thought to be frivolous strike suits. Lawyers have incentives to bring marginal cases because the combination of complex facts, huge potential damages, uncertain legal standards, and the general unpredictability of juries make settling even a weak case attractive to many defendants. In practice, virtually all cases are settled, in

of control limited to actual working control, ideally with safe harbor examples of actions that do not, without more, constitute working control. The safe harbor should include efforts to select up to, say, one-third of the board of directors.

Any line drawn between voice and influence, on the one hand, and control, on the other, will inevitably both chill voice to some extent, and fail to capture all instances of control. But this mix of over- and underinclusion is far preferable to the current grossly overbroad definition. And the severe liability placed on controlling persons will ensure ample deterrence of misdeeds, even if *ex post* liability is uncertain.

A related problem, if institutions select some corporate directors, is that the director may well be part of a controlling group (the board) under any definition of control. That creates risk for the institution, because the director's actions may be imputed to the institutions, under the deputization principle that the SEC has articulated under Exchange Act Sect. 16(b). The institution then becomes a deep pocket that can be sued if the company gets into trouble.

The SEC has been unwilling to provide any guidance on how or when deputization takes place. The standardless case-by-case determination that the Commission favors, though, creates a strong chilling effect, when one couples extreme potential liability with the randomness of jury decisions. There is strong need for a Chinese wall safe harbor rule that will let the institutions select directors while insulating themselves from liability, much as investment banks use Chinese walls to insulate themselves from insider trading liability.

Conclusion

The central problem of corporate governance, for most of this century, has been who, if anyone, will watch the managers who run our large public companies. Institutional oversight, through a combination of formal voting initiatives and informal persuasion, can serve as one strand in a web of imperfect constraints on managerial discretion. Other constraints include the product, capital, and labor markets, corporate takeovers, management-

---

ways that benefit the plaintiffs' bar even if not their nominal clients. *See* Alexander, "Do the Merits Matter? A Study of Settlements in Securities Class Actions," 43 *Stanford Law Review* 497 (1991); and Romano, "The Shareholder Suit: Litigation Without Foundation?," 7 *Journal of Law, Economics & Organization* 55 (1991).

incentive-compensation arrangements, creditor oversight, bankruptcy risk, fiduciary duty, and cultural norms.

Institutional oversight can sometimes complement, sometimes replace, and sometimes strengthen other constraints. Consider, for example, the interplay between institutional oversight and takeovers. Institutional oversight can *complement* takeovers by permitting a change of *management* or closer oversight of the current managers, without the need for a costly, disruptive change of *ownership*. Oversight, if effective, can partly *replace* takeovers by reducing the number of firms that are managed badly enough to justify a takeover at a typical 50-percent premium to market. Oversight can also *strengthen* the takeover constraint by limiting defensive tactics and discouraging misguided acquisitions, so that the takeover mechanism operates more smoothly.

Institutional voice can become an important influence on corporate managers, though, only if legal rules permit it to. Today, a complex array of legal rules discourages institutional oversight. The SEC's expansive views of 13(d) disclosure and control-person liability are among the major obstacles to institutional oversight. By selectively narrowing its rules, the Commission could sharply reduce their chilling effect on institutional voice, while preserving their deterrent effect for the core problems that the underlying statute sought to address.

The line between influence and control is inevitably fuzzy. Thus, the SEC faces a tension if it tries to encourage shareholder influence while retaining burdens on the exercise of control. Any disclosure or liability rule for which control is the touchstone will inevitably be both over- and underinclusive—will both chill some desirable oversight and not reach some actions that, with the benefit of hindsight, should have been covered. In the past, the SEC has drafted overbroad rules, that ensure disclosure of actions by 5-percent shareholders that are even remotely related to control and that create control-person liability for persons who come anywhere near to having actual control, at the cost of strongly chilling oversight. The challenge for the Commission is to recognize the cost of overbreadth and craft rules that *both* encourage oversight and discourage abuse of control as best it can.

References and Suggested Readings

Alexander, Janet. 1991. "Do the Merits Matter? A Study of Settlements in Securities Class Actions." *Stanford Law Review* 43:497.

Black, Bernard. 1990. "Shareholder Passivity Reexamined." *Michigan Law Review* 89:520.

——. 1992a. "Agents Watching Agents: The Promise of Institutional Investor Voice." *UCLA Law Review* 39:811.

——. 1992b. "The Value of Institutional Investor Monitoring: The Empirical Evidence." *UCLA Law Review* 39:895.

——. "Securities Regulation and corporate Governance: Adapting Old Rules to a New Paradigm."

Conrad, Alfred. 1993. "Control, Responsibility and Abdication: A Dilemma of Securities Regulation." *Journal of Corporation Law* 17:539.

Gilson, Ronald, and Reinier Kraakman. 1991. "Reinventing the Outside Director: An Agenda for Institutional Investors." *Stanford Law Review* 43:863.

Gilson, Ronald, and Mark Roe. 1993. "Understanding the Japanese Keiretsu: Overlaps Between Corporate governance and Industrial Organization." *Yale Law Journal* 102:871.

Hansmann, Henry, and Reinier Kraakman. 1991. "Toward Unlimited Shareholder Liability for Corporate Torts." *Yale Law Journal* 100:1879.

Kester, Carl. *Japanese Takeovers: The Global Contest for Corporate Control.*

Leebron, David. 1991. "Limited Liability, Tort Victims, and Creditors." *Columbia Law Review* 91:1565.

Millstein, Ira. 1992. "The Evolving Role of Institutional Investors in Corporate Governance." Unpublished manuscript.

Roe, Mark J. 1991. "A Political Theory of American Corporate Finance." *Columbia Law Review* 91:1.

——. 1993. "Some Differences in Corporate Structure in Germany, Japan, and America." *Yale Law Journal* 102:1927.

Romano, Roberta. 1991. "The Shareholder Suit: Litigation without Foundation" *Journal of Law, Economics & Organization* 7:55.

Sommer, A. A. 1966. "Who's `in Control'—S.E.C." *Business Lawyer* 21:559, 568.

U.S. SEC v. Amster & Co. 1991. 762 F. Supp. 604 (S.D.N.Y.).

15

Regulating the Equity Component of Capital Structure: The SEC's Response to the One Share, One Vote Controversy

Ronald J. Gilson
Stanford University and Columbia University

Over the years, capital structure regulation and research has been consumed with the search for the optimal capital structure, more specifically, for the right debt-equity ratio. A number of regulatory regimes were premised on the belief that one could identify the "right" amount of debt. Until 1979, the Securities and Exchange Commission rendered advisory reports concerning the feasibility of a plan of reorganization under Chapter X of the Bankruptcy Act. Feasibility meant "that the proposed capital structure should be sound."[1] The Public Utility Holding Company Act of 1935 required the SEC to disapprove the issuance of securities by utility holding companies if the security was "not reasonably adapted to the [company's] security structure." In both cases, the focus was on the level of debt. Section 18(a) of the Investment Company Act of 1940 is more direct; it prohibits an investment company from issuing debt securities unless after the issuance "it will have an asset coverage of at least 300 per centum."

Nor did this fixation on debt levels change with the 1958 publication of Modigliani and Miller's irrelevance propositions.[2] Rather than putting aside questions of debt levels as irrelevant, financial economists spent the next thirty years rising to the challenge: How could the presence of debt in the capital structure alter a corporation's return stream, or the market's

[1] *In re* Broadway-Exchange Corp., 15 S.E.C. 256, 267 (1944).

[2] Modigliani & Miller, "The Costs of Capital, Corporation Finance, and the Theory of Investment," 48 *American Economic Review* 261 (1958).

expectation of that return stream, so that the level of debt would once again matter.[3]

During this same period, equity's role in the capital structure was largely ignored. As Holmstrom and Tirole recently put it, "The finance literature has traditionally ignored the fact that a share does not merely confer a right to a residual return stream. It also gives a vote."[4]

The 1980s changed that. With the rise of hostile takeovers, control of a corporation—and, hence, the voting characteristics of equity—became a central focus of analysis, and both academics and regulators took notice. Most significantly, the SEC undertook in July, 1988, a bold regulatory initiative --the adoption of Rule 19c-4—the goal of which was to influence, although not to specify, the make up of the equity component of the capital structure. The initiative proved unavailing, as a Federal Court of Appeals promptly concluded that the SEC lacked the statutory authority to pursue it.[5]

But while the court's action swept away the SEC's response, the problem remained and has again been brought to a head by the efforts of one securities exchange to change its rules concerning voting rights. Because the SEC must approve or reject this proposed rule change, the Commission is back to where it stood in 1987, before Rule 19c-4's adoption. In this essay I want to recount the SEC's efforts at regulating the equity component of capital structure and suggest that the odyssey continue but with a change in venue: Congress.

1. Background: One Share, One Vote and Dual Class Recapitalizations

Financial economists' general disinterest in the terms of the equity contract is understandable. For most of the twentieth century, common stock appeared to have invariant and uncontroversial attributes: the residual-profits interest and one vote for each share. Beginning in 1926, the New York Stock Exchange (NYSE) prohibited the listing of nonvoting common stock

---

[3] *See, e.g.*, Miller, "The Modigliani-Miller Propositions After Thirty Years," 2 *Journal of Economic Perspectives* 99 (1988); Bhattacharya, "Corporate Finance and the Legacy of Miller and Modigliani," 2 *Journal of Economic Perspectives* 135 (1988).

[4] Holmstrom & Jean Tirole, "The Theory of the Firm," in *Handbook of Industrial Organization* 63, 85 (Schmalensee & Willig eds., 1989).

[5] *See The Business Roundtable v. Securities and Exchange Commission*, 905 F. 2d 406 (D.C. Cir., 1990).

or the common stock of companies with multiple classes of voting stock whose votes were not proportionate to their equity. The American Stock Exchange (AMEX) also prohibited nonvoting stock but was more lenient with respect to multiple classes of voting stock.[6] None of this seemed to matter very much, because very few companies evidenced any interest in varying the familiar characteristics of the equity component of the capital structure. Between 1940 and 1978, only thirty issuers of nonvoting or multiple voting common stock were the subject of secondary trading; in no single year did the number of such issuers exceed eleven.[7]

The advent of hostile takeovers in the 1980s made the terms of the equity contract a matter of intense concern. Between 1976 and 1979, only four firms recapitalized to change the equity component of their capital structure from a single class of common stock with each share having one vote to two classes of common stock with disparate voting rights. Between 1980 and 1987, 93 firms recapitalized in this fashion, with 43 dual-class recapitalizations occurring in 1986 and 1987 alone.[8] And while these recapitalizations took a number of different forms, the outcome was always the same. The transaction resulted in management or a dominant shareholder group holding shares of high- voting-rights stock and the public shareholders holding shares with reduced voting rights.[9]

At this point, listing requirements governing voting rights became a subject of competition between the exchanges, and the more lenient AMEX standards were seen by the NYSE as conveying an advantage. In September 1986, the NYSE responded by announcing the abandonment of its 60-year commitment to one share-one vote. The exchange proposed to amend its listing requirements to allow the creation of a class of limited voting right common stock by reducing the voting rights of existing common holders,

---

[6] Seligman, "Equal Protection in Shareholder Voting Rights: The One Common Share, One Vote Controversy," 54 *George Washington Law Review* 687 (1986), carefully sets out the history of the voting rights standards of the stock exchanges.

[7] Lease, McConnell & Mikkelson, "The Market Value of Control In Publicly-Traded Corporations," 11 *Journal of Financial Economics* 439, 450 - 52 (1983).

[8] Lehn, Netter & Poulson, "Consolidating Corporate Control: Dual-Class Recapitalizations versus Leveraged Buyouts," 27 *Journal of Financial Economics* 557, 570 (1990)(Table 1).

[9] *See* Gilson, Evaluating Dual Class Common Stock: The Relevance of Substitutes, 73 *Virginia Law Review* 807 (1987).

provided that a majority of independent directors and public shareholders approved.

Because the NYSE is a self-regulatory agency under Section 19 of the Securities Exchange Act of 1934, the proposed change in its rules required SEC approval. The Commission's initial strategy was to defer action on the NYSE's proposal while it urged the NYSE, AMEX, and NASDAQ to negotiate among themselves a common position that could be jointly presented for approval. When these negotiations failed, the SEC began the process of formulating its own rule.

2. SEC Rule 19c-4: Forcing a Separation of a Pooling Equilibrium

The NYSE's proposed rule posed a real quandary for the Commission: Was there any reason to interfere in the competition between the exchanges over listing standards concerning the terms of the equity contract? Certainly, the SEC had no reason to enshrine a particular kind of equity structure as optimal; thus, there was little to commend Commission action to assure continued prohibition of the original issuance of common stock with low or no voting rights.[10] However, the competition between exchanges did not really concern new issuances of low voting stock. The conflict was over dual-class recapitalizations by which a publicly held company changed the equity component of its capital structure to replace a single class of voting stock with two classes, one of which—given to management or an existing shareholder group—has voting power substantially disproportionate to its interest in equity.

The stated justification for such a recapitalization is that centralizing control in those receiving the superior-voting-rights stock will increase the value of the corporation and, it follows, the value of the limited-voting-rights shares. However, the substance of the dual-class-recapitalization transaction is identical to an alternative transaction form: a leveraged buyout that also shifts control to a participating management or an existing shareholder group. In a dual-class recapitalization, shareholders whose voting rights are reduced typically receive nothing more for the transfer of control than a small dividend increase. In contrast, shareholders of companies subject to an LBO

---

[10] Some academic support remained for prohibiting dual-class common stock structures: *See* Lowenstein, "Shareholder Voting Rights: A Response to SEC Rule 19c-4 and to Professor Gilson," 89 *Columbia Law Review* 979 (1989).

typically receive a very substantial premium. From this perspective, dual-class recapitalizations hardly seemed worthy of encouragement.[11]

In favor of approving the NYSE proposal to extend listing to companies that undertake a dual-class recapitalization—and thereby allowing competition to take its course—was the equity version of the Miller-Modigliani irrelevance propositions. In a perfect capital market the arbitrage mechanism that drives the Miller-Modigliani result would also cause dual-class recapitalizations and LBOs to have the same impact on firm value. The relative prices of the two classes of common stock following the dual-class transaction would reflect the same sharing of the gains from shifting control that is reflected in the premium shareholders receive in an LBO.

Suppose the transaction is cast as a dual-class recapitalization in which public shareholders receive an increase in future dividends as compensation for reduced voting rights. If a shareholder prefers cash, as would have been received for his or her voting rights in an LBO, the shareholder can sell the limited-voting-rights stock at a price that reflects the present value of the increased dividend. The difference in market price between shares of the single class of common stock before the recapitalization and shares with lower voting rights but a higher dividend after the recapitalization reflects the portion of the gain from centralizing control that accrues to the shareholder receiving lower voting stock.

In a perfect market, selling limited voting shares after a recapitalization should yield the same amount of cash as selling them after an LBO. In both cases, the increase in value results from fixing control in a particular group, and the size of the premium and its sharing among those who lose and acquire control should be the same, whether reflected as an increase in a stream of dividends, as in a recapitalization, or as a premium over market as in an LBO. Put differently, the increase in value of the noncontrolling shares following a recapitalization transaction should be the same as the premium paid in an LBO, and noncontrolling shareholders should be indifferent. If equivalence did not hold, then arbitrage would correct the imbalance.[12]

The regulatory implication of perfect market equivalence is to stay out of the way; there is no reason to prefer any particular equity structure,

---

[11] *See* Gilson, supra note 9, 816-20.

[12] The transactions should be identical from the perspective of those acquiring control as well. If the transaction is initially cast as an LBO, the same result as a recapitalization can be achieved by a subsequent public offering.

nor any reason to prefer one means of getting there. The problem, of course, is that markets are not perfect. In fact, the impact on the value of noncontrolling shares differs substantially when control is centralized through an LBO and when it is centralized through a dual-class recapitalization. In an LBO, public shareholders earn very substantial premiums on the order of 30 to 40 percent. In a dual-class recapitalization, shareholders at best earn no premium at all.[13] Just as the regularity of observed capital structure suggested that information and incentive effects resulting from market imperfections may explain why capital structure is not irrelevant,[14] the regularity of the differential experience of shareholders depending on the method of consolidating control suggests that information and incentive effects resulting from market imperfections may explain why the difference between an LBO and a dual-class recapitalization is not irrelevant. And if that is the case, then the difference may have regulatory implications. If the empirical patterns simply represent an efficient market response to the presence of transaction costs, no case for regulation exists and the Commission has no reason to interfere with competition between the exchanges. Alternatively, if the empirical patterns evidence coercion of public shareholders by inside shareholder groups taking advantage of the fact that LBOs are mediated through a market while dual-class recapitalizations are mediated through the corporate proxy process controlled by the inside group, then regulation may be necessary to avoid a race to the bottom.[15]

The difficulty confronting the SEC was that the existing data were consistent with both efficient self-selection and shareholder coercion. The more benign explanation for the different patterns contemplates two types of companies that stand to benefit in very different ways from fixing control in the hands of inside shareholders. The first consists of stable, successful firms with high market share in slow growing mature industries. Their market share and the absence of market growth generate substantial amounts of free cash flow. Centralizing control over these companies eliminates the agency problem Michael Jensen has identified: the misuse of free cash

---

[13] *See* Gilson, supra note 9, 816-820 and Lehn, Netter & Poulsen, supra note 8.

[14] *See, e.g.*, Holmstrom & Tirole, supra note 4, 78-86.

[15] The coercion explanation for dual class recapitalizations is developed in Gordon, "Ties That Bond: Dual Class Common Stock and the Problem of Shareholder Choice," 76 *California Law Review* 3 (1988); Ruback, "Coercive Dual-Class Exchange Offers," 20 *Journal of Financial Economics* 153 (1988).

flow.[16] An LBO is the appropriate mechanism because the monitoring and incentive features of debt serve to increase firm value by eliminating free cash flow. And the operation of the market for corporate control—through the potential for competitive bidding—assures that public shareholders will participate meaningfully in the gains from the transaction. A dual-class recapitalization could not achieve the same benefits for this type of company. Giving management of a company with substantial free cash flow more voting control than residual equity would serve only to strengthen management's incentive and ability to favor itself through the corporation's capital budgeting decisions. No gain would result in which public shareholders could participate.

The second type of company that might stand to gain from fixing control in an inside group is quite different. These companies suffer not from free cash flow but from a capital shortage. They are in an earlier stage of development, both in terms of the market in which they operate and in their own organization. Entrepreneurial company founders remain in a dominant position and face a dilemma when they seek to finance growth. Sale of new equity will dilute their control, but if they avoid dilution by purchasing a proportionate amount of the new shares, the cost is an uncompensated increase in the unsystematic risk associated with already undiversified portfolios.

For these companies, a dual-class recapitalization positions the company to secure capital for positive net present value projects without forcing the dominant shareholder group either to dilute their control or bear a disproportionate amount of the cost. The empirical evidence is consistent with this explanation of the type of firms that centralize control through dual-class recapitalizations rather than LBOs. Megan Partch found that companies that effected dual-class transactions were relatively young—half had been publicly traded for less than ten years and 27 percent for less than five years. Virtually all companies in her sample stated that a main purpose for the transaction was to allow additional capital to be raised without diluting a dominant group's control. And that justification was more than just boilerplate; in the two years following the dual-class transaction, almost 40 percent of the sample companies made public offerings of limited voting

---

16 Jensen, "Agency Costs of Free Cash Flow, Corporate Finance and Takeovers," 76 *American Economic Review* 245 (Papers & Proceedings) 323 (1986).

rights securities.[17] Similarly, Lehn, Netter, and Poulsen found that companies effecting dual-class recapitalization were very likely to issue new lower voting equity after the transaction, and to have significantly higher growth of sales and number of employees, higher ratios of research and development and advertising to sales, and lower rates of undistributed free cash flow than firms that consolidate control through an LBO.[18] Finally, Gilson presents data suggesting that firms engaging in dual-class transactions are in markets with relatively high growth rates.[19]

From this perspective, the empirical pattern of transaction forms that develops when transaction costs are introduced provides no justification for regulatory action by the Commission. The manner by which consolidation of control occurs depends on the presence or absence of an otherwise unconstrained agency conflict between management and shareholders: control is consolidated through a market by means of an LBO when agency costs are significant and through a corporate election by means of a dual-class recapitalization when, because of the discipline of competition in a fast-growing product market, agency costs are insignificant.

This efficient self-selection story has an appealingly happy ending: the presence of transaction costs simply leads companies to select the most appropriate transaction form. But this is not the only story that is consistent with the observed transaction patterns; there is also a dark side to the data. Here the critical distinction is not the economic characteristics of the firm, but the presence of a pretransaction dominant shareholder group. The story is one of coercion. A dual-class recapitalization will be selected when, because of an existing control group, public shareholders would have difficulty resisting the transaction. This explanation for dual-class transactions focuses on public choice defects in the corporate electoral process that prevent shareholders from protecting themselves. From this perspective, a justification for regulation appears. As with efficient self-selection, the move from a perfect to an imperfect market results in a systematic pattern of transaction forms. But in this darker view, the pattern reflects not efficiency, but coercion: if a dominant shareholder group exists, it uses its position to exploit public shareholders by a dual-class

---

[17] *See* Partch, "The Creation of a Class of Limited Voting Common Stock and Shareholders Wealth," 18 *Journal of Financial Economics* 313 (1987).

[18] Lehn, Netter & Poulsen, supra note 8.

[19] *See* Gilson, supra note 9, 832 n. 66.

recapitalization. In the absence of recourse to coercion, control can only be consolidated by paying for it through a market transaction like an LBO.[20]

The presence of conflicting explanations for the transactional regularities associated with dual-class recapitalizations and LBOs presented a serious problem when the SEC took up the question of whether to regulate the equity component of the capital structure. Based on the empirical evidence, one cannot confidently determine whether the observed choice of transaction form reflects efficient self-selection, based largely on whether the product market—quickly expanding or mature—in which the particular company participates adequately constrains agency costs, or whether the chosen transaction form instead reflects inefficient self-selection based on the pretransaction distribution of shareholdings; when a dominant shareholder group exists, public shareholders are coerced. A successful regulatory effort had to operate as a kind of forcing contract, requiring companies to reveal their true characteristics through the transaction form they chose. That is, a rule should differentiate between those companies for whom a dual-class recapitalization reflected efficient self-selection and those for whom it reflected only coercion.

This was the clever twist that shaped Rule 19c-4—the Commission's regulatory response to dual-class recapitalizations. The key to the efficient self-selection explanation for dual-class recapitalizations is the firm's ability to raise equity for positive net present value projects without forcing the dominant shareholders to bear a disproportionate amount of the cost either through a dilution of their position or, if dilution is avoided by additional investment, through an uncompensated increase in their unsystematic risk. In turn, the key to the coercion story is a dominant shareholder group's ability to force public shareholders into further strengthening the dominant shareholders' position by reducing the public shareholders' voting power.

So put, it is apparent that the efficient self-selection explanation requires only that it be possible to raise new equity without diluting the dominant group's position; their control need not be strengthened. In contrast, coercion can operate only if the dominant group's position is affirmatively strengthened. A rule that allowed the public offering of a new class of low- or nonvoting common stock would allow new equity to be raised without dilution. Yet, because such a public offering would not affect the voting rights of existing public shareholders, the offering could not be coercive. Thus, prohibiting the alteration of the voting rights of existing

---

[20] Gilson, supra note 9, 833-39, discusses the empirical support for the coercion explanation of the incidence of dual-class recapitalizations.

public shareholders, but not the sale of a second class of limited or nonvoting common stock, precisely threads the needle between efficient self-selection and coercion.

The Commission took just this tack in Rule 19c-4. New issues of low- or nonvoting common stock were allowed. Transactions that reduced the voting rights of existing common shareholders were prohibited. The result was a quite limited incursion into the realm of capital structure regulation. The Commission's rule made no effort to identify an optimal equity contract; it recognized that in some circumstances two classes of common stock with differential voting might be efficient, while in others a single class was the best result. Rather, it regulated only the governance process to force a separation between companies motivated by efficient self-selection and companies motivated by coercion.

3. The Exchanges' Puzzling Response to the Judicial Invalidation of Rule 19c-4

The court's decision in *Business Roundtable* should have been a non-event. The court did not hold that the exchanges and NASDAQ were prohibited from adopting listing standards that reflected Rule 19c-4. The decision concluded only that the Commission lacked the power under the Securities Exchange Act of 1934 to *force* the rule's adoption. Thus, a fitting end to the story might have been that the exchanges and NASDAQ adopted the substance of Rule 19c-4 voluntarily. The Commission had always preferred a cooperative solution reflecting an agreement among the NYSE, AMEX, and NASDAQ, undertaking the rulemaking process in the first place only after the three parties were unable to agree on a common position.

For a time, it seemed that a cooperative solution would prevail. Because the NYSE had modified Section 313 of its *Listed Company Manual* to conform to Rule 19c-4, the court's decision did not alter the voting-rights standards applicable to NYSE companies (although *Business Roundtable* left the exchange free to modify those standards). At least at the outset, the NYSE remained committed to the substance of Rule 19c-4. The NASD followed a similar course. While the immediate effect of the decision was to leave NASDAQ without a voting rights standard, the NASD then elected to adopt a 19c-4 type rule.

That left only the AMEX. Because it had never adopted Rule 19c-4, the *Business Roundtable* decision's invalidation of Rule 19c-4 reinstated the previous AMEX rule that allowed dual-class recapitalizations subject to specified director and shareholder approval. Thereafter, the AMEX created a special committee to study the matter. Based on that committee's recommendation, the AMEX adopted a voting-rights standard that was filed with the SEC for its approval in June, 1991.[21] The Commission had yet to act on that proposal.

The AMEX proposal takes a very different tack than Rule 19c-4. Rather than prohibiting dual-class recapitalizations, the AMEX's proposed standard only sets certain shareholder-approval requirements for transactions that reduce the voting power of existing public shareholders. Specifically, a disenfranchising transaction requires the approval of either two-thirds of the outstanding shares including the votes of the dominant shareholder group or a majority of the shares not held by interested shareholders.[22]

After the AMEX proposal, the NYSE gave up the fight, although to be fair, the approach ultimately proposed by the NYSE was more restrictive than that of the AMEX. Growing out of a series of symposia on corporate governance, the NYSE proposed to allow disenfranchising transactions subject to approval by a majority of a committee of independent directors, a majority of the full board of directors, and a majority of the shareholders who are not interested in the transaction.[23]

The puzzle is why the NYSE backed away from its support for prohibiting dual-class recapitalizations and joined the AMEX in allowing such transactions to go forward provided that public shareholders have a

---

[21] American Stock Exchange, Rule 19c-4: Proposed Rule Change by American Stock Exchange, Inc., File no. SR-Amex-91-13 (June 11, 1991)(amending Section 122 of the AMEX Company Manual).

[22] This requirement sounds more restrictive than it is. If a dominant group already owns 30 percent of the outstanding stock, than it needs the votes of only 51 percent of the public shareholders to meet the test. If the group held 40 percent, then only 44.5 percent of public shares need be voted in favor of the transaction. The AMEX considered but rejected a rule that would require a majority of the unaffiliated shares because that would "impose a tyranny of the minority" (AMEX proposal, supra note 21, 9).

[23] New York Stock Exchange, Inc. Symposium on Corporate Governance, "One Share-One Vote" Summary, Discussion Draft (May 29, 1992). Note that the NYSE proposal is more restrictive than that of the AMEX in two important respects. First, the NYSE required a majority of the unaffiliated shares, thereby rejecting the AMEX's concern with "a tyranny of the minority." Second, the NYSE required approval by a committee of independent directors. In contrast to the backing away from Rule 19c-4 by the NYSE and the AMEX, the NASD continues to support its own 19c-4 type rule. *See* Report, New York Stock Exchange, Inc. Symposium on Corporate Governance 7-8 (March 29, 1992).

sufficient say in their approval. Interestingly, both exchanges offered the same explanation for rejection of the Rule 19c-4 approach, a cryptic reference to the same perceived flaw in the rule: "It did not afford corporations sufficient flexibility to meet their needs."[24] As used, however, the term *flexibility* seems to be a euphemism.[25] The concern could not be over flexibility in adopting an optimal equity contract; Rule 19c-4 did not restrict the substance of the capital structure a company selects. Rather, the rule restricted only the process by which multiple class capital structures could be adopted—by market-mediated sales of new shares not electoral-mediated disenfranchisement of existing shares. But this restriction was central to the SEC's concept of a forcing regulation—one that separated transactions involving efficient self-selection from those involving coercion. Under the Commission's approach, reducing the voting rights of existing shareholders, as opposed to issuing a new class of low- or nonvoting stock, served no special efficiency purpose; all efficiency goals could be achieved by new issuances that did not serve to increase the control of a dominant shareholder group. The distinction has nothing to do with flexibility of capital structure; it has to do with shifting control.

So what "flexibility" did Rule 19c-4 deny companies? The answer reflects the same phenomenon that first initiated the interest in the equity component of the capital structure: the fear of hostile takeovers. A dual-class recapitalization is a foolproof defensive tactic. Once a dominant group has absolute voting control, the company cannot be taken over without the group's approval. But Rule 19c-4 essentially eliminated dual-class recapitalizations as a defensive tactic. Dual-class *capital structures* remained viable, but dual-class *recapitalizations* were prohibited. The difference, of course, is that issuing a new class of low- or nonvoting stock is not a

---

[24] New York Stock Exchange, Discussion Draft, supra note 23, 2. In rejecting the substance of Rule 19c-4, the AMEX spoke in terms of "the desirability of flexibility in creating capital structures." AMEX proposal, supra note 21, 22-3.

[25] In the edited transcript of the proceedings of the NYSE Symposium on Corporate Governance, Stephen Friedman, the chair of the AMEX committee, expanded somewhat on the flexibility concept. He expressed concern that Rule 19c-4 would lead to a situation where "some companies could have multiple class capital structures and others could not." In his view, the AMEX proposal reflected the benefit that there was "a fair way to convert an existing publicly-held company from a single class to a multiple class structure." Yet Rule 19c-4 allowed any company to adopt a multiple class structure by a perfectly fair means: the issuance of new stock in a market-mediated transaction. Something other than flexibility was of concern.

defensive tactic at all; issuing new securities allows new capital to be raised without diluting the existing dominant shareholder group, but it does not allow the dominant group to *increase* its control at the expense of other shareholders. If the dominant shareholder group wants to increase its level of voting control, Rule 19c-4 required that it be paid for.

Thus, the SEC is really back to where it started concerning dual-class recapitalizations. The issue is not specifying the optimal capital structure—that is, what the terms of the equity contract should be. Nor is it protecting capital structure flexibility. Neither the AMEX proposal nor the NYSE discussion draft explains what flexibility in choosing a capital structure Rule 19c-4 restricted. Reading between the lines, however, we unmistakably see entrenchment at work. The issue seems to be whether management can insulate itself from takeovers by acquiring control without paying for the privilege. Both the new NYSE and the AMEX proposals contemplate that shareholders can be coerced into agreeing to reduce or give up their voting rights. Rule 19c-4 had largely eliminated that possibility.

4. Conclusion: Where Does the SEC Go from Here?

Rule 19c-4 represented a clever, narrowly focused regulatory initiative. By eschewing any interest in regulating the substance of the equity contract, the Commission left the market to determine what equity terms best fit particular corporations. And by prohibiting not the issuance of new low voting or nonvoting common stock, but only the disenfranchisement of existing common stockholders, the Commission forced a separation between companies seeking a more efficient capital structure and companies seeking to coerce shareholders into giving up voting rights in favor of an existing group. Rule 19c-4 restricted only the companies with coercion on their minds. Thus, despite the NYSE and AMEX bemoaning the loss of "flexibility" to build defenses, Rule 19c-4 remains the right approach. The only question now is, Where does the SEC go from here? How should the Commission respond to the court of appeals holding in *Business Roundtable* that the SEC lacked the statutory authority to impose Rule 19c-4 on the exchanges and NASDAQ?

The obvious next step is for the SEC to request new legislation from Congress. But the framing and orchestration of that request is a sensitive task. What the SEC does not need is a congressionally mandated one-share-one-vote rule. That would put Congress in the role that the Commission has declined for itself: the role of defining the optimal equity component of the capital structure. The Commission needs only the authority to impose Rule 19c-4, an approach that facilitates, rather than displaces, market determination of efficient capital structure.

References and Suggested Readings

American Stock Exchange, Inc. 1991. "Rule 14c-4: Proposed Rule Change by American Stock Exchange, Inc." File no. SR-AMEX-91-13, June 11, (Amending Section 122 of the AMEX Company Manual.

Bhattacharya, Sudipto. 1988. "Corporate Finance and the Legacy of Miller and Modigliani." *Journal of Economic Perspectives* 2:135.

The Business Roundtable V. U.S. SEC. 1990. 905 F.2d 406 (D.C. Cir.).

Gilson, Ronald J. 1987. "Evaluating Dual Class Common Stock: The Relevance of Substitutes." *Virginia Law Review* 73:807.

Gordon, Jeffrey. 1988. "Ties That Bond: Dual Class Common Stock and the Problem of Shareholder Choice." *California Law Review* 76:3.

Holmstrom, Bengt, and Jean Tirole. 1989. "The Theory of the Firm." In *Handbook of Industrial Organization*, ed. R. Schmalensee and R. Willig, 63–85.

Jensen, Michael. 1986. "Agency Costs of Free Cash Flow, Corporate Finance, and Takeovers." *American Economic Review* 76:323–29.

Lease, Ronald, John McConnell, and Wayne Mikkelson. 1983. "The Market Value of Control in Publicly-Traded Corporations." *Journal of Financial Economics* 11:439, 450–52.

Lehn, Kenneth, Jeffry Netter, and Annette Poulson. 1990. "Consolidating Corporate Control: Dual-Class Recapitalizations versus Leveraged Buyouts." *Journal of Financial Economics* 27:557, 570.

Lowenstein, Louis. 1989. "Shareholder Voting Rights: A Response to SEC Rule 19c-4 and to Professor Gilson." *Columbia Law Review* 89:979.

Miller, Merton H. 1988. "The Modigliani-Miller Propositions After Thirty Years." *Journal of Economic Perspectives* 2:99.

Modigliani, Franco, and Merton Miller. 1958. "The Costs of Capital, Corporation Finance, and the Theory of Investment." *American Economics Review* 48:261.

New York Stock Exchange. 1992a. Symposium on Corporate Governance Report, March 29, 1992.

——. 1992b. Symposium on Corporate Governance, "One Share-One Vote" Summary. Discussion Draft, May 29, 1992.

Partch, Megan. 1987. "The Creation of a Class of Limited Voting Common Stock and Shareholders Wealth." *Journal of Financial Economics* 18:313.

Rubach, Richard S. 1988. "Coercive Dual-Class Exchange Offers." *Journal of Financial Economics* 20:153.

Seligman, Joel. 1986. "Equal Protection in Shareholder Voting Rights: The One common Share, One Vote Controversy." *George Washington Law Review* 54:687.

16

Multiple Listing Standards: Freeing Exchanges and Investors to Make Efficient Decisions in the Modern Securities Market

John Pound
Harvard University

Exchanges are buffeted by new competitive pressures. From some quarters come calls for more stringent listing standards, to hold U.S. companies to higher levels of accountability. Pressure for increased stringency has been felt in the areas of corporate governance standards, such as the independence of board members, and in auditing, particularly in the wake of recent highly publicized cases in which the auditing mechanism clearly failed. Concurrently, there are also pressures for easing listing standards, in order to accommodate foreign companies with different accounting and reporting standards.

Rigorous analysis of the true role of an exchange in the modern era suggests the answer is neither tighter nor looser listing standards per se. Rather, it is a rethinking of the entire concept of listing standards. The listing-standards concept as we now apply it dates quite literally from before the time of organized securities regulation in the United States. Seen in light of the modern era and economic reasoning, it is inefficient to impose strictures on the exchanges that neither improve efficiency nor accomplish regulatory objectives. A modern approach to listing standards would replace mandatory with voluntary listing standards in a broad set of areas that can be termed "corporate conduct." This shift would increase efficiency and help all market participants—investors, corporations, and the exchanges themselves—in the increasingly competitive market.

The argument for multiple listing standards begins with the reality that for a major U.S. company, there are two broad sets of standards associated with a listing on a major U.S. exchange. The first set pertains directly to the market process and trading environment that the exchange creates. These are the key issues for an exchange, whose purpose is to make a market in shares and offer corporations and investors a liquid and low-cost mechanism for trading. Exchanges compete by offering different market structures that are differentiated by aspects such as reliance on dealers or specialists, reliance on auctions or quotes, trade reporting requirements, and technical capabilities to fill orders and handle order volume. Through these aspects of the market mechanism, exchanges compete directly for customers by offering a better market—more liquidity, more information, better price discovery.

There is then a second set of standards associated with an exchange listing. In this second category falls a broad variety of matters that do not pertain to trading, liquidity, or the underlying market mechanism at all. Rather, they pertain to the *conduct* of listed companies. Included are listing standards on matters such as corporate governance, disclosure, proxy solicitation policies, and so forth. Broadly, these standards define what kind of company is traded on the exchange, as opposed to the kind of market the company is traded in. Such standards are clearly not a part of the market mechanism itself, nor are they a basis on which exchanges compete. They impose an additional layer of requirements on companies that might choose to avail themselves of a particular market mechanism while having nothing at all to do with the operation or the role of that market mechanism.

To see the difference starkly, consider a company with substandard reporting practices, a lax auditor, and a penchant for fraud. Suppose that a large number of investors wish to buy this company's stock nonetheless, because they believe that management, dishonest as it is, has a tendency to make money. They would prefer to see this company list with the exchange that allows them to trade this company's shares for the lowest cost, offers the most liquidity. The best mechanism helps them no matter how bad the company. In the extreme, in response to a disclosure of massive fraud, investors will be able to get out of the stock on a liquid exchange with a good market mechanism.

The conduct standards of exchanges date from before the time of the U.S. Securities and Exchange Commission, when exchanges were literally the only way to enforce such conduct standards on publicly traded companies. Then, a few exchanges had a monopoly position, so that access to national markets could be predicated on meeting standards. In 1991, we are entering an era in which the latter conduct standards cannot be enforced by a listed exchange. No exchange has the market power with which to do so. In a world of competing market mechanisms and competing jurisdictions, any arbitrary set of requirements for companies listed on an exchange will only impose costs that will drive them away from that particular exchange.

Concurrently, in the modern era, there is no reason why an exchange *should* serve as the venue for enforcing corporate conduct. In the 1920s, other venues for conduct enforcement, including federal regulation and investor activism, were weak. Exchanges were thus in a natural position to set conduct mandates in response to broad political sentiment. In the past fifty years, a set of mechanisms has grown up through which corporate conduct is set and monitored, including state law, federal securities regulation, independent organizations such as FASB, and direct negotiation between investors and individual corporations. Indeed, one important part of the institutional investment revolution is that there is more concentrated power among shareholders to negotiate and set specific standards of conduct at particular companies.

To compete in the modern era, thus, it is both possible and efficient to "unbundle" issues of conduct from the more fundamental issue of the market mechanism. Such unbundling would help investors, by allowing them access to the best market while leaving the job of conduct enforcement to them and to relevant regulatory bodies. Concurrently, such a change would help the exchanges, by allowing them to concentrate on providing the best market rather than on dictating the terms on which U.S. corporations are run, an issue that is wholly ancillary to the market mechanism.

This does not mean that exchanges can or should wholly abandon the notion of trying to improve listing standards for corporate conduct. In the real world this is not possible, because the political process would not tolerate a wholesale rollback or abandonment of the present concept of listing standards. How then should and/or can exchanges address issues of corporate conduct in the modern environment? The key is altering the concept of listing standards. Exchanges need to maintain a baseline set of standards, if for no other reason than that the political process would react adversely to a rollback. Above that baseline, exchanges can and should offer one or several additional packages of standards that member companies can subscribe to. These additional standards, however, should be offered and adopted on a *voluntary* rather than a mandatory basis. Voluntary classes of listing standards would be distinguished by letters appearing next to the company's name and ticker symbol.

From the viewpoint of the exchanges, offering different voluntary listing classes would allow product differentiation; each exchange would be able to attract a more diverse group of listed corporations. Under multiple listing classes, any company could choose to avail itself of the particular exchange's market characteristics, and these market-making issues would not be "bundled" in with issues of conduct. But concurrently, the multiple-standards approach would require that a listing company self-select across a series of categories of conduct. This would "pigeonhole" it for investors. Potential traders would not be guaranteed that only one kind of company listed on the exchange, as in the old days; but they would be afforded an opportunity to know, in simple and summary fashion, "what kind" of company they were dealing with.

There is reason to believe that multiple listing classes would offer significant benefits to corporations and their shareholders. The scheme would provide companies with a simple and easy way to disseminate a broad and complex set of information about conduct issues such as their internal governance structure and/or their disclosure policies. This information is not readily available to many investors and is not easily understandable to the average investor even when available. Many companies wish to disseminate such information but have a very difficult time doing so in the present environment. By boiling this kind of information down into simple listing classes, thus, exchanges would be providing a function in this area similar to that which they provide by making an efficient trading market. They would be serving as efficient, centralized processors and providers of information.

Critics might argue that this effectively guts the listing standards by substituting voluntary for mandatory compliance. There are two responses. First, stringent mandatory standards have reached extinction as a concept; exchanges simply cannot enforce stricter listing requirements without eliminating their commercial appeal. Second, given this constraint, voluntary standards are a way of providing an important, alternative kind of enforcement in the modern era. By providing increased information, exchanges would help all investors impose a "market test" on various different standards of conduct. If such issues do in fact matter, then presumably, companies opting voluntarily for the "higher" listing standard would increase investor confidence and thereby lower their cost of capital. Other companies might observe this evidence and ultimately follow suit, thereby prompting the de facto establishment of a higher standard. Or, some companies might choose to live with a less stringent listing class, presumably incurring a higher cost of capital—but they and their investors could choose to strike that bargain, and still have access to a particular exchange's market-making qualities.

To make these arguments concrete, let us consider one specific example—that of the listing standards on corporate-governance issues. For all exchanges, these standards are likely to be a continuing and contentious source of lobbying pressure from both listed companies and shareholders.

Governance is well suited to gradations offered by voluntary listing standards. Suppose an exchange surveyed its members and found, for example, that a significant proportion would be happy to adhere to a more stringent set of governance requirements–including, for example, a mandatory majority of outside directors. This exchange could develop a class G listing standard, which would involve a more stringent set of governance requirements than the exchange's current requirements and would have the endorsement of a significant number of listed companies. The exchange could then announce the establishment of a new option for listed companies–the opportunity, but not the mandate, to list under the G scheme. Companies choosing this option would be denoted by a special G symbol after their ticker symbol; other than this distinction, their rights and privileges on the exchange would remain the same.

Over the next few years, the G class would offer two real-time experiments. First, for companies, the scheme would make available a signalling mechanism whereby they could distinguish themselves as having a "better" governance structure. This could offer them significant benefits in terms of investor support and the cost of capital. Second, for the exchange, the G scheme would allow an experiment in policy and market structure, whereby feedback would occur about whether more listings would be attracted if the baseline standards were complemented with additional voluntary packages.

Multiple listing standards are an efficient way to update the now-archaic concept of stringent corporate-conduct requirements for listing on a national stock exchange. Multiple standards would allow the exchanges to play a valuable role in disseminating information to shareholders, while concurrently separating corporate-conduct issues from the issues fundamental to an exchange, namely, the structure and operation of the market mechanism itself. This separation would help the exchanges compete, by freeing them from their traditional role as conduct enforcers. Concurrently, it would help investors, by assuring them the most efficient market mechanism.

17

Mutual Funds in the Boardroom[1]

Mark J. Roe
Columbia University

We need to examine mutual fund regulation not only with the goals of protecting the small investor and fostering corporate democracy in mind, but also keeping in mind corporate governance as part of the mission. Mutual funds could be more useful in corporate boardrooms. But do the Investment Company Act of 1940 and subchapter M's tax rules make a useful role more difficult than it must be?

The dominant paradigm for understanding the large public firm was articulated by Berle and Means just prior to passage of the 1933 Act and the founding of the SEC. Huge capital needs dictated by technology required that large enterprise raise money from farflung investors who, with their own diversification needs, took small bits of a company's equity. This atomization of shareholding shifted power from shareholders to managers. The securities laws mitigate many problems from that shift, facilitating and mandating information flow from inside to outside the firm. Since the shift has, until recently, been seen as inevitable, we could pursue goals such as protecting the small investor and fostering corporate democracy without wondering if protective rules also facilitated a shift in power to managers. If the shift was inevitable, a rule that underscored it merely hastened or intensified the inevitable.

A closer reading of history and a quick look at other nations suggests that there is more to the story than technology and scale economies dictating an inevitable shift from shareholders to managers. Firms could have raised capital from farflung investors *through* financial intermediaries. The intermediaries could then have sat in corporate boardrooms and balanced authority with the CEO. Moreover, if there's a short-term bias in the stock

---

[1] This paper is based on Roe, "Political Elements in the Creation of a Mutual Fund Industry," 139 *University of Pennsylvania Law Review* 1469 (1991) and Roe, "A Political Theory of American Corporate Finance," 91 *Columbia Law Review* 10 (1991).

market, intermediaries with big blocks could help remedy the problem. Soft and proprietary information does not flow easily to securities traders. It would flow better to big, stable blockholders who sit in the boardroom.

For better or worse, Germany and Japan have had financial institutions—usually banks or insurers—with a big role in firm governance. We could not, even if we wanted to, replicate the foreign systems here, because U.S. banks and most insurers are not now strong enough. Bank regulation and extensive deposit insurance make the task too risky.

If there is value in institutions with big blocks sitting in the boardroom, mutual funds are a good place to start, because for them the costs of error are low. If an experiment fails with mutual funds they are easily disbanded or reconstructed. Failed banks with deposit insurance cannot so easily be changed.

Mutual funds rarely participate in corporate governance. They are intermediaries, channeling funds from disparate individuals into investments. They gather and process information about industrial investments that their owners cannot easily gather and process. They do the paperwork that individuals begrudge. Yet they are not intermediaries in the sense that they take the funds of disparate investors, invest them in concentrated holdings, and then enter the corporate boardroom to represent their shareholder beneficiaries.

In the 1930s some mutual funds began to act as monitoring intermediaries. They underwrote securities, became active players in bankruptcy reorganizations, and participated in management.[2] The 1936 tax act, followed up by the 1940 Investment Company Act, induced them to stop and become more passive. Passivity rules were not unintended. The administration and Congress *wanted* to eliminate mutual-fund (and other banker) control of industrial companies. Explanations for the severance can be seen in (1) popular opinion that mistrusted large financial institutions, (2) public-spirited rules intended to foster stable mutual funds for the average investor, (3) the accidents of tax doctrine, and (4) a glimmer of an interest-group story as some political actors decided to favor local managers over Wall Street.

While chair of the SEC William O. Douglas said:

---

[2] *See* U.S. SEC, Report on the Study of Investment Trusts and Investment Companies 370-371 (1939–1942); hereafter: "SEC Investment Company Study"; U.S. SEC, "Abuses and Deficiencies in the Organization and Operation of Investment Trusts and Investment Companies," Pt. III, H.R. Doc. No. 270, 76th Cong., 1st Sess. 2501 (1939); "Investment Dilemma: Trusts Forced to Choose between Drastic Reorganization and High Tax, under New Law," *Business Week* July 11, 1936:45, 46.

> The banker [should and will be] restricted to . . . underwriting or selling. Insofar as management [and] formulation of industrial policies . . . the banker will be superseded. The financial power which he has exercised in the past over such processes will pass into other hands.[3]

The 1940 Investment Company Act Restrictions

When the 1940 Act was passed, cognoscenti recognized that the mutual fund offered a third function, beyond diversification and expert management: "[the investor] may be able to join in the purchase of control of one or more other corporations."[4] But Congress disliked mutual funds with control. Only unscrupulous financiers mixed investment with control: "The investment company [has] bec[o]me the instrumentality of financiers and industrialists to facilitate acquisition of concentrated control of the wealth and industries of the country."[5] Congress must "prevent the diversion of these [investment] trusts from their normal channels of diversified investment to the *abnormal* avenues of control of industry."[6] Congress might

---

[3] Douglas, "Democracy and Finance" (1940) from a speech Douglas gave in 1937 to a stunned audience that included nearly every important Wall Street investment banker.

[4] *See* Jaretzki, "The Investment Company Act of 1940," 26 *Washington University Law Quarterly* 303, 305 (1941). Jaretzki represented a group of investment companies at congressional 1940 Act hearings.

[5] U.S. Congress, Committee on Banking and Currency, "Stock Exchange Practices: Report of the Committee," Senate Report No. 1455, 73d Cong., 2d Sess. 333-34, 363 (1934). Hereafter: Pecora Report, (in reference to its final chief counsel).

[6] Id., 393 (emphasis supplied). *See also* Hearings on S. 3580 Before a Subcommittee of the Senate Committee on Banking and Currency, "Investment Trusts and Investment Companies," Pt. I, 76th Cong., 3d Sess. 36 (1940). Hereafter: 1940 Act Hearings.

have "to completely divorce investment trusts from investment banking."[7] The SEC was later directed to draft legislation.

The SEC declared in its proposed bill that "the national public interest . . . is adversely affected . . . when investment companies [have] great size [and] have excessive influence on the national economy."[8] A good many of the 1940 Act rules (and perhaps other early SEC rules) should be seen as coming out of this now-forgotten goal. In 1935, 56 investment companies had controlling interests in 187 portfolio companies.[9] Little good could come out of investment company control over portfolio companies.[10] The investment company might fail, because of the lack of diversification. It might pump money into the portfolio company to protect a large position. It might unwisely change the financial policy or capital structure of the portfolio company; it might force dividends out at too high a rate. Finally, it might force a merger on terms disadvantageous to minority interest in the controlled company.[11]

The SEC conceded that mutual fund control could help resolve the informational and organizational problems of scattered shareholders; as it comprises sophisticated investors with specialized personnel, the investment company would have expertise, the motivation to improve managerial

---

7 Pecora Report, supra note 4, 393.

8 1940 Act Hearings, supra note 5, 434. The statement of purpose also showed concern for efficient investment management and protection of investors.

9 SEC Investment Company Study, supra note 1, 8; Wharton School of Finance and Commerce, "A Study Prepared for the SEC," House Report No. 2274, 87th Cong., 2d Sess. 399 (1962). Hereafter: Wharton Investment Company Study.

10 SEC Investment Company Study, supra note 1, 2624.

11 SEC Investment Company Study, supra note 1, 22; Wharton Investment Company Study, supra note 9, 400.

performance, and the financial clout to see its views implemented.[12] Nevertheless, the disadvantages of investment companies with the power to control outweighed the advantages. The SEC wanted mutual fund directors and employees off the boards of all portfolio companies; they wanted a Glass-Steagall-type severance.[13] Eventually the SEC had to compromise with the mutual fund industry, but it still achieved a great deal of severance.

Diversification

A mutual fund cannot advertise itself as diversified if it owns in the regulated part of its portfolio more than 10 percent of the stock of any company. Three-quarters of the portfolio is subject to this fragmentation rule, *even if* that influential block of stock is a small portion of the fund's portfolio.

The disclosure element makes sense. The 10-percent limit does not. A mutual fund might be diversified yet hold a big percentage of a firm, with that block still a small percentage of the fund's portfolio. The hidden goal was to disable control, not to promote diversification. (The big block might raise liquidity disclosure problems, to be discussed below. But this is a different problem.)

Networks and Affiliates

The 1940 Act leaves one-quarter of the portfolio not subject to the fragmentation rules, and, theoretically, the fund could choose not to call itself diversified and then not be subject to the fragmentation rules. (I say theoretically because, as the next section shows, penalty-tax rules track the 1940 Act rules.)

For the portion of the portfolio that could be concentrated, other restrictions apply. True, the 1940 Act does not expressly prohibit a mutual fund or its employees from sitting on the board of a portfolio firm. But if a fund owned 5 percent of a portfolio firm's stock, or sat on its board, the firm would become a statutory affiliate of the fund *and* others owning 5

---

[12] SEC Investment Company Study, supra note 1, 371; Wharton Investment Company Study, supra note 9, 400.

[13] 1940 Act Hearings, supra note 6, 216-20.

percent of the portfolio firm.[14] Various recapitalizations could not then go forward without SEC exemption. The SEC's blanket exemptions seem not to apply if anyone involved in a recapitalization, such as a deputized director, receives incentive compensation.[15] SEC rules also prohibit joint affiliate action without SEC exemption; again blanket exemptions may not cover what could be typical efforts at joint influence.[16] To be effective in the boardroom, mutual funds might ally with others. Moreover, the statute and the SEC's Section 17 rules here are unusually opaque.[17] While joint action has the potential for abuse, blanket rules similar to those promulgated in the 1980s, but improved, might exempt those settings in which abuse is unlikely.

Interplay with 16B and 13(d) is a problem. If a director's seat is attributed to the fund, it must return short-swing trading profits. But the open-end mutual funds cannot help some trading, which can be determined or influenced by their own shareholders' redemptions and purchases. Moreover, group action triggers filing requirements, if 16(a) tracks 13(d), meaning that the funds must constantly file and refile and worry that others in the group might forget a timely filing.

Subchapter M of the Internal Revenue Code

The mutual fund that would control would be taxed unfavorably on its *entire* portfolio, as the tax code allows only *diversified* mutual funds to pass income through to shareholders, untaxed to the conduit mutual fund. The 1936 Revenue Act provided a notion of diversification that was repeated in the 1940 Act; its notion of diversification is not that found in a modern

---

[14] Investment Company Act of 1940, Sect. 2(a)(3); 15 U.S.C. Sect. 80a-2(a)(2) (1988); 17 C.F.R. 17a-6 (1990).

[15] 17 C.F.R. Sect. 270.17a-6(a)(5), (b)(1)(iii); Gilson and Kraakman, "Investment Companies as Guardian Shareholders: The Place of the MSIC in the Corporate Governance Debate," *Stanford Law Review*. n.70 (1993) (forthcoming).

[16] 17 C.F.R. Sect. 270.17d-1.

[17] Id.; 17 C.R.F. Sect. 270.17d-1(d)(5)(i). *See also* Gormley, "On the Same Side of the Table: Is Investment Company Act Rule 17d-1 Partly Invalid?," 20 *Securities Regulation Law Journal*. 115, 117-18 (1992). Section 17d rules are "a morass of unascertainable depth", SEC acknowledges 17d as "uncertain"; ultimate legal advice was "prayer consistently applied."

textbook on corporate finance: mutual funds at that time were required to have their investments in companies constituting no more than 5 percent of the portfolio *and* constituting no more than 10 percent of the *portfolio company's* outstanding stock. Later, in 1942, the tax code was amended to allow half of the portfolio to be more concentrated; for that other half, no more than 25 percent of the fund's assets could go into a single company's stock.[18]

Pass-through tax status is necessary for a mutual fund to work. Therefore, if a mutual fund wished to sell services as an intermediary-monitor, dividing its portfolio into four or five stocks, it could not get the advantage of subchapter M. Further, no mutual fund could *ever* threaten a portfolio company to which it would devote more than a quarter of its assets to obtain a majority of the portfolio company's stock and oust management. That threat, and the influence it would yield, is *always* prohibited for a subchapter M mutual fund.[19]

Investment Trusts: Carrying on a Business?

In the 1930s, mutual funds' pass-through status as untaxed vehicles was challenged. The key issue was whether the trust carried on a separate business. If it controlled an operating company and affected its policies, then it was carrying on a business of managing companies.[20] Trusts in the 1930s said that when they only assembled a passive portfolio, they were not carrying on a business and were not taxable. But the IRS said that providing

---

[18] I.R.C. Sect. 851(b)(4). Venture capital firms, which would provide monitoring for *small* firms, not the large firms that are our subject, are partially exempt from the no-control provision. I.R.C. Sect. 851(e).

[19] I.R.C Sect. 851(b)(4)(B). Nor can mutual funds issue senior securities to enhance absolute size, and hence the size of the chunk that goes into any single company. Investment Company Act of 1940, Sect. 18(a), 15 U.S.C. Sect. 80a-18(a) (1988).

[20] Article 1504 of Regulation 69, quoted in Wallstein, "Some Legal Questions in Relation to Investment Trusts" 9, #11 (1928) ("the trustees did not `manage the mills', i.e., carry on a business."); *Hecht v. Malley*, 265 U.S. 144 (1924). Case law suggested that if "the trustees were, in substance, merely holding property for the collection of the income and its distribution among the beneficiaries and were not engaged, either by themselves or in connection with the beneficiaries, in the carrying on of any business," then it was not carrying on a business of managing companies. Id., 9. The other critical tax distinction was whether the beneficiaries controlled the trustees.

diversified investments was itself a business[21] and in 1935 the Supreme Court agreed.[22]

Only the unit investment trust was left insulated from corporate taxation,[23] because it ordinarily does not buy or sell securities, once *someone else* assembles the trust.

Liberalization in the 1936 Code

The 1936 tax code "liberalized" these tax results, by expanding pass-through status to funds that fragmented and took no 10 %+ positions; that is, positions that would yield influence. Yes, such funds were carrying on a business. But it was not a "real" business. It was the business of picking stocks and bonds, not of making operating decisions.

Legal Change

The fragmentation rules in the 1940 Act and the tax code should be dropped. In the modern securities market, the central protection to buyers of the fund is adequate disclosure of the structure of the fund's portfolio.

The basic concept of diversification in the two acts is well meaning but antiquated. The law's notion of diversification—no more than 5 percent of a single issuer—offers little in the way of investor protection; the mutual fund could put all of its monies into a single industry, making the fund ridiculously undiversified.

Protecting Unsophisticated Investors

Congress feared that unsophisticated investors would invest in mutual funds expecting diversification but would be unable to evaluate the portfolio. The SEC testified that a mutual fund's *only* positive function was

---

[21] Treasury Department, General Counsel Memorandum 1881 (1928); Wallstein, supra note 20, 19-22.

[22] *Morrissey v. Commissioner of Internal Revenue*, 296 U.S. 344 (1935).

[23] *See* Wallstein, supra note 20, 23.

to provide diversification—any extension risked thievery.[24] Keeping mutual fund managers out of controlling positions kept them free from conflicts of interests. The funds' investment adviser, an investment bank, would use the control exerted by the mutual fund to obtain securities-underwriting business from the controlled portfolio company.[25] Or the investment vehicle that controlled industry would be used to unload unwholesome securities onto a gullible public.[26] These are serious problems, but they can be addressed without a blanket prohibition on influence.

Deregulation could be coupled to a back-scratching prohibition: no 5 %+ ownership if the fund, or an affiliated group, sells pension services to the 5 %+ company. Moreover, owners of a mutual fund have more power to deal with the conflicts of interest of *mutual fund* managers than they have to deal with the conflicts of interest of *corporate* managers. To sever ties with conflicted and underperforming corporate managers, shareholders must overcome a severe collective-action problem. They must mount a takeover or proxy contest to get rid of the offending managers. True, they can sell their shares to others. But those others are inextricably bound to the offending managers, unless they can overcome the collective-actions problems. Since the buyers will be bound, they will only pay the shareholders for the value of the package: a pro rata interest in the firm *with these managers*. But owners of the typical open-end fund can *redeem* their shares. They can send the shares into the company, *and get their money back from the company*. The offending managers could quickly find themselves with no assets to manage. Redemption is a serious risk for subpar mutual fund managers.

Interval Funds

Regulation forces an extreme trade-off for investors that might make big-block funds difficult to use. Highly liquid open-end funds that redeem

---

[24] 1940 Act Hearings, supra note 6, 131, 132 (statement of George Matthews, Commissioner of the SEC), 807 (reiteration by David Schenker, Chief Counsel, SEC Investment Trust Study).

[25] Pecora Report, supra note 5, 333; 1940 Act Hearings, supra note 6, 36, 206, 207 (statement of I.M.C. Smith, Associate Counsel SEC Investment Trust Study).

[26] Pecora Report, supra note 5, 381-82.

overnight provide excellent discipline to fund managers: Make a big error and the fund will find itself with no assets.

As noted above, the interplay of boardroom seats with 16B is a problem for mutual funds that must stand ready to redeem. Closed-end funds are an alternative, but they do not discipline fund managers as well as the open-end structure, because the assets cannot move out easily. And persistent discounts[27] make the structure unpopular.

Business entails trade-offs. But the 1940 Act does not allow a trade-off here. It does not allow the investor to buy a vehicle where the fund would take big illiquid blocks and the investors could redeem only on, say, three months notice. Such vehicles would be particularly useful for retirement money, for which the investor has a long horizon and does not expect to spend for decades.

The SEC staff's recent proposals to permit interval funds[28] are good ones. If put in tandem with portfolio rule changes and general joint action exemptions and coordination with 16B, allowing funds to take big blocks and ally with other institutions to put agents into the boardroom, they could help improve corporate governance and informational flow. A plausible argument could be made that they will lift some of the useful features of German and Japanese corporate governance, without the accompanying heavy baggage, to facilitate in a U.S. context more and better relational investing between financiers and corporate managers.

Anticartel Theory

In 1942, Congress slightly liberalized the portfolio fragmentation requirements at the behest of the mutual fund industry. But it said no more than 25 percent could go into the stock of two or more controlled companies "engaged in the same or similar trades or businesses or related trades or businesses."[29] Owning 20 percent of the stock of a portfolio company gave

---

[27] Kraakman, "Taking Discounts Seriously: The Implications of `Discounted' Share Prices as an Acquisition Motive," 88 *Columbia Law Review* 891, 902–05 (1988).

[28] Division of Investment Management, U.S. SEC, "Protecting Investors: A Half Century of Investment Company Regulation" (May 1992), 425, 442.

[29] Revenue Act of 1942, Sect. 170(a), Pub. L. No. 77-753, 56 Stat. 798, 878 (1942), codified at I.R.C. Sect. 851(b)(4)(B).

the mutual fund control for purposes of the fragmentation requirement. The legislative history shows an example:

> Investment company W . . . has its assets invested as follows: . . . 10 percent [of its assets] in corporation B, 25 percent in corporation C. . . . Investment company W owns more than 20 percent of the voting power of corporations B and C. Corporation B manufactures radios and corporation C acts as its distributor and also distributes radios for other companies. Investment company W fails to meet the requirements of section 361(b)(4) since it has 35 percent of its assets invested in the securities of two issuers which it controls and which are engaged in related trades or businesses.[30]

Boardroom presence might need industry knowledge. If the fund cannot concentrate its influential blocks in a single industry, or its vertically related parts, assembling a staff would be difficult or impossible. There is some reason to think that foreign financial institutions link customers and suppliers, as much as they engage in what we think of as boardroom corporate governance.[31] This residue of linkage prohibition raises the costs of such linkages here. Antitrust should be the standard to judge such linkages. Subchapter M is overkill.

Subchapter M produces odd results. If the mutual fund keeps its entire portfolio fragmented, it can put its entire portfolio into a single industry. A few mutual funds do this, giving their shareholders little diversification. But the fund managers cannot put more than 25 percent of their fund's assets into control blocks in a single industry; the fund *cannot concentrate* investments in a single industry without tax penalty. The result is no diversification *and* no influence.

---

[30] U.S. Congress, House of Representatives, "Revenue Revision of 1942: Hearings Before the Committee on Ways and Means," 77th Cong., 2d Sess. 122 (1942).

[31] Gilson and Roe, "Understanding the Japanese Keiretsu: Overlaps Between Corporate Governance and Industrial Organization," 102 *Yale Law Journal* (1993) (forthcoming).

Why Not to the Limits of Subchapter M?

The SEC might view reform as unnecessary, if the institutions will ask for relief. There is much to be said for not fixing it until someone in the industry tells the SEC it is broken. But any gains from shareholder blocks and boardroom representation are shared by all shareholders, and to some extent by employees and customers of the firm. The blockholder can only capture part of these gains. The cost of getting out front, of paying to petition the SEC for what might only be a small part of one's business, may be a sufficient deterrent. Yet any gains accrue not only to the mutual fund beneficiaries, but also to other shareholders, employees, and those who deal with the portfolio firm.

True, mutual funds do not use what leeway they have to take big blocks. But, subchapter M requires that a fund be a fragmented fund and big block fund simultaneously, and joint-action limits (under 13D, 16A and the 1940 Act's Rule 17) and interplay with 16B raise the cost of bulking up of votes. And with the stark choice between closed- and open-end, trade-offs cannot be made between liquidity and easy fund accountability (by investor ability to redeem).

With other larger U.S. financial institutions—banks, for example—largely precluded, perhaps for good reason, from action, mutual funds may need more leeway to be effective. Moreover, there is reason to believe that institutional investor voice works if—and perhaps only if—there are *multiple* big blocks.[32] But with banks and insurers out of the picture and with investor communication costly (in part because of the 13D rules, recently reformed sensibly), multiple blocks simply have not been there. This problem will continue for banks and insurers. But we have to start somewhere. Mutual funds are a good place to start.

Conclusion

Just when Berle and Means were announcing the emergence of the public corporation with uncontrolled managers at the helm, Congress raised the cost of mutual fund influence in industry. The restrictions in the 1936 tax code and the 1940 Act make it impossible to deploy a majority of the fund's portfolio in control blocks. The 1940 Act raises the cost of control

---

[32] *See* Roe, "Some Differences in Corporate Governance in Germany, Japan, and America," 102 *Yale Law Journal* (1993) (forthcoming).

with the unregulated portion of the portfolio by regulating or prohibiting activities with affiliates.

In other countries, powerful financial institutions influence firms with big blocks of stock. The United States with its much more highly developed mutual fund industry, may have a chance to leapfrog some foreign nations in corporate governance. Fractional reserve banks are inherently unstable and are not well suited to take big blocks of stock. Mutual funds, properly regulated, may give us some of the benefits of big blocks without some of the institutional costs that foreign nations must incur.

References and Suggested Readings

Gilson, Ronald J., and Reinier Kraakman. 1993. "Investment Companies as Guardian Shareholders: The Place of the MSIC in the Corporate Governance Debate." *Stanford Law Review* 45:993.

Gilson, Ronald J., and Mark J. Roe. 1993. "Understanding the Japanese Keiretsu: Overlaps Between Corporate Governance and Industrial Organization." *Yale Law Journal* 102.

Gormley, R. James. 1992. "On the Same Side of the Table: Is Investment Company Act Rule 17d-1 Partly Invalid?" *Securities Regulation Law Journal* 20: 115, 117-118.

"Investment Dilemma: Trusts Forced to Choose between Drastic Reorganization and High Tax, Under New Law." 1936. *Business Week*, July 11, 45, 46.

Jaretzki, Alfred. 1941. "The Investment Company Act of 1940." *Washington University Law Quarterly* 26:303, 305.

Kraakman, Reinier. 1988. "Taking Discounts Seriously: The Implications of `Discounted' Share Prices as in Acquisition Motive." *Columbia Law Review* 88:891, 902–5.

Roe, Mark J. 1991a. "Political Elements in the Creation of a Mutual Fund Industry." *University of Pennsylvania Law Review* 139:1469.

——. 1991b. "A Political Theory of American Corporate Finance." *Columbia Law Review* 91:10.

——. 1993. "Some Differences in Corporate Governance in Germany, Japan, and America." *Yale Law Journal* 102:1927.

Wallenstein, Leonard. 1928. *Some Legal Questions in Relation to Investment Trusts.*

Executive Compensation

18

An Overview of the Executive-Compensation Debate

Gregg A. Jarrell
University of Rochester

1. Introduction

In recent years, executive pay has come under increasingly heavy criticism from many quarters. Graef Crystal's 1991 book *In Search of Excess* did much to foster the recent popular outcry against high executive pay. Subsequent events have attracted first the media and then the politicians to this issue. These events include the January 1991 trip to Japan by President Bush and several top auto executives for the ostensible purpose of encouraging the Japanese to compete less effectively in the U.S. auto market. The high recent compensation of the U.S. CEOs was contrasted in the press to both the recession and layoffs in the auto industry and to the relatively low pay of their more successful Japanese CEO counterparts. Within months, several Congresspeople were proposing measures that would limit top executive pay using crude formulas apparently based on what they had learned in the press about Japanese CEO pay levels.

Also fueling the public outrage were several examples of astronomical pay during 1991 and 1992 as executives cashed-out stock options. The booming stock market contributed to several examples of lucrative stock-based CEO pay while at the same time the recession was restricting real earnings growth among working-class citizens. This contrast contributed to many media stories about the fundamental inequity of the entire system for setting executive pay and fostered the continuing criticism of the performance of managers and directors of public firms. This mounting criticism has resulted in significant pay disclosure reforms being passed by the Securities and Exchange Commission (SEC), numerous shareholder proxy challenges, and a campaign promise by President-elect Clinton to take more dramatic regulatory steps to discourage "excessive" executive pay, such as limiting corporate tax deductibility to executive compensation below one million dollars yearly.

My purpose here is to reflect on this widespread criticism and on the recently enacted and proposed reforms regarding executive pay in light of the academic literature on the topic. During the last decade, academic economists have developed a considerable literature on managerial pay and performance, both theoretical and empirical. Indeed, economists have long been among the leading critics of executive pay and of the effectiveness of directors in setting pay and monitoring executive performance. I wish to contrast the criticisms of these scholars to the more populist criticisms that are being reflected in policy. Although, for now, many academic critics are applauding recent policy reforms, I fear that there is a fundamental inconsistency between the politically motivated policy reforms, both implemented and proposed, and the policy implications of the scholarly research. Moreover, I specifically challenge the conclusion reached by some academic critics that this body of scholarly research implies that the current system of setting executive pay needs major reform.

I proceed by first outlining traditional practice in the U.S. for setting executive pay and then reviewing the positions of three different groups of commentators to the executive-pay debate. The first group is the political reformers—activists seeking to use the political process to reform the system of determining executive rewards. Next, I review some of the writings of the financial economists, and of the accounting economists, to lend some perspective on the political debate. I close with some concluding remarks about what I view as the central policy implications of these academic studies, and I contrast these implications with the assumptions underlying the policy reforms being pushed by the political activists.

2. The Traditional Practice for Paying Top Executives

Common practice in the U.S. is for top-executive compensation to be comprised of salary, bonus, and long-term incentives. Salary generally accounts for about 45–60 percent of total compensation, with the rest fairly evenly split between bonus and long-term incentives. Executive salary payments are predetermined contractually and do not appear to be directly tied to year-to-year company performance. So the pay-for-performance characteristics of executive pay plans typically depend on the specific features of the bonus and/or the long-term incentive plan.

The annual bonus is commonly based on accounting-earnings performance over the year, although other accounting measures may also be used as triggers. The most common formula is to make the bonus pool for top executives a fixed percentage of profits in excess of a specified return on capital. The exact definitions of earnings and return to capital vary somewhat across firms, but most plans do specify a lower bound on the return to capital and/or earnings. According to data from The Conference Board, the percentage of companies having annual bonus plans rose steadily from under 40 percent in 1960 to 99 percent in the late 1980s.

Long-term incentives (usually) specifically link payouts to the financial performance of the company through the use of stock options, stock appreciation rights, restricted stock, and/or phantom stock. According to The Conference Board survey, over 80 percent of company plans use stock options, and this has held roughly constant from 1960 to the late 1980s. Restricted stock and phantom stock plans have increased from 20 percent in 1980 to about 35 percent in the late 1980s. Long-term performance plans have increased in popularity, occurring in under 10 percent of plans in 1974 to nearly 40 percent by the late 1980s.

Long-term performance plans reward executives in cash or stock shares for attaining long-term, multiyear accounting goals, most generally growth in earnings-per-share over three to five years. A new performance period begins every fiscal year, so that any particular year is included in between three to five overlapping years.

Therefore, as a general rule, the pay of top executives outside of fixed salary appears to be heavily dependent on accounting measures of performance and less heavily dependent on stock-price performance. Murphy (1985) reports that annual bonus payouts account for over 25 percent of total executive compensation, while stock options account for only about 10 percent on average. This option component has probably increased somewhat in recent years. Moreover, the recent highly visible examples of huge yearly payouts are the result of the executive's choosing to exercise options that had become valuable as a result of stock-price increases from the time of grant.

According to a survey by the United Shareholders Association of the CEO compensation of the 1,000 largest U.S. public companies, the average salary and bonus for 1991 was $901,000. In addition, about 30 percent of these CEOs received salary and bonus payments for 1991 in excess of $1 million. These figures exclude payouts from stock options and other long-term incentive plans as well as any dividends or capital gains from owning stock in their company.

3. The Political Activists and Their Reform Agenda

The political activists include shareholder-rights organizations, institutional investors and their lobbying associations, some shareholder-value consultants, and certain politicians and regulators that desire to implement new policies that are intended to correct an assumed market failure in the labor market for CEOs. These various constituents apparently share the assumption that the board of directors, and other potential competitive forces for CEO discipline, generally fail to adequately bring to bear on top management of large public firms the rigorous reward-and-punishment system for corporate performance that would be consistent with a genuinely competitive marketplace. The usual argument is that shareholders are too diffuse and ill-informed to use the proxy machinery to adequately monitor top management and that the board is also successfully neutralized by most CEOs (who are usually also the chairman of the board).

The symptoms of this market failure allegedly include numerous incidents of egregiously large financial rewards to certain CEOs (recently through the exercise of long-term stock options), widespread and steady pay raises for CEOs even when corporate performance is poor (inadequate pay-for-performance linkage), infrequent dismissals of top management by the board (and then only for the most highly publicized and long-run failures of policy), and across-the-board excessive rewards in the form of financial rewards and perquisites for top management of large U.S. firms. Critics point out that CEO pay rose about 7 percent in 1991 even as corporate profits declined about 7 percent. They rail against the several examples every year of multimillion dollar payouts received as a result of exercising options, and they complain that the pay of U.S. top executives as a ratio of the pay of average workers is roughly double the ratio for top executives in Japan.

If these charges that the top management market is badly flawed are true, then the economic ramifications are indeed quite serious. Although the actual pay levels of top CEOs are but a trivial fraction of a typical large firm's total stockholder equity, a market failure also implies that the wrong executives have the decision rights over the allocation of a large fraction of the United States' corporate resources. The debate would seem to deserve the serious attention it has been receiving in the media, corporate boardrooms, and universities.

In response to pressure from political activists, the SEC recently enacted new disclosure rules governing executive compensation, and it liberalized certain proxy rules to provide institutional investors with more leverage over corporate policy through the use of the proxy machinery. The disclosure rules generally become effective in 1993 and mandate the use of tables, graphs, and reports to describe and rationalize executive compensation in place of the narrative description of plans. In addition, firms must present stock performance graphs—a line graph comparing the firm's stock returns over the last five years to the general market and to a relevant peer portfolio, according to the new disclosure and proxy rules.

The policy solution reveals how political activists and the SEC view the problem of executive compensation. They believe that the market failure can be alleviated, at least in part, by new disclosures of pay levels and of stock-price performance in combination with new proxy leverage for institutional shareholders. The theory is that the institutional shareholders, armed with the necessary data on pay and performance, can offer counter-balancing power to top management by using the proxy machinery to discipline and monitor the board of directors. The new regulations are clearly intended to harness the growing clout of institutional investors to effectively represent the interests of all shareholders and to prod the board of directors into performing better its function of monitoring and disciplining top management. The new disclosure rules also impose significant burdens on the use of stock options, which reflects the regulatory conclusion that options have been a special source of compensation abuse. The new rules mandate that the firm show the potential realizable value of options granted to executives. Ostensibly, the rules allow firms to avoid valuing options; instead they can simply show the end-of-term values based on assumed annual appreciation rates for the stock price of 5 percent and 10 percent, compounded annually. Since this end-value approach will involve disclosing some very large numbers, it is easy to predict that most firms will opt to use present value models, such as the SEC-approved Black-Scholes model, to place a value on the options it grants to its executives. It is also likely that the new rules will discourage the use of options and stock-appreciation rights, since the disclosure costs of substitute long-term incentive plans are much less. I also expect the new SEC rules will virtually eliminate the practice of repricing options, since to do so now triggers extremely burdensome disclosure requirements.

The political activists applaud the new SEC rules for encouraging greater institutional investor involvement and board oversight of executive compensation practices. In my view, the new SEC disclosure rules show more concern with the level of compensation than with promoting greater pay-for-performance linkage. I also think these reforms accurately reflect the criticism of the activists. Promoting greater pay-for-performance linkage is given lip service, but the source of the political appeal of the activist's message is the populist anger at high executive pay. Greater linkage is desired as long as it leads to reduced levels of executive compensation. After all, the SEC rules discourage the use of options, which have been the most effective and popular method of linking executive pay with stock-price performance over the last decade. Further, proposed reforms include President-elect Clinton's promise to discourage public firms from paying executives compensation in excess of $1 million. Indeed, many executives are following the lead of Walt Disney's Michael Eisner and Frank Wells, who last week exercised stock options worth about $187 million to protect shareholders from a possible large tax bill in the future. Clearly, regulations of this kind are not passed out of a concern for pay-for-performance linkage, but rather to satisfy the populist demand for equity.

4. The Financial Economists' Empirical Work

In 1984, the University of Rochester hosted a conference on executive pay to promote and disseminate scholarly research on what was then a subject treated with fascination by the media but neglect by academics. Murphy (1985, 1986) presented data based on 1,200 firms over a ten-year period showing that executive pay was positively correlated, and significantly so, to shareholder returns, over two five-year periods (1975–79 and 1980–84). Not only was salary and bonus strongly related to stock performance, but factoring in for 73 large companies the wealth changes stemming from executive stock holdings showed that total compensation was rather dramatically affected by shareholder returns. This research convinced Murphy that "Top Executives Are Worth Every Nickel They Get" (the title of his 1986 *Harvard Business Review* piece). At the same conference, Coughlan and Schmidt (1985) corroborated Murphy's results and further found that executive turnover was significantly higher during 1978–80 for firms that had relatively low stock returns. Taken together, the research presented at the Rochester Conference seemed to refute the popular-media critics, such as Loomis (1982), by showing that the cross-sectional pattern of executive reward and shareholder performance generally reflected an efficient labor market.

This early conclusion from the Rochester Conference research apparently was not widely accepted by financial economists. Indeed, this conclusion of an efficient labor market for top CEOs was somewhat inconsistent with the blizzard of research being produced by financial economists during 1983-90 on mergers and takeovers. The main message of the takeover studies was that most of the booming M&A activity resulted from an inefficient top-management labor market. This market suffered from large agency costs that separated the survival interests of incumbent CEOs from the maximize-stock-price interests of outside shareholders. Specifically, this literature attributed much of the conglomerate merger activity and value-decreasing friendly combinations, the resistance by target incumbents to hostile takeovers at a premium, and the huge gaps in value between stock prices and takeover prices to the existence of significant agency costs and an inefficient labor market for top executives. This M&A research, which dominated the activity of financial-economic scholars during this time, was at odds with the conclusion of the fledgling executive-pay literature that the executive labor market exhibited strong signs of economic efficiency and insignificant agency costs.

This tension between the two literatures of financial economists was completely eliminated, however, with the publication of Jensen and Murphy (1990a and 1990b). Using data, methodology, and results that are remarkably similar to those of Murphy (1985, 1986), the conclusion was essentially reversed. The Jensen and Murphy research also found that pay and turnover rates are significantly linked to shareholder returns, but they focuses attention on a new measurement that was absent from the earlier work. Jensen and Murphy measured the dollar change in CEO compensation for every $1,000 change in total shareholder wealth. The average result over a large sample of CEOs and a long time period was that total executive compensation increases about $3.00 for every $1,000 increase in shareholder wealth. Although this result is perfectly consistent with the earlier findings of a positive relation between *percentage* stock returns and CEO pay, computing this relation as the change in dollar compensation to the change in total dollar shareholder wealth apparently convinced Jensen and Murphy that the typical executive's stake in changing shareholder wealth is insufficient to align the financial interests of top management with shareholders.

They reach the same "cup is now half empty" conclusion regarding executive turnover rates. Although they corroborate earlier work that turnover is higher (the lower the shareholder returns) they assert that the actual odds (the absolute level) of being dismissed are so low that the market for top executives must be extremely inefficient and uncompetitive. They speculate that this failure of the CEO labor market is a long-term result of the interaction of mandated disclosure of executive pay and misapplied egalitarian principles by the press and political forces.

> By aiming their protests at compensation levels, uninvited but influential guests at the managerial bargaining table (the business press, labor unions, political figures) intimidate board members and constrain the types of contracts that are

> written between managers and shareholders. As a result of public pressure, directors become reluctant to reward CEOs with substantial (and therefore highly visible) financial gains for superior performance. Naturally, they also become reluctant to impose meaningful financial penalties for poor performance. The long-term effect of this risk-averse orientation is to erode the relation between pay and performance and entrench bureaucratic compensation systems. (Jensen and Murphy 1990b, 139).

Thus, financial economists such as Jensen and Murphy agree with the political reformers' general assessment that the executive-compensation system is badly flawed. They also agree that the inadequate empirical link between executive reward and stock performance is the main evidence that the CEO labor market is uncompetitive. But, Jensen and Murphy part company with the political reformers regarding the fundamental cause of the problem and its solution. The implication of the Jensen and Murphy theory is that correcting the problem involves huge potential payoffs to CEOs for improved stock performance. Providing a meaningful stake in future shareholder wealth gains to CEOs using new "super-linkage" compensation contracts would spur CEOs to create shareholder value, which in turn would trigger large financial rewards to CEOs. This solution is, of course, quite at odds with the policy goals of the political reformers, who believe that reform should lower CEO pay generally.

5. The Accounting Economists' Empirical Work

The accounting economics literature generally follows the positive methodology espoused by Watts and Zimmerman (1986). The basic thesis is that accounting methods evolve to provide cost-effective measures of managerial performance, absent regulation, or tax effects. By this view, accounting earnings has evolved and survived as the nearly universal measure of firm performance because it is a cost-effective, efficient measure of managerial performance. As such, it can hardly be a criticism of modern CEO compensation contracts that they rely heavily on accounting earnings to judge managerial performance.

The empirical literature on the association between accounting earnings and stock returns is well developed and methodologically sophisticated (*See* Ball, Kothari, and Watts 1990 for a current example). This literature specifically defends the traditional practice of basing executive rewards such as yearly bonuses and many long-term incentive plans on accounting earnings. Sloan (1991) presents evidence in favor of the widely held view that using earnings shields executive compensation from marketwide fluctuations in equity values. Moreover, he reviews some possible reasons why options indexed to measure only net of market (or industry) stock returns are not rationally used as substitutes for accounting earnings. These reasons include institutional costs, such as tax losses, disadvantageous reporting requirements, and adverse-incentive costs (see Dye 1988, and Gibbons and Murphy 1990 for examples).

The accounting studies are often cited by critics of executive-compensation practices as showing that accounting earnings are only marginally related to stock returns on a year-to-year basis. These critics consider pay plans that rely on earnings-based incentive features, therefore, to automatically fail to meet their pay-for-stock-performance standards. In a recent working paper, however, Jarrell and Dorkey (1992) show that, after grouping the data into five-year averages, accounting earnings and stock returns are very significantly correlated. In fact, for a sample of 576 large firms covering 1963 to 1990 the accounting-based performance measures, such as earnings per share before extraordinary items, have a higher positive correlation with stock returns than does the value-weighted market index.

Also, consistent with the work of Sloan and others, Jarrell and Dorkey (1992) find that the accounting returns are not strongly related to the market index, using five-year averages. This evidence that longer-term accounting measures are not influenced much by macroeconomic "noise", but are highly correlated with the net-of-market component of individual firm stock returns provides support for the widespread use of accounting measures in incentive-pay contracts. This kind of evidence also explains why Murphy (1985) and others consistently find that actual yearly executive compensation (whether just salary and bonus or including stock compensation) is positively and significantly correlated with yearly stock returns. Although most yearly incentive pay is literally linked to accounting earnings and not stock returns, there is a strong enough correlation between net-of-market stock returns and accounting earnings that, in the final analysis, executive pay turns out to be significantly related to stock returns.

6. Conclusion

Academic research on executive pay has consistently shown that both pay and turnover rates are positively related to stock returns. In large samples, these positive correlations between pay and performance are statistically significant according to the usual standards. Accounting research has consistently shown that accounting earnings and stock returns, too, are positively related and are statistically significant. Recent research shows that for five-year averages, firm stock returns are more highly correlated with earnings-per-share than to the returns to the value-weighted market portfolio. Moreover, earnings are not influenced greatly by macroeconomic "noise", as are firm stock returns. Consistent with this evidence, traditional pay practice is to base most bonus payments on accounting performance and secondarily to utilize stock-price options to link long-term stock returns with executive pay. The empirical findings of the academic research would appear on the surface to lend significant support to the view that common practice for rewarding top executives is consistent for both competitive markets and the basic principle of pay-for-performance.

Yet there is much criticism about examples of allegedly excessive executive pay and widespread concern that the market for selecting and rewarding top executives is uncompetitive and inefficient. Recent SEC disclosure reforms on executive pay, increased regulatory burdens placed on the granting on new options to executives, and promises of new tax penalties on above–million-dollar executive pay packages testify to the political weight behind these criticisms.

Why is this evidence pointing to the competitiveness of the CEO labor market not reflected in the policy debate? The main reason may be that the academics themselves ignore it, or at least contribute to its misinterpretation. The financial economists in particular complain that the degree of pay-for-performance linkage revealed in the historical data is insufficient. This normative charge is made in good faith, even though it is not analytically rigorous. After all, noting that executives receive only a small (but significantly positive) fraction of changes in total shareholder wealth is not sufficient grounds to conclude that top executives are not paid in relation to their marginal product. Total shareholder wealth is influenced by the productivity of CEOs, but rarely is it accurate to equate the two. Common practice in the U.S. and elsewhere is to rely on accounting earnings directly to set incentive pay, but to supplement this with stock options. This would seem to be perfectly consistent with setting pay that reflects the measurable, controllable marginal productivity of CEOs.

Academic critics of executive pay might be correct when they claim that the market operates uncompetitively, but the empirical record reviewed here does not persuasively support that claim. In fact, I think that the academic record more persuasively indicates important signs that the market operates with reasonable efficiency overall. More important, the academic complaints about the inefficiency of the CEO labor market has unintentionally contributed to the recently enacted and proposed policy reforms. This is unfortunate, because the policy implications of the academic criticism is the exact opposite of the actual policy reforms. The academic critics are actually calling for greater pay-for-performance linkage and much higher executive pay. In contrast, the actual policies being followed are attempting to cap CEO pay and will contribute over time to a reduced pay-for-performance linkage.

References and Suggested Readings

Adams, H. 1987. "Factors Affecting the Use of Performance Variables in Executive Compensation Contracts." Working paper, Northwestern University. Evanston, IL.

Agrawal, A., A. K. Makhija, and G. N. Mandelker. 1991. "Executive Compensation and Corporate Performance in Electric and Gas Utilities: Some Empirical Evidence." Working paper, University of Pittsburgh.

Baker, George P., Michael C. Jensen, and Kevin J. Murphy. 1988. "Compensation and Incentives: Practice vs. Theory." *The Journal of Finance* 435 No. 3: 593–616.

Benston, George J. 1985. "The Self-Serving Management Hypothesis: Some Evidence." *Journal of Accounting and Economics*:67.

Bernard, V. 1989. "Capital Markets Research in Accounting During the 1980's: A Critical Review." In *The State of Accounting Research as We Enter the 1990's*, T. Frecka, ed. Urbana-Champaign, Illinois: University of Illinois: 72-120.

Brickley, James, S. Bhagat, and R. C. Lease. 1985. "The Impact of Long-Range Managerial Compensation Plans on Shareholder Wealth." *Journal of Accounting and Economics*:113.

Byrne, J. A., D. Foust, and T. Therrien. 1992. "Executive Pay." *Business Week*, Mar. 30.

Crystal, Graef S. 1991. "Executive Compensation in Corporate American 1992." *Executive Compensation 1000*:3–31.

Comment, R., and G. A. Jarrell. 1991. "Corporate Focus and Stock Returns." Working paper, University of Rochester.

Coughlan, Anne T., and R. M. Schmidt. 1985. "Executive Compensation, Management Turnover, and Firm Performance: An Empirical Investigation." *Journal of Accounting and Economics*:43.

Dechow, P., and R. Sloan. 1991. "Executive Incentives and the Horizon Problem: An Empirical Investigation." *Journal of Accounting and Economics* 14:51–89.

Gibbons, R., and K. Murphy. 1990. "Relative Performance Evaluation for Chief Executive Officers." *Industrial and Labor Relations Review* 43:30–51.

Grinblatt, M., and S. Titman. 1989. "Adverse Risk Incentives and the Design of Performance-Based Contracts." *Management Science* 35:807–22.

Jarrell, Gregg A., and Frank C. Dorkey. 1992. "The Longer-Term Relation Between Accounting Performance and Stock Returns." Working paper, University of Rochester.

Jensen, Michael C., and Kevin J. Murphy. 1990a. "CEO Incentives - It's Not How Much You Pay, But How." *Harvard Business Review* (May–June): 138–153.

——. 1990b. "Performance Pay and Top-Management Incentives." *Journal of Political Economy* 98, no. 2: 225–64.

Lambert, R., and D. Larcker. 1987. "An Analysis of the Use of Accounting and Market Measures of Performance in Executive Compensation Contracts." *Journal of Accounting Research* 25:85–129.

Loomis, Carol. 1982. "The Madness of Executive Compensation." *Fortune*:42.

McCartney, R. J. 1992. "Executives Quietly Defend Top-Dollar Pay Packages." *The Washington Post,* (Feb. 21).

Murphy, K. 1985. "Corporate Performance and Managerial Remuneration: An Empirical Analysis." *Journal of Accounting and Economics* 7:11–42.

Murphy, Kevin J. 1986. "Top Executives Are Worth Every Nickel They Get." *Harvard Business Review* (Mar.–Apr.): 125–32.

O'Byrne, S. 1990. "Shareholder Return and Management Performance." *Compensation and Benefits Review* (Jan.):30–37.

Rappaport, A. 1986. *Creating Shareholder Value.* New York, New York:The Free Press.

Sloan, R. J. 1991. "Accounting Earnings and Top Executive Compensation." Ph.D. Diss., University of Rochester.

"The Wall Street Journal Reports: Executive Pay." 1990. *The Wall Street Journal,* Apr. 18.

Watts, Ross L. 1992. "Accounting for Executive Compensation." Working paper, University of Rochester.

Watts, R. L., and J. L. Zimmerman. 1986. *Positive Accounting Theory.* Englewood Cliffs, N. J.:Prentice Hall.

Corporate Takeovers

19

SEC Neglect and the Extinction of the Hostile Takeover

Michael Bradley
University of Michigan

For all intents and purposes, the hostile takeover is a thing of the past, an antiquated transaction of a bygone era. The transaction that shook corporate America to its very core and epitomized Wall Street in the eighties has become extinct. How did this happen? Why did this happen? Was its extinction the result of reasoned debate and extensive deliberations? Was eliminating hostile takeovers deemed to serve the public interest? Were congressional hearings held and expert testimony given? Did the SEC decide that the Williams Act was insufficient protection for corporate stockholders? Were the manifest horrors of corporate takeovers so great and so dastardly that public outcry demanded that the transaction be driven out of existence? Unfortunately, the answer to all of these questions is no. Rather, the extinction of the hostile takeover is the result of parochial state laws, pro-management state bars, and, most important, the neglect of the SEC.[1]

The hostile takeover bid (a.k.a. interfirm tender offer) was virtually unheard of before the mid-sixties. Prior to this time, most corporate control disputes were handled through proxy contests. Dodd (1980) attributes the advent of the tender offer to a tightening of the rules governing proxies. Bradley and Kim (1984) argue that the rise in the popularity of the tender offer corresponds to the increased importance of institutional investors. Whatever the reason, by the late sixties the tender offer had usurped the proxy as the preferred mechanism for removing corporate managers.

---

[1] For a firsthand account of the SEC's involvement in the regulation of takeovers, *see* Jarrell (1992). Jarrell was the Chief Economist at the SEC during much of the time covered by this note.

The advantage of the cash tender offer is that it transfers the risk of a takeover from the stockholders of the target firm to the managers (stockholders) of the acquiring firm, the party to the transactions that has the specialized resource required to improve the allocation of the target firm. Instead of having to convince the stockholders of the target firm that they could run the firm better through a proxy contest, rival management teams can offer the stockholders cash for their shares and remove the target management directly. Target stockholders are cashed out and therefore have no stake in the ability of an acquiring firm to run the target firm more profitably. That risk lies with the managers and stockholders of the acquiring firm.

With the sharp rise of tender offer activity in the mid-60s, came the horror stories of "Saturday Night Specials"—deals made on Friday afternoon and closed on the following Monday—that allegedly stampeded target stockholders into tendering their shares for fear that they would be left holding the shares of an empty corporate shell. Offers were frequently made on a first-come, first-served basis. Bidders were not required to identify themselves or their intentions should they obtain control of the firm.

In the mid-sixties there were no securities laws governing interfirm cash tender offers. The SEC was involved in mergers and exchange offers, since these transactions usually required the issuance of new securities. But since the cash tender offer is a secondary market transaction, made between consenting traders, it fell outside of the legislative mandate of the SEC.

To fill this perceived regulatory void, Congress, in July 1967, passed the Williams Act, which brought the cash tender offer within the purview of the SEC.[2] The major features of the act were to impose disclosure and delay requirements on bidding firms. Offers had to remain open for a minimum amount of time and bidders had to disclose their intentions in seeking shares of a target firm. In addition, oversubscribed offers had to be effected on a pro-rata basis; target stockholders were given withdrawal privileges; and bidders that raised their offer price were required to pay the higher price to all stockholders, even those who had tendered at a lower price.

There has been vigorous debate as to whether the Williams Act evened the playing field between the managers of the target and bidding firms or tipped the balance of power too much in favor of incumbent target managers. In either event the empirical evidence suggests that the stockholders of target firms have done better and those of acquiring firms

---

[2] For a discussion of the regulations and economic effects of the Williams Act *see* Jarrell and Bradley (1982).

worse since the passage of the Williams Act. By mandating a waiting period, target managers are given time to seek other bidders or formulate defensive tactics. As a result, premiums have soared since the enactment of the act; so much so that many acquiring firms in the post-act period paid too much for their targets and suffered a significant decrease in market value.

In the late sixties states began passing anti-takeover legislation. In general the state statutes were more draconian than the provisions of the Williams Act. Most required extended waiting periods and pre-offer notification. Some even required a merit review by a legislative committee.

The encroachment of state governments into the market for corporate control came to an abrupt halt in 1988 when the Supreme Court struck down the Illinois anti-takeover statute in *Edgar v. Mite*. The court ruled the law unconstitutional on the grounds of both the Commerce Clause and the Supremacy Clause.

Having been rebuffed at the state-house door, an unlikely alliance of corporate managers, social reformers, and Wall Street lawyers began to formulate market-oriented anti-takeover defenses. Golden parachutes, Pac-man, greenmail and other exotic tactics were developed. By far the most effective defensive tactic devised was the poison pill. As its name implies it became, and remains today, the most effective defense against a hostile bidder.

While there are several versions of the poison pill, all work in basically the same way. The pill is a convertible security that becomes a liability of any firm that succeeds in obtaining control of the issuing firm. The fact of the matter is that nobody really knows exactly what would happen if a firm went ahead and "swallowed a pill." Aside from a single case that has since faded into obscurity, there is no account of a firm taking control of a target with a poison pill still intact.

No doubt much of the potency of the pill derives from the shroud of uncertainty that surrounds it. In many acquisitions, the assets of the target firm serve as collateral on the funds borrowed to finance the transaction. If provisions in the pill prevent a successful bidding firm from redeploying the assets of a target, then this collateral is at risk and discourages (precludes) investors from financing the deal. Most tender offers are made on the condition that the target management rescind all poison pills. For this reason, bidders often couple tender offers with a proxy campaign to rescind the firm's poison pill.

The test case for the poison pill was *Moran v. Household International, Inc.* The board of Household International had installed a poison pill and was sued by a board member and derivatively by a Household stockholder for a breach of fiduciary duty by precluding a hostile takeover. The SEC filed an amicus brief on behalf of the plaintiffs but elected not to get involved directly. This was a serious error on the part of the SEC. Some have expressed an opinion that the government could have prevailed on the theory that the poison pill is nothing more than a sham security that serves no purpose but to protect and entrench corporate managers. With no serious opposition from the SEC, the Supreme Court of Delaware held that the adoption of a poison pill was not a breach of fiduciary duty.

While the poison pill reigned supreme as the most effective defensive tactic, a series of court rulings began to lessen its effectiveness. Indeed, the seeds of judicial controls of the poison pill were sewn in the *Household* opinion itself. While the Court ruled that the enactment of a poison pill was protected by the business judgment rule, it went on to state that corporate managers who adopt poison pills would be held to a higher standard (the duty of loyalty) in responding to an actual takeover bid. In dicta, the court stated that if Household were to be the target of a takeover bid and refused to rescind the poison pill, the Court would be willing to review the behavior of the firm's management in light of the higher duty of loyalty standard.

Subsequent litigation in the Delaware courts produced a tripartite standard in evaluating the use of defensive tactics in general and the poison pill in particular. First, the defensive tactic had to be designed to combat a real threat (*Household*). Second, the response had to be proportional to the threat posed (*Unocal Corp. v. Mesa Petroleum*). And finally, in what became known as the Revlon Standard, courts would force managers to rescind all defensive tactics if the managers had conceded that the firm was indeed up for sale (*Revlon v. MacAndrews & Forbes Holdings, Inc.*). Once managers made this concession or took actions that indicated that they had, the managers were forced to rescind their defensive tactics and become efficient auctioneers for the firm's shares. In a series of related opinions, the Delaware court began viewing the poison pill defense as an acceptable means of initiating an auction. However, once an auction had ensued, the court began exerting pressure on the target board to rescind the defensive tactic.

While the Delaware courts had reached some consensus regarding defensive tactics, other jurisdictions continued to wrestle with the issue. In Indiana, a series of decisions regarding the use of poison pills would prove to be the beginning of the end for the hostile takeover. The litigation was an outgrowth of an attempt by Dynamics Corporation of America (DCA) to acquire control of CTS Corporation. In April of 1986, the Seventh Circuit Court of Appeals affirmed a lower court ruling that forced CTS to rescind a poison pill that stood in the way of a tender offer made by DCA for 28 percent of the firm's outstanding shares. After the offer had been completed, CTS instituted a second poison pill that had the effect of precluding DCA from buying any additional shares of CTS. DCA filed suit to have the second pill rescinded as well.

In the second round, CTS found a more sympathetic lower court that ruled that the second poison pill was protected by the business judgment rule. DCA appealed to the Seventh Circuit Court of Appeals. Writing for the majority, Judge Posner remanded the case back to the lower court (*Dynamics Corporation of America v. CTS Corporation*). He argued in part that the lower court had erred in dismissing the request for a temporary restraining order against the CTS pill on the basis of business judgment. In dicta, Judge Posner stated that while the adoption of a poison pill was protected by the business judgment rule, the management's use of the pill, *once an offer had been made*, should be evaluated in light of the stricter duty of loyalty standard. While not ruling on the issue per se, Judge Posner made it clear that, from his perspective, the managers of CTS, in this instance, would not survive such a test. Since the plaintiff was not permitted to pursue a duty of loyalty cause of action, no evidence regarding the management's behavior in this regard was submitted at trial. Consequently, Judge Posner deemed the record to be stale and incomplete and remanded the case to the lower court. While not ruling on the merits of the case, Judge Posner left no doubt whatsoever that as far as he (and presumably the rest of the Seventh Circuit) was concerned, poison pills in general, and the version adopted by CTS in particular, were a prima facia breach of the fiduciary duty of loyalty. He clearly stated that he thought that their adoption reduced shareholder wealth and entrenched (inefficient) corporate managers.

This was perhaps the low point for advocates of takeover defenses. It is no coincidence that 1986 was the high water mark for corporate takeovers.

Perhaps anticipating the Seventh Circuit's attitude toward poison pills and other defensive tactics, CTS mounted a legislative front as well. At the behest of CTS, on March 4, six days before the first DCA tender offer, the Indiana State legislature passed what was to become known as the first Control Shares Acquisitions Act. Primarily, the act restricted the rights of so-called controlling stockholders to reallocate the assets of the firm unless certain conditions were met. The most notable was the acquiescence of the target managers.

DCA challenged the constitutionality of the Indiana statute. No doubt still smarting from the reprimand from the Seventh Circuit, the lower court sided with DCA and ruled that the law was unconstitutional for many of the same reasons cited in *Edgar v. Mite*. CTS appealed the decision to the Seventh Circuit, which predictably affirmed the lower court ruling. But in a shocking turn of events the U.S. Supreme Court ruled the statute to be constitutional (*CTS*). The court conceded that the statute would deter takeover bids for Indiana corporations, but ruled that such regulations were the purview of the states and not preempted by federal law.

It is remarkable that the SEC did not play an important role in this series of litigation. Indeed, why did it not play the central role? Of course the Commission filed amicus briefs. But where were the public hearings? Where was the public outcry? Where were the champions of competitive markets and shareholder rights? They were nowhere to be found.

The role of the Seventh Circuit Court of Appeals and the history of defensive tactics did not end with *CTS*. Ironically, it was this court, this defender of stockholder wealth, that finally put the last nail in the coffin of the hostile takeover.

In the wake of the Supreme Court ruling, other states began to enact anti-takeover statutes. It became easier and less costly for corporate managers to enlist the support of a state legislature than to pay the exorbitant fees charged by Wall Street lawyers and investment bankers. Perhaps the most creative was the bill passed in Washington state. The bill is so crafted that it pertains to only one company - Boeing. The legislation was drafted and enacted in the four days following a request by Boone Pickens to the Department of Transportation to buy a 20 percent stake in the firm. One of the most draconian laws was the Wisconsin statute, which simply stated that target managers can just say no to any takeover bid. Managers were not required to respond in any way to a takeover proposal. The law did not prevent the purchase of a controlling block of a target's outstanding shares. However, these so-called Merger Moratorium or Business Combination Statutes did prevent the controlling entity from altering, in any way, the configuration of the target assets for five years. Of course, the conditions of the statute are waived if the target managers give prior approval to the acquisition.

Amanda Acquisitions Corp. v. Universal Foods became an early test case for the new, third-generation Merger Moratorium Statutes. Having survived constitutional hurdles in the lower court, the case was appealed to the Seventh Circuit. In an act reminiscent of Lee's surrender at Appomattox, Judge Easterbrook, writing for the majority, ruled the statute constitutional. No doubt smarting from the reversal of its decision in *CTS*, the court was not going to be second-guessed again. In a masterful stroke of disdain and resignation, Judge Easterbrook opined that while the statute may be economic folly it was not unconstitutional.

Again, where was the SEC? Why was the defense of the tender offer left to the Seventh Circuit?

Back in Delaware, the courts began to assume the attitude of the Seventh Circuit regarding the use of poison pills. Recall that in *Household*, the court stated that it would treat differently the adoption of a poison pill and the use of a poison pill once an offer had been made. In a series of rulings, the Delaware courts began to pressure target management to rescind a poison pill in the face of a valid, fully financed, cash offer, and certainly if there was an open auction for the firm's shares.[3]

In a blatant move to soothe the nerves of the managers of Delaware corporations, the Delaware bar urged the state legislature to pass a Business Combination Statute of its own. There was a genuine fear that unless the legislature acted, firms would move out of Delaware and reincorporate in states with Merger Moratorium Statutes. The Delaware legislation, coupled with subsequent acceptance by the Delaware courts of the statute and the "just-say-no" defense (*Paramount Communications, Inc. v. Time Incorporated*), virtually eliminated the hostile takeover. The Delaware statute was ruled constitutional in *BNS, Inc. v Koppers Co.* Subsequent state legislation and court rulings have driven hostile bidders from the market. States rights protectionism has given corporate managers veto power over all takeover bids. This is an unhealthy situation.

While horror stories abound, there is no systematic evidence that hostile takeovers destroyed corporate wealth. To the contrary, there is almost universal agreement that the takeovers of the eighties created significant corporate wealth.[4] Michael Jensen (1991) estimates that over the 14-year period 1976–1990, the $1.8 trillion of corporate control transactions—that is, mergers, tender offers, divestitures, and LBOs—created over $650 billion in value for selling-firm stockholders. And this estimate includes neither the gains to the buyers in such transactions nor the value from more efficient management as a result of the discipline exerted by the threat of an outside takeover.

---

[3] *See*, for example, *Staley, Interco, Grand Met.*

[4] For a description of the rationale behind and empirical effects of interfirm tender offers, *see* Bradley, Desai, and Kim (1983, 1988).

The SEC must reassert itself into the regulation of corporate control transactions. The SEC should seek whatever authority is required to nullify state statutes.

The U.S. has a tradition of regulating security markets on a national level. Indeed, the SEC is a manifestation of this attitude. It is time to recognize that the market for corporate control is a national market, if not an international market. For all the reasons we do not allow states to interfere with interstate commerce, we should not let them interfere with transactions in the market for corporate control. The SEC should declare that poison pills and like securities are sham securities and serve no purpose except to interfere or preclude control transactions. The Williams Amendment with its disclosure and delay and pro-ration requirements should be the law of the land regarding corporate takeovers. Such a regime would allow for the free flow of corporate assets, while protecting shareholder interests and the integrity of the process.

Some commentators have given up on the hostile takeover as a useful monitoring device. For example, John Pound (1992) argues that we have entered into a new era of corporate democracy, in which active institutional investors use the proxy machinery to monitor the behavior of corporate managers. He argues convincingly that the takeover is too blunt an instrument to do the fine tuning that is often required in directing corporate management. I agree. But sometimes a blunt instrument is just what is needed.

The threat of a hostile takeover is an important check on the behavior of corporate managers. A well-functioning national market for corporate control is critical for the optimal allocation of corporate resources. If we are to have a free, competitive corporate economy, corporate managers must be exposed to the discipline of external competition. Hostile takeovers are important safeguards of our competitive economy, and for the SEC to allow the extinction of this most important control transaction through regulatory neglect is irresponsible and inconsistent with its congressional charge.

References and Suggested Readings

Bradley, Michael, Anand Desai, and E. Han Kim. 1982. "The Rationale Behind Interfirm Tender Offers." *Journal of Financial Economics* 11.

——. 1988. "Synergistic Gains from Corporate Acquisitions and Their Division Between the Stockholders of Target and Acquiring Firms." *Journal of Financial Economics* 21:20.

Bradley, Michael, and E. Han Kim. 1984. "The Tender Offer as a Takeover Device: Its Evolution, The Free Rider Problem, and the Prisoners' Dilemma." CRSP Proceedings 29, University of Chicago.

Dodd, Peter. 1980. "Merger Proposals, Management Discretion and Stockholder Wealth." *Journal of Financial Economics* 8.

Jarrell, Gregg. 1992. "The 1980s Takeover Boom and Government Regulation." *Regulation*. Summer.

Jarrell, Gregg, and Michael Bradley. 1980. "The Economic Effects of State and Federal Regulations of Cash Tender Offers." *The Journal of Law and Economics* 23.

Jensen, Michael. 1991. "Corporate Control and the Politics of Finance." *Journal of Applied Corporate Finance* 4, no. 2.

Cases

Amanda Acquisitions Corp. v. Universal Foods. 1989. U.S. Ct. Apls. 7 Circuit.

BNS, Inc. v. Koppers Co. 1988. 458 (D. Del.).

City Capital Associates v. Interco Inc. 1988. 551 A.2d 787 (Del. S. Ct.).

CTS Corporation v. Dynamics Corporation of America. 1987. 107 S. Ct. 1637.

Dynamics Corporation of America v. CTS Corporation. 1986. No. 86-1888 (U.S. Ct. Apls. 7 Circuit).

Edgar v. Mite Corp. 1982. 457 S. Ct. 624.

Grand Metropolitan PLC v. Pillsbury Company. 1988. 104 (Del.Ch.).

Moran v. Household International, Inc. 1985. 500 A.2d 1346 (Del. S. Ct.).

Paramount Communications Inc. v. Time Incorporated. 1989. A.2 (Del. Ch.).

Revlon v. MacAndrews & Forbes Holdings, Inc. 1986. 506 A.2d 173.

Tate & Lyle PLC v. Staley Continental, Inc. 1988. 9813 (Del. Ch. May 9).

Unocal Corp. v. Mesa Petroleum. 1985. 493 A.2d 946 (Del. S. Ct.).

20

Regulation of Going Private Transactions

Jeffry Davis and Kenneth Lehn[1]
Securities and Exchange Commission
and University of Pittsburgh

1. Introduction

Going-private transactions, as discussed in this chapter, are corporate control transactions that convert free-standing, publicly traded companies into private entities. Frequently, the acquiring entity in these transactions is a shell company that is wholly owned by members of the incumbent management team. We refer to these transactions as management buyouts (MBOs). Alternatively, the acquiring company may be a separate, privately held operating company or investment firm. We refer to these transactions as third-party buyouts.

There is much disagreement over the desirability of going-private transactions. Some argue that these transactions promote efficiency by strengthening the incentives of managers to maximize firm value. They point to the large premiums paid to shareholders in going private transactions as evidence that these transactions are desirable. Others argue that MBOs "cheat" shareholders of an increase in value that the managers expect to achieve. According to this argument, managers propose these transactions because they have inside information about the prospects of their firms. Since management has a fiduciary duty to maximize shareholder value,

---

[1] The Securities and Exchange Commission, as a matter of policy, disclaims any responsibility for any private publication or statements by any of its employees. The views expressed herein are those of the authors and do not necessarily reflect the views of the Commission or of Mr. Davis' colleagues on the staff of the Commission.

This chapter is adapted from and refers extensively to an earlier paper by the same authors (Davis and Lehn, "Information Asymmetries, Rule 13e-3, and Premiums in Going-Private Transactions," 70 *Washington University Law Quarterly* 587 (1992). Hereafter this paper is cited as Davis-Lehn.

MBOs that profit management necessarily constitute breaches of that duty, according to the critics.[2]

2. Rule 13e-3

The only federal regulation designed to mitigate potential conflicts of interest in MBOs is Rule 13e-3, which was adopted by the Securities and Exchange Commission (SEC) in 1979.[3] Rule 13e-3 attempts to mitigate these conflicts by requiring managers to disclose more information in MBOs than third-party bidders are required to disclose in other corporate-control transactions. In particular, Items 7, 8, and 9 of Rule 13e-3 require disclosure in MBOs that surpasses that required of third-party bidders.

These items require that management disclose detailed information on the structure of the transaction, other structures that were considered, the purpose and effects of the transaction, the managers' opinion concerning the fairness of the transaction, the basis of this opinion, a discussion of the fairness of the transaction relative to an assortment of accounting and stock-price data, and a discussion of any reports, opinions, and appraisals that the managers relied upon in determining their offer price. This augmented disclosure purportedly benefits shareholders in three ways: (1) by stregthening the shareholders' bargaining position vis a vis management; (2) by increasing the likelihood of competing bids, and (3) by enhancing the threat of shareholder litigation in the event of a "low" offer price.

Existing regulations presume that when an acquiring firm is not affiliated with the corresponding target firm or its management, shareholders can rely on the managers' judgment concerning the fairness of the proposed transaction. However, the managers' judgment becomes suspect when the managers themselves are making the offer. Rule 13e-3 seeks to remedy this situation by requiring management to treat an affiliated bid in the same fashion as a third-party bid, at least in terms of performing the same kind of analysis of the bid as would be carried out for a third-party bid and disclosing the findings of the analysis to shareholders. Given this objective,

---

[2] Scholarly articles that discuss the potential conflicts of interest in MBOs include Brudney, "A Note on `Going Private,'" 61 *Virginia Law Review* 1019 (1975); Solomon, "Going Private: Business Practices, Legal Mechanics, Judicial Standards and Proposals for Reform," 25 *Buffalo Law Review* 141 (1975); Greene, "Corporate Freezeout Mergers: A Proposed Analysis," 28 *Stanford Law Review* 487 (1976); and Brudney and Chirelstein, "A Restatement of Corporate Freezeouts," 87 *Yale Law Journal* 1354 (1978).

[3] Securities Act Release No. 6100 (August 2, 1979).

it is not surprising that the key elements of Rule 13e-3 are required disclosures concerning the pros and cons of the proposed transaction and its fairness to shareholders.

Many large leveraged buyouts (LBOs) during the 1980s were structured as third party buyouts in which equity was distributed to the target firms' managers after the deal was completed. For example, many Kohlberg Kravis Roberts'(KKR) transactions, including RJR Nabisco, were structured this way. Since the acquiring entity in these transactions was unaffiliated with the target, no Rule 13e-3 filing was made. Yet, some argue, a management conflict exists in these transactions, since the managers are equity owners in the company after the deal is completed.

Following the RJR Nabisco transaction in 1988, Congress requested that the SEC study a variety of issues related to LBOs, including the adequacy and breadth of Rule 13e-3 disclosure. In 1989, then-SEC Chairman David Ruder indicated that the Commission would consider an extension of Rule 13e-3 to "suspect" third party buyouts of the sort described above.[4] Shortly after this, the LBO market subsided greatly, and congressional (and SEC) interest in this topic waned. When and if the LBO market rebounds, the issue of Rule 13e-3 disclosure is likely to resurface.

3. Empirical Issues

The controversy over Rule 13e-3 involves three empirical issues, which are addressed in this paper:

(1) Are shareholders systematically cheated of value in MBOs?

(2) Does the additional disclosure required by Rule 13e-3 actually mitigate management conflicts of interest in MBOs?

(3) Are shareholders systematically cheated of value in the "suspect," KKR-style transactions?

Regarding the first issue, it seems logical that management faces an inherent conflict in MBOs since managers are serving as both fiduciaries for stockholders (i.e., they are obligated to sell the company for the highest price) and principals of the acquirer (which wants to acquire the company at

---

[4] *See* "SEC May Propose Expanding Scope of Going Private Disclosure Rules," *Securities Regulation & Law Report*, Jan. 1, 1989, 7–9.

the lowest price). However, in the absence of regulation, managers are constrained in their ability to buy their respective companies at cheap prices. The threat of competing bids dampens the managers' ability to redistribute wealth from their shareholders to themselves. In addition, managers are constrained by state law, which provides shareholders with appraisal remedies and private rights of action to challenge violations of managers' fiduciary duties in MBOs. The effectiveness of these forces, and hence the severity of the management conflicts in MBOs, is largely an empirical issue.

Even if management conflicts are empirically significant in MBOs, the effectiveness of Rule 13e-3 in mitigating this conflict is debatable. It can be argued that the information disclosed in Schedule 13e-3 is not particularly valuable to investors, either because it involves boilerplate language, or it already is impounded in stock prices. If the disclosed information is not material in an economic sense, then it will not benefit target shareholders, and shareholders may even bear part of the cost of the rule in the form of lower premiums. Hence, the effectiveness of Rule 13e-3 in counterbalancing information asymmetries also is an empirical issue.

Finally, although some have suggested that shareholders may be cheated of value in the KKR-type transactions, they have offered no evidence in support of this conjecture. Hence, it is of interest to examine premiums paid in these "suspect" transactions vis-a-vis premiums paid in MBOs and other third-party buyouts.

4. Empirical Evidence

Several scholarly law articles have discussed both the efficacy of Rule 13e-3 and the SEC's authority in this area.[5] However, little evidence has been presented on whether management's informational advantage actually works to the detriment of other shareholders in MBOs.[6] This chapter examines this issue and the other two empirical issues presented above. To accomplish this with brevity, we make extensive references to Davis-Lehn (1992), hereafter referred to as DL, which describes the evidence summarized here in more detail.

---

[5] A list of such articles appears in Davis-Lehn (1992), 589, footnote 11.

[6] One exception is DeAngelo, DeAngelo, and Rice, "Going Private: Minority Freezeouts and Stockholder Wealth," 27 *Journal of Law and Economics* 367 (Oct. 1984).

Using a sample of 336 going-private transactions during 1980-1988, DL reports the results of several simple statistical tests that address the following three questions:

(1) Are premiums lower in transactions initiated by management or in which management is an equity participant?

(2) Did premiums in MBOs increase relative to premiums in other takeovers after the adoption of Rule 13e-3?

(3) Are premiums lower in "suspect" transactions than in Rule 13e-3 transactions?

If shareholders are disadvantaged in MBOs, then premiums in these transactions should be lower than the corresponding premiums received by shareholders in buyouts led by third parties. Hence, DL compares premiums paid in two sets of going-private transactions: (a) transactions that are initiated by management versus those that are initiated by third parties and (b) transactions in which management is an equity participant versus those in which management is not an equity participant.

The data reveal only small differences in average premiums across the different categories of transactions—(a) 39.51 percent for management-initiated versus 40.01 percent for third-party initiated and (b) 39.65 percent for transactions with management participation versus 40.31 percent for those without such participation. Neither of these differences in average premiums are statistically significant, suggesting that on average shareholders are not mistreated in MBOs.

The absence of any difference in the average premium paid in MBOs versus other going-private transactions may be due to the fact that the supposed conflicts of interest in MBOs are mitigated by the market and legal forces mentioned above or the fact that Rule 13e-3 has been effective in mitigating these conflicts. If the latter is true, we should find that premiums in MBOs increased significantly relative to premiums in other takeovers after the adoption of Rule 13e-3 in 1979.

To test this, we computed premiums for all MBOs listed in the *Wall Street Journal Index* during 1976–1978 and during 1980–1982. As reported in DL, there was a decline in the average premium, but it was statistically insignificant. To standardize for trends in general takeover premiums during this period, we calculated the ratio of the average premium in MBOs to the average premium in takeovers generally. DL finds a decline in this ratio from 0.79 before Rule 13e-3 was adopted to 0.55 after it was adopted.

Although the sample size in the pre-Rule 13e-3 period may be too small to draw meaningful conclusions, this evidence nonetheless suggests that Rule 13e-3 did not noticeably increase premiums paid to shareholders in MBOs.

A final test focuses on the class of "suspect" transactions noted above. In these "suspect" transactions, members of existing management, though not participating in the going-private transaction, are offered the opportunity to invest in the equity of the company after the transaction and may be offered lucrative employment contracts as well.

Of the sample of 336 going-private transactions, 227 involved the filing of a Schedule 13e-3, 26 fall into the "suspect" class, 63 are strictly third-party transactions, and 20 could not be classified. DL presents the mean percent premiums for each of the three classes of transactions. These data reveal that the average premium is highest for the "suspect" transactions (55.5 percent) and smallest for the Rule 13e-3 transactions (37.9 percent). Notably, the mean premium for the "suspect" transactions is significantly larger than the mean premium for both the third-party transactions (at the 0.10 level) and the Rule 13e-3 transactions (at the 0.05 level). Thus, a simple comparison of mean percent premiums offers no indication that shareholders in these "suspect" transactions are treated unfairly.

An obvious shortcoming of simple comparisons of mean premiums is that they fail to take into account other important differences that may affect premiums. Multiple regression analysis, of course, allows us to hold constant other factors that may have a significant influence on premiums. To test the relation between Rule 13e-3 and premiums, DL regresses the premium paid to shareholders against a set of variables selected to filter out other factors affecting premiums. In the interest of brevity, we focus our discussion on the two variables identifying the Rule 13e-3 and "suspect" transactions.

If management conflicts of interest exist in the "suspect" transactions, and if these conflicts result in harm to shareholders, then we expect a significant negative estimated coefficient for the "suspect" variable. Furthermore, an estimated coefficient insignificantly different from zero for the Rule 13e-3 variable would be a necessary, but not sufficient, condition for finding that Rule 13e-3 has completely countered the conflicts presumed to exist in transactions subject to the rule. It would not be a sufficient condition unless we knew that otherwise identical transactions not subject to the rule had significantly smaller premiums.[7]

---

[7] Some evidence on this issue is presented below.

DL finds that the estimated coefficient for Rule 13e-3 is insignificantly different from zero, meaning that premiums in Rule 13e-3 transactions are indistinguishable from premiums in comparable third-party transactions. The estimated coefficient for the "suspect" variable is positive, but not significantly different from zero. The failure to find a significant negative estimated coefficient for this variable is inconsistent with the view that these transactions involve conflicts of interest that work to the detriment of shareholders.

If we assume for the moment that the above findings with respect to the Rule 13e-3 variable are due to the effectiveness of Rule 13e-3 in combatting the presumed conflicts, then we can use regression analysis to test for the existence of the same conflicts in the "suspect" transactions. If those same conflicts exist, then we expect to find that the premiums in the "suspect" transactions are smaller than in otherwise identical Rule 13e-3 transactions. To test this proposition, DL reestimates the regression model for the sample consisting of only the Rule 13e-3 transactions and the "suspect" transactions.

DL finds that the estimated coefficient for the "suspect" variable is significantly positive at the 0.10 level, which is inconsistent with the argument that shareholders are disadvantaged in the "suspect" transactions. We cannot conclude from this that the "suspect" transactions pose the same potential conflicts of interest presumed to exist in the Rule 13e-3 transactions. Rather, it appears that either the same conflicts do not exist or, if they do exist, that they do not have the same effect on premiums.

5. Conclusion

Critics of management-led going-private transactions logically argue that an inherent conflict of interest exists in these transactions since management simultaneously is an agent for the shareholders and a principal in the acquiring entity. However, since managers are constrained by both market and legal forces in these transactions, it is unclear whether this conflict of interest actually results in harm to shareholders.

We find no empirical evidence that premiums are systematically lower in transactions where this conflict is likely to exist, namely, transactions initiated by management and transactions in which management is an equity participant. Although this result may suggest that Rule 13e-3 is effective in mitigating these conflicts, we are doubtful since (1) premiums in going-private transactions did not increase after this rule was adopted and (2) premiums in transactions that are exempt from Rule 13e-3 and in which management is an equity participant are actually higher than premiums in

Rule 13e-3 transactions. Although the critics' argument seems logical, as an empirical matter their concerns appear to be unfounded.

References and Suggested Readings

Brudney, Victor. 1975. "A Note on `Going Private.'" *Virginia Law Review* 61:1019.

Brudney, Victor, and Marvin A. Chirelstein. 1978. "A Restatement of Corporate Freezeouts." *Yale Law Journal* 87:1354.

Davis, Jeffry, and Kenneth Lehn. 1992. "Information Asymmetries, Rule 13e-3, and Premiums in Going-Private Transactions." *Washington University Law Quarterly* 70:587.

DeAngelo, Harry, Linda DeAngelo, and Edward M. Rice. 1984. "Going Private: Minority Freezeouts and Stockholder Wealth." *Journal of Law and Economics* 27 (Oct.):367.

Greene. 1976. "Corporate Freezeout Mergers: A Proposed Analysis." *Stanford Law Review* 28:487.

"SEC May Propose Expanding Scope of Going Private Disclosure Rules." 1989. *Securities Regulation & Law Report*, Jan. 1, 7–9.

Solomon. 1975. "Going Private: Business Practices, Legal Mechanics, Judicial Standards and Proposals for Reform." *Buffalo Law Review* 25:141.

21

SEC Regulation of Corporate Diversification by Public Utilities[1]

Yash P. Joshi and Anil K. Makhija
Northeastern University and University of Pittsburgh

The value of diversification provided through the conglomerate form of corporate organization is questionable when investors can directly and inexpensively form their desired portfolios. One motivation for adopting the conglomerate form may be the synergy provided by either general management or centralized functions (such as planning, control, information systems, research, and legal service). At any rate, no compelling reason exists to legislate use or prohibit adoption of this corporate form by the typical firm, leaving such decisions to the marketplace. In the case of public utilities, however, Congress has expressly handed the Securities and Exchange Commission (SEC) the authority to disallow significant corporate diversification if it is detrimental to the public interest (investors and consumers). The SEC is currently reviewing the limits and scope of permissible utility diversification; a proposed ruling would grant automatic approval if the non-utility business is not in excess of 10 percent of the consolidated assets of the holding company, provided the interests of ratepayers are safeguarded. The proposal permits other levels of diversification if the state public utility commission (PUC) allows it. Appendix A contains the text of the proposed rule [42 SEC Docket 1520-21].

The SEC proposal has met with overwhelming opposition from the utility industry, which considers it overly restrictive. This paper reviews the

[1] We are grateful to Jeffry Davis (SEC), Daniel Fogel (University of Pittsburgh), Kenneth Lehn (formerly chief economist at the SEC, now at the University of Pittsburgh), Robert Malko (formerly chief economist at the Wisconsin Public Service Commission, now at Utah State University), Michael Spiro (University of Pittsburgh), and Howard Thompson (University of Wisconsin, Madison) for helpful discussions.

issue and concludes that the SEC proposal correctly attempts to limit utility diversification. The analysis here, however, reaches a significantly different conclusion regarding how the limits and scope of diversification should be determined. It is argued here that the state regulatory commissions are in the best position to regulate utility diversification.

The gist of the analysis is that it is difficult to safeguard the ratepayers from the adverse effects of diversification—increases in risk and expropriations. As a result, ratepayers are in a uniquely disadvantageous position, since they can not readily diversify away their reliance on the local (monopoly) utility. In order to assure reliable service, ratepayers may not want the stockholders to undertake ventures with very high risk to the utility, even though the investment promises to produce extremely low prices for services if it is successful. A trade-off between higher risk from diversification activities and lower rates is practically feasible in only a narrow range.

Balanced against the risks are some potential benefits. Diversification can create value if there is synergy between the utility and non-utility businesses (e.g., an electric utility rents poles to a cable company), with possibilities for the PUC to split these gains between stockholders and ratepayers. The need to protect ratepayers from expropriation, however, conflicts with capturing the synergistic gains. Attempts to capture such gains imply integration of activities between the utility and non-utility components. The PUC has important tasks to perform when it permits diversification, if indeed there are synergistic gains to be made— determination of acceptable level of risk and mediation of division of gains between stockholders and ratepayers. These are not unusual tasks for PUCs who routinely oversee the compact between consumers and investors.

If ratepayers share in the risk-return from the diversified activity, it is not critical, apart from an accounting perspective, whether the business is carried out in a separate division of a holding company. The holding company format is no guarantee that the utility component (ratepayers) will be completely protected from the risks of the non-utility business. However, it is a useful device when coupled with monitoring by the PUC. Certain non-utility ventures could be held as separate entities within the holding company so that the risk of spillover to the utility is more easily monitored. A distinction between unrelated and related businesses is useful in this context. Unrelated, non-utility businesses are ideal candidates for holding separately within a holding company (e.g. a gas utility manufactures fiber board). But, they are also the businesses from which the potential for harm to ratepayers is likely to outweigh the small synergistic gains to stockholders.

Consequently, it is harder to make a case for unrelated diversification even within the holding company format. As a practical matter, the relatedness of a proposed venture can be debatable (e.g., suppose an electric utility wants to market payroll services because of related experience in billing).

There is another reason to watch the diversification activities of public utilities. It is unclear whether even utility stockholders are well served by diversification. If past performance is a guide, utility managers seem to have been unprepared for competitive investments. According to a recent article in the *Wall Street Journal*, utility diversification efforts have resulted in "huge writeoffs, dismal earnings, plummeting stock prices and bond ratings, not to mention an occasional bankruptcy." In fact, there is a growing literature in finance that claims that managers should focus on their core business (Comment and Jarrell 1991; Kaplan and Weisbach 1990). In many situations it may be in the best interests of stockholders to undertake these investments through separate, independent firms. The investments will then be subject to a market test, in addition to an internal managerial evaluation.

Utility managers may have a personal stake in the diversification debate. Relative to managers in industrial firms, utility managers have smaller salaries and stock awards (Agrawal, Makhija, and Mandelker 1991), which is partly a reflection of the low growth opportunities faced by utilities. Consequently, managers may be attracted to unregulated businesses that can offer better prospects for growth and compensation, even though it is not in the best interests of stockholders.

We have organized the remainder of this paper in six sections. In Section 1, we elaborate on the issues involved in diversification by utilities. We summarize the relevant history of the Public Utility Holding Company Act and the current SEC proposal in Section 2. In Section 3, we document examples of utility diversification and discuss the motivation behind them. We consider the impact on ratepayers in Section 4, and on stockholders in Section 5. In the final section, Section 6, we make concluding remarks regarding the SEC proposal.

1. Issues Surrounding Diversification by Utilities

The question of diversification by utilities involves a number of specific issues. We present them here in the form of reasons typically offered in support of diversification by utilities. We also offer some summary response, with detailed analyses in the following sections.

Empowered by the Public Utility Holding Company Act (PUHCA) of 1935, the SEC has historically disallowed or restricted the formation of holding companies with utility and non-utility subsidiaries, particularly if the result is a substantial investment in unrelated businesses. Details are provided in the next section. The primary beneficiaries of this regulation are ratepayers, who may otherwise be affected by the risks of investing in unregulated industries and by unjustified transfers to the non-utility subsidiaries.

Advocates for diversification argue, on the other hand, that diversification across subsidiaries within the holding company can be a means to lower cost of capital for ratepayers. Moreover, they claim that sufficient safeguards can be developed to separate and protect the utility within the holding company. They also suggest that diversification into non-utility businesses is desirable for stockholders since it increases rates of return. The growth prospects for utilities are considered to be poor. Finally, with many construction projects completed since the mid-eighties and substantial funds flowing in for future plant decommissionings, diversification is considered an important route for many utilities that have surplus cash in a low–interest rate environment.

We find below that ratepayers have justified fears that diversification can affect them adversely. Variance risk, whether it is rate of return or earnings variability, may be reduced through corporate diversification depending on the correlations among returns or earnings of the subsidiaries (Markowitz 1952). But, reduction of variance risk may not necessarily bring about a lower cost of capital. The cost of capital will depend on the beta riskiness of the subsidiaries, according to the Capital Asset Pricing Model. The evidence suggests that the beta riskiness of the average utility with diversified activities is in fact greater than that of an undiversified utility. Also, diversification can result in the siphoning off of utility assets, cross-subsidization of non-utility operations, and insufficient investments in the maintenance of the utility system. In two major cases reviewed here, the state public utility commissions (PUCs of Wisconsin and California) granted approval but did not erect perfect "firewalls" to protect ratepayers. (Support of the state legislators is obtained typically through promises by the utility that it will reinvest in the state and help local economic development. These promises, even if carried out, are of limited value to the average ratepayer.)

2. Legislative History and Proposed SEC Ruling

In this section we review the legislative history of the regulation of public utility diversification leading to the proposed SEC ruling. The review is based on Chapter 13 of Phillips (1985) and the discussion accompanying the proposed SEC proposal (42 SEC Docket 1515–1519). One purpose for this review is to show that giving the responsibility of regulating public utility diversification to the state PUCs is consistent with the historical development of regulation in this area.

Enactment of the Public Utility Holding Company Act (PUHCA) of 1935

For legislative purposes, a holding company is one that owns 10 percent or more of another company, or exerts controlling influence on another company. In the 1910s and 1920s, there was a rapid growth of holding companies in the electric and gas utilities. This organizational form offered some economies: with the advent of the alternating current, it became economical to produce electricity in large quantities in central power stations and service large areas; larger firms exerted negotiating advantage in securing financing or equipment purchases; large scale operations allowed common engineering departments; and bigger enterprizes could afford more skilled managers.

Holding companies were subject to abuse, however. The abuses came to light after the crash of 1929 when a large number of these firms went bankrupt and investors (stockholders and bondholders) suffered. Multiple layers of holding companies, so-called pyramiding, meant that small investments controlled large amounts of assets, with an excessive leveraging effect on holding company profitability and in many cases insufficient decentralized management control at the local level. For example, Associated Gas and Electric System, with an investment of $300,000, controlled over a billion dollars of assets. In an attempt to seek profits, holding companies disbursed unearned dividends after excessive write-ups through property revaluations. With operations stretched across a number of states, the holding companies were not easy to monitor by the local (state) PUCs. Intracompany transactions, including transfer prices, could not be regulated well by state PUCs with limited interstate authority.

In response to the abuses of the holding company form, Congress enacted legislation to limit sharply use of this form. Title I of the Public Utility Act of 1935 is known as the Public Utility Holding Company Act (PUHCA). PUHCA is considered one of the most stringent corrective laws passed by Congress. The aim of the PUHCA was to remove the "evils . . . connected with the holding company system," through "the simplification of the public utility holding company systems." It sought "to limit the operations . . . to a single integrated public utility system." In a so-called death sentence clause, the PUHCA provided that all holding companies that are twice removed from their operating subsidiaries be abolished. The act was challenged on constitutional grounds but was upheld by the courts.

SEC Implementation of PUHCA

The SEC implemented PUHCA by requiring companies to submit their divestiture plans for a compliance review under PUHCA. It attempted to form integrated public utility systems that were confined to a single geographic area. Exceptions were permitted to the one-system rule when (1) there were strong economic reasons to hold two systems, (2) the systems were located in one state or in adjoining states, and (3) the resulting holding company was not too large. The summary effect of PUHCA was to bring the utilities within the grasp of state regulators.

Intrastate diversification was not prohibited per se by PUHCA, since the operation of holding companies within a state was considered to be regulated by state PUCs. In the spirit of limiting holding companies, however, the SEC opposed the ownership of non-utility enterprizes by public utilities unless the businesses were reasonably incidental or functionally related to its operations. In later years the SEC also allowed retention of functionally unrelated businesses by intrastate holding companies. For example, in the first ten months of 1988 the SEC recieved 88 applications from intrastate holding companies to allow diversification, and about half of these applications pertained to diversification in unrelated areas (34 firms with unrelated business applications were granted permission). In one case, Pacific Lighting Corporation (45 SEC 152, 1973) the Commissioners debated in detail the potential for harm to ratepayers from unrelated non-utility diversification, but, unable to agree among themselves, they approved the diversification request.

SEC Proposal

In the proposed ruling the SEC would automatically permit diversification if:

(a) the non-utility business is in a separate corporate subsidiary of the holding company; there are no contracts between the affiliates or, if there are, they are supervised by the PUC; the utility provides no financial support to the non-utility affiliate except for PUC-authorized dividends; the non-utility affiliates are limited in total size to 10 percent of the consolidated assets of the holding company; and the holding company guarantees that non-utility businesses do not exceed 2 percent of the consolidated assets of the holding company or

(b) the holding company meets the requirements of the state in which it operates and the PUC of the state has considered the issue of utility diversification in the context of PUHCA.

A review of the legislation above shows that one major goal of Congress and the SEC has been to bring utilities within the control of state regulators. Since the primary responsibility to protect ratepayers rests with the PUCs, the SEC is willing to allow diversification to the extent that the relevant PUCs are comfortable with it. Failing explicit treatment of diversification by the PUC, the SEC proposal attempts to provide some protection to the ratepayer before granting a utility permission to diversify.

3. Diversification Practices of Utilities

We describe in this section the diversification activities of utilities. We find the practice to be widespread, with investments in a wide array of related and unrelated businesses.

Utilities are looking at diversification into unrelated businesses because the need for investments in the utility industry has been slowing down. Annual growth in electricity demand has yet to pick up after falling from approximately 7 percent in the sixties and early seventies to about 2 percent in the late seventies and early eighties according (O'Connor, Bussa, and Olson 1986). Moreover, new electric generating capacity is frequently available through Independent Power Producers (who have been provided special incentives through PURPA). Finally, the remaining life of net plant is long: 21.8 years for electric plants, 20 years for electric and gas, and 19.3 years for gas distribution companies (based on data in Turner 1992).

One obvious choice for utilities is to pay higher dividends. Some managers would argue that with payout ratios close to or above 80 percent, they are already paying out large dividends (dividend yields from 6.3 percent to 6.8 percent compared to 2.9 percent for S & P Industrials in 1991, Turner 1992). Reinvesting in themselves by repurchasing their stock is also not an attractive option for utilities, since they do not represent growth businesses (price-earnings ratios of 11.9, 12.2. and 14.7 for electric, electric and gas, and gas transmission utilities compared with a price-earnings ratio of 25.5 for S & P Industrials, as of end-1991, Turner 1992). Moreover, with low interest rates, their cost of capital and allowed rates are likely to be low as well. Financial instruments can be ruled out for the same reason—low interest rates, although successful investments in portfolios of marketable securities were undertaken by some (examples include Potomac Electric

Power, Baltimore Gas and Electric, Tucson Electric Power Company, Minnesota Power and Light Company, and Duke Power.)

Since the mid-eighties there has been a wave of diversification activities among utilities, similar to an earlier wave in the early seventies. Studness (1992) points out several aspects regarding this wave: one-third of the utilities have tested diversification at one time or another and one in four has done so in a significant manner. The twenty utilities with major non-utility diversification, possibly accounting for 90 percent of the common equity invested, spent about $6.5 billion in the period 1985 to 1991.

Examples of Diversification Activities

Utilities have invested in a surprisingly wide variety of unrelated investments. In many of these investments they possess no obvious competitive advantage or expertise. Examples of non-utility businesses include fiberboard manufacture, land development, venture capital for medical equipment and telecommunications (Public Service of New Mexico), thermal window and door manufacture (Florida Progress), drugstore chain (Pacific Lighting Corporation), telemarketing (Iowa Light and Power), savings and loans (Arizona Public Service Company), and sewage treatment, real estate, and paper mill (Minnesota Power and Light Company). Some firms, such as Tenneco and Arkla began in the early eighties to look like industrial conglomerates rather than traditional utilities. Another unrelated business was investments in specialized financial products and strategies: MDU Resources, as well as its Montana-Dakota Utilities Company Division, and Baltimore Gas and Electric invested in dividend capture strategies, exploiting the high corporate tax exemption on dividends.

Frequently, and understandably, public utilities have invested in functionally related businesses: Telco Energy Inc., holding company for Tampa Electric Corporation integrated vertically with its own coal mines and transportation facilities. Telco also owns tugs and barges. Entergy invested in energy audits, foreign power projects, and unregulated independent power production.

4. Impact of Diversification on Ratepayers

We analyze here the consequences of diversification for ratepayers.

Diversification can have a negative impact on ratepayers in three ways: (1) the risk of the utility and hence its cost of capital and rates can be adversely affected by diversification; (2) its assets can be siphoned off to the non-utility subsidiary or to the holding company; and (3) ratepayers may end up paying higher rates if the transactions of the utility with its affiliates are not at arms length and it cross-subsidizes them.

Cost of Capital of the Diversified Holding Company

One benefit of corporate diversification that has been suggested is that it can lower the risk of the holding company and consequently the cost of capital of the utility. Reduction in variability of earnings and rate of return are possible through corporate diversification, but they do not necessarily represent a reduction in relevant risk. According to the Capital Asset Pricing Model (Sharpe 1964), the undiversifiable risk is captured by the beta coefficient. Assessed with this measure, diversified utilities are actually riskier, based on the estimates in Hanley and Harris (1991). Hanley and Harris (1991) find that the average beta for a sample of 113 diversified utilities is significantly greater statistically than that for a sample of 102 undiversified utilities (0.5773 versus 0.4939), using Merrill Lynch adjusted betas. This should not be surprizing, though. The beta of S & P Industrials—a proxy of alternative opportunities—is likely to exceed one, whereas the betas of the regulated businesses are expected to be considerably less than one. Consistent with this conjecture, Rosenberg (1986) reports the following beta estimates, using quarterly data for the period 1977–1983: 1.029 for S & P Industrials, 0.339 for electric utilities, and 0.474 for gas utilities. If the cost of capital for the utility is calculated using the holding company beta, ratepayers will pay higher prices on average. The cost of capital of the utility should be determined based on its own riskiness. If the risk effects of the non-utility business are to be separated out, at least the holding company form makes it theoretically possible to do so.

In practice, the estimation of the cost of capital is complicated. To see how the cost of capital may be estimated it may be useful to distinguish the three forms within which a utility typically diversifies: (1) diversification within utility, when the amount of diversification is too small to separate out or to be concerned about, (2) utility with subsidiary, and (3) holding company with utility subsidiary with non-utility affiliates. When the utility creates its own subsidiary the diversified activity is an integral part of the operations. The utility wholly owns the subsidiary, and the management of the utility serves the subsidiary as well. The cost of capital cannot be separately estimated and the operations freely subsidize each other (cross-subsidization). In the third form the holding company owns stock, and theoretically the risks and benefits of the diversified activity can be separated from the utility operations. But in practice, expert witnesses first determine the holding company cost of capital and then *subjectively* mark it down for the utility cost of capital. Since the stock of the holding company is typically traded, it is easier to work from the estimate of its cost of capital. In an alternative procedure, a group of utilities comparable to the target utility is identified, and their average cost of capital is applied to it. Subjectivity enters the picture this time through the choice of comparable firms.

Cross-Subsidization and Transfer of Assets to Non-utility Affiliate

In principle, the affairs of the utility and non-utility affiliates can be separated to prevent subsidization of and unjustified transfers of assets to the non-utility affiliate. A review of attempts by two state PUCs to protect the ratepayers shows that this is difficult to achieve in practice.

Wisconsin PUC and Wisconsin Electric Power (Malko and Edgar, 1986). The State of Wisconsin passed legislation (1985 Wisconsin Act 79) that made it possible for the PUC to approve in May 1986 an application by Wisconsin Electric Power (WEP) to reorganize and form a holding company, Wisconsin Electric Corporation (WEC). The general principles upon which approval was granted are that (1) utility ratepayers are not made worse off by the formation of the holding company, (2) utility ratepayers should benefit from activities of the holding company, at least indirectly, as tax payers and community members, (3) non-utility operations of the holding company or its non-utility affiliates should not be regulated, and (4) the formation and operation of the holding company shall in no way diminish the authority of the commission over its activities. Generally, the provisions with the state approval provide access to information, minimize transfers, and require that the formation of the holding company will not harm the credit, capital, or service of the utility materially. The specific requirements are as follows:

1. No affiliated interest transactions (sharing officers or other items of value) should occur without commission permission.

2. WEP and WNG (Wisconsin Natural Gas, another utility within WEC) shall maintain a balanced capital structure. (In another case, involving Wisconsin Power and Light, it was required that the utility meet a target common equity ratio of 50 percent before funds can be transferred to the holding company. Until the target is met, all dividends are to be distributed to shareholders.)

3. WEP and WNG shall set dividend policy based on their own financial health and not that of the holding company.

4. WEP and WNG shall submit long-term financial strategic plans in rate cases.

5. Non-utility assets are not to exceed 25 percent of the utility assets (WEP and WNG).

6. WEC must share holding company and affiliate records, or it must show why the sought information deserves confidentiality.

7. WEC shall submit for commission staff review procedures for transactions between affiliates.

8. WEP and WNG shall submit plans for maximum separation of officers and staffing of employees between affiliates. Plans should indicate transfers and joint use of employees.

9. WEC shall submit (a) accounting data on the formation of the holding company and (b) assets transferred to the non-utility affiliate.

10. WEC shall submit (a) annual reports, (b) explanations and descriptions of all affiliates with relationships, (c) assets of utility and affiliates, with percentage diversification, (d) names of all officers of utilities, holding company, and affiliates, and (e) audited statements.

11. Jurisdiction is maintained.

California PUC and Southern California Edison. In another example, the California PUC approved a request by the Southern California Edison Company (SCE) to place its unregulated businesses in a separate subsidiary, the Mission Group. The PUC felt that bifurcation would help insulate SCE. Major provisions of the approval include

1. Access to information to the Mission Group.

2. A 5-percent markup in services performed by the utility for the Mission Group.

3. The holding company testifies at the rate hearings.

4. Disclosure of holding company's projected capital budgets.

5. Existence of arms-length bargaining for any intercorporate property transfers in the future.

6. Held authority over whether the Mission Group will be allowed to sell electricity to the utility subsidiary from that generated by qualifying facilities for cogeneration.

7. Compensation to ratepayers for SCE's goodwill and intangible assets transferred to the unregulated subsidiary.

8. Sales of equipment and interconnection facilities by the holding company (Progress of Regulation 1988).

Differences between the provisions in the cases show areas in which ratepayers are left exposed in one of the states. Constraints on the capital structure, an important consideration with implications for excessive dividend drains, are directly addressed in the Wisconsin agreement but not in the California agreement. In California, however, a 5 percent mark-up provides protection against subsidized utility services to the non-utility affiliate. Treatment of shared personnel and royalty payments for the intangibles and goodwill of the utility are other examples of differences. (It may be argued that depending on the specific circumstances only the so-called binding provisions are given attention.)

All the possible loop holes, where ratepayers' wealth can be expropriated, cannot be ennumerated. Rather, analogous to bond covenants, some of the constraints are explicitly recognized with the understanding that the PUC will have to monitor the situation. The PUC has the burden of identifying lapses in the defence and take corrective action. For example, if subsidies exist, the PUC may accordingly adjust rates downward. Nevertheless, the summary implication is that ratepayers are exposed and they can be made whole if the problem is recognized and corrective action is taken.

5. Impact on Stockholders

We show in this section that most stockholders have suffered losses on their diversification investments in public utilities.

If the purpose of undertaking diversified activities was to exploit better oppotunities than those available in the utility business, the results have been disappointing. Looking at a sample of 20 utilities that were involved in major diversification investments over the years 1986–1991, Charles Studness (1992) reports that the utilities lost some $387 million on an equity investment of about $20 billion. That is an average rate of return of -1.1 percent per year for the six-year period. Of the twenty firms in his sample, seventeen did not start significant investments until 1980. The remaining three, Montana, Pacificcorp, and TECO, were successful survivors of a previous wave of diversification. These three firms earned an average of 13.4 percent per year during this period. The other firms lost an average of -5.5 percent per year.

The evidence in several studies is consistent with the notion that stockholders are better served through corporate focus, a strategy in which the firm stresses its commitment to its core business. In a study by McKinsey and Company, quoted in Lipnick (1986), only six out of 58 corporate acquisitions between 1975 and 1985 were financially successful. The most successful companies were the ones whose business lines were similar to those of the acquiring company. In similar vein, Kaplan and Weisbach (1990) note that, as far as the subsequent treatment of acquisitions is concerned, those that came from unrelated businesses are far more likely to be divested than those from a related business. Finally, Comment and Jarrell (1991), who compare the value of focus relative to corporate diversification, find that "the view that the trend over the 1980s to increased corporate focus (away from conglomerate diversification) is consistent with shareholder wealth maximization."

6. Implications for Regulation

In this concluding section we note that the case for state level regulation exists on several grounds based on the discussion in this paper.

Managers may stand to benefit from utility diversification. The benefit to managers, however, does not come from the usual sources. Diversification may result in greater variability, not less, since the non-utility businesses are usually riskier. Utility diversification does not necessarily imply less employment risk.

Given the separation of ownership from control, managers may be using the available surplus cash to pursue self-serving goals at the cost of stockholders and ratepayers (Jensen 1986). Managers may be undertaking these diversification activities to expand their perks and prestige. Moreover, non-utility businesses have larger compensation; for example, the total annual compensation of utility managers was only about 34 percent of that of executives in industrial firms in the years 1975–1984 (Agrawal, Makhija, and Mandelker 1991). These agency problems may not be readily resolved in utilities through monitoring by stockholders, since stockholdings may be too widely and thinly dispersed. In fact, it may be the expectation that the state PUCs will monitor and control managerial actions. This supports the case for placing the responsibility for regulating utility diversification with state PUCs for the benefit of stockholders.

State-level regulation is also desirable from the viewpoint of ratepayers. Ratepayers may not be willing to accept any level of risk even if stockholders are willing to compensate them with lower prices for services because assured service is an important priority for ratepayers. There may be acceptable levels of risk, however. The state PUCs are closest to the ratepayers and utilities and, therefore, in a position to determine what the permissible amount and type of diversification may be. Since risks cannot be fully contained, even through the holding company format, the unique ability of PUCs to monitor the investments is another distinct advantage of state regulation.

The SEC proposed ruling recognizes the inherent problems associated with unrestricted utility diversification. It also recognizes the special role of the PUCs, and defers to the local regulators when they set guidelines for diversification. We have argued, in addition, that the level and type of diversification allowable is best determined by PUCs that can take into account the specific circumstances involved, including the acceptable level of risk and the ability of the PUC to monitor the investments. Diversification of up to 10 percent of the consolidated assets, the upper limit in the proposed SEC ruling in the absence of state rules, may entail excessive risk in some cases depending on the nature of the investment.

Appendix A

Text of Rule Proposed by the SEC (42 SEC Docket 1520–21)

Chapter 2 of Title 17 of the Code of Federal Regulations is proposed to be amended as follows (by adding 250.17 and amending 250.2 to read):

250.17 Diversification by intrastate holding companies
(a) On and after three years from (insert date three years after date of publication of the adopted rule in the Federal Register) the Commission, in determining whether to grant, modify, or revoke any order upon application under paragragph (1) of section 3(a) of the Act shall not deem holding company direct or indirect interests in non-utility businesses to be detrimental to the public interest or the interest of investors and consumers, within the meaning of section 3(a) of the Act, if—

(1)(i) All such holding-company interests are segregated from its public utility business through separate corporate subsidiaries;

(ii) There is no service, materials or other contracts between affiliated public utility companies of the holding company or its non-utility affiliates except to the extent such contracts are subject to supervision of a State commission;

(iii) Except for dividend payments to the holding company from its affiliated public utility companies, which dividend payments have not been objected to by the State commission, there is no use of funds, or credit, or of operating management of an affiliated public utility companies of the holding company for non-utility purposes; and

(iv) Holding company interests in non-utility businesses not having a functional relationship, within the meaning of section 11(b)(i) of the Act, to its affiliated public utility companies together with guarantees by the holding company of any obligations of such non-utility businesses constitute not more than 10 percent of the consolidated assets of the holding company; and holding-company interests in, and guarantees of obligations of, any one such business constitute not more than 2 percent of such assets; or

(2)(i) The State of organization of the holding company has enacted a statute governing the formation and/or operations of intrastate public utility holding companies and their affiliates;

(ii) The State has considered, or authorized the appropriate State commission to consider, the issue of diversification of intrastate public-utility holding companies into non-utility businesses in light of the public policy goals of the Act, and the State and/or State commission has written policies with regard to such diversification; and

(iii) The holding company is in compliance with any State statute and any State commission rules, regulations and orders pertaining to diversification activities.

(b) For purposes of paragraph (a)(1)(iv) of this section, holding-company direct or indirect interests in securities which could be acquired by a registered holding company under section 9(c) of the Act, or by rules, regulations, or order of the Commission also under section 9(c) shall be excluded for purposes of computation from the numerator, but not from the denominator, of the fraction in that calculation.

(c) Any holding company exempt under section 3(a)(1) of the Act by order of the Commission on {insert date three years after date of publication of the adopted Rule in the Federal register) shall file with the Commission within 60 days after such date, and on or before March 1 of each year thereafter, a report bearing the file number that had been assigned to the exemptive order by the Commission, containing the information, as of the close of the last calendar year, required by paragraph (4) and Exhibit A, or Exhibits A and B, as appropriate, of Amended form U-#A-2.

(3) Section 250.2 is amended by revising paragraph (a)(1) and adding paragraph (c) as follows:

250.2 Exemption of holding companies which are intrastate or predominantly operating companies

(a)(1)(i) Such holding company, and every subsidiary company thereof which is a public utility company from which such holding company derives, directly or indirectly, any material part of its income are predominantly intrastate in character and carry on their business substantially in a single

State in which such holding company and every such subsidiary company thereof are organized, and

(a)(1)(ii) On or after (insert date three years after date of publication of the adopted Rule in the Federal register) such holding company meets one of the safe harbor provisions of 250.17.

(c) Any holding company which has filed an exemption statement in reliance on paragraph (a)(1) of this section prior to (insert date three years after date of publication of the adopted Rule in the Federal Register) shall file with the Commission within 60 days after such date a special one-time filing of form U-3A-2, as amended, containing only the information, as of the close of the last calendar year, required by paragraph (4) and exhibit A, or by Exhibits A and B, as appropriate, of amended Form U-3A-2.

References and Suggested Readings

Agrawal, A., A. K. Makhija, and G. N. Mandelker. 1991. "Executive Compensation and Corporate Performance in Electric and Gas Utilities." *Financial Management* (Winter): 113–124.

Comment, R., and G. A. Jarrell. 1990. "Corporate Focus and Stock Returns." Working paper, University of Rochester.

Hanley, F. J., and A. G. Harris. 1991. "Does Diversification Increase the Cost of Capital." *Public Utilities Fortnightly,* July 15, 26–30.

Jensen, Michael. 1986. "Agency Costs of Free Cash Flow, Corporate Finance, and Takeovers." *American Economic Review* 76:323–29.

Kaplan, S., and M. S. Weisbach. 1991. "The Success of Acquisitions: Evidence from Divestitures." Working paper, University of Rochester.

Lipnick, B. 1986. "Investment Strategies in an Interval of Cash Surplus." *Public Utilities Fortnightly,* Nov. 13, 34–37.

Malko, R. J., and G. R. Edgar. 1986. "Energy Utility Diversification: Its Status in Wisconsin." *Public Utilities Fortnightly,* Aug. 7, 20–24.

Markowitz, H. 1952. "Portfolio Selection." *The Journal of Finance* 7, no.1 (Mar.): 77–91.

Murray, E. A. C., and M. J. Closterman. 1986. "How Utilities Are Becoming New Conglomerates." *Public Utilities Fortnightly,* Aug. 7, 11–19.

O'Connor, P. R., R. G. Bussa, and Wayne P. Olson. 1986. "Competition, Financial Innovation, and Diversification in the Electric Industry." *Public Utilities Fortnightly,* Feb, 20, 17–20.

Phillips, C. F., Jr. 1985. *The Regulation of Public Utilities*, chapter 13. Arlington, Virginia: Public Utilities Reports.

"Progress of Regulation." 1988. *Public Utilities Fortnightly*, Apr. 14.

Rosenberg, J. 1986. "Risk, Return, and Regulation Among Energy Industries." *Public Utilities Fortnightly,* Aug. 7, 31–38.

Rouffignac, A. D. 1992. "Energy Pursues Tricky Path of Utility Diversification." *The Wall Street Journal,* Dec. 1, B4.

Sharpe, W. F. 1964. "Capital Asset Prices: A Theory of Market Equilibrium Under Conditions of Risk." *The Journal of Finance* 19, no. 3 (Sept.): 425–42.

Studness, C. M. 1992. "Earnings from Utility Diversification Ventures." *Public Utilities Fortnightly,* Sept. 1, 28–29.

Turner, C. A. 1992. *Financial Statistics: Public Utilities.*

York, S., and J. R. Malko. 1983. "Utility Diversification: A Regulatory Perspective." *Public Utilities Fortnightly,* Jan. 6, 15–20.

22

An Appropriate Federal Role in the Market for Corporate Control

Michael Ryngaert
University of Florida

There is a contradiction present in the political rhetoric surrounding regulation of the corporate boardroom. At times corporate managers are viewed as arrogant and unaccountable to their shareholders. Practices such as supposedly excessive managerial pay, "golden parachutes", and corporate "greenmail" are roundly condemned as managerial abuses of power. Yet, actions with the potential to make management more accountable to shareholders such as hostile takeovers and contentious proxy contests are not only criticized but regulated by state anti-takeover laws and federal regulations in a manner that greatly reduces their effectiveness as managerial oversight mechanisms.

In this chapter I argue that federal policy toward the market for corporate control should put more decision-making power about how corporations are governed back into the hands of shareholders, taking it out of the hands of legislatures and courts. This, however, should not be performed through mandated rules of governance. Some firms may be better off with rules that make managers less accountable. If managers of firms can persuade shareholders to accept greater restrictions on the activities of control-oriented investors, so be it.

I will proceed by briefly sketching the workings of the corporate control market and the problems with current regulation of it. I will then present a guiding philosophy for federal regulation of that market and show how that philosophy might be extended to the 13d regulation of the Williams Act, a federal response to state takeover laws and a federal rule for the use of poison pill securities.

The Market for Corporate Control

Stockholders control a corporation through their power to elect a board of directors to oversee management. If management turns out to be self-serving or incompetent, the board must intervene. Some boards fail to carry out this duty. The solution is for shareholders to replace these boards with new directors that will implement value-enhancing changes. This, however, is more easily said than done. It is costly to conduct a proxy contest, and it might be the case that no shareholder owns enough shares to make such a contest worthwhile. Furthermore, shareholders may not have an economic incentive to become informed about who is best qualified to run their firm. It is costly to become informed, and this cost may be too large relative to the expected benefits of becoming informed and voting.

The most obvious solution to the problem is concentrated ownership. If a near majority of votes is concentrated in the hands of a few shareholders, it may be possible to exert pressure on a board of directors to make needed changes. In fact, those with large holdings may serve on the board. Such investors have the right incentives to make sure that firms are run properly and have the clout to do something if they are not.

In cases where shareholdings are not concentrated, a majority of votes can be gathered through purchases of a firm's stock via a tender offer. The problem here is that one can only make money on a takeover by buying shares at a price below what the firm will be worth when value-enhancing changes are made. Again, more easily said than done. There is a free-rider problem inherent in takeovers. Shareholders may refuse to sell shares unless they are paid what the firms' shares will be worth in the event of a successful takeover. This holdout problem can undermine any bid's success.[1]

In spite of the free-rider problem, an acquirer can still profit from a takeover bid if (1) shares are bought before the takeover bid is public knowledge or (2) shares are purchased using a two-tier takeover where the acquirer pays a high price for a majority of the target's shares and then freezes out the remaining shareholders at a lower price once control is taken. Profits from share purchases are necessary to cover the costs of identifying targets and launching a takeover bid. If no profit can be made on shares purchased, profit-maximizing acquirers will not investigate potential takeover targets or pursue takeover bids. This would be bad news for shareholders. Most empirical evidence suggests that target-firm shareholders have done

---

[1] For more on the free-rider problem in takeovers *see* Bradley, "Interfirm Tender Offers and the Market for Corporate Control," *Journal of Business* 53, (1980) 345.

quite well when they are the subject of takeover bids, even during a time period when tender offers were not generally regulated. In fact, even shareholders who do not sell there shares on the front end of a two-tier bid realize capital gains on their shares as a result of two-tier takeover bids.[2]

While most evidence suggests that shareholders gain from hostile takeovers, this has not diminished the criticism that shareholders do not get enough for their shares, because they do not know the value of their shares or they are coerced via two-tier offers into selling too cheaply. If shareholders are selling too cheaply, then bidders must be making out like bandits. The facts prove otherwise. While bidders appeared to earn positive profits on takeovers before the 1968 passage of the Williams Act, those profits began to evaporate in the 1970s. For the early 1980s, even before the widespread introduction of poison-pill takeover defenses and new restrictive state laws, the average bidder's share price dropped when it announced a successful tender offer for control of a target firm.[3]

The dismal profits to bidders suggest that targets are getting all the gains from takeover bids. In spite of this, takeover activity stayed strong throughout the 1980s, but casual empiricism suggests that hostile acquisition activity has been reduced dramatically in the past few years. While some claim that difficulty in financing deals explains this, it is quite clear that even takeover entrepreneurs with large war chests such as Coniston Partners, have essentially "gotten out of the business".

An alternative explanation for the decline in takeover activity is the cumulative effect of federal and state regulation of the market for corporate control. This regulation has tilted the playing field against corporate acquirers. The unfortunate part of this regulation is that, while defense of shareholder interest is often invoked by regulators, shareholders have had very little say in the formulation of the restrictive rules that now regulate the takeover market. While shareholders may benefit from higher takeover premia resulting from takeover regulation, they may be harmed by fewer value-increasing takeovers and less oversight of management. Whether

---

[2] *See*, for instance, Comment and Jarrell, "Two Tier and Negotiated Tender Offers: The Imprisonment of the Free-Riding Shareholder," *Journal of Financial Economics* 19, (1987) 283: they provide evidence for tender offers made during the period 1981–1984. Bradley (1980) provides evidence that target shareholders who did not tender still experienced gains even before the tender-offer market became heavily regulated.

[3] *See* Bradley, Desai, and Kim, "Synergistic Gains from Corporate Acquisitions and Their Division between the Stockholders of Target and Acquiring Firms," *Journal of Financial Economics* 21 (1988), 3.

particular takeover rules are a good bargain for shareholders is something that shareholders should be consulted on.

Thus, I suggest a guiding philosophy for the federal government in its oversight of the market for corporate control. Federal policy should clear the deck of state and federal laws that currently hinder the operation of the takeover market. At the same time, a free hand should be given to shareholders and management to fashion their own set of investor protection measures. Ideally, managers can propose their own anti-takeover amendments, which then can be put to a shareholder vote. Similarly, management can propose that shareholders "opt in" to existing federal and state takeover rules. For firms conducting initial public offerings, anti-takeover amendments are also quite acceptable. After all, if they reduce firm value, the costs are born by the original issuers of stock, and shareholders have priced out the protection afforded management.

The most important aspect of federal policy is that it should avoid the use of mandates that make investor monitoring of companies more costly to undertake. Most federal legislation is of the one-size-fits-all variety. All firms must conform with no or few exceptions. This may not only be detrimental to the participants in the market for corporate control (shareholders and control-oriented investors), it may also be detrimental to society in other respects. It is costly to construct a bureaucracy to oversee federal rules, and litigation stemming from federal rules can add to the burden on federal courts.

Let's look at how this guiding philosophy could be conceivably applied to improve existing law governing the market for corporate control.

The Williams Act and 13d Disclosure

Section 13d under the Williams Act raises the costs of forming large blocks of shares that can be used to influence firm policy or used as a "beachhead" for a future acquisition. This rule forces a control-oriented shareholder to file a disclosure statement with the SEC whenever the shareholder obtains more than 5 percent of a firm's stock. The investor must also disclose the purpose of the investment (e.g., just for investment or to influence control over the firm).

This rule discourages the formation of block shareholdings in two ways. First, if the block is to be used as a base for making profits from a monitoring activity or a takeover bid by having to disclose the existence of the block, the number of shares that can be acquired at a low price is limited. Second, there are potential costs for simply filing a 13d amendment. Besides the physical costs of filing, filers subject themselves to the potential of being sued for false disclosure. Many such suits are simply nuisance suits with little legal merit, but the suits serve their purpose. They impose costs on potential competitors to current management.[4]

One can debate whether shareholders would find it desirable to force control-oriented investors to be subject to Rule 13d disclosure. The problem now is that the rule is a legal mandate that cannot be avoided even if shareholders and management agree that it has ill effects. The general rationale for such a regulation is the protection of small, uninformed investors who are not aware that their stock is under accumulation. In the worst case, small investors could sell out to an investor who obtains control through open-market purchases and pays no premium whatsoever.

While one can debate this contention, a modest rollback of 13d provisions could be a step forward without imposing a serious threat to small shareholders. For instance, the 5 percent reporting threshold could be increased to 10 percent and the disclosure of intent could be dropped from the 13d filing. Small shareholders, who tend to be more passive in their investment strategies, are unlikely to be harmed by such rule changes. Control will not change hands without their becoming informed, and, in any event, it is even unlikely that they will be the ones to sell to an accumulator who is going from 5 percent to 10 percent. It is more likely that active institutional investors will be these sellers.

For those uncomfortable with this proposal, I should hasten to add that provisions can be added that allow firms to elect into current 13d regulation by shareholder vote or by original incorporation at the time of an initial public offering. Similarly, firms could be empowered to create their own 13d type regulations with shareholder consent.

Preemption of State Anti-takeover Laws

The majority of states have introduced an array of laws that make takeovers more difficult and costly. Laws range from the mildly restrictive (Delaware) to the highly intrusive (Pennsylvania). The laws have two common aspects: (1) that they increased the cost of acquiring a target firm and (2) that all were imposed by state law and never voted on by shareholders. Most states allow opting out of their takeover laws if the board of directors deems fit or in the case of a newly incorporated firm. Some states allow shareholders to opt out by changing corporate bylaws

---

[4] *See* Macey and Netter, "Regulation 13d and the Regulatory Process," *Washington University Law Quarterly* 65 (1987), 131.

(Delaware), but others (Indiana and Pennsylvania for example) do not allow any opting out via a shareholder vote. Even states such as Delaware, that allow shareholders to opt out are putting the burden of change (and the costs of generating a proxy ballot initiative) on stockholders.

The fact that most states allow for a new incorporation opt out provision is telling. An entrepreneur who wants to raise new capital will receive a lower price for his or her newly issued shares if a value-reducing takeover law is on the books. In other words, there is a distinct possibility that these laws would flunk the market test. This could discourage new incorporations in a state and cost the state incorporation fees. Thus, state lawmakers leave new incorporators a way to avoid a bad law.

Of course, one might ask where these laws come from. One possibility is that they arose from cases suchas the following: a large firm in a state is threatened by an actual or feared takeover bid (e.g., Goodyear in Ohio, Dayton Hudson in Minnesota, Burlington Industries in North Carolina), which mobilizes a lobbying effort by the firm's management and the community in which it is based. A law is proposed and faces little opposition because managers of firms affected by it can generally opt out of it if they so desire and shareholders of affected firms are too diffuse to lobby against it and may not live in the state.[5]

Shareholders must swallow hard and accept the law. Interestingly, many of these shareholders never contemplated the allowance of restrictive takeover rules to govern their firms. Many firms had no takeover protection of the sort lobbied for by their management teams. Not surprisingly, the evidence seems to indicate that firms that already had shareholder-approved anti-takeover rules do not drop in value when these new laws are put into place, but firms that had no anti-takeover protection experience share price declines when these laws are enacted.[6]

A reasonable federal response to state anti-takeover laws may be new legislation that renders them nonoperative unless shareholders decide to opt into them by a majority vote. If the rules benefit shareholders, then managers have every incentive to propose them and shareholders have every incentive to ratify them. Firms that opted to be covered by the laws at the time of an initial public offering would continue to be covered by the laws,

---

[5] For more on the legislative dynamic that yields state takeover laws, *see* Romano, "The Political Economy of Takeover Statutes," *Virginia Law Review* 73 (1987), 11.

[6] *See* Karpoff and Malatesta, "The Wealth Effects of Second Generation State Takeover Legislation," *Journal of Financial Economics* (1989), 291.

since the pricing of their new issues incorporated the potential effects of the laws.[7]

Poison Pill Securities

The history of poison pill securities differs a bit from state and federal anti-takeover laws. Pill securities make it virtually impossible for a takeover to be consummated without the approval of target management. They are essentially rights issues that are triggered by a takeover event. By designing pill securities as state-contingent securities, their inventors have been able to argue that their use is not inconsistent with most state corporation law. Generally, courts give greater scrutiny to the use of poison pills than they might other corporate actions, but one could argue that their use is largely protected under the business judgment rule.

Arguably, pill securities were an innovation that was unanticipated by security market participants. There is some evidence that their introduction reduces shareholder wealth, and there is no doubt that they can dramatically change the balance of power in a takeover contest.[8] Arguably, states have been reluctant to act against the issuance of pill securities for the same reason that they adopt state anti-takeover laws.

I believe that it is consistent with the regulatory philosophy espoused in this chapter to pass a federal law that prohibits the use of poison pill securities unless they are explicitly approved by shareholders or allowed in a firm's initial incorporation charter. It is doubtful that shareholders of most publicly traded firms ever contemplated the use of pill securities, and, under existing law, about all they can do is call for advisory votes to remove any existing poison pill. In most states, pills cannot be banned in the corporate charter by unilateral shareholder action, because the board of directors must first propose a change in the corporate charter before shareholders can act on it.

---

[7] Note that many managers may be reluctant to take a firm public unless they feel adequately protected from hostile takeovers. Managers in this category should not be forced to seek shareholder approval when they arguably "paid" for the protection at the time of their initial public offering.

[8] *See* Ryngaert, "The Effect of Poison Pill Securities on Shareholder Wealth," Journal of Financial Economics 20 (1988), 357.

Dissenting Voices

While I believe that the policy proposals made here can lead to a better-functioning market for managerial oversight, it is quite clear that some of the above policy proposals are controversial in nature. I conclude, therefore, by addressing some potential objections.

Objections may come from those who believe that competition among the states will provide corporation law that maximizes shareholder value. This presumes that management will seek to incorporate in states with value-maximizing laws. If, however, a state adopts a value-reducing law that tilts the governance balance of power toward management, it is unclear that management has any strong motivation to change to a new state of incorporation. The very feature that may motivate management to maximize value—fear of a takeover—may be eradicated by state law.

There are also those who argue that anti-takeover laws do not exist merely to protect shareholders. It is a common belief that takeovers harm other constituencies within the firm. They are often associated with plant closings, massive white collar layoffs, and attempts to force down labor costs. In some cases, this may be true, though I am aware of no systematic body of evidence that employees of a firm fare worse as the result of a takeover bid than do workers of firms not subject to takeover pressure.[9]

In fact, in many cases takeovers actually compel management to ensure the continued existence of the firm and thus may ultimately create jobs. For example, the takeover rumblings at Disney in the mid-1980's ultimately led to the ouster of a management team that seemed unwilling to fully utilize the assets that Disney had at its disposal. New management took actions that led to greater merchandising of the Disney name and greater use of the Disney film library. This undoubtedly led to more job creation by Disney and better product selection for consumers. On the other hand, if you do not believe that the poor management of firms that are largely exempt from takeover pressure can result in the loss of thousands of jobs, I refer you to the case of General Motors.

Lastly, even those who agree with the contention that current regulations tilt too heavily against acquirers may protest that many of my proposals lean too heavily on the efficiency of the shareholder voting mechanism. There is some evidence that shareholders sometimes vote for

---

[9] For a general response to many of the perceived evils of the takeover market *see* Jensen, "Takeovers: Their Causes and Consequences," *Journal of Economic Perspectives* (Winter 1988), 21.

amendments that reduce firm value. On the other hand, there is also evidence that shareholders do vote against management from time to time.[10] What may be more telling, however, is the votes we never see. Many management teams may refuse to put anti-takeover amendments to a vote if they believe they will lose that vote. Furthermore with the SEC relaxation of shareholder communication rules in October 1992, it is increasingly likely that shareholders will defeat value-decreasing rule changes proposed by management in the future. While I sympathize with those who worry about the efficiency of the proxy voting system, it is my belief that a greater danger lies in relying exclusively on government-made rules that tilt the market for corporate control in any direction without the approval of shareholders.

---

[10] For evidence on the efficiency of the voting mechansim *see* Pound, "Shareholder Activism and Share Values: The Causes and Consequences of Countersolicitations against Management Antitakeover Proposals," *Journal of Law & Economics* 32 (1989), 357.

References and Suggested Readings

Bradley, Michael. 1980. "Interfirm Tender Offers and the Market for Corporate Control." *Journal of Business* 53:345.

Bradley, Michael, Anand Desai, and E. Hun Kim. 1988. "Synergistic Gains from Corporate Acquisitions and Their Division between the Stockholders of Target and Acquiring Firms." *Journal of Financial Economics* 21:3.

Comment, Robert, and Gregg Jarrell. 1987. "Two Tier and Negotiated Tender Offers: The Imprisonment of the Free-Riding Shareholder." *Journal of Financial Economics* 19:283.

Jensen, Michael. 1988. "Takeovers: Their Causes and Consequences." *Journal of Economics Perspectives* 2 (Winter):21.

Karpoff, Jonathan, and Paul Malatesta. 1989. "The Wealth Effects of Second Generation State Takeover Legislation." *Journal of Financial Economics* 25:291.

Macey, Jonathan, and Jeffry Netter. 1987. "Regulation 13d and the Regulatory Process." *Washington University Law Quarterly* 65:131.

Romano, Roberta. 1987. "The Political Economy of Takeover Statues." *Virginia Law Review* 73:11.

Ryngaert, Michael. 1988. "The Effect of Poison Pill Securities on Shareholder Wealth." *Journal of Financial Economics* 20:357.

Bankruptcy

23

The Role of the U.S. Securities and Exchange Commission in Corporate Bankruptcy

Robert Nachtmann
University of Pittsburgh

Participation by the U. S. Securities and Exchange Commission in corporate bankruptcies is established in the bankruptcy legislation of the United States. The evolution of the Commission's role in the context of this legislation has changed over time. This essay reviews the Commission's historical role in the area of corporate reorganizations accomplished through bankruptcy petitions. Recent evidence on reorganization activity is summarized for the reader's review. The essay concludes by outlining an agenda for future developments in Commission activity.

1. The Commission and Corporate Bankruptcy

The Commission's formal presence in bankruptcy proceedings began in 1938. The Chandler Act (1938) amended the Bankruptcy Act of 1898 and prescribed the Commission's activity in the reorganization proceedings for corporations having a public securityholder interest. This position was redefined by two subsequent events. The first was a direct outcome of the passage of the Bankruptcy Code of 1978. The second was the Commission's reassessment in 1983 of its own objectives and procedures regarding corporate bankruptcy. A brief description of Commission activity under each of these three regimes follows.

1.1. Role of the Commission under the Chandler Act

The Chandler Act established two procedures for corporation reorganization under the originating legislation and designated as Chapters X and XI of the Act. Chapter X provided for "impartial and expert administrative assistance in corporate reorganizations through the appointment of a disinterested trustee and the active participation of the SEC . . . ".[1] It conveyed upon the Commission the right to intervene in reorganization cases and entrusted the Commission with the responsibility of preparing advisory reports on plans of reorganization. In practice, this responsibility evolved into two Commission functions: adviser and general expert. The successful outcome of a Chapter X reorganization was a confirmed plan that was found to be "fair and equitable."[2] A fair and equitable finding is synonymous with the application of and adherence to the absolute priority rule.

Chapter XI procedures were substantially different from those of Chapter X. Chapter XI proceedings precluded the Commission's involvement. The scope of the reorganization proceedings was limited to the adjustment of unsecured debts only and proceedings were controlled by the debtor—the petitioning firm—with the permission of the unsecured creditors. The successful outcome under Chapter XI was an approved plan consistent with a finding in the "best interests of the creditors."[3] *No provisions* for an independent study by the court, *the Commission*, or any other agency nor for advisement from any third party to creditors were part of Chapter XI proceedings. More than 90 percent of all business reorganization cases filed over the period 1938 through 1977 were filed under Chapter XI.[4]

1.2. Bankruptcy Code of 1978

The Bankruptcy Code of 1978 revised corporate reorganization procedures in several important ways. These procedures are represented in Chapter 11 of the code. The guiding principle is to obtain a consensual plan of reorganization through negotiations. Provisions of both Chapter X and XI of the act are found in Chapter 11 of the code.

The debtor typically remains in possession, manages operations, and is provided with a period of exclusivity for the production of a reorganization plan. Interested parties to the reorganization negotiate with

---

[1] *Securities and Exchange Commission v. American Trailer Rentals Co.*, 379 U.S. 594 (1965).

[2] Bankruptcy Act, Sect. 221.

[3] Bankruptcy Act, Sect. 366.

[4] H.R. Rep. No. 595, 95th Cong., 1st Sess. 222 (1977).

the debtor through *official committees* that *must* be appointed for unsecured creditors and *may* be appointed for equityholders. The absence of an official committee for an interested party impairs that party's ability to participate in the formulation of the reorganization plan. Committee activities conducted are costly. These costs are assigned to the debtor firm after review by the court.

This development of official committees is important for, at the least, three reasons. First, not all claimants on the assets of the firm need be represented by official committees. Second, official committees are authorized by the court through the action of the case judge. Third, the costs incurred by all official committees become the responsibility of the estate of the debtor-in-possession—the firm.

The code resulted in a strengthening in the Commission's right to participate in corporate reorganizations.[5] Furthermore, since the code has consolidated most of the provisions of Chapters X and XI of the act into Chapter 11 of the code, it effectively increased the possibility of the Commission's appearance from the limited frequency of Chapter X cases under the act.

For the period extending from 1979 through 1983, the Commission maintained its presence in reorganization cases but did so selectively. It appeared before the court to express its views on a wide variety of issues. These included appointment of trustees and examiners, interim managerial compensation, employment of professionals, the use of real property, the appointment of shareholder and creditor committees, the appropriateness of administrative fees, and matters pertaining to the confirmation of the

---

[5] Three provisions of the Code specifically address the role of the Commission. They are:

- 11 U.S.C. Sect. 1109(a) reconfirms the role of expert witness and advisor regarding any aspect of a case. It extends to the *Commission* the right to take up any issue regarding a case, appear before the court, and be heard.
- 11 U.S.C. Sect. 1125(d) confers upon the Commission the right to appear and be heard regarding its assessment of the adequacy of the reorganization plan's disclosure statement. This section of the Code formalizes the Commission's appraisal role of the reorganization plan prior to confirmation which had informally become a part of proceedings under Chapter X of the Bankruptcy Act.
- 11 U.S.C. Sect. 1129(d) authorizes the *Commission* to object to the confirmation of a reorganization plan if the principal purpose of the plan is to avoid the registration provisions of the Securities Act of 1933.

reorganization plan. Of the 250 so-called 12g companies (with public securities outstanding and reporting requirements to the Commission) that filed for reorganization, the Commission appeared in 79 of these cases and reviewed all confirmed plans.

1.3. The Role of the Commission following the Longstreth Report

In 1983, Commissioner Bevis Longstreth initiated a self-audit of the Commission's participation in reorganization cases as part of a more general assessment of the Commission's procedures and objectives in fulfilling its statutory role under the Bankruptcy Code. This resulted in the Commission's Report, *The Securities and Exchange Commission's Role in Bankruptcy Reorganization Proceedings*, hereafter referred to as the Longstreth Report. The current program is a direct outcome of the Longstreth Report. The program is limited to three activities: (1) the full participation of Commission counsel in only those cases for which legal precedence is an expected outcome; (2) comments on plan disclosure statements, and (3) the review of reorganization plans in order to assure compliance with Securities Act registration requirements.

In summary, the Commission's role has changed substantially over time. The Commission's right to appear is established in law and is quite broad. Its current role is limited by choice and focuses upon legal precedence and technical accuracy.

2. Summary of evidence of Corporate Bankruptcy Proceedings

It is understood by participants in bankruptcy proceedings that current procedures are costly; that prebankruptcy financial and operating contracts are often rejected, amended, or dissolved by the court; that an improvement in expediting the bankruptcy process is long overdue; and that it is difficult to identify the extent to which the benefits ensuing from the bankruptcy process are related to the degree of interest in the firm.

A brief summary of important attributes of Chapter 11 reorganization cases is presented in order to assist the reader in making his or her own judgment about the efficiency and effectiveness of bankruptcy proceedings. We summarize evidence on (1) the frequency of corporate reorganizations resulting from Chapter 11 petitions, (2) time spent in bankruptcy, (3) adherence to the rule of absolute priority, and (4) the direct costs—accounting, legal, and financial and managerial consulting fees—incurred by firms that complete the reorganization process.

2.1. Frequency of Corporate Reorganizations in Chapter 11 Proceedings

Bankruptcy petitions for the publicly traded firm represent a small percent of all Chapter 11 filings. The most comprehensive summary of Chapter 11 cases is provided in the SARD report.[6] There were 163,515 Chapter 11 case filings during the period October 1, 1979, through September 30, 1988. These included 838 (0.5 percent) publicly traded companies that have reporting responsibilities to the Commission. Table 1 presents the incidence of Chapter 11 filings.

Whereas public corporations represent a small proportion of Chapter 11 filings, they account for a disproportionate amount of asset totals. The combined assets for all case filings under Chapter 11 protection exceeded $200 billion representing an average book value per firm of $1.2 million. The combined assets of public companies with available accounting information was $99.3 billion, for an average value of $182.5 million.[7] Public companies account for more than half of the combined assets and are 152 times the average size of all firms filing for Chapter 11 protection.

The success rate of the statute to date is low. As of January 31, 1989, confirmed plans of reorganization filed between 1979 and 1986 accounted for only 4.3 percent of the 125,638 cases (n=5,334). Still pending were 37 percent of the cases (n=46,727). Unconfirmed were 34 percent and 24 percent were resolved in Chapters 7, 12, or 13.[8]

Public firms fared somewhat better. Of the 838 public companies, 216 (36 percent) succeeded in developing a confirmed plan. Transferred into Chapter 7 and liquidated were 3 percent of the cases. The status of the remaining 71 percent is unresolved.

---

[6] Information regarding all Chapter 11 filings was obtained from *Statistical Analysis of Chapter 11*, the Statistical Analysis and Reports Division of the Administrative Office of the United States Courts, Oct. 1989. This document, which is referred to throughout as the SARD report, was prepared by Mr. Ed Flynn, Management Analyst, Bankruptcy Division of the Administrative Office of the United States Courts.

[7] Accounting information retrieved from Standard & Poors Compustat Services Inc.'s PCPlus for the fiscal year ending just prior to the filing of a bankruptcy petition was available for 544 of the 838 publicly traded companies. These 544 firms account for 0.33 percent of all Chapter 11 cases filed.

[8] Chapter 7 of the Bankruptcy Code governs liquidations; Chapter 12 processes family owned farms; Chapter 13 deals with personal bankruptcy.

2.2. Time Spent in Bankruptcy

Table 2 presents the findings of five studies of the time firms spent in Chapter 11 reorganization proceedings. The simple weighted average of time spent in bankruptcy is approximately two years. There is no doubt an overlap of firms in the samples. The largest sample, of 101 firms reported by MacMillan et al. (1992), reports an average of 682 days or approximately 1.82 years—2 months less than the weighted average of all studies.

2.3. Deviations from the Absolute Priority Rule

A review of bankruptcy law suggests that deviation from absolute priority is the most likely outcome of corporate reorganizations as a matter of procedural regularity. The evidence reported in Table 2 supports this expected outcome.

Significant departures from the absolute priority rule are common. Each study reports a frequency rate of approximately 70 percent. The studies apply different methods for the measurement of deviations from absolute priority. Eberhart et al. (1990) present evidence that minimizes estimation errors. For those cases in which deviations were observed, stockholders received, on average, 10 percent of the reorganized value of the firm.

2.4. Direct Costs of Bankruptcy

Evidence on the direct costs associated with corporate reorganization under Chapter 11 is quite limited. Table 3 provides summary statistics on direct costs. Weiss (1990) and MacMillan, et al. (1992) provide the most recent evidence. A sample of 101 firms includes 56 NYSE and AMEX listed firms and 45 OTC firms. Measure 1 in Panel A, Costs/ReorgValue, reports the dollar cost associated with the production of $1 of reorganization value. The average cost of successfully reorganizing $1 in going-concern, asset value is $0.244, or approximately 24 percent. The median firm expended $0.095 and this cost ranged from a high $8.312 per dollar to a low of $0.004 per dollar. Other constructions of cost measures are provided to assist readers in forming their own comparison. The conclusions are similar. Chapter 11 reorganizations are costly.

3.0. A New Agenda for the Commission

The Commission is reviewing its policy regarding publicly traded firms that seek the U.S. Bankruptcy Code's Chapter 11 protection. Recall that the Commission plays two significant roles: ensuring the establishment of a stockholders' committee for a firm that petitions for Chapter 11 reorganization and setting legal precedents. I suggest that the Commission broaden its agenda in order to facilitate Chapter 11 avoidance and Chapter 11 revision. This broader agenda should include (1) identification and reduction of transaction costs associated with consensual nonbankruptcy restructuring of public securities, (2) expansion of an advocacy position in Chapter 11 for the public securityholder, and (3) development of a national forum for the revision of Federal Bankruptcy Law in the context of firms with a public securityholder interest.

3.1. Identification and Reduction of Transaction Costs Associated with Chapter 11 Avoidance

The evidence summarized in Section 2 suggests that liquidations are the most likely outcome of a Chapter 11 petition filing. The process consumes significant amounts of the cash reserves of debtor firms. The length of time required for completed reorganizations extends from three months to approximately seven years and averages two years. Financial contracts are revised, and deviations from the absolute priority rule are the norm in completed reorganizations. Finally, the postbankruptcy performance of the reorganized firm as a going concern is not documented. These facts describe a costly but unsuccessful process. Chapter 11 avoidance is a reasonable goal of policy revision.

The Commission can make significant advances in facilitating avoidance of Chapter 11 through the recognition of the value of reducing the costs of consensual nonbankruptcy restructuring. I suggest that the Commission charge its General Counsel to coordinate an effort to focus on increasing the flexibility of firms, securityholders, and exchanges in the area of distress management. This analysis should involve the Divisions of Corporate Finance, Investment Management, and Market Regulation as well as the Offices of the Chief Accountant and Economic Analysis. A possible outcome of such an endeavor might be a classification of financially distressed firms that relaxes Securities Exchange Act constraints on firms appealing for such status.

Three current activities of the Commission are on point. First, the Commission is establishing procedural protection for investors in connection with tender and exchange offers for noninvestment-grade debt securities, which would lead to a revision in Rule 10b-13. Rule 10b-13 outlines purchase prohibitions during tender or exchange offers. Chapter 11 avoidance should be one guiding principle in the formation of this ruling. A ruling that would inhibit consensual nonbankruptcy restructuring or increase the cost of such restructuring can be expected to lead to an increase in Chapter 11 activity.

Second, the Commission's current revision of shareholder communication rules and the proxy reform have significant implications for firms in financial distress. The Commission should be applauded for this effort. Institutional investors are playing an increasing role in the governance of the public corporation. Decreasing the costs faced by institutions regarding information transfer, trading, and the consolidation of positions in the securities of financially distressed firms will enhance bankruptcy avoidance and reduce the costs associated with consensual nonbankruptcy restructuring.

Third, the office of the Chief Accountant recently released a staff bulletin regarding quasi reorganizations. The quasi reorganization permits firms to restate their financials consistent with a "fresh start". This restatement does not require a Chapter 11 petition.

Other recent initiatives to reduce the transaction costs of financial distress management should be promoted. For example, the NYSE has moved to reduce the cost of bond trading, thereby improving the level of market transparency in the trading of bonds. Self-regulatory organizations should be encouraged to adopt similar strategies. Professional institutes have proposed solutions to unique conditions, such as the American Bankruptcy Institute proposal for a procedure to accommodate product-liability suits for asbestos makers. This proposal would establish a separate trust for the financing of suits separate from the going concern. Product liability cases tend to require the most amount of time in Chapter 11 reorganizations. Innovations in the management of financial distress conditional upon asset specific factors lead to specialized solutions best provided by the markets, not the courts.

3.2. Expansion of the Advocacy Program

The Commission commits limited resources to a public securityholder-advocacy program. This program attempts to ensure that the exercise of the bankruptcy option by management does not preclude a public securityholder from access to the Chapter 11 reorganization process. The role of the Commission as an advocate can be debated. Nonetheless, access to the Federal court by management and inclusion of the Federal court as a participant in bankruptcy induces a complex structure of agency problems. These problems are too extensive to detail in this essay. (The Commission may be an effective means of reducing the costs associated with these problems.)

I highlight three areas of concern. First, filing for Chapter 11 is a board-approved action, which at any point in time may not represent the best interests of public securityholders. Second, management typically retains its role as operating manager of the firm and has the authority to petition for Chapter 11. This function is subject to continual approval of the court, or more specially, the judge assigned to the case. Management teams now service a broader stakeholder constituency. In order to maintain its control of the firm, management can be motivated to satisfy the court's interests in contradiction to its role as an agent for securityholders. Third, the court often attempts to disallow the formation of an equity committee by fiat. This denies the extension to all claimants of the consensual-negotiation objective of Chapter 11 reorganizations. The Commission may here serve as the advocate of last resort for public securityholders once the firm comes under the aegis of the court.

3.3. Bankruptcy Legislative Reform

Senator Howell Heflin and Representative Jack Brooks of the Senate and House Judiciary Committees have proposed reform of U.S. bankruptcy law. Their goal is to amend the Bankruptcy Code of 1978 in several ways. The first is to establish a Bankruptcy Commission to review the Bankruptcy Code. This is long overdue. Their efforts are also directed toward amending certain aspects of the code with regard to its application to cases involving commerce and credit and individual creditors and to add a temporary chapter to govern the reorganization of small business.

The recent spate of Chapter 11 bankruptcies in the airline industry is one example of the need for amendment of the code. Chapter 11 provides to the airline in financial distress the ability to reduce current costs and thereby reduce the price for services. In order to compete, healthy airlines must reduce fares to levels that are often below variable costs, further deteriorating the financial quality of the industry. One suggested amendment would require that firms with fungible and tradable assets such as equipment leases and airport gates be required to turn over these assets upon Chapter 11 filing. This speaks to the use of Chapter 11 as a stalling tactic for the inevitable and in the process impairing the security values of competing firms through predatory pricing.

I suggest that the Commission support the initiative to revise corporate bankruptcy. The public corporation is the most successful entity in effecting a reorganization in Chapter 11. It would seem reasonable that Chapter 11 be decomposed not only on the basis of firm size but on the basis of public-securityholder ownership. For the privately held firm, the court in many ways substitutes for a market in focusing the activity of claimants on the firm. The public corporation need not avail itself of this device when nonbankruptcy restructuring is feasible and less costly.

Conclusion

Corporate reorganization under Chapter 11 bankruptcy attempts to bring the Federal Bankruptcy program into the twentieth century. The problem is that we are moving into the twenty-first. The success of corporate reorganization under Chapter 11 is debatable. The U.S. Securities and Exchange Commission is in a position to improve the economic processing of financial distress. Failure as well as success is symptomatic of a competitive economic environment. The Commission can affect the costs of achieving a healthy economy in several important ways. I suggest that the Commission pay attention to the direct as well as the indirect costs of financial distress.

Table 1
Chapter 11 Case Filings by Year for the Period 1979–1988

Year of filing	Total cases filed	12(g) companies	12(g) as % of Total
1979–1980[a]	7,944	70	0.87
1981	10,085	66	0.65
1982	18,915	72	0.38
1983	20,351	94	0.46
1984	20,311	97	0.48
1985	23,376	146	0.63
1986	24,773	117	0.47
1987	20,070	99	0.49
1988[b]	17,690	76	0.43
Total	163,515	837	0.51

[a] Number of cases filed are for the periods October 1, 1979, through December 31, 1980.

[b] 12(g) cases include only those firms that filed through September 1988.

Table 2
Recent Evidence on Time Spent in Chapter 11 and the Occurrence of Deviations from the Absolute Priority Rule in Corporate Reorganizations.

Study	Sample period	Length (yrs)[a]	Sample (#)	Dev. from APR[b]		
				#	%	Equity/Reorg[c]
Franks and Torous (1989)	1970–1978	4.76	15	10	67	.35
	1979–1983	2.57	15	11	73	.29
Daigle and Maloney (1990)	1981–1987	1.83	56	40	71	.28[d]
Eberhart, Moore, and Roenfeldt (1990)	1979–1986	2.10	30	23	77	.10
Weiss (1990)	1979–1986	2.50	37	29	78	n/e[e]
MacMillan, Nachtmann & Phillips-Patrick (1992)	1979–1989	1.82	101	n/a	n/a	n/a

[a] Length reported in years refers to time spent in reorganization proceedings measured from the petition filing date to the confirmation date of the reorganization plan for firms in Chapter 11.

[b] Deviation from the absolute priority rule (Dev. from APR) is measured differently in each of the studies reported in Table 2. We report the authors' findings with respect to number (#) and frequency of incidents identifying cases where absolute priority is not maintained, but we construct from their results the ratio of common equity to the reorganized firm's value (Equity/Reorg). The reorganized value is measured as the value of claims distributed through the reorganization plan.

[c] Equity/Reorg is the average value of the equity to reorganized value ratio for all firms identified by the authors as having confirmed a plan that deviated from the absolute priority rule.

[d] Daigle and Maloney (1990) do not specifically identify which plans include a measured deviation from absolute priority. Rather, they report the percentage of common stock retained by common stockholders. This is not direct evidence of a deviation from the absolute priority rule. We report the average value of percentage common retained for all firms other than those (N=6) that were liquidated.

[e] n/e: not estimable. Weiss (1990) does not provide measures of the reorganized value of the firm.

Table 3
Direct Costs Associated with Corporate Reorganizations under Chapter 11

	Mean	Median	Low	High	St. Dev.	N	Period
MNP (1992):							
1. Costs/ReorgValue[a]	.244	.095	.004	8.312	.910	101	1979–88
2. Costs/Value[b]	.113	.089	.004	.893	.132	101	1979–88
3. Costs/Assets[c]	.059	.033	.029	10.000	1.102	101	1979–88
Weiss (1990)[d]	.028	.025	.009	.070	n/a	31	1980–86

[a] Costs/ReorgValue is the nominal sum of direct costs divided by the reorganization value of the firm as measured by total assets on exit from Chapter 11.

[b] Costs/Value (defined as Costs+ReorgValue) is nominal sum of direct costs divided by the sum of resources available, including the ReorgValue plus the costs associated with establishing the reorganization.

[c] Costs/Assets is the nominal sum of direct costs divided by the book value of total assets at the fiscal year end prior to bankruptcy.

[d] Costs identified from court dockets divided by the book value of total assets at the fiscal year end prior to bankruptcy.

References and Suggested Readings

Daigle, Katherine, and Michael Maloney. 1989. "Residual Claims in Bankruptcy: An Agency Theory Explanation." Working paper, Clemson University, Clemson, S.C.

Eberhart, A., W. Moore, and R. Roenfeldt. 1990. "Security Pricing and Deviations from the Absolute Priority Rule in Bankruptcy Proceedings." *Journal of Finance* 45:1457–70.

Flynn, Ed. 1989. "Statistical Analysis of Chapter 11." Report of the Statistical Analysis and Reports Division of the Administrative Office of the United States Courts. Washington, D.C.: U.S. Government Printing Office.

Franks, Julian, and Walter Torous. 1989. "An Empirical Investigation of U.S. Firms in Reorganization." *Journal of Finance* 44:747-769.

Longstreth, B. 1983. "The Securities and Exchange Commission's Role in Bankruptcy Reorganization Proceedings." U.S. Securities and Exchange Commission, Washington, D.C.: U.S. Government Printing Office.

MacMillan, Henry, Robert Nachtmann, and Fred Phillips-Patrick. 1992. "Costs of Reorganizing Under Chapter 11: Some Evidence from the 80's." Working paper, University of Pittsburgh.

Weiss, Lawrence. 1990. "Bankruptcy Resolution: Direct Costs and Violation of Priority Claims." *Journal of Financial Economics* 27: 85–314.

Whitford, W., and L. LoPucki. 1989. "Settlements Without Entitlements: Bargaining Over Equity's Share in the Bankruptcy Reorganization of Large, Publicly Held Companies." Unpublished manuscript, University of Wisconsin.

V

MARKET STRUCTURE AND PERFORMANCE

The Structure of Securities Markets and the SEC's Market 2000 Report

24

Market 2000

Allan W. Kleidon
Cornerstone Research and Stanford University

Introduction

In a July 1992 release, the Securities and Exchange Commission (SEC) announced that the Division of Market Regulation was undertaking "a study of the structure of the U.S. equity markets and of the regulatory environment in which those markets operate" (SEC 1992, 1524). This followed SEC Chairman Breeden's announcement of Market 2000 (the study) to the Securities Industry Association in December 1991.

The stated motivation for the study is the extensive change that has occurred since the early 1970s when the SEC last examined the securities markets in detail, which resulted in the 1973 Policy Statement on the Structure of a Central Market System and the subsequent establishment of the National Market System (NMS) for securities. That regulatory framework, with various modifications, has been the dominant mold within which the securities markets have operated for twenty years. The question is, is it appropriate for the next century?

The Study's timing is not coincidental, given the strains on the existing system caused by the globalization of markets and trading, the emergence of vigorous markets in "derivative" securities such as options and futures, and the enormous technological changes reflected in both computer systems and competing market mechanisms. Winners and losers under potential new rules have every incentive to argue their particular cases forcefully.

Overall Reaction to the Release

What role does the SEC play in such a situation? On one hand, it has the luxury of substantial largesse at its disposal, and, given the absence of categorically correct answers to the questions being posed, it can dispense favors to various constituents without obvious partiality. On the other hand, it suffers from the standard asymmetry of incentives faced by regulatory authorities, with the attendant propensity to tinker at the margin.

The current Market 2000 release appears to be a sincere attempt to ask the right questions about potential regulatory changes in the U.S. equity market. It is apparent from the release that the issues selected are those that have caused some trouble for the SEC and on which various representations from interested parties have been made. This is appropriate in at least one sense: these wheels are squeaking for good reasons.

Nevertheless, the release is more a recitation of current ills or issues, with reasonable evenhandedness in stating alternate cases, than it is a blueprint for progress. It is true that the 1992 release is not the final report but rather a call for response and reaction. However the extent to which the release is a *tabula rasa* leaves the impression that the SEC has little by way of a conceptual framework with which to organize, let alone resolve, the disputes that are coming before it.

My primary reaction to the release is to urge the SEC to take the discussion one level higher (or deeper) before attempting to address the specific issues raised in the study. For example, the release asks commentators whether any current regulations should be removed because they are impediments to the proper working of the industry. The prior question, in my view, is: What is the purpose of regulation in this industry? Without an adequate answer to that question, the SEC has little to guide it if commentators come down on different sides of a particular issue. And, of course, there *will* be parties on opposite sides in almost any case—first, because there are so often wealth transfers consequent on regulatory changes and second, because, even if some regulation would be regarded by all as unnecessary in the abstract, its very existence for an extended period will have evoked reactions that are costly to implement and hence provide a current competitive edge to whoever has best worked out how to accommodate the regulation.

The release would have been much different, and in my view much better, had an overall rationale for regulation in this market been in place before the release were written. For example, the issues could have been better organized. Much of the Release is initially confusing because the same issues appear to be repeated under various guises.[1] Moreover, ostensible regulatory goals, such as competition and efficiency, are stated simultaneously and often as being in actual or potential conflict, for example in discussions of market fragmentation. The apparent acceptance of many equally valued goals means that the study will lose effect if it does little more than allow for arbitrary choice from multiple goals to justify whatever the SEC ultimately chooses to do.

The rest of this paper attempts to provide some framework for evaluating the issues raised in the release and to address the specific issues in terms of the framework.

Regulatory Principles

Why have the SEC in the first place? The fact that the SEC was created along with so many other agencies in the golden regulatory period following the Depression raises general questions such as those addressed by Stigler (1971) and Peltzman (1976). For example, Peltzman considers regulation to be the equilibrium outcome of forces of supply and demand where the regulator, when considering regulatory changes that will favor one group, weighs the potential benefits (often pecuniary, including, e.g., financial electoral support for legislators) against the potential costs imposed by those who are disadvantaged.

Within this somewhat cynical (albeit often realistic) framework, the SEC must ask itself whether the changes to which it is currently reacting have altered the clientele for its regulatory services. For example, institutions have increased in relative trading and ownership importance in the stock market since the 1970s and are becoming increasingly vocal in their opposition to current regulations that implicitly equate their importance with that of an individual investor (e.g., regulation of block trade executions).

The SEC touches on these issues when it invokes "equity" as a criterion for regulatory justification. While political realities may dictate ultimate decisions, this paper leaves such matters to the private calculus of the SEC and focuses instead on textbook rationales for regulation. Three issues seem particularly pertinent: competition, property rights, and externalities.

---

[1] E.g., subsection A, *Market Structure and Operations,* of Section IV. *Issues*, concludes with a litany of concerns and the statement: "All these issues are discussed more fully below."

Competition

The benefits of competition need not be reiterated here. However, two matters warrant emphasis.

First, the primary regulatory issue concerning competition is cause, not effect; that is, are there the barriers to entry that create a noncompetitive situation? If the SEC wishes to address questions of competition, then it should focus on the identification and elimination of barriers to entry. For example, the prices of NYSE seats (which capitalize expected rents) indicate that NYSE specialists enjoy some market power, and the behavior of intraday prices also provides indirect evidence of market power. For example, Stoll and Whaley (1990) estimate the bid-ask spread implicit in opening NYSE prices and conclude that the implied cost of immediacy is significantly higher at open than at close, which they attribute in part to temporary price deviations at open induced by the exploitation of market power by the specialist.

An alternative source of potential information on barriers to entry in the U.S. equity market that is not exploited in the current release, is the characteristics of overseas markets or U.S. markets for derivatives.[2] For example, Brock and Kleidon (1992) provide evidence on U.S. equity spreads that is consistent with market power of specialists; additional evidence is provided by examination of U.K. equity markets, which are organized along the lines of NASDAQ (see Kleidon and Werner 1992) and the foreign exchange market (see Bollerslev and Domowitz 1990) and Hsieh and Kleidon 1992).

Second, the benefits of competition (assuming adequate protection of property rights), such as innovation and efficiency, should not be confused as regulatory goals with the same priority as competition itself. This seems possible in the current release (1992, 1527):

> A focus of the study will be to ensure that regulators and others continue to craft an approach preserving the contributions of alternative systems, such as competition, innovation and reduced costs, while taking into account their overall effect on the fairness and efficiency of the market as a whole.

---

[2] *See* SEC (1992, 1528), which states that derivative and international markets are not examined except for any direct impact they might have on U.S. equity markets.

Property Rights

Innovation in a competitive market requires adequate definition and enforcement of property rights, such as patent laws. Enforcement of property rights in such standard legal forms as prohibition of fraud clearly underlies well-functioning securities markets, and it may be efficient for the SEC to specialize in related laws concerning securities. More general, however, is the question of property rights over innovations and technologies that have some public good aspect, for example, the quotations generated on an exchange floor such as the NYSE.

This question is particularly pertinent given technological innovations allowing competitors to base the prices offered to customers on the quotation stream from, say, the NYSE. For example, one NYSE competitor, an automated execution system for listed stocks operated by Bernard Madoff and Co. (Madoff), offers rapid execution of relatively small orders at the best current exchange quotes, which presumes access by Madoff to those quotes. Issues of possible externalities tied to discrimination based on transactions size are discussed below; but clearly the NYSE (or more generally the NMS, to the [limited] extent of price discovery from exchanges other than the NYSE) is producing a product that is invaluable for Madoff's operation and for which the NYSE could conceivably receive direct compensation. Inadequate compensation may push more than a competitive amount of order flow to Madoff (which pays for order flow) and conversely.

Similar issues have been faced in the past, for example, the competition from bucket shops faced by the Chicago Board of Trade (CBOT) during the nineteenth century when the telegraph was developed, which had the effect of dramatically increasing the value of the quotes. Mulherin, Netter, and Overdahl (1990) provide an excellent analysis of the issues, both legal and economic. They conclude: "By establishing property rights to exchange-generated quotations, the courts enabled the CBOT to reap the gains from investing in new trading technology ... new trading technology, *combined with both well-defined and well-enforced property rights*, can lead to cost-reducing innovation" (p. 21, emphasis added).

The release adequately identifies the issue of property rights in quotes and seeks comment. The ultimate response to the conflict between those who generate and seek compensation for the quotes and those who have an incentive to free-ride may depend on the SEC's presumptions. Bureaucratic conservatism may imply that the status quo remains intact until clearly inadequate—which may be too late for those bearing the costs but not full benefits of quote generation, if they lose the competitive struggle (to either domestic or foreign competitors). My personal presumption is that those generating quotes have property rights over them and should be compensated by those seeking to compete based on the quotes themselves. The question of a fair price will no doubt arise, but that is at least the right question.

Externalities

These questions are complicated by the externalities that are inherent in securities markets, especially given the importance and ubiquity of asymmetric information. Since market prices can move continuously and rapidly as information changes, potential traders naturally seek up-to-date price and volume information. Those producing quotes have a private incentive to provide these to customers—but not to rival market makers. On the other hand, depending on their production, quotes have public-good qualities that may suggest their free release to all. The example of possible free-riding on exchange generated quotes illustrates the additional complications of asymmetric information in the securities context.

As articulated by Bagehot (1971), trades by those with superior information will always be at the expense of the other party (or the trade would not occur); consequently, a price will be charged for transactions services (the spread) to recoup sufficient profit from uninformed liquidity traders to compensate for losses to informed traders.[3] If there are inadequate numbers of uninformed traders to offset losses to the informed, the market may close.

There is evidence that the trades that convey the most information, that is, that are most heavily based on private information, are those of intermediate size (Barclay and Warner 1992). This means that the small trades "picked off" by the Madoff system are likely to be those based on little or no private information. However, the spreads set in the exchange are in part designed to protect against informed trades. The logical consequences of losing a stream of uninformed trades to Madoff are reasonably straightforward; since the ratio of informed to uninformed trades increases, the exchange spread may rise, giving Madoff (which guarantees the current quotes) a greater incentive to purchase more (uninformed) trades, since more can be made on each round-trip transaction.

If this were to siphon off more uninformed trades, the exchange spread might rise further, and so on. Ultimately, the exchange may prove

---

[3] This concept has been extensively exploited in recent literature; *see*, e.g., Glosten and Milgrom (1985), Kyle (1985), and the review by Admati (1991).

unprofitable, but, if it dies, then so does the source of quotes that is the basis of Madoff's system. Clearly this increases the importance of protecting property rights in quotes that have been generated through costly transactions with better-informed traders.

Two other externalities also relate to quotes and information. First, some standards of "truth in advertising" may be appropriate. For example, the NYSE strongly emphasizes the frequency of NYSE transactions between the inside quotes, in contrast with either the NASDAQ or Madoff systems.[4] It is quite possible that many ultimate customers of transactions services are unaware of the potential differences in indirect execution costs across market structures and hence focus on direct commission costs (especially if some market structures charge little commission or even pay for orders). A useful role for the SEC may be to define criteria on which the alternate exchanges must credibly report, with possible certification procedures (either public or private). Disclosure requirements in this context may reasonably include the total product actually being sold.[5]

The second issue concerns fragmentation of the market. The potential externality if transactions are made in various sectors of a fragmented market is that price discovery may be impaired if information-based trades are not observed by all relevant players. This argument originally formed the basis of the NMS, and in general it makes sense. However, we are gaining new evidence about which trades convey the most information, and this may allow informed reaction to different forms of fragmentation (and its cousin, transparency, i.e., immediate reporting of trades).

For example, institutions currently account for about 70 to 80 percent of NYSE trades and about 50 percent of ownership (see Securities Industry Association 1991 and Fabozzi and Modigliani 1992, 225). Various off-floor procedures have developed to accommodate institutional interests, including trades on regional or overseas markets.[6] Whether this is a problem

---

[4] *See*, e.g., NYSE (1992). *See also* Lee (1991), Blume and Goldstein (1992), and Petersen and Fialkowski (1992).

[5] This general argument may apply to many of the issues about which different groups claim the consumers are ignorant because of market complexities.

[6] E.g., if a large block trade was split up by NYSE floor-trader participation under rule 72, the trade was often made on regional exchanges. The recent amendment to Rule 72 to allow clean crosses on the NYSE (*see Wall Street Journal*, Oct. 26, 1992) was sought in response to the loss of trades to other exchanges and off-exchange markets

for price discovery will depend on whether there was much information in institutional trades that are diverted from public view in a single market. Similarly, from a pure price discovery viewpoint, the cost of any siphoning of small trades from the NMS will depend on whether any information was conveyed by those trades.

Conclusions

The Market 2000 release cites the following as issues to be addressed by the study:

Market structure and operations

Market competition

Market fragmentation
- Multiple markets—linkages
- Proprietary trading systems

Best execution
- Payment for order flow

Transparency
- Overseas trading

Regulatory oversight

The release concludes with a set of related questions on which it invites commentary, many of which are stimulated by pressures felt by the SEC as the 1970s National Market System is strained by subsequent changes in markets and technology.

The questions are good, and the issues are real. What is missing from the release is a structured approach to economic regulation in general and to the specifics of the securities markets in particular. The ultimate success of the study may well depend on its ability to find the right balance between general statements that are unobjectionable, yet broadly irrelevant, and the attendant minutiae of regulatory bureaucracy.

---

and electronic trading systems.

If the SEC does not have a clear conceptual framework, the Market 2000 study runs a very real risk of generating partisan comment with little agreement across commentators (which is simply a magnified picture of the current situation that has led to the study) and with little or no progress on answering the questions it raises. It is one thing to ask the right questions, especially if they are dictated by current pressures, it is another to provide a leadership role in dealing with the frictions created by evolutionary market conditions.

References and Suggested Readings

Admati, A. R. 1991. "The Informational Role of Prices: A Review Essay." *Journal of Monetary Economics* 28:347–61.

Bagehot, W. [pseud.]. 1971. "The Only Game In Town." *Financial Analysts Journal* 27:12–14, 22.

Barclay, M. J. and J. B. Warner. 1992. "Stealth Trading and Volatility: Which Trades Move Prices?" Working paper, Simon Graduate School of Business Administration, University of Rochester.

"Big Board Set to Allow Bypass of Floor Trades." 1992. *Wall Street Journal*, Oct. 26, C1.

Blume, M. E., and M. A. Goldstein. 1992. "Differences in Execution Prices Among the NYSE, the Regionals and the NASD." Unpublished Working paper no. 4-92, White Center for Financial Research, Wharton School, University of Pennsylvania, Philadelphia.

Bollerslev, T., and I. Domowitz. 1990. "Trading Patterns and the Behavior of Prices in the Interbank Deutschemark/Dollar Foreign Exchange Market." Working paper no. 119, Kellogg Graduate School of Management, Northwestern University, Evanston, IL.

Brock, W. A., and A. W. Kleidon. 1992. "Periodic Market Closure and Trading Volume: A Model of Intraday Bids and Asks." *Journal of Economic Dynamics and Control* 16:451–89.

Fabozzi, F. J. and F. Modigliani. 1992. *Capital Markets: Institutions and Instruments*. Englewood Cliffs, N. J.: Prentice Hall.

Glosten, L. R., and P. R. Milgrom. 1985. "Bid, Ask and Transaction Prices in A Specialist Market with Heterogeneously Informed Traders." *Journal of Financial Economics* 14:71–100.

Hseih, D. A., and A. W. Kleidon. 1992. "Determinants of Bid-Ask Spreads: Evidence from Foreign Exchange Markets." Working paper, Graduate School of Business, Stanford University.

Kleidon, A. W., and I. W. Werner. 1992. "Round-the-Clock Trading: Evidence from U.K. Cross-Listed Securities." Working paper, Graduate School of Business, Stanford University.

Kyle, A. S. 1985. "Continuous Auctions and Insider Trading." *Econometrica* 53:1315–35.

Lee, C. M. C. 1991. "Purchase of Order Flows and Favorable Executions: An Intermarket Comparison." Working paper, Graduate School of Business Administration, University of Michigan, Ann Arbor.

Mulherin, J. H., J. M. Netter, and J. A. Overdahl. 1990. "Who Owns the Quotes? A Case Study into the Definition and Enforcement of Property Rights at the Chicago Board of Trade." Working paper, Office of Economic Analysis, U.S. Securities and Exchange Commission. Washington, D. C.: U.S. Government Printing Office.

Peltzman, S. 1976. "Toward A More General Theory of Regulation." *Journal of Law and Economics* 17:211–40.

Petersen, M. A., and D. Fialkowski. 1992. "Price Improvement: Stock on Sale." Working paper, Graduate School of Business, University of Chicago.

Securities Industry Association. 1991. *Trends*. New York.

Stigler, G. J. 1971. "The Theory of Economic Regulation." *Bell Journal of Economics and Management Science* 1:3–21.

Stoll, H. R., and R. E. Whaley. 1990. "Stock Market Structure and Volatility." *Review of Financial Studies* 3:37–71.

U.S. Securities and Exchange Commission. 1992. "Market 2000." *U.S. Equity Market Structure Study*, Exchange Act Release No. 34-30920, 51 S.E.C. Docket 1524 (July 14).

Wall Street Journal. 1992. "Big Board Set to Allow Bypass of Floor Trades." October 26, C1.

25

Market Transparency: Pros, Cons, and Property Rights

J. Harold Mulherin
Dartmouth College

1. Introduction

Transparency in securities and futures markets describes the extent to which information about trading is made publicly available on a real-time basis. A perfectly transparent market would be an environment in which all relevant information including transaction prices, trading volume, quotes, order flow, and trader identification is instantaneously available to all potential investors. In many respects, therefore, a perfectly transparent market resembles the economist's notion of a perfectly competitive market, in which knowledge is equally available and completely dispersed to all market participants. In current discussions of securities markets, much of the debate on transparency involves questions on the degree to which off-exchange, after hours, and foreign activity in U.S. equities should be publicly regulated and incorporated into the consolidated tape that compiles information from U.S. securities exchanges.

The entry of the specific term transparency into the lexicon of securities and futures markets appears to be relatively recent. A review of studies ranging from the Securities and Exchange Commission's 1963 *Special Study* and 1971 *Institutional Investor Study* to the New York Stock Exchange's 1990 report *Market Volatility and Investor Confidence* finds no topical heading for transparency. Of course, these studies do discuss issues such as market fragmentation, automation, sales and quote dissemination, and the openness of the specialist's book, which all are integral to the current debate on transparency. Hence, the concepts tied to market transparency and the associated policy debate are not new. Why is it, therefore, that transparency now deserves its own section in the SEC's current review of the structure of U.S. equity markets?

At least four related factors contribute to the current emphasis on transparency. First, ongoing improvements in technology facilitate the implementation of real-time price, and quote and volume dissemination. Second, the advancing technology together with a continued growth in the demand for trading services has raised the value of the information produced by equity markets. Third, the sizable growth in the value of the information generated by financial exchanges has made the issue of transparency a central choice variable for the various exchanges. Finally, many of these same forces are bringing more direct competition across previously uncrossed international boundaries, making the strategic choices of financial exchanges regarding transparency even more important.

In spite of, or perhaps instead because of, the importance of these transparency-related issues, the debate on transparency has not had a consistent focus. Indeed, the exact meaning of transparency remains elusive. Similar to the difficulties with the related concept of perfect competition, there has been confusion as to whether transparency should be a specific objective of regulators or instead should be a result of the process of competition between financial exchanges. Indeed, regulators seem unaware that complete transparency is not necessarily optimal.

This essay addresses the pros and cons of seeking various levels of market transparency as well as the incentives of financial exchanges to provide transparency on their own intitiative. The guiding framework in the analysis is the premise that financial exchanges such as the New York Stock Exchange are best viewed as competitive firms having the objective of producing prices in their traded instruments. Since exchanges compete on various margins of price quality such as transparency by weighing the costs and benefits of the quality components, the analysis indicates that perfect transparency, even if attainable, is not necessarily desirable and that financial exchanges have strong private incentives to provide the appropriate level of transparency to investors.

2. Transparency, Price Informativeness, Liquidity, and Regulation

Perfect transparency, like perfect competition, is an ideal that is rarely obtained in actual markets. In securities markets, however, innovations in technology as well as innovative implementation of such technology are placing perfect transparency within reach. But even as the costs of transparency fall, is 100 percent transparency a desirable goal? Several factors suggest a negative response to this query. Beyond a certain point, greater transparency can actually lessen the informativeness of securities prices, impede the provision of liquidity, and hinder the regulation of the exchange process.

2.1. Transparency and Price Informativeness

Conceptually, if securities prices were perfectly transparent, then investors would know, at any time, the fundamental value of any public issue. While an apparently laudable goal, this perfect transparency sets up a paradox—as securities prices become perfectly known, there is less individual return to discovering new information. The quicker revelation of information lessens the incentives of an individual investor or analyst to search out fundamental information. But if less effort is devoted to analyzing fundamentals, prices will be less informative. This indicates that attempts to mandate transparency can actually impede price informativeness.

The impediments to price informativeness become especially onerous if mandated transparency implies that an exchange must give away its prices. The information contained in equity prices is a valuable product and exchanges invest time and effort in advancing the technology of trading in order to improve upon existing price quality. Certainly, competitors and customers of a particular exchange might reap short-term gains from not having to pay for information that they value highly. Yet the mandated provision of price information at less-than-market clearing levels will significantly reduce the long-term incentive for exchanges to improve the quality of the financial instruments and trading procedures available to investors, ultimately hurting all participants in securities markets.

Trade secrets provide a good analogy. If a company's trade secrets were mandated to be readily transparent to its competitors, then no individual company would have an incentive to innovate. Viewing the prices produced by a given exchange as a trade secret, one can see that perfect transparency would impede the price-discovery process in equity markets.

Of course, viewing equity prices as trade secrets or even more generally as the property of a particular financial exchange runs counter to the public-good view of securities markets that is promoted by the concept of a National Market System. But assuming that prices are public property will neither produce prices nor provide transparency. Indeed, maintaining a view that the prices produced on U.S. exchanges are public property may only decrease the informativeness of the prices.

2.2. Transparency and Liquidity

Transparency is thought to attract investors and thereby improve liquidity. But as prices become more transparent, the individual investor must make a decision between making use of a given exchange's prices when making investment decisions and avoiding the fees for trading on the exchange. Transparency can, therefore, lead to off-exchange trading that can reduce liquidity on organized exchanges. Indeed, the traders most injured by a decline in liquidity would be individual investors who have limited access to off-exchange trading.

Moreover, not all investors prefer to have information on their trading habits made immediately available to other investors. For example, an investor with a large trade to complete may prefer some anonymity to reduce the market impact of his or her trades. This desire for anonymity is not peculiar to securities markets and also appears in settings as diverse as artwork and oil tankers. Indeed, the preference for anonymity is one reason for the pervasiveness of brokers in a variety of market settings. Mandates of transparency that lessen anonymity will reduce the trades made by some investors. This reduction in trades will lessen liquidity and also reduce the overall information reaching the market.

Consider the issue in terms of the specialist's book. Moving toward greater transparency would imply making information on the limit orders available to all investors. But since some of those presently placing limit orders may prefer that their orders not be made public, they would place fewer orders in a more transparent market, thereby reducing liquidity. Hence, providing transparency entails trade-offs involving liquidity, which a given exchange will have to weigh as part of its business decisions.

2.3. Transparency and Regulatory Monitoring

While transparency is generally felt to facilitate regulation and, in doing so, ensure fairness in securities trading, movement toward complete transparency on regulated exchanges can actually impede the regulatory process. If enhanced transparency allows unregulated, off-exchange locations to obtain price information from organized exchanges, then more trading will occur in the unregulated setting. This is exactly what happened following the introduction of the stock price ticker in the 19th century. Off-exchange bucket shops gained access to exchange quotes via the telegraph and conducted trade under less-than-desirable conditions. Only after the U.S. courts acknowledged property rights in price quotes did the freeriding by off-exchange locations decline.

Ironically, it is the growth in after-hours trading, proprietary systems, and fourth-market strategies that has heightened the debate on transparency in U.S. markets. These nonexchange venues for trading are said to create a gap in regulatory coverage that lessens transparency. One possible response in this current gap is to record the off-exchange trades on a run-off tape that would be consolidated with currently recorded transactions.

Portraying these off-exchange transactions as a hole in current regulation is misleading. Instead, these off-exchange trading locations can be thought of as a reaction to transparency,—that is, investors prefer these locations because of the explicit lack of mandated transparency. Any attempt to export transparency to these locations may push some investors even further outside the SEC's control, much like the movement from regional exchanges to the over-the-counter markets after the creation of the SEC in the 1930s.

This threat of a flight from transparency regulations appears real and is one reason for the attractiveness of London over New York for some trades in U.S. securities. This attraction of order flow by London suggests that exchanges have incentives to explicitly develop a strategy toward transparency. Indeed, the NYSE has responded to London's strategy by structuring one of its after-hours sessions to accommodate some institutional investors' preference for anonymity when making large trades.

3. Incentives for Financial Exchanges to Provide Transparency

The property-rights perspective in this essay treats a financial exchange as a competitive firm and contrasts with the historical perception that poses securities markets in a public goods framework with a mandate to raise capital. The public goods approach probably stems from the historical view that the U.S. stock market had many natural monopoly characteristics and that regulation was necessary to enhance efficiency in securities trading. But given the current cross-border competition and the variety of trading venues, the monopoly paradigm of securities markets is outmoded.

It is much more useful to view financial exchanges as competitive firms producing a number of complementary products, such as liquidity, trade processing, and dispute resolution, that attract investors and lead to the valuation of traded instruments. Indeed, financial exchanges can be thought of as firms that produce prices. This price production is a direct source of value for exchanges and continues to be of growing importance.

In their role as price producers, financial exchanges face trade-offs. To attract business, the exchanges disseminate information on recent prices and volume as well as the level and depth of price quotes. But the exchanges do not reveal all information for free, as the information is costly to produce and is also of direct value to investors. Because full information might dissuade some investors from submitting orders in the first place, exchanges must estimate how much as well as what information dissemination will maximize total exchange profits coming from sales of quotes, fees for trading, and so forth. In addition to direct decisions on transparency, the exchange will also choose rules on minimum ticks, where and when members can trade (e.g., NYSE Rule 390), and other operation procedures. In making such decisions, an individual exchange is competing against the services provided by other exchanges as prescribed by the competitors' choice of products and own internal rules related to transparency. Through this competitive process, exchanges will respond to the desires of their customers and, among other things, provide the amount of transparency that is most valued by investors.

This framework, in which financial exchanges are viewed as firms competing for business, offers little room for regulators to dictate levels of transparency. The choice of transparency is instead guided by competitive forces that match the transparency provided by exchanges with that desired by investors at prices that reflect the costs and benefits of the desired level of transparency. Any role for legal oversight of transparency by regulators is limited to the protection of property rights to the products of an exchange and the enforcement of contracts between a given exchange and its individual members and between the exchange and its customers.

Even within this limited oversight role, a number of issues will arise regarding transparency. For example, the NYSE has suggested to the SEC that foreign trades in U.S. stocks be reported to the NYSE. However, to the extent that such trades are being conducted by its own members, the NYSE appears to have direct contractual ability to implement such reporting. More generally, the NYSE could contract with the London Stock Exchange to facilitate such reporting. Of course, the international nature of such contracting suggests less-than-perfectly defined property rights, placing the NYSE in a similar situation to the one it faced in its 19th century battles with bucket shops. But the policy on resolving such issues should focus on the enforcement of property rights in prices rather than placing transparency as the primary objective.

4. Concluding Comments

As in many industries, the securities business continues to change and prosper from advancements in technology. Modernization brought about by computerization allows financial exchanges to reach more investors and conduct greater business with products that are more sophisticated than ever before. This same technology also allows greater choices in the level of transparency provided to investors.

The technological feasibilty of greater market transparency, however, should not be confused with its economic desirability. Greater transparency brings direct costs in terms of technology as well as indirect costs, which can lessen price informativeness and lower liquidity. Individual financial exchanges have the incentive to balance the costs and benefits of transparency, just as they have for any of the other services that they provide. Of course, relying on the incentives of individual exchanges rests on the premise that the exchanges are competitive firms. Given such a premise, the role of regulators is merely to enforce property rights rather than to set broader goals such as promoting transparency in markets.

Setting a narrow role for regulation rests, not on economic philosophy, but on the plain fact that attempts at a broader regulatory effort can lead to conflicting actions. For example, at the same time the SEC is considering actions to increase transparency, it is also reviewing the desirability of Rule 390, which requires NYSE members to trade NYSE securities only on registered exchanges. Obviously, Rule 390 adds to transparency by bringing the information from all member trades directly to the floor. But since Rule 390 restricts the actions of individual members, the rule is considered evidence of market power that lowers the welfare of securities investors. This latter view follows from the outmoded notion that the NYSE is a monopoly. But, by maintaining this view, regulation is likely to offer inconsistent policies if it tries to artificially promote competition while also setting specific targets for transparency.

To allow a more consistent approach to understanding financial exchanges, one should adopt a property-rights perspective. Indeed, if one is to address how financial exchanges are to take risks and innovate so as to remain competitive, one cannot help but adopt a property-rights–oriented framework. Under such a perspective, the regulatory objective is not to provide detailed procedures for the operations of exchanges but is to regulate through the use of a hands-off approach that preserves the private incentives of exchanges to adapt to new technology.

References and Suggested Readings

Bronfman, Corinne, and James A. Overdahl. 1992. "Would the Invisible Hand Produce Transparent Markets?" Working paper no. 92-10, Commodity Futures Trading Commission, Division of Economic Analysis, (June).

Coase, R. H. 1992. "The Institutional Structure of Production." *American Economic Review* 82 (Sept.):713–719.

Franks, Julian, and Stephen Schaeffer. 1991. "Equity Market Transparency." Working paper, London Business School, (June).

Grossman, Sanford J. 1992. "The Informational Role of Upstairs and Downstairs Trading." *Journal of Business* 65 (Oct.): 509–28.

Madhavan, Ananth. 1991. "Security Prices and Market Transparency." Working paper, Wharton School, University of Pennsylvania, Philadelphia (Nov.).

Mulherin, J. Harold, Jeffry M. Netter, and James A. Overdahl. 1991. "Prices Are Property: The Organization of Financial Exchanges from a Transaction Cost Perspective." *Journal of Law & Economics* 34 (Oct.): 591–644.

——. 1991. "Who Owns the Quotes? A Case Study into the Definition and Enforcement of Property Rights at the Chicago Board of Trade." *Review of Futures Markets* 10:108—29.

26

Competition and Efficiency

Robert A. Schwartz
New York University

The SEC states that the purpose of its Market 2000 study is to assess regulatory structure, not market structure per se. "The Division is not trying to dictate what the structure of the equity markets should be in the year 2000. That determination should be made by the markets and their participants as a result of competition. However, that competition should not be skewed by inequitable regulation or allocation of self-regulatory costs, beyond that which is necessary for the protection of investors." (Release No. 34-30920, 14).[1]

Following through with this important intention will not be simple. New systems (like the proprietary markets) do not fit easily into the existing regulatory structure, and the regulatory environment will have to accommodate the new systems to allow the competition they provide. It is extraordinarily difficult for a new system, irrespective of its inherent efficiency, to attract order flow until it has achieved critical mass order flow; therefore, particular care must be taken not to impose excessive regulatory burdens on a new venture. And, because competition between alternative market centers fragments the order flow for individual issues, some fragmentation must be accepted as the price that must be paid to achieve progress through competition.

A diversity of trading systems exists in the United States. The New York Stock Exchange's agency/auction market and NASDAQ's competitive dealer market are different trading environments. The recent emergence of proprietary systems such as Posit, Instinet, and the Arizona Stock Exchange have introduced additional ways in which orders can be handled and trades made. To the benefit of users–the investors and listed companies–the

---

[1] A copy of my letter to the SEC regarding the Market 2000 study is appended to this paper.

various U.S. markets have put competitive pressure on each other and will continue to do so as long as they remain free of legislative interference.[2] This is highly desirable. A market that faces competitive pressure will more readily listen to the needs of its users and innovate when a good business reason to do so exists.

The Commission's eagerness to strengthen the competitive environment will depend on how clearly it recognizes that, from the point of view of public customers, our markets are not maximally efficient. Unfortunately, the prevailing academic opinion is that markets are efficient. However, with intraday price, quotation, and volume data becoming increasingly available to both practitioners and academic researchers, statistical evidence is beginning to emerge that prices are excessively volatile in short time intervals, that price discovery is imperfect, and that trading costs are unduly high.

There are other indications that the markets are not producing textbook results. Despite their extensive use of computer technology, our major market centers have not yet automated the point of sale; the reason is that trading and price determination are very complex processes. Current price and volume data supplied by Bloomberg, Bridge, Reuters, Telerate, and other vendors is of enormous importance to traders. Would this be the case if prices really followed a random walk? Would technical analysis be as prevalent as it currently is? What would be the economic value of traders on the exchange floors and upstairs trading desks if we really were operating in a random-walk world?

A broader understanding of market inefficiencies has been impeded by the difficulty of comprehending their source and of accurately measuring the trading costs they impose. Market impact, for instance, has proven extraordinarily hard to quantify. There is scant recognition that order flow is fragmented and transparency obscured, not just because markets are geographically (spatially) fragmented, but because they are also fragmented over time (temporally) in our continuous trading systems.

The fragmented, relatively opaque environment of our continuous markets benefits intermediaries but is not desirable for public customers. And the importance (and complexity) of price discovery, a major service provided by a market center, has not been clearly perceived by many students of the market.

---

[2] The threat of order flow going to foreign markets also intensifies the competitive pressure on our domestic systems.

Transparency

Most of the issues raised in the Market 2000 release relate to transparency. Transparency, itself, has largely been considered with regard to the reporting of trade and quote information and the spatial integration of markets. Although little discussed, participants' reluctance to disclose their orders is perhaps the greatest impediment to transparency.

Picture a set of traders, each holding orders that the others cannot see. At least some must announce the prices at which others can trade if a market is to form. But each participant, while individually preferring that the market be transparent, is reluctant to disclose his or her own order. A bid that is too high, or an ask that is too low, will be picked off immediately; an unexecuted limit order extends an option to others that may be exercised to the trader's detriment upon the arrival of adverse news; or a limit order may fail to execute following the arrival of favorable news. Participants must therefore be compensated in some way if they are to announce the prices at which others can trade.

In a dealer market such as NASDAQ, public participants do not, as a rule, place priced orders. Instead, market makers post the quotes at which the public may trade. Accordingly, a dealer system is sometimes referred to as a quote-driven market. Dealers are compensated for their services largely by the bid-ask spreads they set and the short-term trading profits they realize from their superior knowledge of the order flow.

In an agency/auction market such as the New York Stock Exchange, public participants commonly do use limit orders. These orders (along with those of the exchange specialist) establish the prices at which other public participants may transact by market order. Consequently, the exchange system is sometimes referred to as an order-driven market. Limit-order traders can save paying the spread. Moreover, intraday price volatility, which is greater than it would be if prices followed a random walk, compensates the limit-order traders by enabling their orders to execute at better prices.[3]

---

[3] Intraday price volatility is high (relative to longer term volatility) when relatively few limit orders have been placed and the book is thin; it is low when many limit orders have been placed and the book has depth and breadth. Because high intraday volatility attracts limit orders and, conversely, because limit orders are not desirable when volatility is low, an equilibrium balance can exist between short-term volatility and the number of limit orders that are placed. In this equilibrium, a relatively high intraday volatility (compared to a random walk environment) is a necessary property of the continuous market. See Handa and Schwartz (1992) for further discussion.

Call auctions, where orders are batched over time for simultaneous execution at a single price, deal with the situation differently.[4] Order disclosure can be rewarded by using time priorities and by charging lower commissions for orders that have been placed earlier in the entry period that precedes a call.[5] Further, because limit orders execute at a common clearing price, participants can put prices on their orders without extending an option to others or risking being picked off (as long as enough participants are present at the call).

Moreover, the need for transparency is less with call-market trading. Participants can more easily scale their orders (i.e., place an order in parts, at more than one price), and put contingencies on their orders (e.g., make a buy order contingent on the existence of a counterpart sell order). Essentially, a trader can specify his or her parameters and then rely on the computer to work out the trades. A contingent order may not be revealed to other traders until its conditions have been satisfied, but, most importantly, it is entered into the system. Because the system knows of contingent orders on both sides of the book, trades can be made that otherwise might not have been found.

If transparency is desirable, should it be legislated? Rules might be instituted that require posted quotes to be broadly displayed and last sales to be reported, but traders cannot be forced to reveal their intentions. However, the trading system, if properly designed, might encourage participants to display their orders. A trading system that handles this delicate design feature will prosper, and one that does not will lose order flow in a competitive environment. But an attempt to achieve the objective by legislative mandate risks being counterproductive.

Price Discovery

One might expect that transparency would be an important determinant of the accuracy of price discovery in a market center. That this is indeed the case is not always recognized. I have often heard the comment, "If a buy and sell order cross and a company's shares trade at $24, the stock must be worth $24." What does it mean for "a stock to be worth

---

[4] I have long been a proponent of call markets (*see*, for instance, Cohen and Schwartz 1989 and Schwartz 1991), and am currently a consultant to the Arizona Stock Exchange, which is an electronic call market.

[5] The Arizona Stock Exchange's electronic call uses both price- and time-priority rules for execution and time dependent commission rates for this purpose.

\$24"? Many students of the market would interpret the statement as meaning, not simply that the stock's equilibrium price is \$24, but that its shares have an *intrinsic value* of \$24. If shares have intrinsic values, share prices need not be discovered in the marketplace—they can be assessed by security analysts.

The converse is also true—if shares do not have intrinsic values, they must be priced in the marketplace. I believe price discovery occurs as orders meet in the market. If so, this has major implications for market structure and regulation. A simple security valuation model, the dividend discount model (DDM), can be used to suggest that security analysts cannot individually determine the price of an asset.

Assume a dividend of 45¢ per share has just been paid and that shares have been trading in the \$23 to \$24 range. Consider two funds: Fund 1, which forecasts a growth rate of 10.0 percent, and Fund 2, which forecasts a growth rate of 9.8 percent. Let both funds use 12 percent as the appropriate risk-adjusted discount rate for the stock. The "intrinsic value" for the two funds would be \$25.00 and \$22.68, respectively.[6]

How many shares should each fund hold? The dividend discount model does not say. One might presume that an asset that can be bought at a price less than its intrinsic value should be purchased in unlimited amounts and that an asset that can be sold at a price higher than its intrinsic value should be sold in unlimited amounts. Should the first fund go infinitely long and the second infinitely short? This would be absurd because of the risks involved.

Perhaps Fund 1 will buy up to some fixed number of shares, say 100,000, if the price is less than \$25.00, and Fund 2 will sell up to a fixed number of shares, say 75,000 if the price is greater than \$22.68. How will

---

[6] The DDM equation is

$$SHARE\ PRICE = \frac{NEXT\ PERIOD\ DI\ \ IDEND}{DISCOUNT\ RATE - GROWTH\ RATE}$$

Thus the evaluations are

$$\frac{.5000}{12 - .10}\ for\ Fund\ 1\ and,\ 22.68 = \frac{.4990}{.12 - .098}\ f($$

the two funds disclose their willingness to trade to each other? As suggested above, their actions will depend on the trading environment within which they are operating (dealer market, continuous auction, call auction, etc.). At what price will they trade? This can only be determined in the marketplace.

Expectations constant, a fund might also seek to acquire more shares as the stock's price falls or to lighten its position as the price rises.[7] For instance, Fund 1 might wish to hold up to 100,000 shares at a price of $25, up to 200,000 at a price of $24, and so on. Generalizing, we might state, using economic parlance, that the fund has a downward-sloping demand to hold shares. This willingness to make incremental rather than all-or-nothing decisions is profitable in an environment where price changes are not caused by informational change alone.[8] While many funds may not make such refined decisions with respect to individual shares, they commonly do so with respect to their aggregate equity position.

Whether investors individually seek to acquire more shares of a stock at lower share prices or make all or nothing decisions but at different prices, the market's demand to hold shares is downward sloping. With downward sloping market demand, share prices can be determined only in the marketplace. But trading is costly and equilibrium values are not known to participants before their orders are written and submitted to the market. Consequently, equilibrium values are not readily attained in the marketplace. Only when this is recognized will the regulators realize that the quality of price determination we are currently achieving in our major market centers is an important issue.

---

[7] Requiring a lower price to hold more shares is simply a reflection of the fact that risk, and therefore the fund's risk-adjusted discount rate, increases with the size of its position.

[8] Investors should not and do not accept that every change in a stock's price during a trading day is a reflection of new information. Prices also change with the receipt of orders that reflect participants' individual reassessments of existing information, liquidity needs, and/or desires to rebalance their portfolios. For the analyst who does not change his or her beliefs concerning the expected future value of a stock, a price decline in the market that results in a cheaper purchase implies an increased expected return to a long position, and a price rise that enables a better sale implies an increased expected return to a short position. The increased return associated with the price change compensates a fund for the greater risk of a larger position (long or short).

The Demand for Immediacy

Far too little attention has been given to improving the accuracy of price determination, and far too much importance has been attached to the supply of immediacy (the ability to trade at any time in the continuous market) and to bid-ask spreads (the price of immediacy). Unfortunately, participants pay a price to trade whenever they wish during a trading session: the components include the bid-ask spread, market impact, and commissions. In addition, the temporal fragmentation of orders in our continuous markets makes the markets more opaque.

Thus far, the assumption that participants demand transactional immediacy has gone practically unquestioned. Would some asset managers choose not to pay the price of immediacy if they truly understood the cost of the service, and if they had an alternative?[9] Immediacy is clearly important to a participant seeking to trade on information that has not yet been reflected in market prices. And many participants, most notably the mutual funds, do have to trade certain amounts each day because of deposits, redemptions, or other cash flow needs. This does not mean, however, that they must be able to trade at any given moment during the day. It is conceivable that the provision of immediacy, because it temporally fragments orders, actually makes it more difficult for these participants to "get the job done" at a reasonable cost by the end of the day.

Yet asset managers, including informationless traders, demand immediacy. I suggest that, to a significant extent, this demand is a result of the continuous market, rather than the other way around. Trading decisions are commonly made not because of the receipt of news but because a portfolio position has been reassessed. Whether the reassessment is made and implemented an hour sooner or an hour later may not matter to the asset manager. However, once a decision to trade has been made, participants are pressured to transact quickly in an environment in which prices are continuously subject to change, and where orders can be front-run. The process of transacting should be unbundled from the provision of immediacy. This can be accomplished by offering both call markets and continuous trading. Doing so could be likened to giving commuters the alternatives of traveling between home and office by train or by private car. The call market is equivalent to commuting by train—everyone travels according to a

---

[9] I am currently planning to investigate, through the use of a questionnaire, asset managers' demand for immediacy. This research is being undertaken with a colleague, Nicholas Economidies.

common time table at relatively low cost. The continuous market is equivalent to commuting by car—everyone travels according to his or her own personal schedule, but at higher cost. I suggest that a good transportation system, for both commuters and shares, should include both alternatives.

Consolidation of the Order Flow

Consolidating the order flow is desirable so that counterparties to a trade might be more easily found and for reasons relating to order exposure and price priority, the imposition of orderly secondary priority rules (such as time priority), the consolidation of floor information, and price discovery. As more efficient trading systems emerge, it would be best for those systems to be instituted in a major market center such as the New York Stock Exchange or NASDAQ. However, if the established market centers choose not to adopt a system, the freedom must exist for that system to be introduced elsewhere.

Until now, the consolidation-fragmentation debate has focused virtually exclusively on the spatial consolidation of orders. Orders can also be consolidated temporally in call-market trading.[10] The introduction of electronic call market trading into either an agency/auction market such as the NYSE or a competitive dealer market such as NASDAQ would be one of the most important steps that currently could be taken with regard to market design. I have suggested that an electronic call be used three times a day: to open a continuous market, at twelve noon, and to close the market.[11]

The call is not just an opening or closing mechanism. It is an alternative trading environment. The environment is particularly suitable for computerization and, in fact, must be computerized to be efficient. The electronic call is highly cost efficient, is an explicit price-discovery mechanism, and provides a suitable environment for stabilizing orders to be entered. These attributes are largely due to how order flow is consolidated in call market trading. With orders consolidated at the market calls, the

---

[10] For this reason, proprietary systems such as Posit, Instinet, and the Arizona Stock Exchange that cumulate orders for multilateral crosses at a single price in fact consolidate the order flow temporally, and perhaps even spatially since a variety of trading venues currently exist (i.e., the upstairs block trading market, the London market, the regional exchanges, the Over-the-Counter market, etc.).

[11] *See* Schwartz (1991).

computer is used to compute the appropriate clearing prices. When computer technology has been applied to the continuous market, on the other hand, it has served largely to accelerate the pace with which orders are submitted to the market and translated into trades. Under stressful conditions, this acceleration may be destabilizing.

If consolidation is desirable, must it be legislated? With regard to temporal consolidation, no market center should be forced to institute a call market if it chooses not to adopt the system. However, the call market should be allowed to compete in the marketplace. If it is responsive to customers and truly satisfies their needs, it will gain order flow. If not, it will cease to exist. Again, competition not legislation should be relied on to drive the market toward greater efficiency.

Must spatial consolidation be enforced? I have long supported the New York Stock Exchange Rule 390. My reasons can be summarized as follows.[12] Two forces are at work: a gravitational pull (order flow attracts order flow), and a centrifugal force—(order flow fragments as satellite systems offer cheaper, faster service while freeriding on the price discovery and other services provided by a major market center.)

Prices can be pirated with relative ease in a continuous market, both between markets and within a market center. A trade in the continuous market establishes a price, and the posting of quotes gives the price continuing validation until new quotes and/or a new transaction price are set. Prices established on the New York Stock Exchange thus become the benchmarks against which orders can be executed on the regional exchanges or elsewhere, and trades can be negotiated in the upstairs market. Floor traders also commonly negotiate transactions among themselves with reference to the posted quotes. These trades do not contribute to price discovery and are of no benefit to those participants who have actively participated in price discovery by posting quotes on the market.

Freeriding occurs in the continuous market because trading actually takes place while prices are being set. In contrast, with call-market trading, orders are batched together, a clearing price is found, the trades are made, and the market is closed. The indicated price before the call is only tentative, and the transaction price after the call is given no continuing validity. The simultaneity of the system results in all orders collectively determining the price and eliminates freeriding on price discovery.

---

[12] With Ernst and Bloch I wrote in defense of the rule in "The Battle Over Rule 390," Op. Ed. Page, *The Wall Street Journal*, Sept. 11, 1978. *See also* Bloch and Schwartz (1978) and Cohen, Maier, Schwartz, and Whitcomb (1986), ch. 8.

Market Structure

Does market structure matter? Some academicians think not; I disagree. The costly trading and imperfect price discovery I perceive are attributable to broad structural deficiencies in market design, not to the pernicious behavior of any individuals or groups of individuals. The trading system affects how orders are written, handled, and translated into trades. This determines which trades are made, who participates in the trades, the prices that are set, and the trading costs that are incurred. In short, the trading system affects how efficiently information (both fundamental information and market information) is processed and translated into price.

The translation of information into prices is imperfect in our markets, and better systems are needed to (1) reduce trading costs and improve portfolio performance for investors and (2) increase share values and reduce the cost of capital for listed companies. These changes would benefit the aggregate economy, as more efficient financing would result in faster economic growth. Although markets should not be designed for intermediaries, the intermediaries themselves might also benefit; if payments for their services were properly structured, their income receipts could be less risky and their commission income higher.

However, impediments to change exist. One is technological inertia—the difficulty of switching people to a new technology and the difficulty for a new market to receive order flow when it does not have critical-mass order flow. Another is the vested interests of intermediaries—the broker-dealer firms have become increasingly proficient at finding their profits in the inefficiencies of the continuous market.

And misconceptions persist. Academicians continue to believe that our security markets are efficient. Institutional investors accept, without questioning, that immediacy is critical despite the costs incurred. And the listed companies rely too exclusively on third-party market makers to make markets fair and orderly. Hopefully, the SEC's Market 2000 study will identify the serious impediments to change that do indeed exist and clarify that the regulatory environment might best counter these impediments by allowing competition among alternative systems.

Appendix A

Letter to Jonathan G. Katz, secretary
U.S. Securities and Exchange Commission

October 19, 1992

Mr. Jonathan G. Katz
Secretary
Securities and Exchange Commission
Mail Stop 6 - 9
450 Fifth Street, NW
Washington, D.C. 20549

Re: Market 2000, the U.S. Equity Market Structure Study, Release No. 34-30920; File No. S7-18-92

Dear Mr. Katz:

I appreciate this opportunity to convey my comments to you concerning the SEC's Market 2000 study.

The most fundamental issue from the SEC's point of view is the following: How active a role should the Commission play in controlling the development of market structure? I believe that the Commission's number one responsibility should be to insure that proper and adequate competition exists in the industry so that innovations which may increase the efficiency of the markets can be made. Beyond this, competition, rather than regulatory interference by the SEC, should be relied on as much as possible to drive markets toward greater efficiency.

I believe the most effective form of competition in the securities industry is *intermarket competition*, not interdealer competition. Alternative trading systems offer participants alternative ways of submitting orders and having their orders translated into trades. Only when these alternatives exist, may competition lead to meaningful change in our securities markets. By fostering such competition, the Commission may be far more successful in realizing its goal of enhancing market performance, than if it were to rely primarily on discretionary, legislative interference.

Whatever the role played by the SEC, competition will continue to intensify between market centers internationally. With electronic technology, orders will flow to those systems that provide investors with the environment they most desire, regardless of where the centers are around the globe. We do not at this time know which systems will win, and which will loose, in the international competition for order flow. But the Commission can spur competition within our own borders, and I urge that this be done. This is the most reliable way to ensure that the U.S. equity markets remain vibrant in the global arena.

Various proprietary trading systems have emerged in the U.S. in recent years to challenge the preeminence of older, established systems. A new venture may use a system that the established exchanges will not adopt. In so doing, a proprietary system can be a very effective source of competition in the marketplace. It is important that the regulatory authority recognize this.

The Market 2000 release raised the issue of price discovery. I consider price discovery one of the most critical functions of a securities market. Recognition of the complexity and importance of accurate price discovery is now emerging among market participants and others concerned with the operations of a market center. Nevertheless, insufficient attention is still being given to it.

A more commonly emphasized objective of systems design is to accelerate the speed with which orders can be submitted and translated into trades. I believe the emphasis is misplaced and does not accurately reflect the needs or desires of investors. Far too much attention has been given to the provision of immediacy, the price of which includes not only high commissions and spreads, but also excess volatility. This extra volatility is the product of inaccurate price discovery. I believe that accurate price discovery is more important than immediacy. Emphasis on the provision of immediacy can damage the accuracy of price discovery and drive up the costs of trading.

While some investors can be expected to demand immediacy some of the time, I believe that much of the demand for immediacy is induced by the dynamics of the continuous market. Would traders pay for immediacy if it could be unbundled from the making of a trade? We will not know the answer definitively unless investors are given a choice between continuous and non-continuous markets. Traditional markets have little incentive to provide such a choice, because the primary service provided by dealer-members is the provision of immediacy. Consequently, competition from new exchange structures may be necessary if the needs and preferences of investors are to be served.

The release also underscores issues concerning consolidation/fragmentation. Order flow can be consolidated in two ways: geographically and over time. Thus far, attention has been given almost exclusively to the spatial dimension. Consequently, the emergence of proprietary systems may appear to fragment the market. However, certain proprietary systems (Posit, Instinet's Crossing Network, and the Arizona Stock Exchange) bunch orders for simultaneous execution at a single price. In this regard, a proprietary system may consolidate rather than fragment the order flow.

Consolidation of the order flow is desirable—it strengthens competition between public orders and facilitates price discovery. For this reason, competition for order flow between *very similar markets* may decrease the efficiency of the broader marketplace. On the other hand, competition between *truly different trading systems* should be encouraged to counter technological inertia.

What if a proprietary market's trading system is, in fact, more efficient than the system used by a major exchange? It would be preferable for that system to be used by the major exchange itself. But what if the major exchange chooses not to use the system? The exchange should not be forced to adopt it. On the other hand, however, the proprietary system should be allowed to compete for order flow. Even though spatial fragmentation will result, stifling such competition would block progress unduly, thus impairing the efficiency of the market. Intermarket competition, between alternative trading systems, is one of the most powerful engines that will drive us to greater efficiency.

I have been a proponent of electronic call market trading, and have been a consultant to the Arizona Stock Exchange (AZX) which runs an electronic call market. I have suggested that such a system be instituted by the New York Stock Exchange, and that it be used three times during the

Exchange's trading day: to open the market, at noon, and to close the market. In my opinion, the electronic call market is an extremely efficient trading environment in terms of costs (development costs, operational costs, and user costs), price discovery, and price stability. I believe the introduction of an electronic call in a major market center such as the NYSE would be one of the most far-reaching, powerful innovations that could be made in the design of a trading system. The innovation should be of great value to institutional investors, retail customers, and to the listed companies. The NYSE, however, has not adopted this system. The Arizona Stock Exchange has. AZX should be free to compete with the NYSE (and others) for order flow. AZX will get the orders if it provides traders with an environment that is suitable for their needs. If it does not provide this environment, it will not get the order flow. Ultimately, the efficiency of a trading system can be determined only in the marketplace.

An analysis of the complexity of price discovery is developed in "Price Discovery Noise," a 1992 New York University working paper I have coauthored with Corinne Bronfman. My thoughts on electronic call market trading are further developed in "Integrating Call and Continuous Markets," *Securities Traders' Monthly,* September 1991. I have enclosed copies of both of these papers for your interest. Should further information or comment be desired, I would do my best to be of service.

Sincerely,

Robert A. Schwartz

References and Suggested Readings

Bloch, Ernest, and Robert Schwartz. 1978. "The Great Debate over NYSE Rule 390." *Journal of Portfolio Management* (Fall).

Bronfman, Corinne, and Robert Schwartz. 1992. "Price Discovery Noise." Working paper, New York University.

Cohen, Kalman, Steven Maier, Robert Schwartz, and David Whitcomb. 1986. *The Microstructure of Securities Markets*. Englewood Cliffs, N. J.: Prentice Hall.

Cohen, Kalman, and Robert Schwartz. 1989. "An Electronic Call Market: Its Design and Desirability." In *The Challenge of Information Technology for the Securities Markets: Liquidity, Volatility, and Global Trading*, Henry Lucas and Robert Schwartz, eds. Homewood, IL: Dow Jones-Irwin.

Handa, Puneet, and Robert Schwartz. 1992. "Limit Order Trading." Working paper, New York University.

Ho, Thomas, Robert Schwartz, and David Whitcomb. 1985. "The Trading Decision and Market Clearing Under Transaction Price Uncertainty." *Journal of Finance* (Mar.).

Lucas, Henry, and Robert Schwartz, eds. 1989. *The Challenge of Information Technology for the Securities Markets: Liquidity, Volatility, and Global Trading*. Homewood, IL: Dow Jones-Irwin.

Schreiber, Paul, and Robert Schwartz. 1986. "Price Discovery in Securities Markets." *Journal of Portfolio Management* (Spring).

Schwartz, Robert. 1991. *Reshaping the Equity Markets: A Guide for the 1990s*. Cambridge, MA: Harper Business.

27

Organization of the Stock Market: Competition or Fragmentation?

Hans R. Stoll
Vanderbilt University

Common stocks, historically traded almost exclusively on the New York Stock Exchange (NYSE) can now be traded in a variety of markets—on a regional exchange, in the NASDAQ market, in a foreign market, or on a proprietary trading system such as POSIT, the Wunsch auction system, or Instinet. Large blocks are traded in an upstairs dealer network even though transactions are brought to the floor for execution. Similarly, NASDAQ stocks may be traded on regional exchanges or on other systems. Options on common stocks and index options will be tradable on the five different option exchanges under the SEC's decision to allow multiple trading of options. Stock index futures and futures options, which can substitute for positions in stocks, are traded on several futures exchanges. Tailored equity derivatives are created in OTC dealer markets. The dispersal of equity trading and the new forms in which equity positions can be established has led to a debate between those who consider these trends to be a sign of dangerous fragmentation and those who consider them a healthy sign of increased competition.

Economic Forces

To understand this debate, one must understand the economic forces giving rise to new trading markets and new trading instruments. Automation and improvements in communications technology have dramatically reduced the cost of providing standardized trading. Firms such as Bernard Madoff, operating in NASDAQ, or other firms operating through regional exchanges claim to offer low cost, automated execution of orders at prices equal to or better than NYSE quotes. As an inducement to retail brokerage firms to send customer orders to these off-exchange markets rather than to the NYSE, rebates amounting to one or two cents per share are offered. Standardized, automated trading services are also being offered to institutional investors by systems such as Instinet, Posit, and the Wunsch Auction System.

In parallel to the development of low-cost, standardized trading systems is a trend toward tailored trading services aimed primarily at large institutional investors. Block trading has long been carried out in upstairs trading rooms. In recent years, research sales and trading operations of investment banking firms have become more integrated as trading strategies are devised to implement the portfolio objectives of institutional investors.

In effect, recent trends in equity trading reflect an increased range of trading services—from low-cost, standardized trading aimed at both individual and institutional investors to specialized trading for large institutional investors who can bear the set-up costs of a tailored service. The NYSE, still the dominant market in equity trading by far, has lagged in responding to these developing clienteles; and it serves none of them very well. Like the Bell System, threatened by low cost producers such as MCI on the one hand and by tailored PBX products for large customers on the other, the NYSE is threatened by automated trading systems on the one hand and by tailored trading services provided by large dealers on the other. The implications of these developments are profound.

Implications for the Specialist System

The specialist is the custodian of a disappearing franchise. Institutional trading in large blocks is carried out in upstairs dealer markets in which the specialist cannot participate effectively. The increased "dealerization" of the NYSE is reflected as well in the recent acquisition of specialist firms by upstairs investment banking firms such as Bear Stearns, Merrill Lynch, and Paine Webber. As specialist firms sell out to larger financial institutions, it is not farfetched to anticipate a time when the dealer function of the specialist is carried out in upstairs trading rooms, as is presently the case in London or in the NASDAQ system. Since large dealer firms do not want to be restricted in the stocks in which they can make a market, the exclusive franchise of specialists in certain stocks is also likely to disappear. Instead, one can expect competing upstairs dealers not only in block trades, as is now the case, but also in a wider range of institutional orders.

The role of specialists in the execution of smaller orders is also declining. In 1980, the NYSE accounted for 85.4 percent of the number of consolidated tape trades; in 1990, 66.2 percent. In response to this declining market share, the NYSE has automated trading of small orders in its DOT system, but the DOT system does not allow for automated execution as is possible, for example, on the Toronto CATS, Paris CAC, or Tokyo CORES. Instead, intervention by the specialist is required. To hold on to the trading business in small- to medium-sized transactions, the NYSE will have to substitute computers for high-cost labor. Inevitably, the point of sale, at least for small orders, will be automated. As this occurs, the role of the 420 or so specialists will become increasingly tenuous. The exchange's recently introduced after-hours execution systems, by bypassing the specialist, move in this direction.

Implications for the NYSE

The NYSE has held a dominant position in equity trading because of natural advantages. An exchange tends to be a natural monopoly because investors want to trade where other investors already trade. However, advances in communications technology have weakened the NYSE's natural monopoly. Satellite market makers can observe NYSE quotes in real time and can therefore match them. Investors are assured of receiving nearly the same prices as on the NYSE, and they can monitor prices on different markets to assure the quality of execution.[1]

Instantaneous communication and the ability to match quotes are necessary but not sufficient conditions for the growth of competing markets. Even if a satellite market can match the quote on the NYSE, investors would prefer to trade on the NYSE unless trading costs were lower or quality of service higher in the satellite market. If the NYSE were the low cost producer, it would retain the order flow.

The task of the NYSE is to find ways to adjust to the new realities of upstairs dealer markets and automated auction markets in a way that minimizes costs and assures investors of quality markets. This means moving in two directions: (1) recognizing the important role of an upstairs dealer market, and (2) automating the execution of standardized trades at lowest possible cost.

Implications for Brokers and Customers

For brokers and their customers, the new world of fragmented markets increases the range of available trading services, although it can be argued that it also increases the cost to brokers of ensuring that customers

---

[1] Execution is nearly the same because transactions might be inside the quote in one market and at the quotes in another.

receive the best price. It is worth remembering that fragmentation occurs only because customers or their brokers choose to trade in a satellite market rather than in the primary market. They choose to do so only because they receive at least as good a price as on the primary market and at a lower transaction cost. Paradoxically, fragmentation has increased in recent years because its adverse effects have decreased. To the extent that satellite markets guarantee price priority, the task for brokers of finding the best price is no more difficult under fragmented markets than in a single market.

In the new, more fragmented markets, brokers will buy execution services from different entities including regional exchanges and proprietary trading systems. Individual customers can shop among brokers on an increasing dimension of cost and service. Institutions can deal directly with broker-dealers who trade as principals or as agents and who are capable of tailoring a trade the institutions needs. All these decisions can be made because markets are, in fact, integrated by high-speed communications links, though many are physically fragmented.

Implications for Regulators

For regulators, the increasing range of trading services and the dispersal of trading among different market centers poses some tough questions.

Is fragmentation harmful?

Fragmentation may be defined as the inability of an order in one market to trade with an order in another market. The fact that orders cannot meet does not mean that prices in the two markets are misaligned. Real-time communication among markets and monitoring by investors ensures that prices in the two markets are the same. Fragmentation is often said to result from the freeriding of satellite markets on the prices displayed in the central market. But the ability to freeride cannot alone fragment markets because investors want to trade where other investors already trade. Only if satellite markets have lower costs than the central market is fragmentation feasible, for then a satellite market can trade at better prices or lower commissions. If the central market enjoys economies of scale in processing transactions, it can always underprice a satellite market. Fragmentation may, of course, be induced by differential regulatory costs. If the central market incurs regulatory costs that are not incurred by a satellite market, fragmentation will be subsidized. It is unlikely that differential regulatory costs can explain the observed dispersal of trading. It appears more likely that the observed fragmentation of markets reflects competition in the provision of trading services that arises from the development of more efficient trading procedures.

If the SEC considers the evils of fragmentation to outweigh the benefits of competition, one can expect increased regulatory involvement in the shape of trading markets. The SEC will become involved in specifying computer links among related markets in order to limit fragmentation or it may directly limit the establishment of off-exchange trading systems. A case study of the issue as it applies to the five option exchanges is now before the SEC. Under recent SEC rulings, an option may be traded on any or all of the five option exchanges. Concerned about fragmentation, the SEC has asked the option exchanges to establish a costly system to link the floors of the five option exchanges. Linking exchange floors has some beneficial effects, but it also limits competition among the exchanges and may create barriers to new trading systems. The alternative to the proposed linkage of exchange floors is not the absence of linkage. Markets are already linked by high speed, real-time communications systems of broker-dealers. It may be sufficient to leave with brokers the task they already have to shop around for the best price among markets.

What is an exchange?

Many of the new trading systems do not fall easily into the current regulatory cubicles of broker-dealer or exchange and are presently operating under no-action letters from the SEC. For example, new trading systems are not exchanges since they may simply be computer facilities and have no members. While some trading systems are operated by registered broker-dealers, the system itself need not be a broker-dealer that has contact with customers. A related concern is how the costs of regulation should be distributed between existing and new markets. This issue is complicated by the fact that existing exchanges combine the roles of self-regulatory organization and profit-making business entity, whereas new markets are focused on providing trading services for a profit. Regulators will have to draw a clearer distinction between the business entity providing trading services and the self-regulatory organization through which regulatory policy is implemented.

Should payment for order flow be permitted?

Satellite markets sometimes offer inducements in order to send orders to attract order flow. Certain NASD market makers, for example, offer one to two cents per share for orders in NYSE stocks sent to them. Other markets offer services, such as clearing, to attract order flow. Payment for order flow is criticized for at least two reasons. First, it is said to fragment markets, but this fragmentation is the result of a lower trading cost, which makes it possible to pay inducements. If the primary market is equally efficient, it too can lower trading costs. Second, inducements are paid to brokers not to customers. Critics are concerned that brokers may choose to execute at an inferior price in order to receive payment for order flow or other inducements. It is feared that the broker, who is the customer's agent, may not act in the best interests of the customer, who is the principal. The principal-agent problem occurs in many aspects of financial markets (and other areas of commerce). Investment advisers help structure portfolios and select securities; brokers execute trades; clearing agents facilitate clearing; and so forth. At each step in this chain, a fee is paid, either directly or indirectly. Investment advisers are compensated in part through commissions because they use commissions to purchase soft-dollar services. Brokers may be compensated in part by payment for order flow or by services such as clearing. Investors must determine if the package of services received is worth the final price and whether their agents are acting in their interests. Regulatory limitation on the ability of dealers to cut prices by paying for order flow would result in a too direct interference in business arrangements.

What rules of best execution should regulators promulgate?

Should the SEC specify in detail what constitutes best execution or should evaluation of a broker's execution be left to the customer? The evaluation of best execution is complicated by the fact that the customer's net price depends not only on the spread but also on commissions, on other costs incurred in the trade, and on the services provided by the broker (research services, for example) that the investor would otherwise be required to pay for. The SEC's determining whether an investor paid the right price for a share of stock is like someone's determining whether a customer paid the right price for a television. Prices will differ across customers according to the services received and other factors.

The principal-agent problem is ever-present in the securities industry, and concerns that unsophisticated investors will be unable to monitor their agents are natural. Yet it is well-nigh impossible for a regulator to clearly identify whether a package of services is worth the price paid. General standards of best execution should apply to brokers as they make decisions on the markets in which to trade, but detailed best-execution rules put a straitjacket on the markets, invariably favor established markets, and are almost impossible to oversee. In a free market, the evaluation of best execution should be left to the customer, and competition for customers will push markets toward high speed, low cost trading arrangements.

Is Transparency Advantageous?

Regulatory policy ought to aim at facilitating monitoring by customers and competition by providers of transaction services. Both competition and monitoring are made easier in transparent markets. In a transparent market, customers can assess the quality of execution because they can compare their price to that of other trades at the same time. In a transparent market, brokers and market centers can observe opportunities for providing lower cost trading services and can display the prices at which they will trade. Competition would not be possible if markets were not transparent.

Conclusions

Competition fragments markets in the sense that orders in one market do not have the opportunity to trade with orders in another market, but modern communications technology keeps prices aligned and makes it possible to assure investors that they receive price priority even when they trade in a satellite market. New markets can arise only if their costs of operation are lower than existing markets or their services and range of products superior. The new competition puts pressure on the NYSE and the specialist system to adapt. It offers brokers and their customers a wider range of vendors from whom transaction services may be purchased. It raises some tough questions for regulators. When there is more competition, direct regulation is less necessary, but the increased complexity of financial markets makes standard setting and transparency desirable. Transparent markets allow customers to monitor their brokers and allow competition to take place.

References and Suggested Readings

Harris, L. 1990. "Liquidity, Trading Rules, and Electronic Trading Systems." In *Monograph Series in Finance and Economics* 1990–94. New York: New York University, Salomon Brothers Center.

Huang, R., and H. R. Stoll. 1991. "Major World Equity Markets: Current Structure and Prospects for Change." In *Monograph Series in Finance and Economics* 1991–93. New York: New York University, Salomon Brothers Center.

Stoll, H. R. 1992a. "Principles of Trading Market Structure." *Journal of Financial Services Research* 6:75–107.

——. 1992b. *Equity Trading Costs.* Charlottesville, Va.: The Research Foundation of the Institute of Chartered Financial Analysts.

U.S. Securities and Exchange Commission, 1992. *U.S. Equity Market Structure Study*, Release No. 34-30920; File No. S7-18-92. Washington, D. C.: U. S. Government Printing Office (July 14).

28

If It Ain't Broke, Don't Regulate It

Corinne M. Bronfman[1]
University of Arizona

1. Introduction

Supporters of a strong regulatory presence in the financial markets often argue that conflicting needs among market participants require an arbitrator to assure fairness in order that one group not be disadvantaged by another.[2] Those who support more limited regulation do not feel that differences among market participants lead to a market failure but feel that market solutions are an efficient means to determine the appropriate balance. In this paper, I lend support to the second view. While the stated goals of regulation are hard to fault, its gross effects are often unpredictable and counter to the original intent.

This paper is motivated by the policy debate over how to regulate proprietary trading systems in the securities markets (electronic trading networks operated as private businesses and not as nonprofit organizations) and the extent to which they should be allowed to compete with the

[1] This paper was written while the author was visiting at the Commodity Futures Trading Commission. The views expressed in this paper are those of the author and do not necessarily reflect those of the Commission.

[2] "All those interested in the development of healthy equity markets—investors, issuers, the SRO's, market professionals, and Congress—have frequently looked to the Commission to resolve or mediate the seemingly intractable market issues that continually arise." (U.S. Securities and Exchange Commission [SEC], Equity Market Structure Study, Release No. 34-30920).

established exchanges.[3] For an economist, the issue appears straightforward; entry makes markets competitive and results in efficient outcomes. However, differential regulation of alternative trading systems *within a single regulatory jurisdiction* can be seen as subsidizing (or imposing a burden on) one system relative to another. Moreover, technological progress has permitted the development of cross-border, screen-based trading systems that have the capacity to link market participants *across regulatory jurisdictions*, giving rise to jurisdictional and other regulatory issues. And while proprietary trading systems (PTS) make at least some investors better off, they also fragment the order flow.[4] Although economists feel markets are better able to internalize the costs and benefits of any trade-off, regulators have displayed a tendency to doubt the ability of markets to arrive at a satisfactory solution. The issues raised by PTS prompt a reassessment of the role of the regulatory authorities in the financial markets.

The U.S. exchanges are self-regulatory organizations (SRO) with rules designed to "prevent fraudulent acts and practices, to promote just and equitable principles of trade, to foster cooperation and coordination with persons engaged in regulating, clearing, settling, processing information with respect to, and facilitating transactions in securities."[5] Subject to their self-regulatory obligations (and to the self-interest of their members), the exchanges structure a market with rules and procedures that facilitate the trading of financial assets. The actual microstructure can be assumed to balance the costs and benefits of different aspects of market design, including the level of market transparency, priority rules, trade practices, the option of continuous or periodic trading, and so on. Why should additional regulation and oversight by a government agency be necessary?

---

[3] See the International Organization of Securities Commissions Report of the Technical Committee, June 1990, "Screen-Based Trading Systems for Derivative Products," and the SEC's Equity Market Structure Study, Release No. 34-30920; File No. S7-18-92.

[4] PTS are often designed to attract some portion of the order flow, for example, institutional portfolio managers (POSIT) or patient traders who do not value the immediacy of the continuous market (AZX, Inc.'s Arizona Stock Exchange).

[5] *See* SEC Release No. 34-27445 16/11/89 and SEC Release No. 34-29185 15/5/91. Self-regulatory exchanges in the U.S. include the New York Stock Exchange (NYSE), the American Stock Exchange (AMEX), the over-the-counter (OTC) market (NASD), five regional exchanges (Boston, Cincinnati, MidWest, Pacific, and Philadelphia) and the Chicago Board Options Exchange (CBOE).

One argument for at least some level of regulation is that, while an exchange may maximize its own profits (or the profits of its members), it may disadvantage another group of market participants. Regulation is needed to ensure "fairness."[6] This argument for regulation regards the regulatory authorities as serving as referee for diverse interests groups. But does diversity of self-interest among market participants justify regulatory intervention? In Bronfman (1992), I argue that the ability of financial market regulators to finetune the markets and predict the final outcome is questionable. In this paper, I argue that deficiencies in an auction design may be helped by regulation, but regulation is a poor substitute for a well-designed auction. Moreover, in a well-designed auction, regulation can diminish performance. Therefore, the question of what and how to regulate must be answered with respect to a particular market structure, and in a properly designed system the need for regulatory intervention should be limited.

To analyze the role of regulation in the financial markets, I focus on an important aspect of market design—the level (and timing) of the information provided to market participants. This issue is what is meant by the term *market transparency*. In a transparent market, *real time* information on orders, quotes, and trades is publicly disseminated; in a less transparent system, the information is released with a lag or perhaps only in summary form (such as aggregate volume and/or high low prices) or only to certain participants. In Section 2 of this paper, I review the policy issues involved in the regulation of the level of market transparency and show how this regulation has caused problems for the U.S. securities exchanges, both domestically and internationally. In Section 3 of the paper, I discuss results from a laboratory asset market experiment that allows comparison between the impact of regulation (i.e., externally imposed rules) on auction performance under alternative levels of market transparency. In Section 4, I argue for a less interventionist regulatory policy: If it ain't broke, don't regulate it.

---

[6] The study *Derivative Markets, Products, and Financial Intermediaries*, compiled by the Commodity Futures Trading Commission, March 1992, provides the consensus view of IOSCO members that regulation should consider the public interest in regulating markets and generally construes that interest to encompass, to various degrees, the general objectives of *fairness* (including fiduciary and related customer [investor] protection), *market efficiency*, and *financial safety* (including the integrity of clearing houses and market participants, credit and systemic risk). Bronfman (1992) examines the arguments for regulation in the public interest, and demonstrates that the generally accepted policy goals of fairness and efficiency are often inconsistent.

2. Market Transparency[7]

In the United States, the wide dissemination of market information was mandated by Congress in 1975 in the Securities Acts Amendments legislating the development of a National Market System (NMS). Congress and the SEC argue that markets, in which quotes, transaction prices, and transaction volume are reported contemporaneously, are fairer and more efficient in that they (1) allow all market participants access to current market information, (2) allow some level of monitoring of execution quality and broker performance, and (3) improve brokers' ability to achieve best execution for their customers.[8] As might be expected, however, there is a trade-off; although in a continuous auction, greater transparency *may be* fairer to retail investors, it may also be less efficient for large institutional investors. Moreover, the regulations can (and have) caused problems for the New York Stock Exchange (NYSE), both domestically and internationally.

The U.S. securities exchanges are required to report full price, volume, and firm quotation information contemporaneously, and the *price* at which the information can be sold is subject to regulatory oversight as well.[9] In a ruling dated April 17, 1984, the SEC determined that "because Instinet sought to distribute certain NASDAQ quotation information in competition

---

[7] For a more detailed discussion, see Bronfman and Overdahl (1992).

[8] Best execution requires that a broker execute a customer's order "so that the customer's total cost or proceeds are most favorable under the circumstances." Both transaction price and commission costs are therefore included. See SEC Release No. 34-30920, Equity Market Structure Study.

[9] This dual regulation resulted from efforts to implement the NMS by enforcing linkages between markets. Congress was not concerned with compensating the producers of the information for their price discovery, but it was concerned with assuring that all securities information processors distribute and publish this information *on fair and reasonable terms*. Congress took the position that an information processor was a "public utility, and thus it must function in a manner which is absolutely neutral with respect to all market centers, all market makers, and all private firms." (Senate Committee on Banking, Housing, and Urban Affairs, Report to accompany S. 249: Securities Acts Amendments of 1975, Senate Report No. 75.) Securities information processors are defined in Section 3a of the Securities Exchange Act as "any person engaged in the business of (i) collecting, processing, or preparing for distribution or publication . . . transactions in or quotations for any security . . . or (ii) distributing or publishing . . . on a current and continuing basis, information with respect to such transactions or quotations" (Federal Register 49, no. 50 [April 24, 1984], 17640 n. 3).

with the NASD, which is an exclusive processor of that information, the proposed fees must be cost-based to ensure the neutrality and reasonableness of the NASD's charges to Instinet and its subscribers."[10] The SEC ruled that the only costs that were relevant in the determination of the fee were the costs incurred by NASD in collecting the information and passing it on to vendors.[11] By requiring the NASD to charge no more than its costs for the collection and dissemination of quotation data, the SEC, reflecting the wishes of Congress, decreed that the prices produced by an exchange, once produced, were part of the public domain. In so doing, a public-goods–problem was created where none needed to have existed (because information can be priced). Lower cost transaction services were thus able to freeride off the price discovery of the exchanges.

Internationally, a similar problem has arisen because of differences in the required level of transparency among regulatory jurisdictions. The Securities Industries Board in London requires only that firm quotes be displayed on the Stock Exchange Automatic Quotation (SEAQ) system screens. Transaction price and volume information is released, but with a lag, currently ninety minutes. Because the London market is a dealer market, NYSE members who route their orders to London when the NYSE is closed do not run afoul of NYSE Rule 390.[12] London's International Stock

---

[10] Federal Register 49, no. 80, [April 24, 1984]: 17643. *NASD* was organized to provide self-regulation of the OTC securities market. To this end, it owns and operates the NASDAQ system, a computerized securities information service. NASDAQ collects price quotation information from market makers (broker-dealers who hold themselves out as willing to buy and sell particular securities on a regular basis). The information is processed by the NASDAQ computers and made available to the public. *Instinet* is a registered broker-dealer offering computerized execution facilities and securities information services.

[11] The ruling is based on utility-rate regulation where costs of common or integrated facilities must be allocated among different groups of customers. It is well known in the industrial organization literature that cost-based methods of price regulation may involve incorrect signals to consumers about the incremental costs of production and incorrect incentives for the regulated firm. For further discussion and references see Spulber (1989).

[12] As explained in footnote 24 in the SEC Equity Market Structure Study, Rule 390 prevents NYSE members from effecting transactions in any NYSE listed stock in the OTC market *either as principal or agent*. The rule contains certain exceptions such as trading an NYSE stock on an organized exchange in a foreign country or the trading of NYSE-listed stocks in a foreign OTC market outside of NYSE trading hours.

Exchange (ISE) thus competes directly with the NYSE for order flow (and the resulting trading volume). The competition arises, in part, because of differences in the microstructure of these market centers. The willingness of dealers in London to put large amounts of capital at risk allows large traders to minimize the market impact of their orders and thus reduces an implicit cost of trading. Because the dealers take large positions to accommodate these traders, the exchanges differ significantly in terms of the level of transparency; a dealer who has a large inventory (long or short) will want to be able to unwind that position before the trade is publicly revealed. These differences in the levels of transparency cause problems, however.

In addition to the cost imposed on the NYSE because of the ISE's freeriding off its price discovery and the loss of order flow to London, such asymmetry means that the opaque exchange, London, has better information. While market professionals in London can monitor the prices set on the NYSE, the NYSE is less aware of the market activity in the ISE. Knowledge of the prices set on the transparent market, NYSE, and a portion of the order flow to the opaque market enable members of the opaque exchange to exploit price differentials between the exchanges. At least some portion of the costs that the opaque market imposes on the retail market could be recovered if the transparent NYSE could charge appropriately for the contemporaneous dissemination of its market data.

By regulating both the level of transparency and the price at which the information can be sold, the U.S. Congress through the agency of the SEC has prevented market-based contracting solutions to problems between competing exchanges, necessitating more involved regulations.[13] By precluding a market solution, the dual regulation—(regulation of the level of transparency and of the price at which the information can be sold)—has created a public-goods-problem, with the regulators now facing the problem of how to regulate the proprietary trading systems, several of which freeride off the price discovery of the NYSE.

3. Regulation versus Market Design

Any trading system has different means of addressing issues of efficiency or fairness. For example, rules can be imposed from without (regulation) or the auction can be modified by exchange members or by the

---

[13] For example, the SEC has approved lower levels of transparency for the after-hours session on the NYSE, in part to help the exchange recapture some portion of the order flow that has migrated to the ISE.

system sponsor (market design). Regulation brings benefits, but it also imposes costs. The cost of regulation includes both its impact on the performance of the underlying system and the costs of enforcing and monitoring compliance. Often the benefits of a regulation are clear, but the costs on the performance of the underlying system are less easily identified. Theory is not always helpful; for example, an important weakness of the perfectly competitive model when applied to the financial markets is that it is institution free. But experimental market economists have found that the choice of institutions is often the essential factor in determining how well a market works and that small changes in auction rules can result in very large changes in traders' behavior and/or in the market's performance.[14] This suggests that the impact of regulation on the performance of a trading system be a consideration before the imposition of new rules or modification of existing ones.

The experimental methodology allows economists to test the predictions of economic theories or to assess the performance of an auction under alternative rules or procedures.[15] For example, we could design an experiment to test the impact of some new regulation on a Walrasian tatonnement (an auction design that, in introductory or intermediate economics classes, is commonly used to explain the price discovery process).

---

[14] *See*, for example, Bronfman, McCabe, Porter, Rassenti, and Smith (1992), McCabe, Rassenti, and Smith (1991), Plott (1989), and Smith and Williams (1992). Auction theory provides similar results; important early papers are by Vickrey (1961) and Smith (1982). Milgrom and Weber (1982) and MacAfee and McMillan (1987) each provide an overview of the literature and a bibliography.

[15] For the reader who is not familiar with the experimental methodology, I will describe this research tool briefly. For a more complete introduction, see Plott (1989) and Smith (1982, 1989). Laboratory experiments in economics allow the experimenters to observe the behavior of human subjects who are following a set of instructions. The instructions place the subjects in an abstract version of some naturally occurring economic environment in which they play the role of specific economic agents, such as consumers or firms. Using monetary incentives, underlying demand and supply conditions can be induced so that the equilibrium price and quantity exist and are known to the experimenter. Payoffs are structured so as to induce preferences. For example, a seller will earn the difference between the sale price and his cost or the purchase price; therefore, he will prefer to sell high. Similarly, a buyer will earn the difference between the purchase price and her resale value; therefore, she will prefer to buy low. Given the induced supply and demand, performance of an auction in terms of the efficiency of price discovery and in the allocation of asset holdings can be assessed. Additionally, the strategic behavior of subjects can be compared relative to fully revealing strategies.

In this auction, an auctioneer calls out a price and observes how many units are sought for purchase relative to the number offered for sale at that trial price. He or she adjusts the price in the direction of excess demand (downward if there are more sells than buys, upward if there are more buys than sells) based on the reported demand and supply responses at announced prices.[16] When the market clears (no imbalance), that trial price is the equilibrium price.

In economic theory (and in textbook economics), it is implicitly assumed that traders reveal fully and truthfully their supplies and demands at the announced price. However, the world of theory is not always consistent with observed behavior. Direct observation of the behavior of buyers and sellers in a controlled experiment would allow us to assess whether, in fact, they do behave as in the stylized model, and whether the level of information provided (for example, the excess demand at a price or the rate of arrival of buy and sell orders during the price search procedure) affects their willingness to reveal their order quantities and the time required to find the price that clears the market. If we were to hold a Walrasian tatonnement auction under different informational conditions (levels of market transparency), we could observe and document any differences.

In a recent paper, Bronfman, McCabe, Porter, Rassenti, and Smith (hereafter: BMPRS 1992,) discuss their experimental test of a computerized Walrasian tatonnement auction. Their experiments are designed to assess the impact of multi-unit supply and demand as well as the role of information on supply and demand conditions on the performance of the tatonnement auction. The results of their experiments show that when traders each wish to trade more than a single unit, attempts to manipulate the price by under revealing supply and demand are widespread. This strategic behavior results in inconsistent bidding and offering behavior and an inefficient price search that backtracks. Thus, the tatonnement process fails to coordinate traders' expectations. Perhaps the auction could be improved by imposing a rule to enforce consistency in traders' behavior. But would this regulation otherwise affect the auction's performance?

---

[16] In many respects, the opening procedures on the NYSE are similar to a Walrasian tatonnement. After considering the limit orders (priced orders) on the book and any imbalance in the flow of orders to purchase or sell at market, the specialist lets the brokers on the trading floor know an indicated price and they respond with the quantities they are willing to buy and sell at that price. If there is an imbalance of buy and sell order quantities, the specialist will raise or lower the price to discover the price that best reflects the consensus among active participants.

Table 1 below provides an overview of the experimental treatments and the number of experiments conducted per cell in the design. There were two treatments (regulation and type of information provided). In some replications, neither was in effect (no order flow information and no regulation), both were in effect (order flow information and regulation), or one or the other was in effect.

Table 1
Experimental Treatments of a Computerized Walrasian Tatonnement Auction

Regulation	Minimal Information	Order Flow Information
No	4	3
Yes	3	3

As discussed above, when individual buyers and sellers each wish to trade more than a single unit, truthtelling is not a dominant strategy in a tatonnement auction because a trader may influence the price by withholding units without being out of the market entirely. This strategic behavior makes if difficult for market participants to coordinate their expectations of the underlying supply and demand conditions. If there is no consistency in traders' messages, there is little information revealed by price and convergence to the equilibrium price is slow or nonexistent. Therefore, in some replications, BMPRS imposed a consistency requirement on participants' bids and offers, analogous to a regulator imposing restrictions on behavior.

In roughly 50 percent of the replications, a one-sided improvement rule was in effect, requiring that a buyer who was willing to purchase *n* units at a price *X* had to be willing to purchase at least n units at a better price, X-ϵ. Similarly, a seller who was willing to sell *n* units at a price *X* had to be willing to sell at least *n* units at a better price, X+ϵ. This rule does not prevent withholding, but it does minimize inconsistency. A buyer who was willing to buy 2 units at 325 is not precluded from revealing later in the period that in fact he or she is willing to buy 3 units at 340. However, a willingness to buy only 1 unit at 320 would not be admissable. A seller who was willing to sell only 1 unit at 325 can in the end agree to sell 4 units at 300; however, he or she would not be permitted to offer no units at 330. The rule is flexible enough to permit traders to explore their relative competitiveness; however, it does limit reneging.

BMPRS also examined the impact of alternative information structures on the auction's performance in both the presence and the absence of regulation, that is, the bid-offer restriction rule explained above. Under the *minimum information condition*, market participants were told (on their computer screens) the current trial price, the number of seconds remaining at a trial price, the adjustment factor for the current trial,[17] and a full history of past trial prices and past order-flow imbalances. However, they were given no information on any imbalance at the current price and, therefore, during a trial they did not know if the market would clear nor the extent of the imbalance if it were not to clear. Under a more *complete information treatment*, buyers and sellers also saw the buy and sell quantities of the other participants as they were entered (each traders' computer display was continuously updated). Thus, each seller and buyer knew whether the market would clear at the current price if he or she were to submit a sell or buy quantity or whether it could be prevented from clearing (or the price-adjustment minimized) by withholding (under-revealing) supply or demand. Allowing participants to see the exact real-time composition of buy and sell imbalances allows individuals to update their strategies. The impact of order-flow information was assessed by comparing the outcomes in identical experiments differing only in whether order flow information was or was not revealed.

All versions of the tatonnement experiments produced prices consistent with the competitive equilibrium predictions, but all were far less efficient in terms of allocations, with too few units traded. Among all the treatments, the ones where participants were provided with full order flow information and where there was no regulation in effect performed the best. The regulation did help in the environment where there was no order flow information provided. Thus, BMPRS conclude

---

[17] The adjustment factor determined by how much the price would be raised or lowered based on the revealed supply and demand at the current price. If there were 4 units sought for purchase and 10 offered for sale and the adjustment factor was 2, the price would be lowered by 12 cents. The sensitivity of the adjustment factor to the current imbalance was decreasing in the number of trial prices, that is, every four prices the adjustment factor was halved.

1. Conditional on having no bid-offer restriction rule, full information helps in allowing more efficient allocations.

2. Conditional on only minimal information being provided to market participants, the restriction rule helps in obtaining more efficient allocations.

In this experimental environment, regulation helps the performance of a poorly designed auction, but reduces efficiency otherwise.

4. Conclusion

This paper has argued for a regulatory agenda that recognizes the self-interest of the markets in finding the appropriate trade-off, and the possibilities offered by technology for competition in trading systems. The problem with more active regulation (beyond the minimum necessary to assure system integrity and oversight of the procedures in place to assure the financial integrity of the participants) is not its stated goal but that its gross effects are often unpredictable and unintended. Moreover, regulation is costly and a poor substitute for a well-designed auction.

Competition for order flow through innovation in the financial markets should result in the development of trading systems that minimize market participants' total costs of trading, including not only the usual focus (i.e., commissions and the bid-ask spread), but also inaccurate price discovery, market impact arising from transitory market illiquidity, and the level of regulatory oversight. This eventuality and the arguments presented in this paper suggest the following policy recommendations:

1. "If it ain't broke, don't regulate it," for those auctions that work efficiently. The level of oversight should differ across trading systems. Bronfman and Lawton (1992) document the appreciable number of regulations developed to enforce the Commodity Exchange Act that would be unnecessary and irrelevant if futures were to be traded in a computerized single price call auction: for example, rules to prevent frontrunning customers' orders, or trading ahead of customers, and rules about cross-trades and out-trades. The

potential for trading abuses by intermediaries in a periodic batched trade is far lower.[18]

2. Where inefficiencies and poor design require a higher level of regulatory oversight, the repair and redesign of the auction are best left to the markets.

3. When the imposition of regulation is necessity, a research tool like experimental economics should be employed to assess the total impact of the regulation on market performance.

---

[18] Of course, it is unlikely that intermediaries would willingly accept a procedure that eliminates a source of profits (the bid-ask spread). Some other payment structure would have to be introduced; fixed commissions are one possibility.

References and Suggested Readings

Bronfman, Corinne. 1993. "Regulation *In the Public Interest*?" Working paper, University of Arizona.

Bronfman, Corinne, and John Lawton. 1993. "Market Structure and Regulatory Costs: The Effect of a Single Price Auction." Working paper, Commodity Futures Trading Commission.

Bronfman, Corinne, Kevin McCabe, David Porter, Steven Rassenti, and Vernon Smith. 1992. "An Experimental Evaluation of the Walrasian Tatonnement Mechanism." Working paper, Economic Science Lab, University of Arizona, Tucson.

Bronfman, Corinne, and James A. Overdahl. 1992. "Would the Invisible Hand Produce Transparent Markets?" Working paper no. 92-10, Commodity Futures Trading Commission, Division of Economic Analysis; Washington, D. C. (June).

International Organization of Securities Commissions. 1990. "Screen-Based Trading Systems for Derivative Products." *Report of the Technical Committee* (June).

MacAfee, E. P., and J. McMillan. 1987. "Auctions and Bidding." *Journal of Economic Literature* 25.

McCabe, Kevin, Steven Rassenti, and Vernon Smith. 1991. "Testing Vickrey's and Other Simultaneous Multiple Unit Versions of the English Auction." In *Research in Experimental Economics* vol. 4, 45-79, JAI Press.

Milgrom, P. R., and R. J. Weber. 1982. "A Theory of Auctions and Competitive Bidding." *Econometrica* 50.

Plott, C. 1989. "An Updated Review of Industrial Organization: Applications of Experimental Methods." In *Handbook of Industrial Organization,* vol. 2, Richard Schmalensee and Robert D. Willig, eds. Elsevier Science Publishers B.V.

Smith, V. 1982. "Microeconomic Systems as Experimental Science." *American Economic Review* 72.

——. 1989. "Auctions." In *Allocation, Information, and Markets,* J. Eatwell, Murray Milgate, and Peter Newman, eds. New York: W. Norton and Company.

Smith, V., and Arlington W. Williams. 1992. "Experimental Market Economies." *Scientific American* (Dec.).

Spulber, Daniel F. 1989. *Regulation and Markets.* Cambridge: MIT Press.

U.S. Securities and Exchange Commission. 1992. Equity Market Structure Study, Release No. 34-30920, File No. S7-18-92 (July 14).

Vickrey, W. 1961. "Counterspeculation, Auctions, and Competitive Sealed Tenders." *Journal of Finance* 16.

29

Why the National Exchanges Provide Superior Information Flows and Pricing

Lawrence M. Benveniste
Boston College

Introduction

Dramatic developments in the secondary equity markets over the past two decades have weakened the position of the national exchanges (The New York Stock Exchange [NYSE] and the American Stock Exchange [AMEX]). For example, the exchanges have lost market share of volume in listed stocks to competitors such as the over-the-counter market and fourth-market trading systems like INSTINET and POSIT. The exchanges have also been increasingly challenged for listings by the development of the National Association of Securities Dealers Automated Quotation System (NASDAQ) and its National Market System (NMS).

Despite these trends, most of the markets' constituencies recognize the public-good value of an integrated national market. The focus of debate is on the market structure that can best serve the function of a national market. Proponents of the national exchanges claim that floor trading with a specialist at the center is the optimal national market structure. Critics of the exchanges argue that the exchange trading mechanism with a monopoly specialist at the center is a dinosaur that has outlived its usefulness. An electronic trading mechanism like the NASDAQ that fully integrates multiple competitive dealers into a national market is most often mentioned as the alternative.

This paper will argue that technology is not the real issue. Rather, the relevant distinction between the markets is their ability to efficiently incorporate information into prices. In this regard, the self-regulatory and trading traditions of the exchanges with the specialist playing an important role give the exchanges an advantage. A byproduct though is that the exchanges create incentives for certain users to seek alternative trading mechanisms; a trend that could eventually destroy the exchanges' effectiveness.

The paper concludes by suggesting that regulators should consider some limited protection of the integrity of the exchanges. However, since the goals of the exchanges are not entirely aligned with those of the public, regulators should seek to create a balance of competition, which along with regulatory oversight would assure that the markets best serve the public good.

Focusing the Debate on the Public Good

Much of the debate regarding the markets has concentrated on which market structure uses resources most efficiently. For example, NASDAQ has proudly promoted its highly sophisticated computer system for its speed, access, and cost efficiency. The NYSE has countered with its own promotion of the capability of its systems such as the SuperDOT.

But, in fact, comparing performance along these dimensions is virtually impossible because the products can be so different. Liquidity consists of a bundle of services tailored to characteristics of the individual stock, and costs on the two markets cannot be directly compared. Issues of stock can vary greatly in volume of trade, relative risks, and other characteristics that affect the cost of providing liquidity. And, in any case, the competition has already served the public well by providing incentives to develop faster, cheaper, and more responsive methods of servicing trades, and both markets have responded reasonably well.

It is more important that the debate be guided by an understanding that markets provide *public goods* that may not be given proper weight in the marketplace.

Secondary equity markets principally provide two services: liquidity and price discovery.[1] Both benefit investors directly and the public at large indirectly. Investors benefit because the markets allow them flexibility in their holding period and the opportunity to rebalance risk exposure without paying prices that differ too greatly from true values.

The public benefits from the markets because both liquidity and price discovery contribute to more efficient capital flows. The cost of equity

---

[1] Price discovery occurs as equity prices reflect all current information that might have an impact on firm values.

capital has been shown to be directly related to the cost of liquidity.[2] Thus, the markets make it cheaper for firms to raise equity capital, benefitting all segments of the economy. Price discovery assures that successful firms are rewarded with lower costs of equity. In essence, secondary equity markets are a form of voting booth with results that assist in the efficient allocation of scarce equity capital. In the language of economists, the secondary equity markets create positive externalities and society has a significant interest in how they operate.

The following section will explain why the costs of liquidity and price discovery are inseparable. It will also demonstrate why markets have difficulty arriving at a socially desirable balance of the two.

How Information Flows Affect the Secondary Equity Markets

The prices of equity issues are constantly in a state of flux. Like all financial instruments, equity values depend on a combination of anticipated future cash flows and required yields. In both dimensions, however, equities are especially hard to pin down. Dividends, for example, depend almost entirely on the uncertain profitability of the issuing firm, and yields can vary greatly across equities. There is no equity analogue to bond coupons and the yield curve. This makes equity prices especially sensitive to tangible information and intangibles like the "mood" of the market.

A challenge to secondary equity markets is to discover the evolution of prices on a timely basis. In this effort, market makers access all channels of publicly available information and adjust prices accordingly. The problem is that much information is first discovered by investors who then trade on it and realize profits that come at the expense of market makers and indirectly at the expense of liquidity traders.

When investors acquire information prior to the market, they are referred to in the vernacular of economists as asymmetrically informed investors. Such knowledge can be attained, for example, through research, observations of changes in order flow, knowledge of large trades that can move the market, and knowledge of the change of a major analyst's forecast.[3]

---

[2] *See* Amihud and Mendelson (1986).

[3] The basis for the legal use of asymmetric information was established in the federal case of *Vincent F. Chiarella v. the United States*. This case confined the definition of an insider as one who has a "relationship of trust and confidence with shareholders." The courts have also distinguished between the use of private information and insider information. Trading on private information is legal.

Casual observers believe that using any form of asymmetric information in trading should be illegal. Realistically though, such laws would be impossible to enforce.

This view also ignores the benefits of improvements in information flows brought about by asymmetrically informed investors. The potential for trading profits create incentives for market makers to learn what investors know as quickly as possible and to adjust prices accordingly. They also provide incentives for investors to search for new information.

In this spirit, one should view the trading profit generated by a legitimate information advantage as the markets' payment for information. The policy question can then be restated as follows: Do the markets pay the "right price" for information? Unfortunately, the markets' weakness is that without external impediments (like those provided by the exchanges as described below) the prices paid for information are uncontrollable, despite the efforts of market makers. The potential costs can be so great as to cause the markets to close; this is the ultimate externality. Such is the case, for example, when significant new information about an issuing firm is rumored or publicly released or when the markets suffer extreme volatility like that of October 1987.

The markets and regulators have partially diffused the problem through advances in reporting requirements and tougher standards and stronger enforcement of insider-trading rules. These initiatives seek to separate information flows from trading. But they can only go so far because there will always be information that smart investors will (and should be encouraged to) discover. Market institutions must carry the ball beyond this point. It is in this regard that floor exchanges with the specialist at the center provide unique services.

The National Exchanges as Self-Regulating Organizations

The original development of the NYSE can be traced to the Buttonwood Agreement of 1792, in which 24 brokers signed an agreement to give each other preference on stock deals. Although they were motivated by interests that are not entirely in line with the public good, these brokers founded the exchange as an institution that would represent their interest as a group in competition with the interest of the members individually. It is sometimes referred to as a Self-Regulating Organization (SRO) to capture the exchange's role as monitor of its membership.

The exchanges are a microcosm of the markets because various segments of the membership trade on behalf of clients (as brokers). They therefore have an interest in keeping the cost of liquidity down while encouraging the processing of information. At the same time, individual members seek information advantages, which they would fully exploit if they were given the opportunity.

So the challenge of controlling the profits from information is an example where the interests of the membership conflict with those of individual members. To this end, the exchanges have taken a number of formal steps to control their members' trading practices, including reporting requirements, the tick-test rule, and electronic monitoring of trades.

But the real distinction of the exchanges is the informal control provided by the trading mechanisms anchored by the specialists on the exchange floors. Members of the exchanges have had a tradition of linking trades with reputation.[4] Members form relationships that are based on trust and cooperation. And the specialists continue this tradition and, by virtue of their position, provide unique monitoring and pricing services.

To support their price setting function, specialists have access to unique and concentrated sources of information. For example, the specialist is informed of every trade executed for exchange members. They also have continuous access to electronic information on the flow of smaller trades and they know of most proposed trades through the limit order book.[5] In this way, the specialists enhance the efforts of the regulators and the exchanges to bypass investors as much as possible in gathering information.

Specialists can also use their control over trades to cultivate relationships with members and encourage additional flows of information. For example, specialists will commonly offer prices inside the quoted spread or other favors like filling larger orders without changing the price and working block trades. They also work to match buyers and sellers without themselves taking any profit. As evidence, according to one sample, some 15 percent of NYSE transactions are done at the midpoint of the bid-ask spread.[6] Using these powers as both carrots and sticks, specialists

---

[4] An example of this is the way the outdoor curb market (which eventually became the AMEX) developed. Around the turn of the century Emanual S. Mendels and others set up an informal screening committee and refused to trade with dishonest brokers.

[5] The NYSE executes small trades electronically over the SuperDOT system and the specialist has a screen that constantly reports trades being executed there.

[6] *See* Hasbrouck (1988).

compensate traders for being forthright and honest and punish traders who do not cooperate.[7]

As a result, it is not uncommon for brokers to share their knowledge of future order flows or other information with the specialist. Such information is not available to market makers in an anonymous competitive trading mechanism such as NASDAQ and permits the specialists to adjust prices more quickly to reflect the changing markets.

A recent paper by Benveniste, Marcus, and Wilhelm (1992) explains the benefits markets can derive from market-making specialists. The paper shows, for example, that specialists can reduce the profit realized by traders with information. More importantly, the paper shows that specialists can actually enhance incentives to gather information while at the same time reducing the cost of liquidity. It is a classic case of a win-win outcome that would not occur without the institution of the specialist. The important element in the theory is the specialist's ability to receive the information directly, rather than disguised in a trade. In essence, this allows the specialist to pay for information directly and therefore control the externality. The paper also shows how the added flow of information allows the specialist to maintain open markets even at times when markets would otherwise close. This is at least a partial explanation of why the NYSE continued to execute trades in October 1987 when other markets like NASDAQ were virtually shut down.

The structure of the exchanges, including the specialist system, grew from the tradition of the exchanges as SROs. The structure has an advantage in price discovery and in avoiding the externality of asymmetrically informed investors. However, the interests of the exchanges have not always been aligned with those of the public, which suggests a role for regulation.[8] The following section will discuss the current trends and suggest why some form of limited protection of the exchanges may be desirable.

---

[7] The specialist knows the identity of traders executing orders on the SuperDOT system. Thus, members are not able to avoid the watchful eye of the specialist by trading over SuperDOT.

[8] For example, the original Buttonwood agreement established minimum commission rules that served as anticompetitive regulations until 1975. The exchanges have also maintained closed shops that limit members' ability to trade exchange-listed stocks off exchange. And, in its early days, the NYSE was extremely secretive about transactions.

Discussion

The exchanges are able to utilize their institutional structure to provide efficient price discovery because most trades in exchange-listed stocks are executed there. Unfortunately, the trend is for trades to move outside the network of the exchanges. The movement is partially the result of some traders' ability to avoid the information costs by avoiding the exchanges. An analogy can be found in the automobile insurance industry. The incentive in that market is for good drivers to distinguish themselves from high-risk drivers to avoid the externality costs they would otherwise bear. Therefore, one finds signals such as age, sex, and driving record determining insurance premiums.

Likewise, traders in secondary equity markets are often able to signal that they are not trading on asymmetric information. For example, it is less likely that a trader will have asymmetric information about a portfolio than a trader will have asymmetric information about an individual stock. Thus, the movement toward portfolio trading in both the fourth market and at the exchanges can be partially explained as a signaling device that can reduce the cost of the trade.

The danger, however, is that if this trend continues the only trades left to be executed on the exchanges will be the ones most unable to signal their trading motive. These will mostly be the smaller individual traders and those that are informed. The result could be a form of lemons problem in which the exchanges are the place where trades are done that cannot be done anywhere else.

If this outcome is realized, the ability of the exchanges to conduct orderly markets and to lead the way in price discovery will be significantly weakened. As trades move off the exchange, the information content of these trades will become unavailable to the specialists. Also, as the ratio of informed to uninformed traders at the exchanges decreases, it will be more difficult for specialists to generate the flow of information and more difficult for them to keep markets open at times of great uncertainty.

In the end, it will likely be up to the regulators to determine the future structure of the national markets. The exchanges are not by themselves the model structure. They have adapted to better meet the market's needs partially as a result of the threat of competition and by the force of regulation. To their credit though, the strength of the exchanges lies in their ability to self-regulate. The resulting institutional structure provides an effective way of providing efficient price discovery and of conducting orderly markets.

References and Suggested Readings

Amihud, Y., and H. Mendelson. 1986. "Asset Pricing and the Bid Ask Spread." *Journal of Financial Economics* 17 (Dec.):223–49.

Benveniste, Lawrence M., Alan J. Marcus, and William J. Wilhelm. 1992. "What's Special About the Specialist." *Journal of Financial Economics.*

Hasbrouck, Joel. 1988. "Trades, Quotes, Inventories and Information." *Journal of Financial Economics* 22.

Schwartz, Robert A. *Equity Markets: Structure, Trading, and Performance.* New York: Harper and Row.

30

Auction Market Trading at the New York Stock Exchange

James E. Shapiro
New York Stock Exchange

1. Introduction: Types of Securities Markets

The debate over the relative merits of auction and dealer markets is a perennial one in regulatory circles. Numerous public policy issues in the securities industry are closely intertwined with the presumed advantages of one market structure over another or the concern that certain policies may favor a specific structure. For this reason, in the context of current policy discussions, it is useful to try to clarify some of the important differences between auction-market and dealer-market trading.

Dealer Markets

In dealer markets, the counterparty in a trade is almost always a dealer, that is, a market professional trading for his or her own account. There is generally no order-flow centralization in dealer markets—actively traded securities have multiple quotes as competing market makers attempt to attract orders by advertising buy and sell prices and by other means. Finally, dealer markets typically, but not necessarily, have no floor trading.

Examples of dealer markets include the over-the-counter market (NASDAQ) in the United States, SEAQ in Britain, the secondary U.S. Treasuries market, and the global spot market in major currencies. In all these markets, quotes are advertised on screens and transactions are typically consummated over the telephone. NASDAQ and SEAQ rely heavily on electronic screens for quote dissemination. Decentralized, multiple-quote dealer markets, however, can be high tech or low tech. Many countries, for example, have dealer markets without electronic screens: everything is done over the telephone. On the other extreme, the whole process—including trade execution—can be automated.

To many people, dealer markets are the most desirable way to organize markets because they encourage competition between many dealers. This is true, although it is also true that there may be costs to this competition in terms of efficiency—each dealer must make a profit. This can be costly. Dealer markets may be most desirable when there are relatively few buyers and sellers in a market at any one time. Where buyers and sellers are more concentrated and numerous, auction market trading is more feasible and may be preferable.

Auction Markets

The essential feature of most auction markets is that investors have the opportunity to trade *directly* with each other. In dealer markets, investors rarely trade directly with each other—a dealer is on at least one side of virtually every trade. Auction markets, again in contrast to dealer markets, aim for order-flow consolidation and have one bid and one ask quote per security.

There are many types of auction markets. Auction markets can be *continuous* auctions or periodic call auctions. In a continuous auction, trading can take place at any time during the trading day. In a call auction, orders are combined for simultaneous execution at prespecified times, usually once or twice a day. Some auctions have trading floors, while other auctions do not (i.e., the auction is completely automated). Finally, auction markets may have one or more designated market makers in each security.

New York, Tokyo, and Toronto have continuous auction markets with floor-based trading and (in New York and Toronto) one designated market maker per stock. Futures trading at the Chicago Mercantile Exchange takes place in a floor-based continuous auction market with competing market makers in each contract—the locals in an open-outcry system. Tokyo's CORES, Toronto's CATS and the French CAC systems are automated, continuous auction markets with no floor trading. Finally, in the United States, the Wunsch system (since March 1992 the Arizona Stock Exchange) is a call auction with no floor trading and no designated market makers.

Is there an absolutely best market system? No. Each system has advantages and disadvantages. Each system reflects the history and circumstances of a particular market for a particular security at a particular time. Markets evolve and change, adapting to the realities of the marketplace. As in any business, in the business of running a marketplace, the pragmatic approach may be the best. The best market in theory may not prove the most liquid and attractive in practice.

Pure auction markets, while attractive in theory, in practice are often supplemented with designated market makers who stand ready to act as dealers-of-last-resort, providing liquidity when there is an insufficient concentration of investors. Automation and high levels of technology are also clearly attractive, but floor trading has provided flexibility—for example, in the strategic handling and display of a customer's order—that computerized trading systems simply have yet to match.

2. The Advantages of Auction Markets

Investors Collectively Supply Liquidity and Do Not Pay the Dealer Spread

At the NYSE and in other auction markets, investors typically trade directly with each other so that the investor community as a whole avoids paying the dealer spread—the difference between the highest bid (to buy) and the lowest offer (to sell). For example, if an investor wishes to buy 100 shares of Coca Cola at $40 per share and another wishes to sell that amount at the same price, the trade can be executed on the floor of the NYSE without a dealer acting as intermediary. This is what is meant by an auction market.

In a dealer market, such as the over-the-counter market for stocks in the United States, investors might buy at 40 1/8 and sell at 39 7/8. The difference between the buying price and the selling price—the spread—would go to the dealer, as compensation for his or her willingness to trade at a posted price and supply liquidity. Dealer markets are typically organized to maximize competition between dealers. Thus, at least in theory, when dealer markets are highly competitive—and when this competition works to narrow the spread between the prices paid by buyers and the prices paid by sellers—dealer markets serve investors by maintaining a narrow spread.

Auction markets, on the other hand, are typically organized to maximize the competition between orders. When this competition works well—and when there are sufficient natural buyers and sellers—it too narrows the spread between the prices paid by buyers and the prices paid by sellers. In fact, by matching buyer and seller, auction markets often eliminate this spread.

Order Exposure and Price Improvement

In auction markets, in contrast to dealer markets, each order is exposed to all the other participants in the market—not just to the dealer to whom the order is sent. This means if there are investors willing to buy at $50 then no one can sell at $49 7/8, without first offering the trade to them. Order exposure also gives investors the opportunity to meet and trade between the quotes. This narrows the effective spread, the actual difference between transactions prices for buyers and sellers. Studies of transaction data for NYSE-listed stocks show that between-quote negotiation and interaction is quite common. Approximately one-third of all volume on the NYSE is executed between the quotes. And when the spread is greater than the minimum one-eighth of a dollar ($0.125), the proportion of NYSE volume occurring between the bid and the ask quotes is much higher—nearly 60 percent.[1]

Designated Market Makers in Auction Markets

In many auction markets, certain individuals or firms are assigned the function of dealer-of-last-resort so that there will always be someone willing to buy and sell. In this way, auction markets supplement the liquidity provided by investor limit (or priced) orders. But the role of dealers in auction markets is subordinate to public investors. On the NYSE, investor orders take precedence over specialist quotes. For example, if the bid is $50 and the offer is $50.25, with no one but the specialist bidding, when a public investor's limit order arrives to buy at $50, that limit order must be satisfied before the specialist can buy for his or her own account at $50.

---

[1] *See*, for example, Lee, "Market Integration and Price Execution for NYSE-listed Securities," Working paper (Oct. 26, 1992), University of Michigan; Blume and Goldstein, "Displayed and Effective Spreads by Market," Working paper (Nov. 10, 1992), the Wharton School, University of Pennsylvania; and Petersen and Fialkowski, "Price Improvement: Stock on Sale," Working paper (June 1992), Graduate School of Business, University of Chicago. In 1991, investors sending orders through the NYSE's SuperDOT electronic order processing system saved $331 million by trading inside the quoted bid or offer prices. Because SuperDOT orders account for only 30 percent of total NYSE volume, these numbers can be viewed as a minimum estimate of actual price improvement in the NYSE auction market.

Dealer markets do not typically give investors precedence over dealer trading. For example, for *unlisted* stocks traded in the over-the-counter dealer market, if there is a dealer bid for $50 and an offer at $50.25, the dealer can buy at $50 without executing a public limit order to buy at $50. The dealer is required to fill such an order only when his or her *offer* reaches $50.

3. Diversion of Orders in NYSE-Listed Stocks

In the United States, auction markets compete with dealer markets. The competition takes place at two levels. First, the NYSE competes with the over-the-counter dealer market for the listing of companies. In deciding where to list, large and small companies weigh the benefits of a NYSE listing versus an over-the-counter listing. The NYSE also competes with the over-the-counter dealers for order flow in NYSE-listed stocks. This second form of competition—referred to as third-market trading—raises several interesting issues and deserves closer scrutiny.

Even though auction markets may be attractive to investors and even though investors may have a collective interest in concentrating their trading in a single auction so as to maximize order exposure, dealers will inevitably try to divert orders away from the auction market in order to capture the spread for themselves. The NYSE quote, for example, is the best consolidated bid or offer around 90 percent of the time. In other words, it typically has a higher bid or lower offer or is firm (i.e., guaranteed) for a larger amount than other competing quotes. These findings are not particularly controversial and have been borne out in numerous empirical studies.[2] Despite the superiority of NYSE quotes, however, small retail trades are increasingly diverted away from the NYSE to dealer markets because dealer markets provide profitable opportunities for dealers to trade for their own account. Own-account trading has become increasingly important as competition has sharply reduced commission income—currently around 15 percent of gross income for NYSE-member firms.

This dealerization is further fueled by the growing institutionalization of equities investment and trading. Institutions, because they are large customers, are far less wary of dealer markets than small investors. In the foreign exchange market, for example, large customers pay extremely small spreads in transactions with the dominant dealers. But for

---

[2] *See*, for example, Blume and Goldstein (1992).

small retail transactions, the difference between the selling price and the buying price—the spread—can be enormous in percentage terms.

Agency Problems

One of the most important reasons for the diversion of small retail trades away from the NYSE is a potentially serious agency problem. When brokers buy or sell stock on a customer's behalf, they act as agents. When the interests of an agent are different from those of the agent's customer, there is what is called an agency problem. Most investors do not choose the market in which they trade; their brokers do. When retail investors give their orders to their brokers, they rarely specify where the order should be executed. Retail customers typically either assume that NYSE-listed stocks are always traded on the NYSE or do not care because they assume that as long as they get the best consolidated bid or offer they receive the best execution possible.

Unfortunately, the assumption that where a small order executes does not affect the quality of execution is mistaken. Several empirical studies using trade-by-trade transaction data have found that small orders sent to the NYSE receive, on average, better executions than those sent elsewhere.[3]

This is particularly disturbing because small investors in particular are the least able to effectively monitor the quality of their trading through agents. As additional empirical evidence accumulates, policy makers will be better able to judge the degree to which retail investors are disadvantaged by the diversion of their orders from the NYSE.

Encouraging Competition

Increasingly, the NYSE must compete for order flow. This is good. Competition—or at least the constant threat from potential competitors (what economists call contestable markets)—gives customers greater bargaining power over the dominant market and encourages innovation and efficient service. Competition has brought tremendous benefits to the industry and has been a force for change and technological advancement. Care is needed, however, to ensure that public policies that encourage competition benefit investors (through, for example, quote competition) and do not merely enrich

---

[3] *See*, for example, Lee (1992), Blume and Goldstein (1992) and Petersen and Fialkowski (1992).

intermediaries (by, for example, increasing the percentage of trading done through dealers).

There is a trade-off between increasing competition among markets and increasing order-flow fragmentation. When competition among markets leads to order-flow fragmentation, the effectiveness of order exposure is reduced: each sell order, for example, is exposed to fewer potential buyers. Pricing efficiency and investor protection may both suffer as a result. To claim that one is procompetition is not enough. Public policy must weigh the benefits of competition between markets against the benefits of competition between orders.

References and Suggested Readings

Blume, Marshall E., and Michael A. Goldstein. 1992. "Displayed and Effective Spreads by Market." Working paper, the Wharton School, University of Pennsylvania, Philadelphia.

Fialkowski, David, and Mitchell A. Petersen. 1992. "Price Improvement: Stocks on Sale." Working paper, Graduate School of Business, University of Chicago.

Lee, Charles M. C. 1992. "Market Integration and Price Execution for NYSE-listed Securities." Working paper, University of Michigan, Ann Arbor.

Circuit Breakers

and Rule 80A

31

Regulatory Responses to Program Trading and Index Arbitrage: Circuit Breakers and Rule 80A

Henry McMillan[1]
Transamerica Occidental Life Insurance

The 1980s saw the widespread adoption of innovative trading strategies, such as portfolio insurance and index arbitrage, that rely on program trading and stock index futures contracts. Program trading, index arbitrage, and portfolio insurance have all been associated with the stock market crashes of 1987 and 1989. In the eyes of many observers, these trading practices caused these crashes and need to be restricted. This paper reviews how and why program trading came to be blamed for the crashes and why limits on program trading are perceived as beneficial. The paper evaluates the trading restrictions implied by circuit breakers and Rule 80A and briefly reviews the empirical evidence on these subjects.

1. Program Trading

Program trading is the simultaneous purchase or sale of a group of securities. The New York Stock Exchange (NYSE) defines the group to be 15 or more stocks with a total value of $1 million or more. In principle, the program trade could include futures contracts, option contracts, or other securities or synthetic securities. The average index-related program trade executed on the NYSE in early 1990 included 167,000 shares among 280 stocks with a value of $7.25 million (Sofianos 1990).

Program trading is a simple application of modern portfolio theory. For example, if the program trade involves the market basket, then an investor is simply adjusting his or her exposure to nondiversifiable market

---

[1] The views expressed here are those of the author and do not necessarily reflect the view of Transamerica Life Companies or its employees.

risk. This is what modern portfolio theory argues the investor should do. We can view program trading as a financial innovation evolving from financial theory.

Program trading, however, is more commonly associated with index arbitrage, portfolio insurance, and computers. Index arbitrage is nothing more than a program trade that includes the stocks that comprise the Standard and Poor's 500 Index (S&P 500) and the S&P 500 futures contract of the Chicago Mercantile Exchange (CME). If the futures contract is relatively cheap, the arbitrageur buys it, sells the cash index, and makes a riskless profit. Index arbitrage can involve other futures contracts, such as the Major Market Index Contract, or futures and options contracts. Portfolio insurance is an investment strategy that increases the exposure of a portfolio to market risk as the market return increases. Exposure to market risk can be adjusted with program trades using stocks only or with program trades involving stocks and futures contracts. Program trading typically uses computers to calculate arbitrage opportunities, evaluate proper exposure to market risk, and submit buy and sell orders to the NYSE floor and CME trading pits.

2. Policy Pressures and Issues

On October 19, 1987, the Dow Jones Industrial Average fell 508 points. Trading volume on the New York Stock Exchange was an extraordinarily high 604 million shares. Program trading accounted for almost 20 percent of total share volume and as much as 60 percent when the market was falling rapidly. On Friday, October 13, 1989, the Dow fell 190 points and the S&P 500 fell thirty points in the 90 minutes before closing. Program trading accounted for over 30 percent of S&P share volume during this time.[2]

In the subsequent analysis, program trading in general and its association with portfolio insurance and index arbitrage in particular came to be blamed for these crashes. The association begins with a simple empirical fact: when markets were most volatile, program trading was more common and constituted a larger fraction of total trading.

Two critical studies (the report of the Preidential Task Force on Market Mechanisms [hereafter referred to as the Brady Report or Presidential Task Force. . . 1988] after the market break of 1987 and the report of the

---

[2] For further details, *see* Presidential Task Force on Market Mechanisms, (1988) and Securities and Exchange Commission (1990).

Division of Market Regulation of the SEC after the market break of 1989 [SEC 1989]) point to anecdotal evidence suggesting a tendency for futures prices, alleged to be excessively volatile as a result of inadequate margin and regulatory requirements, to gain momentum and "overshoot" their "correct" values during times of rapid moves in the market. Program trading and especially index arbitrage, according to this view, transfer "excess volatility" from the futures market to the stock market. The SEC's approval order of NYSE Rule 80A specifically cites minimum margin levels and restrictions on short selling as examples of regulatory differences that contribute to overshooting:

> Low margin levels on stock index futures encourage speculative trading in such futures, which creates the appearance of deep liquidity during normal market conditions. When markets are stressed and prices begin to fall rapidly, however, the illusion disappears. Liquidity in the stock index futures markets evaporates, causing price declines that are already occurring to accelerate. These price declines are transmitted almost instantaneously through index arbitrage to the stock market. The resulting index arbitrage can drag the stock market past the equilibrium price. The October 1987 Market Break and the rapid decline on October 13, 1989, are the two most glaring examples of these phenomena.[3]

In addition to the overshooting argument, some critics allege that index arbitrage causes excess volatility by generating surges of one-sided market orders (either buy orders or sell orders) straining cash market liquidity. The SEC's approval order for Rule 80A expresses this concern:

> Index arbitrage can exacerbate dramatic price declines during volatile market conditions by transmitting volatility surges from the stock index futures market to the stock market. These surges can overwhelm the capacity of the market to meet instant liquidity demands and taxes liquidity in the stock market when it is needed most.[4]

---

[3] Securities and Exchange Act Release No. 34-28282, 55 FR 31471.

[4] Securities and Exchange Act Release No. 34-28282, 55 FR 31471-2.

The implication of this reasoning was that the futures and stock markets, having different market mechanisms, either needed coordination to prevent destabilizing interactions between the markets or separation to insulate the stable (stock) market from the unstable (futures) market. Index arbitrage was and is the most direct link between the markets and was singled out as the villain that transmitted volatility from the futures market to the stock market.

How program trading and index arbitrage could be the villains is a mystery to most economists. Program trading is simply an effective way to rebalance a large portfolio between debt and equity in response to fundamental macroeconomic news. Portfolios and prices should react quickly to fundamental news in an efficient securities market. Arbitrage is simply the simultaneous purchase and sale of the same commodity at two different prices. It generates riskless profits at zero net cost. If you buy in one market, you sell in the other. In theory, index arbitrage should have no net effect on the stock and futures price levels, since any change in one price is offset by an equal and opposite change in the other price.

Furthermore, while program trading and index arbitrage occur more frequently when markets are volatile, that does not mean that they cause volatility. Instead, program trading and index arbitrage might respond to volatility. As Furbush (1991) notes, index arbitrage may be like fire fighters to a fire: "An observer of a forest fire will see lots of fire fighters. They did not cause the fire; they responded to it."

Additional issues became wrapped into the subsequent debate. Arguments were raised that the NYSE wanted to retain market share being lost to the CME and that restricting program trading would help do this. The SEC and Commodity Futures Trading Commission (CFTC) battled each other to protect or expand their regulatory powers.

3. Policy Prescriptions

3.1. The Brady Report

The Brady Report made four broad recommendations: (1) establish a single regulatory agency for all equity-related markets; (2) establish circuit-breaker mechanisms to shut down panicked markets; (3) unify and fix problems in the clearing and settlement systems; and (4) establish consistent margin requirements across futures and stock markets.

The recommendations were not a direct attack on program trading or index arbitrage. The recommendations called for greater coordination and linkage among futures and stock markets. Indeed, the recommendations were criticized for failing to recognize the differences in the markets and for inappropriately trying to establish uniformity where uniformity was not warranted. This criticism was especially made with respect to consistent margins.[5]

As time wore on, consistency and market linkage were replaced with separation of markets as the desired goal among some policy makers. As described in the SEC order on Rule 80A, the linkage of futures and stock markets would be undesirable if the futures markets were unstable. Rules were passed to decouple the markets, to inhibit order submission from program trades, and to shut down futures markets before stock markets were shut down.

3.2. Circuit Breakers

Circuit breaker is a generic term attached to a variety of mechanisms that alter trading rules under specified circumstances. The Brady Report argues that circuit breakers offer three major benefits. Circuit breakers can

> (1) . . . limit credit risks and loss of financial confidence by providing a `time-out' amid frenetic trading to settle up and insure that everyone is solvent.
>
> (2) . . . counter the illusion of liquidity by formalizing the economic fact of life . . . that markets have a limited capacity to absorb massive one-sided volume.
>
> (3) . . . facilitate price discovery by providing a `time-out' to pause, evaluate, inhibit panic, and publicize order imbalances to attract value traders to cushion violent movements in the market.[6]

The CME instituted circuit breakers for its S&P futures contract effective October 20, 1988. A price floor (not a trading halt) would be imposed for 30 minutes if the contract price had fallen 12 points during the day, and a

---

[5] *See* Miller (1991, Ch. 4).

[6] *Report of the Presidential Task Force on Market Mechanisms*, 66.

second price floor would be imposed for an hour if the futures price had fallen 30 points during the day. At the same time the NYSE agreed to halt trading in all stocks for one hour if the Dow Jones Industrial Average had declined 250 points from the previous day's close. The CME's circuit breakers for the S&P futures contract were first triggered on October 13, 1989; the NYSE circuit breakers have never been triggered.[7]

3.3. Rule 80A

In July 1990, amidst the controversy, the NYSE amended its Rule 80A to restrict stock index arbitrage on days of large stock price movements. The amended rule requires that, on days when the Dow declines (or increases) by 50 points or more from the previous day's closing value, all index arbitrage sell orders using component stocks of the S&P 500 be entered with the instruction "sell plus" ("buy minus").[8] The tick restrictions apply to all index arbitrage orders in component S&P 500 stocks traded at the NYSE, regardless of the means by which the orders are routed to the specialist's post. The rule was implemented in August 1990 for a one-year trial period and became permanent in 1991 after formal approval from the SEC. The amended rule makes index arbitrage program trades difficult and slow to execute, which effectively eliminates their value for many market participants.

4. Evaluation

4.1. Index Arbitrage and Market Volatility

An evaluation of circuit breakers and Rule 80A necessarily begins with how index arbitrage and program trading affect market volatility. In my view the weight of the evidence does not indicate that program trading or index arbitrage cause market volatility. Among the many studies see Harris,

---

[7] *See* Appendix E of NYSE report, "Market Volatility and Investor Confidence" (1990).

[8] "Sell plus" means that the order can be executed on a plus or a zero-plus tick. A plus tick is a price above the price of the preceding sale. A zero-plus tick is a price equal to the preceding sale if the last transaction at a different price was at a lower price. "Buy minus" means that the order can be executed on a minus or a zero-minus tick. A minus tick is a price below the price of the preceding sale. A zero-minus tick is a price equal to the preceding sale if the last transaction at a different price was at a higher price.

Sofianos, and Shapiro (1990) and Neal (1992). If program trading and index arbitrage do not cause market volatility, then circuit breakers and Rule 80A are unnecessary to correct the problem of excess volatility. These rules may have other benefits, or the rules themselves may induce volatility.

4.2 Circuit Breakers

The CME circuit breaker is an example of price limit rules frequently adopted by futures exchanges to assure contract performance and clearing house solvency. However, solvency was an unlikely motive for adopting the original CME circuit breakers. Because contract performance and clearing house solvency depend on the magnitude but not the direction of price changes and because the CME circuit breakers applied to price declines only, the likely motive was an assessment of the regulatory and political costs of failing to adopt such a rule.

There is little empirical evidence on the CME circuit breakers, largely because the limits have been triggered only a few times in their first four years of existence. In research begun at the SEC (see McMillan 1991), I found that circuit breakers appear more likely to have increased volatility than to have decreased it during October 1989. First, volatility, as measured by the dispersion of minute-by-minute futures price changes, increased after circuit breakers were lifted on Friday, October 13, 1989, and remained large on Monday morning, October 16, 1989. In contrast, futures price dispersion did not increase on October 16, 1987 (the Friday before the crash), even though the market decline would have triggered a 12-point circuit breaker had it been in place. Second, price dispersion did not increase after a long run-up of futures prices on October 24, 1989, that would have triggered a price ceiling had the circuit breaker been symmetric. This implies that runs by themselves do not increase price dispersion but do increase dispersion when coupled with circuit breakers. Together, these two findings suggest that volatility increased as a result of lower liquidity and lower informativeness of futures prices. Third, two empirical specifications indicated that circuit breakers exerted a gravitational effect on futures price changes, pulling futures prices down toward the limit, on October 13, 1989. However, because a gravitational effect has not been found in other commodities markets with price limits, we might expect the gravitational effect to lose its strength after its initial episodes as stock index futures traders will become accustomed to the price floor.

4.3. Rule 80A

Rule 80A restricts index arbitrage trades that link stock and futures markets. By linkage we mean that cash and futures prices reflect the same information and thereby satisfy the law of one price. Index arbitrage makes the cash and futures prices equal and so assures that the markets are linked. By restricting index arbitrage, Rule 80A could weaken or eliminate this linkage, thereby insulating one market from the volatility of the other, which would be a good thing according to some observers. Other observers feared that the stock and futures markets might wander apart, destroying the law of one price that economists cherish. In fact, the linkage was hardly disturbed at all. To see why, it is useful first to analyze Rule 80A in the context of two firms producing similar but different products.

Index arbitrage links two markets (stock and futures) that have different trading structures produced by different firms (the NYSE and the CME). Each exchange's rules and trading structure reflect the specific preferences of their customers and the nature of their products. The CME's customers largely are institutional investors and professional traders who wish to trade marketwide risk. The NYSE's customers are institutions and individual investors who wish to trade individual company risk. The CME has developed rules for its stock index futures contract that are designed to allow prices to move rapidly, something that its customers value. The NYSE has developed rules for the trading of individual stocks that are designed to dampen rapid price movements, something that its customers value. That the CME's customers value the properties of the S&P 500 futures contract is revealed by the product's success: within three years the daily share-equivalent trading volume of the S&P 500 futures contract was greater than daily volume of the NYSE. The NYSE's success is witnessed by its continued robust activity after 200 years of trading. Undoubtedly, the NYSE specialist's obligations to provide price continuity and continuous market presence play a significant role in this success.

On days on which prices move rapidly in one direction, the different adjustment speeds can create problems. The NYSE's price quotes adjust less quickly to new marketwide information than do the CME's futures prices, creating a profit opportunity that arbitrageurs attempt to exploit. The resulting arbitrage trades, which are typically market orders, demand liquidity from the stock market. By providing price continuity, specialists and other traders who place limit orders lose to index arbitrageurs whenever the market is trending in one direction.[9]

If index arbitrage trading volume reduces the specialist's profits, then the specialist can attempt to regain these profits elsewhere. This compensation could take the form of higher bid-ask spreads and smaller commitments even during less stressful times and a greater willingness to quit the market altogether when large price changes occur. Alternatively, the specialist can seek protection through state-contingent trading rules.

Rule 80A is a state-contingent rule; it is invoked only when specialists would otherwise absorb large losses by maintaining price continuity. Rule 80A rations the liquidity of specialists during peak-demand times. In this respect it is similar to a brownout in the provision of electricity or admission limits for the use of ski slopes. These nonprice rationing mechanisms impose costs on those who wish to trade at the peak time but reduce costs of providing services during normal times by eliminating the need for seldom-used capacity.

Rule 80A effectively reduces the profitability of index arbitrage by raising its costs and increases its risk by slowing the execution time. Eliminating index arbitrage need not eliminate the linkage between cash and futures markets, however. Since arbitrage will be permitted after the market has stabilized (under Rule 80A, typically the next day), the futures and cash prices will come together in the future. Specialists can continue to revise quotes in anticipation of arbitrage orders to align cash prices with futures prices. Specialists will have pressure to do so from "smart shoppers" (Miller 1992) who choose to sell where prices are high and buy where prices are low. Market makers whose prices are out of line will receive one-sided orders and will be forced to adjust their prices as an inventory control measure. Thus, eliminating index arbitrage need not eliminate market linkage.

Three studies—NYSE (1991), Kuserk et al. (1992), and McMillan and Overdahl (1992)—find that Rule 80A weakens, but does not eliminate, the linkage between stock and futures markets, where linkage is measured by the adjustment speed of cash prices to futures prices. However, there are significant changes in index arbitrage volume. The NYSE report and Overdahl and McMillan find that index arbitrage trades are about 25 percent

[9] Program trading does not necessarily hurt the specialist who provides price continuity. Because program trades are not done for stock-specific reasons, the specialist need not be concerned with asymmetric information issues. Consequently, in stable markets, program trades provide profitable order flow to the specialist.

of what would otherwise be expected. Agency index arbitrage (performed by NYSE firms for outside firms) is essentially eliminated while principal index arbitrage (performed by NYSE firms for their own account) is reduced but persists.

5. Summary

The evidence as a whole indicates that index arbitrage is not destabilizing. Circuit breakers and limitations on index arbitrage trading were not needed to promote market stability. However, while unnecessary, circuit breakers and Rule 80A have not adversely affected market stability, although may have reduced efficiency in market price quotations to some extent. The primary effects of circuit breakers and especially Rule 80A have been in the composition of trade, which is consistent with an adjustment of wealth distribution from trade.

Trading rules can have public-relations benefits not measured in financial studies. Some market participants most definitely believe that program trading and index arbitrage increase market volatility and are destabilizing. Circuit breakers and Rule 80A restrictions might calm their fears during volatile market episodes. Consequently, circuit breakers serve a useful purpose by acting as a placebo for those investors.

References and Suggested Readings

Furbush, Dean. 1991. "Program Trading in Context: The Changing Structure of World Equity Markets." *Cato Review of Business and Government* (Spring): 71–77.

Harris, Lawrence, George Sofianos, and James Shapiro. 1990. "Program Trading and Intraday Volatility." Working Paper, New York Stock Exchange (Feb.).

Kuserk, Gregory, Peter Locke, and Chera Sayers. 1992. "The Effects of Amendments to Rule 80A on Liquidity, Volatility, and Price Efficiency in the S&P 500 Futures." *Journal of Futures Markets* 12, no. 4 (Dec.).

McMillan, Henry. 1991. "Circuit Breakers in the S&P 500 Futures Market: Their Effect on Volatility and Price Discovery in October 1989." *Review of Futures Markets* (forthcoming).

McMillan, Henry, and James Overdahl. 1992. "NYSE Rule 80A: An Evaluation of Its Effects on Trading Costs and Intermarket Arbitrage." Working paper, Commodity Futures Trading Commission, Washington, D. C. (Aug.).

Miller, Merton. 1991. *Financial Innovations and Market Volatility.* Cambridge: Basil Blackwell.

——. 1992. "Volatility, Episodic Volatility, and Coordinated Circuit-Breakers: The Sequel." *Pacific-Basin Capital Markets Research* 3:11–21.

Neal, Robert. 1992. "Program Trading on the NYSE: A Descriptive Analysis and Estimates of the Intra-day Impact on Stock Returns." Working paper, University of Washington, Seattle (June).

New York Stock Exchange. 1990. *Market Volatility and Investor Confidence.* New York: New York Stock Exchange.

——. 1991. "The Rule 80A Index Arbitrage Tick Test." Working paper, New York Stock Exchange (July).

Presidential Task Force on Market Mechanisms. 1988. *The Report of the Presidential Task Force on Market Mechanisms* [Brady Report]. Washington, D.C., U.S. Government Pringting Office (Jan.).

Sofianos, George. 1990. "Index Arbitrage Profitability." Working paper 90-04, New York Stock Exchange (Nov.).

U.S. Securities and Exchange Commission. Division of Market Regulation. 1990. *Trading Analysis of October 13 and 16, 1989.* Washington, D. C.: U.S. Government Printing Office (May).

Multiple Trading of Options

32

Multiple Listing of Stock Options

Robert Neal[1]
University of Washington and
Securities and Exchange Commission

Exchange trading of most U.S. securities is governed by the Securities and Exchange Acts of 1934 and 1975. An important objective of these laws is to encourage competition among exchanges. While this objective has been attained in the equity markets, trading for most stock options is limited to a single exchange by the options allocation plan. This rule, administered by the Securities and Exchange Commission, gives an exchange exclusive rights to trade particular options. The allocation plan was formally adopted in 1980, two years after the SEC had requested the exchanges voluntarily refrain from listing options traded on another exchange. In June 1989 the SEC adopted Rule 19c-5 which rescinded the allocation plan, allowed for new options to be multiply listed, and gradually allowed multiple listing for options previously restricted to a single exchange. Through administrative procedures, however, the SEC has delayed full implementation of Rule 19c-5. As of November 1992, most options are still restricted to a single exchange. This chapter discusses the history of the allocation plan and summarizes the empirical evidence of its consequences.

1. History of Options Regulation

The regulatory history of U.S. stock option trading involves innovation, competition, and politics. Stock options began trading at the Chicago Board Options Exchange (CBOE) in June 1973. Within two years, options were also trading at the American Stock Exchange (AMEX), the

---

[1] The views expressed here are those of the author and do not necessarily reflect the views of the Securities and Exchange Commission.

Philadelphia Stock Exchange (Phlx), and the Pacific Stock Exchange (PSE). By February 1976, the exchanges had initiated options trading in most of the actively traded stocks and began to compete with each other by trading options that were listed on a rival exchange. By July 1977, 22 options were listed on multiple exchanges. During this period, competition was viewed favorably by both the exchanges and the SEC. For example, in March 1977 the CBOE stated:

> Experience in multiple trading in options to date has shown that, largely in response to the forces of competition, markets have improved and costs have been reduced on the exchanges that have been involved in this competition. Although these benefits have been concentrated in the option classes that have been the subject of dual trading, in many cases they have also carried over to classes of options that are not dually traded. Market improvements are reflected in narrower bid-ask spreads, better price continuity between consecutive transactions, and greater depth and liquidity. Cost savings have resulted from, among other things, reduction in charges by CBOE board brokers and AMEX specialists, and by reductions in floor brokerage.[2]

Fifteen months later, however, the CBOE, Phlx, and PSE became concerned about the adverse consequences of competition and sought regulatory intervention. For example, the CBOE stated:

> we believe . . . that further expansion of multiple trading should not be permitted unless and until a national market system for options, and the resulting creation of a fair field of market competition, have been substantially achieved. In the absence of the latter, expanded multiple trading would inevitably result in (1) further undesirable fragmentation of the market, and, at times, disorderliness and confusion; (2) problems of best execution, and (3) a

---

[2] Report of the Special Study of the Options Markets, United States Securities and Exchange Commission, 808.

gradual decline in effective competition because of the absence of a fair field of competition.[3]

Their justification for these concerns was twofold. First, the exchanges believed that brokers executing orders for customers always sent the order to the primary exchange, without considering whether an alternative exchange had more favorable prices. Thus it was pointless for an exchange to compete with another exchange for trading volume in an established option. Second, the exchanges were concerned that options might simultaneously trade at different prices on different exchanges. For example, on September 1, 1978, the price of Bally call options appeared to differ substantially between AMEX and CBOE.[4] Without a linkage among exchanges, options investors could not expose their orders to all available supply and demand.

In response to these concerns, the SEC accepted the reasoning of these exchanges and requested they voluntary refrain from trading options that were listed on another exchange. Part of the SEC's motivation was to give the exchanges time to develop a computerized linkage similar to the current Intermarket Trading System (ITS) for stocks. This linkage would display the best bid and ask quotes for all markets, report transaction prices, and provide automatic execution for small orders. The SEC gave tentative approval of multiple trading restrictions in 1978 and formally adopted the options allocation plan in March 1980. To encourage option trading, the allocation plan allocated the pool of available options to the exchanges in a manner similar to the National Football League draft. The options that were multiply listed prior to July 15, 1977, however, were exempt from the allocation plan and continued to be listed on multiple exchanges.

The SEC's position changed over time toward favoring multiple listing. In June 1985 the SEC allowed options to be traded on OTC stocks. These options were outside the domain of the allocation plan and were therefore permitted to be multiply listed. The allocation plan was formally

---

[3] Report of the Special Study of the Options Markets, United States Securities and Exchange Commission, 806.

[4] *See* U. S. SEC, 840–43 for additional discussion. It should be noted that at least some of the AMEX prices reported in the study appear to violate arbitrage relationships. For example, at 11:15 the May 60 call traded at $13 with the stock price at 60 7/8. In the previous minute, with the stock price at 61 1/4, the May 70 call traded at $14 1/2. I doubt these prices reflected the true state of the market.

rescinded in May 1989 with the adoption of Rule 19c-5. This rule provided for multiple listing of options listed after 1989 and, for singly listed options, a gradual phase-in of multiple listing beginning January 1990 and complete multiple listing by January 1991.[5]

While the allocation plan could have been viewed as a pragmatic compromise for an interim period, the SEC was reluctant to permit direct competition among exchanges. This occurred for two reasons. First, some of the exchanges successfully lobbied to preserve the allocation plan. They employed leading academic researchers to dispute the SEC's findings on multiple trading and obtained the support of key senators and representatives to delay the SEC.[6] Second, the exchanges used the computerized linkage as a strategic issue. The exchanges adopted the position that a linkage must be in place prior to multiple listing. As one might have predicted however, the exchanges could never agree on the form of the linkage. In 1991 the exchanges finally agreed on a common linkage[7] only to discover that it could not be implemented because its costs would outweigh its benefits.

One reason the exchanges have successfully preserved the allocation plan is because the SEC commissioners change every several years. The incoming commissioners have demonstrated a willingness to reconsider the same arguments. SEC Chairman Richard Breeden has delayed full implementation of Rule 19c-5 through at least November 1992 and President-elect Clinton will likely appoint a new chair in early 1993. The future of the multiple listing restrictions will likely be determined by the next chair.

2. Economic Analysis of the Allocation Plan

Evidence on the consequences of the allocation plan is valuable to both the study of multiple listing and as a controlled experiment for analyzing market structures. Comparing the transaction costs of options eligible for multiple listing with single listed options provides insight into the consolidation-fragmentation debate and the necessity of intermarket linkages.

---

[5] *See* U. S. SEC (1989) for additional discussion of Rule 19c-5.

[6] *See*, for example, the letter from the Subcommittee on Oversight and Investigations of the Committee on Energy and Commerce (John Dingell, Chairman) to SEC Chairman Richard Breeden on October 21, 1992. A copy of this letter is available from the Subcommittee.

[7] *See* U. S. SEC (1992) for a discussion of one proposed plan.

Contrasting single listed options traded in alternative market structures provides a precise comparison of these market structures.

The empirical evidence suggests that multiple listing restrictions impose significant costs on options investors. In December 1978 the SEC published the *Special Study of the Options Markets*. Chapter 8 provides a pre–multiple listing and a post-multiple listing comparison of options listed on either AMEX or CBOE prior to multiple listing and listed on both AMEX and CBOE following multiple listing. The study finds that the mean spread for these options fell from 20.1 cents in the three months prior to multiple listing to 15.0 cents in the three months following multiple listing. Consistent with the decline in spreads, a measure of trade-to-trade volatility exhibited a similar decline. While these results persist in multiple price categories, the study does not control for the substantial increase in trading volume during the post–multiple listing period. Other things constant, the increased volume should also narrow the spreads.

A second study of multiple listing is by Lightfoot, Davis, and Martin (1986) of the SEC's Directorate of Economic Policy Analysis. Unlike the before and after comparison in the *Special Study*, Lightfoot et al. provide a cross-sectional analysis. Specifically, they contrast the transaction costs of options on OTC stocks with a control group of AMEX single listed options. Their results, summarized in Table 1, show that options eligible for multiple listing have significantly smaller bid-ask spreads than options restricted to a single exchange. After controlling for factors likely to influence spreads (price, trade frequency, trade size, and price volatility) they find that the coefficient for a multiple listing dummy variable is negative and significant. The spreads for the OTC multiple listed options are about 20 percent lower than for the single listed options.

The most detailed analysis of the options allocation plan is contained in Neal (1987) and Neal (1992). The 1987 study focuses on AMEX options that are single or multiple listed. The multiple listed options include both the OTC options and the options that were multiple listed prior to the allocation plan. The comparison of single and multiple listed transaction costs occurs long after AMEX became the primary market and therefore provides a measure of the sustained impact of the exchange level competition. The results from this study are summarized in Table 2. After controlling for factors that affect bid-ask spreads, the multiple listing dummy coefficient is negative and statistically significant. The coefficient on a variable that interacts trading volume and the multiple trading dummy is positive and significant, suggesting that high volume drives spreads toward the minimum tick size and thereby reduces the effect of multiple listing. Consistent with the Lightfoot et al. (1986) study, spreads for low volume multiple listed options are about 20 percent smaller than for comparable single listed options.

The analysis in Neal (1992) compares the transaction costs of single listed options in two alternative market structures: the CBOE competitive market maker structure and the AMEX specialist structure. The results are summarized in Tables 3 and 4. After controlling for factors that affect spreads, Table 3 shows that the AMEX dummy coefficient is negative and significant. When trading volume is low, the bid-ask spreads for AMEX options are about 20 percent smaller than for CBOE. As volume rises this difference diminishes and may even reverse for high volume options. These findings are consistent with a model by Grossman and Miller (1988) and suggest that investor transaction costs would be reduced if options were free to migrate to their optimal trading environment.

Table 4 shows that the difference between competitive market maker and specialist structures is not confined to bid-ask spreads. A greater fraction of the AMEX trades are executed between the current bid and ask than for the CBOE trades. In addition, the average trade size, a proxy for liquidity, is larger in the AMEX sample. These results show that the difference in spreads presented in Table 3 understate the transaction cost differences between AMEX and CBOE.

3. Conclusion

The options allocation plan is an SEC-administered rule that prohibits, with some exceptions, an exchange from trading an option that is currently traded on another exchange. The empirical evidence suggests that the restriction on multiple listing has two effects. First, bid-asked spreads of options that are eligible to trade on multiple exchanges are significantly smaller than options that are confined to a single exchange. It is important to note that this effect occurs without a computerized linkage among exchanges and without any significant trading volume on the nonprimary exchange. Since competing market centers produce lower transaction costs, this suggests that policies designed to prevent market fragmentation will not be in the best interests of investors. Second, forcing options to trade in a particular market structure will, on average, increase transaction costs. When trading volume is low, a specialist structure has lower transaction costs than a competitive market maker structure. This advantage narrows as trading volume increases and may reverse when volume is sufficiently high. Allowing options to migrate to their optimal trading environment can also reduce transaction costs.

In 1989 the SEC adopted rule 19c-5, which rescinded the allocation plan and provided for the elimination of the multiple listing restrictions. Through administrative procedures, the SEC has maintained these restrictions for most options. It is difficult to say when the SEC will fully implement Rule 19c-5 and permit direct competition among options exchanges.

Table 1
A Cross-sectional Comparison of Bid-Ask Spread between OTC Options and Single–Listed Options

Sample Period	β_0	β_1	β_2	β_3	β_4	β_5	R^2	Obs.
June 17	0.340	-0.165	-0.059	0.080	0.000	-0.047	.77	263
and 26 1985	(25.4)	(-28.2)	(-8.8)	(1.7)	(0.3)	(-3.2)		
Sept 9 - 13 1985	0.313	-0.153	-0.053	0.095	0.000	-0.039	.76	759
	(39.2)	(-44.1)	(-14.4)	(3.3)	(0.04)	(-5.0)		

Source: U.S. Securities and Exchange Commission, Directorate of Economic and Policy Analysis (written by L. Lightfoot, J. Davis, and P. Martin), "The Effect of Multiple Listing on the Market for OTC Options," (Washington, D.C.: U.S. Government Printing Office, November 1986).

Table 2
A Cross-sectional Comparison of Bid-Ask Spreads between Multiple-Listed and Single-Listed Options

β_0	β_1	β_2	β_3	β_4	β_5	β_6	R^2	Obs.
0.1847	-0.0025	0.0011	0.0519	-0.0493	0.0003	-0.0439	.22	4426
(15.5)	(-10.5)	(3.19)	(18.7)	(-4.92)	(0.40)	(-5.11)		

Source: R. Neal, "Potential Competition and Actual Competition in Equity Options," *Journal of Finance* 42 (July 1987).

Table 3
A Comparison of Bid-Asked Spreads between the AMEX and the CBOE

β_0	β_1	β_2	β_3	β_4	β_5	β_6	λ	δ	R^2	Obs.
0.2985	0.0889	0.0011	0.0102	-0.0048	0.0014	-0.0551	.520	.348	.50	7337
(25.2)	(23.5)	(2.40)	(3.57)	(-15.1)	(3.49)	(-4.53)				

Source: R. Neal, "A Comparison of Transaction Costs in Competitive Market Maker and Specialist Market Structures," *Journal of Business* 65 (July 1992).

Table 4
Distribution of AMEX and CBOE Transaction Prices and Trade Size

	Trades below the bid	Trades at the bid	Trades between the bid and ask	Trades at the ask	Trades above the ask	Obs.
AMEX trades	0.5%	26.0%	40.0%	32.3%	1.1%	3396
CBOE trades	2.9%	22.5%	29.5%	40.1%	5.0%	3941
AMEX trade size in contracts per trade	12.9	17.5	21.3	17.3	19.3	3396
CBOE trade size in contracts per trade	9.4	14.1	14.6	7.8	8.3	3941

Source: R. Neal, "A Comparison of Transaction Costs in Competitive Market Maker and Specialist Market Structures," *Journal of Business* 65 (July 1992).

References and Suggested Readings

Grossman, S., and M. Miller. 1988. "Liquidity and Market Structure." *Journal of Finance* 43 (July): 617–633.

Lightfoot, Lois, Jeff Davis, and Peter Martin. 1986. *"The Effect of Multiple Trading on the Market for OTC Options*. U.S.Securities and Exchange Commission staff study, Division of Economic Analysis. Washington, D. C.: U. S. Government Printing Office (Nov.).

Neal, R. 1987. "Potential Competition and Actual Competition in Equity Options." *Journal of Finance* 42 (July): 511–37.

——. 1992. "A Comparison of Transaction Costs between Competitive Market Maker and Specialist Market Structures." *Journal of Business* 65 (July): 317–334.

U. S. Securities and Exchange Commission. 1989. Securities Exchange Act Release 26871. Washington, D. C.: U. S. Government Printing Office (June 5). 43 SEC Docket 1807-1816.

——. 1992. Securities Exchange Act Release 34-30187 Washington, D. C. : U.S. Government Printing Office (Jan. 22). 50 SEC Docket 1162-1166.

——. *Report of the Special Study of the Options Markets*. Washington, D.C.: U.S. Government Printing Office.

Broker-Dealer

Capital Requirements

33

The Economics of Risk-Based Capital Requirements

Stephen Craig Pirrong
University of Michigan

1. Introduction

The cost of capital is a major component of the total costs that broker dealers, market makers, and specialists incur in order to supply liquidity and access to financial markets. Capital requirements imposed by the Securities and Exchange Commission on some securities market participants have an important effect on the amount of capital these firms must hold. As a result, these requirements influence directly the costs of market access and liquidity and thus help determine the efficiency and competitiveness of securities markets.

It is certainly true that these requirements serve a legitimate function; specifically, they reduce the costs of trading by increasing the probability of contractual performance. Unfortunately, given the existing means of determining firm capital for regulatory purposes, the requirements do not perform this function in an efficient fashion. Most importantly, the existing means of calculating regulatory capital do not adequately reflect the true riskiness of security firm portfolios. Altering capital requirements calculations in order to do so could therefore allow broker-dealers, specialists, and market makers to offer their services at both lower cost and lower risk. A movement to these truly risk-based capital requirements would thus improve the efficiency of U.S. financial markets. This would redound to the benefit of all users of these markets—including investors large and small, as well as the firms, governments, and government agencies that utilize these markets to raise capital for productive investment.

2. The Economic Function of Capital Requirements

No financial market can operate unless those that participate have a high degree of confidence in the ability of those who they trade with or trade through (e.g., securities brokers) to perform on their contractual obligations. As a result, over the years securities and commodities market participants have devoted massive resources to the task of designing institutions intended to improve contractual performance. These institutions include clearing houses and the margin system.

Regulatory capital requirements, which date from the Securities Exchange Act of 1934, represent the U.S. government's contribution to the goal of assuring low cost contractual performance. The SEC's Net Capital Rule requires registered broker-dealers conducting a general securities business to maintain a cushion of liquid assets that it can draw upon to satisfy the claims of customers and creditors.

Capital requirements would be superfluous in a world in which information about the financial condition and riskiness of firms providing liquidity and access to financial markets could be obtained costlessly. In such a world, investors and other market participants would simply observe the characteristics of the firms they may trade with or trade through and make their decisions concerning which firms to patronize by weighing the trade-off between price and the probability that a firm will be unable to meet its financial obligations. Under these conditions, poorly capitalized firms would either be forced out of the industry or could survive only by discounting the prices of their services in order to compensate their customers and counterparties for the greater likelihood of default.

When information is costly to obtain, however, capital requirements can lower the costs of operating a financial market. First, repeated verification of a firm's financial condition by numerous investors and counterparties is duplicative and wasteful. Moreover, since broker-dealers have claims against other firms, verification of the creditworthiness of firm *A* requires knowledge of the creditworthiness of firms *B*, *C*, *D*, and so on, with which *A* deals. This daisy chain problem further increase the costs of evaluating the riskiness of a given firm. The daisy chain effect also introduces an externality; a firm that increases its riskiness may not consider the effects of this action on the riskiness of other firms with which it deals.[1]

Capital requirements economize on information costs; one agency monitors an important determinant of creditworthiness: capitalization. This reduces (but does not eliminate) search and evaluation by private parties. Moreover, the imposition of universal requirements reduces the importance of the daisy chain problem, as capital requirements provide some assurance that a particular firm's other counterparties are viable and/or solvent, thereby reducing the necessity of evaluating the creditworthiness of these other firms.

It is important to note that capital requirements are a common feature of private clearing organizations, such as the Chicago Board of Trade Clearing Corporation or the Options Clearing Corporation. This voluntary adoption of capital requirements suggests they serve an important efficiency function. Since government plausibly has a comparative advantage in organizing capital requirements across markets and across a large number of geographically dispersed market participants, there is a strong presumption that (in principal) government capital regulations can improve market performance by reducing the costs of improving contractual performance.

3. Current Capital Requirement Regulations

The Net Capital Rule requires firms to maintain a specified minimum amount of net capital. Under the Rule's so-called basic method, broker-dealers must maintain net capital in excess of the maximum of (a) 6.67 percent of its aggregate indebtedness (which essentially consists of all unsecured borrowings including some debt that does not appear on a firm's balance sheet) or (b) $25,000. Under the alternative method, the firm must maintain net capital in excess of the maximum of (a) $100,000 or (b) 2 percent of customer-related receivables.

A firm calculates its net capital by adjusting its GAAP (generally accepted accounting principles) net worth. Most importantly, for the purposes of this analysis, a firm must reduce its net worth for the purposes of computing regulatory capital by making certain percentage deductions from the value of its securities and derivative positions. These

---

[1] It should be recognized that firms do expend resources to evaluate the creditworthiness of their trading partners, and this reduces the importance of the externality. Nonetheless, capital requirements may perform the same function at lower cost.

deductions—called "haircuts"—are intended to reflect the riskiness of the security positions. Thus, a security that the SEC considers risky is assessed a large haircut (e.g., some short equity positions have a 30 percent haircut), while one that is perceived as less risky is assessed a relatively small one (e.g., short-term government debt).[2]

4. A Critique of Current Capital Requirements

In theory, at least, the principal of risk-based capital requirements is sound. Other things being equal, firms with riskier portfolios are more likely to fail; they therefore require more capital in order to reduce the probability of default. Thus, capital requirements that vary with risk force firms to bear a cost at the margin for increasing default risk. Unfortunately, under existing capital requirement regulations, haircuts are not necessarily related to the *true* riskiness of a broker-dealer's securities and derivative positions. This is due to three basic features of the capital calculation methodology.

First, and most importantly, haircuts are largely calculated on a security-by-security basis. Although the SEC has increasingly recognized the risk-reducing effects of offsetting positions (e.g., long and short positions in different but related securities or derivative instruments)[3] and has adjusted haircuts accordingly, it is nonetheless true that a firm's capital requirements are largely determined by calculating haircuts on each of a large number of rather narrow categories of securities. Moreover, these categories frequently create artificial distinctions between quite similar securities.

Modern finance theory implies that the riskiness of a firm that holds inventories of securities and derivatives depends crucially upon the composition of its entire portfolio. Other things being equal, a firm's riskiness declines as it increases the diversity of holdings in its portfolio. Because of this "diversification effect," the idiosyncratic variations in individual investments tend to offset, and, as a result of the law of large numbers, the variation in a portfolio's value as a result of idiosyncratic (as

---

[2] It should be noted that the methods that are used to calculate haircuts are extremely complex and constantly changing. In addition to its formal rules concerning haircuts, the SEC sometimes allows firms to adjust their computations in order to reflect risk management strategies that they may employ.

[3] Examples include offsets between stock index futures and baskets of equity securities and between government debt securities of different maturities.

opposed to systematic) variations in asset prices declines as the number of different investments increases. Moreover, the variation of a portfolio depends crucially upon the correlations among the returns of the individual investments that it includes. These correlations essentially measure the importance of common sources of security risks; these common sources cannot be diversified away.

The foregoing implies that the marginal contribution of a particular security or derivative instrument to the overall risk of a securities firm depends vitally upon the number and identity of the other instruments it holds in its portfolio. A security-by-security approach to calculating capital requirements does not recognize this interdependency. Therefore, a firm's capital requirements do not necessarily vary with the relevant risk—the risk of its total portfolio. Put another way, two firms with very different risk profiles may receive identical capital requirements when haircuts are calculated on a security-by-security basis. Similarly, different firms holding a given security or derivative may pay an identical haircut on that position even if its marginal contribution to portfolio risk differs substantially between firms. This implies that firms do not necessarily pay the appropriate price at the margin for increasing default risk.

Second, even abstracting from portfolio composition issues, the existing haircut calculation methodology does not adequately recognize the different risk characteristics of securities that fall within a particular class. Thus, for example, two different equity securities with very different risk characteristics may incur the same haircut. For example, a high volatility equity incurs the same haircut as a low volatility equity.

Third, asset riskiness changes over time. This is particularly true for options and assets with embedded options (e.g., mortgage backed securities), as the variability of these assets depends upon the value of the securities or claims underlying them. Asset riskiness may also change because of variations in the riskiness of particular markets, industries, or the economy at large. Again, the existing haircut methodology does not adequately recognize this time variation in asset risk.

Together, these features of the existing haircut methodology imply that a firm's capital requirements do not necessarily vary appropriately with the riskiness of its security and derivative positions. Similarly, they imply that the marginal capital charge associated with a particular trade/position in a given security may bear little relation to the true riskiness associated with it.

These implications may have serious consequences. Most importantly, when making trading decisions, the existing capital requirements do not induce firms to internalize the true costs of default risk associated with these decisions. As a result, firms perceive some trades to be less risky (i.e., less costly) than they truly are, but perceive other trades to be riskier than is indeed the case. This may result in a distortion of trading decisions across markets. Liquidity and access will be underpriced in markets for instruments in which capital requirements are artificially low and overpriced in markets for instruments in which capital requirements are artificially high. Moreover, insufficiently risk sensitive capital requirements can lead to an inefficient allocation of trading activity in a given security/derivative among firms. The true risk associated with a given security for a given firm depends upon the composition of its portfolio, while capital requirements may not. Since portfolios differ among firms, the capital requirement attributed to a position in this security should also vary among them, but may not. Thus, some firms underestimate the true cost of trading/holding a particular security, while other firms overestimate it; as a result, the former firms trade/hold too much, and the latter trade/hold too little.

These distortions in trading activity are costly. Put another way, market participants could enjoy both lower risk of default and lower costs of access and liquidity if capital requirements reflected the true riskiness of security and derivative portfolios held by broker dealers, market makers, and specialists. Thus, a movement to capital requirements that bear a close relation to the true riskiness of a firm's positions would lead to an improvement in the efficiency of U.S. financial markets.

5. Portfolio Risk-Based Capital Requirements

The foregoing discussion suggests that risk-based capital requirements should include three basic features. First, haircuts should be determined on a portfolio wide, rather than a security-by-security, basis. Second, they should recognize the variation in riskiness across securities of a particular class. Third, they should recognize that the riskiness of securities and portfolios can vary systematically over time.

Although the theoretical arguments in favor of a portfolio approach are unimpeachable, it must be admitted that there are some practical difficulties that must be surmounted before this approach can be implemented. Most importantly, as broker-dealers frequently hold large numbers of assets in their portfolios it is necessary to compute the correlations between each of these assets in order to determine portfolio risk. Since the number of correlations that must be calculated rises with the square of the number of the assets in the portfolio, the number of parameters that must be estimated is large for well-diversified portfolios.

In this regard, it should be noted that the data required to calculate most of these correlations are readily available, and these parameters can be calculated at relatively low cost given modern data processing capabilities. It is therefore possible to establish an SEC-certified service that would calculate these parameters (and other necessary parameters such as asset return variances) and then provide them to broker-dealers, who could in turn use them to estimate the riskiness of their portfolios. This service could reestimate these parameters on a regular basis in order to ensure that haircuts reflect changing economic conditions. Alternatively, the service could employ the techniques utilized in the burgeoning literature on time varying volatility and correlations in order to accomplish the same objective.

If the number of parameters is still too large to be manageable, however, it may be necessary to compromise on the goal of calculating a portfoliowide haircut. It should still be manageable, however, to calculate the variability of very broad subcategories of firm portfolios (e.g., equities and equity derivatives, interest rate securities and interest rate derivatives) and establish haircuts for these broader categories. Although such a strategy would not completely achieve the objective of relating capital requirements to overall firm risk, it would still represent an improvement on the existing methodology and reduce the distortions in the relation between a security's marginal contribution to firm risk and its haircut.

Another practical complexity that capital requirements must address relates to options and assets with embedded options (e.g., mortgage backed securities). As noted earlier, the variability of these instruments and their correlation with other assets vary systematically with the value of the underlying security/derivative relative to its strike price. It is necessary to employ an option valuation methodology (such as variants of the Black-Scholes model or finite approximation approaches such as the Cox-Ross-Rubenstein model). The approach pioneered by the Options Clearing Corporation in its proposed risk-based haircuts for options market makers provides a clear example of how to implement such a methodology.

6. Summary

Capital requirements for security firms can improve market efficiency by reducing the costs of enforcing contractual performance. In order to economize on the costs of capital and provide market participants with the appropriate incentives at the margin, capital requirements should depend upon risk. Existing capital requirements for particular securities are ostensibly intended to vary with their riskiness. Since these requirements are calculated (with some exceptions) on a security-by-security (rather than portfoliowide) basis, however, they do not achieve these objectives. The efficiency of the vast U.S. securities and derivatives markets could therefore be improved by implementing capital requirements that depend upon the riskiness of security firm *portfolios*. Such a system would economize on capital costs because a given level of protection against default could be achieved with less capital. Moreover, such a system would give traders and brokers a more accurate signal of the true marginal costs of their trading decisions. This would reduce distortions in the allocation of capital, liquidity, and access among markets for particular securities and derivatives, and among market participants. Although some practical complications may preclude attainment of the ideal risk based capital requirement, exploiting a combination of modern portfolio theory, asset pricing theory, and today's sophisticated data processing capabilities could go a long way toward achieving these goals.

Securities Transaction Taxes

34

Transaction Taxes and Stock Values

Yakov Amihud and Haim Mendelson
New York University and Stanford University

1. Introduction

This paper considers the effects of a securities transaction tax on stock values based on the higher transaction costs that such a tax entails. In particular, we examine the impact of imposing a 0.5 percent transaction tax on the sale of stocks, as was recently proposed. We demonstrate that such a tax will lead to a substantial increase in corporate cost of capital and, correspondingly, to lower stock prices.

The reason that a securities transaction tax affects stock values is its detrimental effect on liquidity through the increase in transaction costs. Transaction costs include the bid-ask spread (the difference between the buying price of an asset and its selling price), brokerage and related fees, and transaction taxes (when they exist). Investors are more willing to commit capital if they know that they will be able to liquidate their investment quickly and at low cost whenever the need arises. Investments that are more costly to trade need to offer higher returns to attract investors and compensate them for the higher costs of transacting.

A transaction tax will cause a significant increase in transaction costs, especially for highly liquid stocks. Recently, average brokerage fees and commissions for stock trading paid by large institutional investors were of the order of 6.5 cents per share or less (White 1990), or 13 cents for a "round trip" transaction. A bid-ask spread of $0.125 brings the total cost of transacting to 25.5 cents, or 0.637 percent of the value for a $40 stock. A 0.5 percent tax will thus almost double the total cost of transacting and will do so for the stocks with the largest capitalization, which constitute the bulk of investors' assets.

An increase in the excess return required by investors because of the tax means that corporate cost of capital will increase and stock values will decrease (for any given cash flow). Put differently, if the required return increases in order to compensate for the higher transaction costs imposed by the tax, the hurdle rates for investment projects will increase, and projects that would otherwise be cost-beneficial will be rejected.

We review in Section 2 theoretical predictions on the relation between transaction costs and securities values. Section 3 presents empirical evidence on this relation and applies it to analyze the impact of a transaction tax on the expected returns and prices of stocks, and Section 4 studies the effect of the tax on New York Stock Exchange–listed stocks. Section 5 examines additional effects of the tax, and our concluding remarks are in Section 6.

2. Transaction Costs and Asset Values: Theory

We have developed a model of asset pricing with transaction costs that shows how asset prices depend on their liquidity (Amihud and Mendelson 1986). The model considers rational investors who take into account the costs of transacting capital assets. A key result of our model is that assets with higher transaction costs have, in equilibrium, higher returns because investors need to be compensated for bearing higher costs. Consequently, higher transaction costs lower the value of any capital asset for a given cash flow that the asset generates.

In addition, in equilibrium there is a clientele effect whereby investors with longer holding periods tend to invest in less liquid assets, because they can depreciate their transaction costs over longer periods. These investors are consequently willing to pay more for illiquid assets than investors with shorter holding periods who bear transaction costs more frequently, and thus these investors end up holding the less liquid assets. Investors whose holding periods are shorter value more highly assets with low transaction costs and will end up holding them. As a result, a given change in transaction costs is of greater importance for highly liquid assets. Thus, while the required yield-premium is an increasing function of asset illiquidity, the incremental premium is decreasing. This gives rise to the liquidity premium (the additional yield required by investors) being an increasing and concave (increasing at a decreasing rate) function of the asset's illiquidity, measured by the cost of transacting. Intuitively, one would expect that an increase of, say, 0.5 percent, in transaction costs should have a greater effect on a highly liquid stock than on a thinly traded stock, whose trading is already subject to high transaction costs.

In conclusion, theoretical considerations show that the functional relation between asset returns and transaction costs is increasing and concave.

We illustrate the large effect of apparently small transaction costs by the following simple example.[1] Consider a perpetuity bond that makes a fixed annual coupon payment equal to the return required by investors; its trading does not entail any transaction costs and its market value is $100. Now, assume transaction costs of $0.5 per trade, and assume that the bond is traded once a year. Then, if we discount at a real rate of return of 4 percent the discounted present value of the infinite stream of transaction costs is

$$(1) \qquad 0.5 + 0.5/1.04 + 0.5/1.04^2 + 0.5/1.04^3 + \ldots = \$13$$

The first term in Equation 1 is the $0.5 paid for the original purchase transaction. The second term is the present value of the $0.5 paid a year later, when the bond is sold. The third term is the present value of the subsequent transaction cost, and so on. Thus, we obtain that transaction costs of only $0.5 translate into a loss of $13 in value. The reason that a small increase in transaction costs results in a sizable decline in value is that transaction costs are incurred repeatedly, which magnifies their effect.

This example provides a simple methodology for assessing the impact of a transaction tax. The price decline it will cause can be obtained by discounting the cash-flow stream of the tax payments at an appropriate rate. We apply this methodology to stocks using the basic discount-valuation model by which the value of a stock is the present value of the expected future cash-flow stream it generates,

$$(2) \qquad P_0 = \sum_{t=1}^{\infty} \frac{D_0 \cdot (1+g)^t}{(1+R)^t} = D_1 / (R-g),$$

where P_0 is the current stock price, D_0 is the stock's previous payout, D_1 is the end-of-period payout (at the end of period 1), R is the required return and g is the growth rate (t is the period index). As Equation 2 demonstrates, the analysis using the discount-valuation model is the same as that of the perpetuity model, except that the required return R is adjusted by the growth rate g. Thus, the two models can be used interchangeably.

Consider, for example, a stock with annual growth rate $g = 0.06$ and with an expected end-of-period cash flow of $D_1 = \$1$. If $\underline{R} - \underline{g} = 0.04$, the stock's market value will be $D_1/(R - g) = \$25$. Now assume that a tax rate

---

[1] *See* Amihud and Mendelson (1988).

of 0.5 percent is applied to each transaction in the stock (including the initial purchase) and that the stock is traded once a year (corresponding to a unit turnover rate). Then, if the current price of the stock is P_0, the present value of the transaction-cost stream is given by

$$(3) \quad \sum_{t=0}^{\infty} \frac{0.005 \cdot P_0 \cdot (1+g)^t}{(1+R)^t}$$

which implies that the stock price will decline to P_0 = \$21.98, or a 12 percent loss in value.

The 12 percent estimate of price decline in the above example is sensitive to the assumed parameters and in particular to the assumed holding period of one year. If the stock is traded once every two years rather than once a year, Equation 3 is replaced by

$$(4) \quad \sum_{t=0}^{\infty} \frac{0.005 \cdot P_0 \cdot (1+g)^{2t}}{(1+R)^{2t}}$$

which yields a value of \$23.36, or about a 6.5 percent value loss due to the tax. Thus, to estimate the price effect using this methodology we need accurate information about stocks' holding periods.

The "average" holding period can be calculated from the turnover rates on the New York Stock Exchange (NYSE), which have been between 46 percent and 73 percent during 1986–1990, implying a transaction every 2.2 to 1.4 years on average. However, this approach does not provide the relevant holding period, because large parts of stock issues are often locked away in portfolios that are not actively traded. It is the behavior of the *marginal* investors that determines the market price of a stock and the size of its illiquidity premium. In many companies, there are shareholder groups that hold large blocks of stocks and trade them rarely. These include insiders, outside investment groups with a permanent interest in the company, corporations that control other corporations, and employees' pension funds that hold their own company's stock, often through ESOPs. Clearly, in companies with a group of interested parties that have stable holdings of the stock, the average turnover rate underestimates the holding periods of those investors whose trading determines the illiquidity premium.[2]

---

[2] The inactive investors in the company gain a surplus because of the higher return required by the active ones.

In addition, to calculate the impact of a transaction tax by the above methodology, it is also necessary to know how the holding periods of each stock will be adjusted in response to the tax.

In the analysis that follows we demonstrate the effect of an increase in transaction costs on stock returns by using our estimates of the relation between transaction costs and stock returns in the NYSE. Our empirical estimates are cross-sectional while our objective is to estimate the effect of a change over time in transaction costs on stocks' expected return. Yet, the empirical evidence we employ in our analysis was observed over a long period of time through which there have been significant changes in liquidity, and thus it provides the long-run effect of transaction costs on stock returns and the resulting adjustments that investors make. For example, by our cross-sectional estimation, if stock A has higher transaction costs than stock B, the trading frequency of A is lower and thus the sensitivity of this expected return to transaction costs is lower. While our method of estimation does not consider the general equilibrium (economywide) consequences of taxing stocks, we expect that if a transaction tax is imposed on stocks, their holding periods will increase, particularly if other liquid assets, such as money (broadly defined) and bills, remain untaxed. In Section 5, below, we discuss additional effects of the transaction tax that suggest that its effect could be greater than we estimate here.

3. Empirical Evidence and Its Implications

The analysis in Section 2 implies that transaction costs, or low liquidity, should have a large effect on asset returns and correspondingly on their values. In this section we present our empirical evidence showing the actual effect of illiquidity costs on stock prices and relate the evidence to the proposed transaction tax.

The analysis is based on our estimates of the relation between securities returns and their bid-ask spreads. The bid-ask spread, which is the difference between the buying price of a security and its selling price, is a major component of the cost of transacting. In organized securities markets there are market makers and traders who quote bid and ask prices at which they are willing to execute incoming orders. These quotes enable investors to immediately buy or sell securities and hence provide liquidity to the market. The narrower the difference between the ask and bid prices, the more liquid the stock, because a lower spread is associated with a lower cost of transacting. Thus, the bid-ask spread provides a measure of a stock's illiquidity.[3] The median quoted bid-ask spread in the NYSE is $1/4, which constitutes 0.625 percent of the price of an average $49 stock. There is a multitude of stocks with relatively wide spreads, but they represent a small fraction of total trading volume. For example, the median spread on the 30 stocks that constitute the Dow Jones Industrial list is about 0.35 percent[4]

We studied the empirical relation between the bid-ask spread and expected returns using 20 years of data (up to 1980) on stocks traded on the NYSE,[5] with the sample size for each year ranging between 619 and 900 stocks. The functional relation between the return and the spread is expected to have the properties discussed in Section 2. First, the average (risk-adjusted) return should increase as the spread increases to compensate investors for bearing higher transaction costs. Second, returns should increase at a decreasing rate because of the equilibrium clientele effect whereby less-liquid stocks are matched with longer holding periods. The resulting functional relation between required returns and illiquidity is increasing and concave. That is, if we plot the return as a function of the spread, the function should be increasing, but its rate of increase should be decreasing.

We tested these theoretical predictions empirically by estimating the relation between the risk-adjusted average returns (in excess of the treasury-bill rates) on NYSE stocks and their illiquidity, measured by their (percentage) spread. We formed 49 portfolios[6] of stocks grouped by their

---

[3] Other attributes of illiquidity are strongly correlated with the bid-ask spread. For example, there is a strong inverse correlation between the stock's trading volume (a measure of liquidity) and the spread. The spread is also narrower for stocks with less insider trading and with many competing market makers. On the cost side, brokerage commissions—the other major component of illiquidity costs—is strongly correlated with the bid-ask spread.

[4] The effective spread at which trades are executed can be smaller than the quoted spread.

[5] Amihud and Mendelson (1986, 1989). We also studied the effect of transaction costs on short-term Treasury securities (1991b), obtaining similar results.

[6] The use of portfolios instead of individual stocks is a commonly used method for reducing estimation errors in econometric research in finance.

bid-ask spreads and by their betas, which measure systematic risk.[7] Then, we estimated the relation between the bid-ask spread and the portfolios' average returns (in excess of the Treasury-bill rate), controlling for risk. The empirical results were consistent with the theoretical predictions: average returns are an increasing and concave function of the bid-ask spread.

The research cited above was intended to quantify in general the relation between transaction costs and the stock's expected returns. The application here treats the transaction tax as an additional component of trading costs. In our detailed econometric estimations (Amihud and Mendelson 1986), we employed a free-form estimation of both the beta and the spread effect and found that the return was an increasing and concave function of the spread. Here, we employ a smooth concave function for the return-spread relation, which enables a full-range comparison between alternative levels of trading costs and (following the Capital Asset Pricing Model) a linear return-beta relation.

We use the following notation:

R_i = the average monthly return on the stocks included in portfolio i in excess of that month's 90-day Treasury bill rate;

β_i = the β (or systematic) risk coefficient of portfolio i,

S_i = the average bid-ask spread (measured as a fraction of stock price) for the stocks in portfolio i.

The estimation results are as follows:

(5) $$R_i = 0.006477 + 0.01012 \cdot \beta_i + 0.002144 \cdot log\ (S_i)$$

[7] The beta of an asset measures the tendency of its return to move together with the market and thus measures its systematic risk. By the Capital Asset Pricing Model it should affect its expected return: the higher the beta, the higher the return. Beta can also be viewed as the relative risk of the asset with respect to the market risk, where the asset risk is defined as the covariance of the asset's return with the market's.

(Adjusted R^2 = 79.24 percent), where the logarithmic function represents the concave return-spread relation in the relevant range.[8] The estimated coefficients are highly significant.

Figure 1 depicts Equation 5 the relation between transaction costs and the excess expected monthly return (for a fixed value of the systematic risk, β). The expected return required by investors is increasing with the transaction cost, but the increase is stronger for stocks with high liquidity (low bid-ask spread), reflecting the effect of transaction costs on the stock's holding period. We use Equation 5 to estimate the effect on required returns of an increase in transaction costs caused by a 0.5 percent transaction tax.[9]

The imposition of a 0.5 percent transaction tax leads to a worsening of other attributes of liquidity. For example, because the trading volume declines when transaction costs increase, market depth decreases and the price-impact of large orders increases. An occasional large buy order will cause a steeper price increase than would be the case in a market with more sellers (who are now inhibited because of the tax), and an occasional large sell order will cause a steeper price decline.[10] These price impacts represent costs that increase with the other transaction costs. In general, the attributes of illiquidity or components of transaction costs are highly correlated with the bid-ask spread (*see* Garbade 1982; Benston and Hagerman 1974; Stoll and Whaley 1983). Therefore, our calculations of the effect of the spread already incorporate the other associated illiquidity attributes that prevailed during the sample period. For example, a higher spread is associated in our sample with commensurately higher brokerage commissions, and thus our estimation measures the effect of the total increase in both components of transaction costs. If the transaction tax will not be accompanied by any increases in the other components of transaction costs, these considerations suggest a more conservative estimate of the effect of the tax on stock prices.

The relation between the bid-ask spread and brokerage commissions and fees can be estimated using Stoll and Whaley's (1983) data on these

---

[8] An alternative form of the return-spread relation which we estimated, a power function, gave practically the same results as model (5).

[9] We follow the common practice of applying cross-sectional estimates to estimated changes over time. The usual caveat regarding this method applies.

[10] Under these conditions, the transaction tax will increase market volatility rather than decrease it. Our research (Amihud and Mendelson 1991a) shows that the greater the trading volume of a stock, the lower the noise in the stock price caused by trading. This important issue is, however, beyond the scope of this paper.

variables for 10 portfolios over the 20 years in our sample (a total of 200 observations). The data show a high correlation between the bid-ask spread and the brokerage commissions and fees. The estimated relation between the two variables shows that an increase of 1 percent in the spread was associated with a 0.405 percent increase in total transaction costs. By this methodology, an additional 0.5 percent transaction tax with no concurrent increase in the other transaction costs is equivalent to an increase of 0.356 percent in the bid-ask spread. 0.144 percent (=0.356x0.405) in spread.

This estimate is conservative because it assumes that when the transaction tax is imposed, transaction costs will increase only by the tax rate while all other costs will remain unchanged. However, making the provision of liquidity to the market more costly will surely reduce the willingness of traders and marketmakers to stand ready and provide immediacy and liquidity. Put differently, if the costs of providing liquidity increase, the supply of liquidity will decrease. The result is that illiquidity will be higher, and therefore other illiquidity costs will increase (e.g., the market-impacts of buy and sell orders will increase). Thus, imputing the 0.5 percent tax as an increase of only 0.356 percent in the bid-ask spread underestimates the detrimental effects of the tax, and we use it as a conservative estimate.

We calculated the effect of the 0.5 percent tax on expected returns and prices for a stock that behaves like the perpetuity in our example in Section 2, with an annual return (or excess return over the growth rate) of 8 percent, and obtained the results in Table 1.

TABLE 1:

Effects of a 0.5 % increase in the bid-ask spread on annual return and on price using the conservative estimate (the tax is not accompanied by an increase in other transaction costs)

For a stock with spread of	The annual return increases by	And the price declines by
0.5 %	1.383 %	14.74 %
1.0 %	0.784 %	8.92 %
1.5 %	0.548 %	6.41 %

Our results on the effect of the transaction tax on the (excess) return required by investors and on stock prices are based on long-term estimates—20 years. Over this sample period, the return differential between the high-spread and the low-spread stocks persisted. For stocks whose spreads changed, trading frequencies were correspondingly adjusted as they moved from one investment clientele to another, because investors adjusted their portfolios so as to minimize the burden of transaction costs. These adjustments and changes over time are already incorporated in our long-term estimates on the effect of transaction costs on stock returns.

4. The Effect of the Tax on NYSE Stocks

In this section we employ the methodology and estimates of Section 3 to assess the impact of a transaction tax of 0.5 percent on the values.

The theoretical analysis of Section 2 as well as the empirical results in Section 3 have shown that the effect of a transaction tax is different for different stocks, depending on their liquidity. The higher the stock liquidity (i.e., the narrower its bid-ask spread), the greater the effect of the tax.

There is a strong relation between stock liquidity and market value: stocks with a higher market value tend to have narrower bid-ask spreads.[11] This is demonstrated in Figure 2. Using a sample of 1400 NYSE stocks with bid-ask spread and price data for the last year of the studied period, we calculated the relation between spread and market value. For each level of the spread variable S, Figure 2 shows the fraction of total market value (or capitalization) that has a spread of up to S. For example, more than 10 percent of total market value is concentrated in eight stocks with spreads below 0.265 percent, about 40 percent of total market value has spreads of less than 0.5 percent, about 80 percent of market value has spreads below 1 percent, and about 98 percent of the market value consists of stocks with spreads below 2 percent!

Because the stocks for which the tax effect is the strongest—the more liquid stocks—also weigh more heavily in investors' portfolios, the effect of the tax on the total value of stocks will be higher than the effect calculated for the average stock. An estimation of the effect of the tax on investors' wealth or on market capitalization should take into account the differential effect of the tax on stocks of different capitalization.

We calculated the impact of the tax on the excess return required by investors, using equally weighted and value weighted portfolios. The

---

[11] *See* Roll (1984).

equally-weighted changes in expected return and price answer the question, "What will be the effect of the tax on a portfolio that has equal dollar amounts invested in each stock, large and small alike?" This measure exaggerates the importance of small-firm stocks; however, an average investor cannot hold an equally weighted portfolio. The value weighted measures answer the question, "What will be the effect of the tax on a portfolio that represents (some fraction of) the total market value of the stocks?" This is the relevant measure for assessing the value effects of the tax on the stock market if the value-weighted measure.

For each stock, we calculated the increase in required return due to the 0.5 percent tax as a function of the stock's bid-ask spread using our conservative estimate. Then, we calculated both the value-weighted and the equally weighted averages of these returns. The increase in the required annual return, value-weighted, was 1.33 percent, compared with an increase in required return of 0.73 percent for the equally-weighted average. That is, the tax will lead to an increase of 1.33 percent in the cost of capital on equity investments in the NYSE.

The tax effect will be particularly strong on companies that weigh most heavily in investors' portfolios. We divided the stocks into four groups ranking from the most liquid (narrowest spreads) in Group 1 to the least liquid (largest spreads) in Group 4. For each group, we calculated the average increase in the return required by investors. Both the grouping and the averaging were performed using both the equally weighted approach and the value-weighted approach. The results are presented in Figure 3.

Consider the quarter of the market that includes the most liquid stocks (quartile 1).[12] Using the equally weighted approach, the average stock in this group requires an increase of 1.24 percent in its annual return due to the tax. But the increase in required return per dollar invested in a quarter of the market value composed of the most liquid stocks is higher: 2.24 percent per annum. At the other extreme, the increase in required return per dollar invested in the quarter of market value composed of the least liquid stocks is 0.63 percent.

Next, we consider the effect of the 0.5 percent transaction tax on stock prices. Figure 4 shows the losses in stock values as a function of liquidity (measured by the spread). For each level of the spread, S, we

---

[12] For the equally weighted measure, each quartile contains one quarter of the stocks. For the value-weighted measure, each quarter contains one quarter of the stocks. For the value-weighted measure, each quarter contains one quarter of the value of the sampled NYSE stocks. Clearly, the number of stocks in value-weighted Quartile 1 is the smallest, and the number in Quartile 4 is the largest.

formed a portfolio of all the stocks whose spreads are less than (or equal to) S, and estimated the decline in market value for that portfolio. The results in Figure 4 show, for example, that for the group of NYSE stocks whose spreads are 1 percent or less (which constitute about 80 percent of total NYSE market value), the decline in total value due to the tax is about 15.6 percent. More liquid stocks will be subject to larger declines in value, while less liquid stocks will lose less as a fraction of their market value. The curve in figure 4 becomes practically horizontal at a level of about 13.8 percent, which is the expected total value loss of all NYSE stocks.

Figure 5 shows the cumulative effects of the tax on NYSE stocks as a function of their liquidity. For each level of the spread variable S, we estimated the fraction of the loss in total NYSE value due to the stocks with spreads up to S. For example, the loss in value of the stocks whose spreads are up to 1 percent in magnitude constitutes about 12.4 percent of the total market value of our NYSE stocks. As we increase S, more stocks are added to the estimate and the calculated loss correspondingly increases. At the limit, we obtain the virtually horizontal section of the curve (for large S) which gives the total value loss for all NYSE stocks, 13.8 percent.

5. Additional Effects

In this section we present a number of issues that bear on the calculation of the effect of the transaction tax on securities returns and values. We first consider the method presented in Sction 2, by which the loss due to the tax is given by the present value of the stream of tax payments incurred whenever the security is liquidated. As discussed in Section 2, investors can mitigate this loss by reducing their trading frequency. For example, if prior to the imposition of the 0.5 percent transaction tax investors traded the stock analyzed in the example of Section 2 once a year, they might decrease the trading frequency to once in two years after the tax is implemented. This would reduce their loss from $3.02, or 12 percent of the $25 stock, to only $1.64, or 6.5 percent of value. The question is whether the $1.64 loss estimate provides a correct measure of the loss to investors due to the tax.

Theoretically, the value loss due to the transaction tax could be reduced to zero if investors held stocks indefinitely and never traded them. But this argument misses the meaning of liquidity and ignores the loss caused by a reduction in liquidity. Liquidity is valuable because investors *need* to trade. They need to convert securities into cash for consumption or change the structure of their portfolios. If there are higher costs of trading and this need is constrained, investors suffer. Therefore, the present value of the tax payments by investors (as in Section 2) underestimates the real cost of the tax to investors.

To illustrate, consider the imposition of a toll of $1 on the use of a road. Assume that a driver used the road 5 times a day. His loss due to the toll will be $5 if he maintained the pretoll frequency of driving. But most likely, the driver will reduce his cost by taking the road less frequently, say only twice a day, in which case he will pay only $2 a day. But is it true that the cost inflicted on him by the toll is only $2? Straightforward economic analysis shows that the driver's welfare loss will be greater than the out-of-pocket $2 he is paying; in fact, his total loss can be anywhere between $2 and $5.[13] The intuition behind this effect is clear: the driver will pay in time and in loss of convenience in addition to the direct payout of the toll. For example, he may reduce the number of trips made to the grocery store, thereby necessitating the purchase of larger quantities. But then, he will incur additional costs of storage, interest and inconvenience that must be added to the toll itself. If these additional costs are worth, say, $1.50, he may prefer to bear them rather than pay the additional $3 in tolls. The additional costs of $1.50, while unobserved, are still very real.

Alternatively, the driver may choose to take a detour route so as to avoid paying the toll. But, given that previously the toll road was his best choice, he will surely incur additional costs in gas, wear of the car and lost time. In any case, the driver's cost due to the imposition of the toll will be greater than the tolls actually collected.

A similar analysis applies to the proposed transaction tax. Therefore, it is not only the out-of-pocket cost of a transaction tax that should be considered. In our example, the investor traded the stock once a year, in which case his loss would be $3.02 or 12 percent, and he reduces his trading frequency to once in two years in order to reduce the present value of the tax payments to $1.64 or 6.5 percent of value. His loss, however, is greater than the observed tax collection of $1.64. The real loss, which is the sum of the out-of-pocket cost and the cost in loss of immediacy can be anywhere between $1.64 and $3.02.

Similarly, if the investor reallocates his wealth to other assets away from the assets on which transaction taxes are imposed, he will save in taxes just as the driver saves in tolls by taking alternative roads. But the investor will then bear the cost of being invested in assets which he considered inferior before the tax. The value of these assets may increase because of

---

[13] For example, for a simple linear demand function that passes through the points described, the welfare loss to the driver is $3.50.

the increased demand, but the investor is certainly worse off being forced to invest in them.[14]

Furthermore, while investors will restructure their portfolio holdings by reducing the proportion of assets subject to the transaction tax, the price of these assets will never recover and the effect of the tax will never dissipate. This portfolio restructuring means that the investment community as a whole will hold a smaller proportion of its wealth in the taxed assets. The price of these assets must decline in order to bring about the decline in holdings, and the price of the nontaxed assets must correspondingly increase.[15] The price of the taxed assets will thus remain lower, and their returns will stay higher, than they would otherwise be.

In sum, the costs imposed on investors due to the tax are only partly reflected in the tax payments. While investors will naturally employ measures to reduce their tax burden, they will remain worse off than they were before the imposition of the tax.

Our estimates of the effect of the transaction tax showed its direct effect on expected excess returns (over the Treasury-bill rate and the risk premium) as observed in the stock and bond markets. These observations reflect the actual market's lower valuation of assets with higher transaction costs, and thus capture more completely the tax effect. While our analysis builds on the relation between cross-asset differences in liquidity and their returns, it does not deal with the broad macroeconomic effect of the tax on asset allocation in the economy. The tax will affect both demand and supply of assets and change the relative returns between the most liquid securities, which will not be subject to the tax (such as Treasury bills), and those that will become less liquid because of the tax.[16] In addition to the upward shift

---

[14] It cannot be claimed that economic welfare is increased because the owners of assets that were previously considered of lower value enjoy the greater demand and higher prices for these assets. Using the toll example, if drivers take longer routes to avoid paying tolls, their demand for gasoline and auto services will increase, which will benefit those who provide these services. But the economy cannot benefit from creating a demand for services that would not have been needed in the first place.

[15] This ignores supply adjustments; but as in the above analysis, these adjustments are valuable only because of the tax and were not valuable before it.

[16] Voyanos and Vila (1992) derived the impact of transaction costs changes in an equilibrium model with fixed supply of liquid and illiquid assets and applied the results to the case of transaction taxes. They found that taxing transactions on part of the assets will increase the return on the taxed assets relative to the return on the untaxed assets, that the return on the untaxed assets will decline, and that the final effect relative to the

in investors' demand for liquid securities, which will reduce their yields, there will also be supply adjustments. For example, banking institutions may develop liquid instruments and funds to respond to the increase in demand for liquidity. On the other hand, because the U.S. capital markets are subject to competition from foreign markets, trading in U.S. stocks can move abroad and will increase the negative effect of the stock transaction tax beyond what we have estimated in this paper.[17] The consideration of the general equilibrium consequences of the transaction tax is beyond the scope of this paper, and we expect these consequences to have conflicting effects on stock prices.

Another broad economic effect of the transaction tax, considered in Section 3, is its effect on the other components of transaction costs. We suggest that some cost components may increase because of the "thinner" market caused by the reduction in trading. Because the brokerage industry is extremely competitive and most of it is using similar technologies, it is reasonable to assume that the brokerage fees and commissions will not decline and the incidence of the tax will be borne by investors. In the last decade, commissions declined significantly, by nearly 50 percent (in cents per share), and there is evidence that they bottomed out (see White 1990) and may rise. In our analysis of the tax effect, we employed the conservative assumption that other transaction costs, other than the tax, will not rise. In fact, this assumption is rather conservative. We were also conservative in translating the effect of the tax in terms of excess returns to the corresponding price effect. We used for the most part a discount rate of 8 percent, which is rather conservative. The effect of the tax on stock prices would be greater than presented with lower discount rates. Also, the historical statistics might have underestimated the effect that the transaction tax would have today because during our sample period, the turnover ratio in the NYSE was much lower than it is today. For example, the average turnover during 1961-1970 was 0.176 and the average turnover during 1971-1980 was 0.238, while in recent years it hovers around 50 percent. As we have shown above, the greater the turnover rate, the higher the impact of a given increase in transaction costs on the required expected returns.

---

pretax situation depends on the proportion of assets taxed.

[17] Sweden experienced a flow of trading to London to avoid the stock transaction tax there. This trend was partially reversed after the tax was abolished.

6. Concluding Remarks

In this study we estimated the effect of a 0.5 percent transaction tax on the expected excess returns required by investors and on stock prices. Because the tax will impose greater transaction costs on investors, they will need to be compensated by higher returns. Our estimates of the effect of the additional transaction costs on asset values show that, for NYSE stocks, the required annual return will increase by 1.3 percent and the market value of NYSE-listed stocks will decline by 13.8 percent These results on the tax effect are based on long-term estimates and already reflect the adjustments in investors' trading frequencies and valuations, assuming all other things constant. As such, we do not consider general equilibrium consequences that, on the one hand, will make the markets thinner and increase the impact of the transaction tax, particularly if trading in U.S.-listed stocks moves abroad and, on the other hand, will induce changes in the return structure on all assets and supply adjustments in the capital markets.

Naturally, the transaction tax will have broader effects on U.S. capital markets and on the economy. Our research on the functioning of capital markets shows that stock liquidity interacts with both the volatility and the efficiency of the market.[18] Regarding volatility, the prices of less liquid stocks overreact and exhibit greater noise than those of liquid stocks. Because the tax will reduce stock liquidity, it can be shown that it will also affect volatility in an undesirable way. Regarding market efficiency, we found that the speed of adjustment of market prices to fundamental values is a function of liquidity. Lower liquidity is associated with slower price adjustment, and it is therefore conducive to greater deviations between prices and fundamental values. In a market economy, prices play a critical role in the allocation of resources. A reduction in liquidity will render the market less efficient and will hamper the allocation of resources in the economy.

There is also an expected capital flight to markets with lower transaction costs. This could exacerbate the negative effect of the tax on market depth and may lead to a further increase in transaction costs and further thinning of the market. Because of the "liquidity externality" (Amihud and Mendelson 1991d), the decline in liquidity may go beyond the initial impact of the tax.

The increase in returns required by investors directly translates into an increase in corporate cost of capital. This implies that some investments

---

[18] For a summary of our findings on this issue and some of their implications *see* Amihud and Mendelson (1991c).

that are now desirable (i.e., their internal yield is sufficient to cover the cost of capital) will no longer be undertaken. The result will be a reduction in the rate of capital formation in the U.S. and an overall decline in the competitiveness of the U.S. economy and its capital markets.

Figure 1
Excess Monthly Return as a Function of the Spread

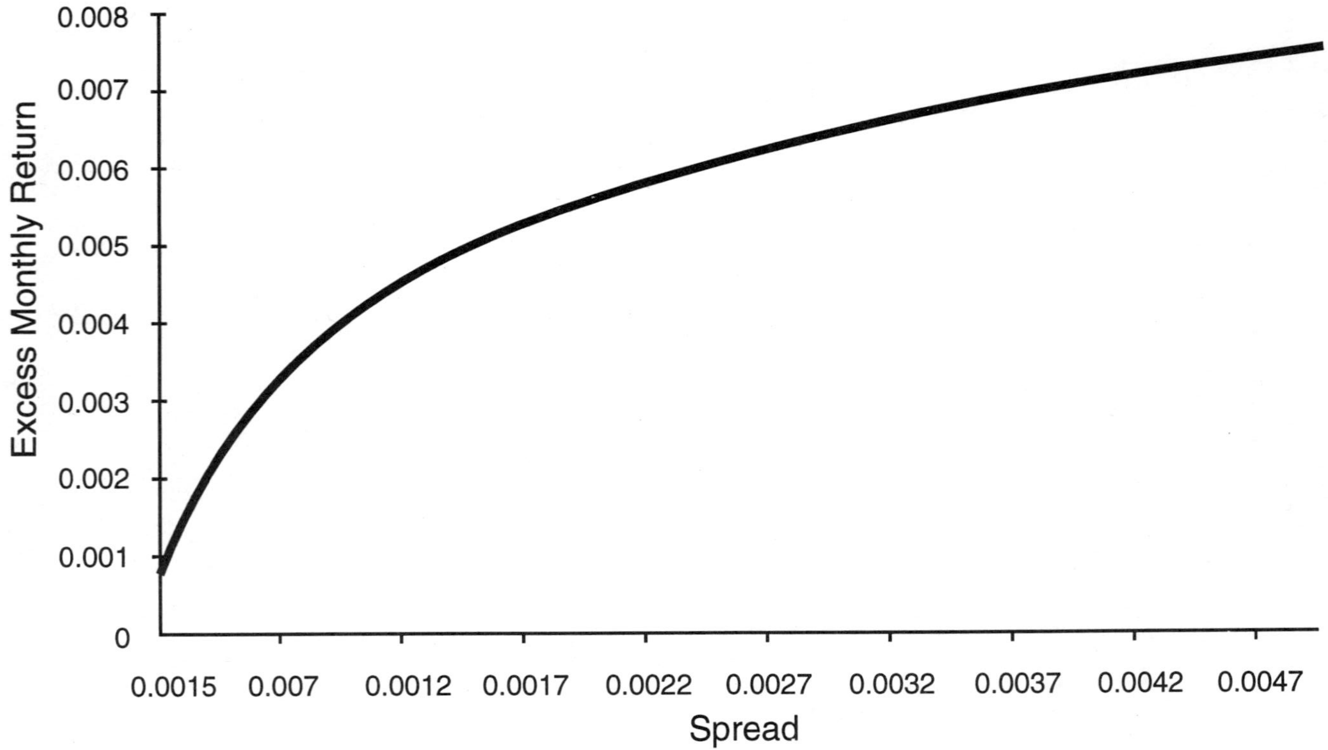

Figure 2
Distribution of the Spread by Market Value of NYSE Stocks

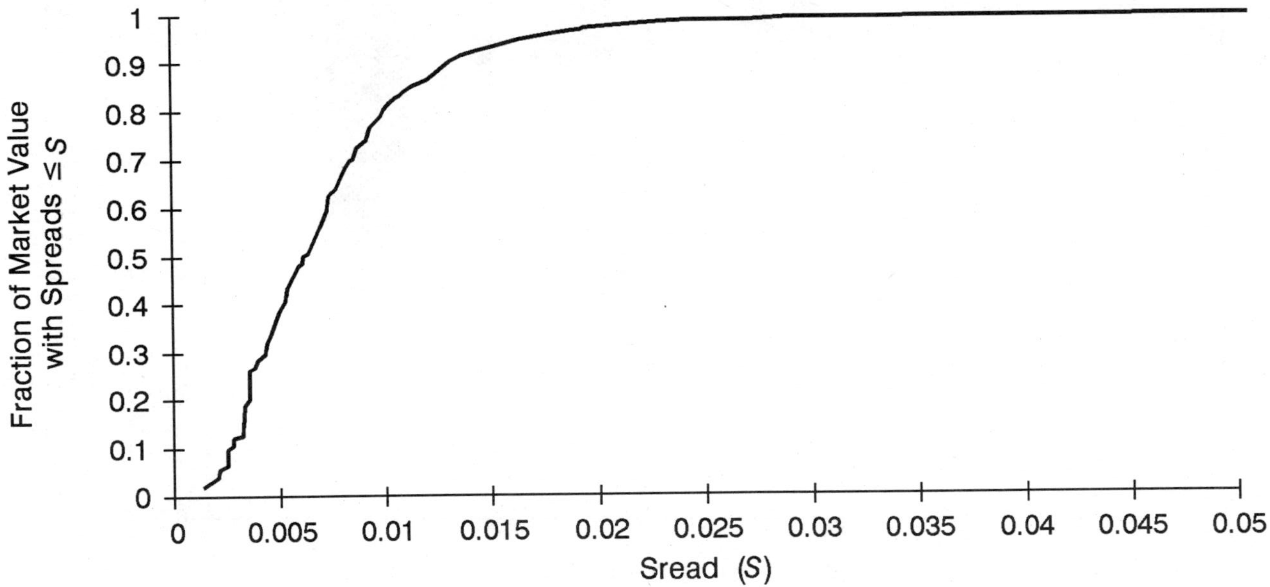

Figure 3
Increase in Required Annual Returns for NYSE Stock Quartiles due to a 0.5% Transaction Tax.

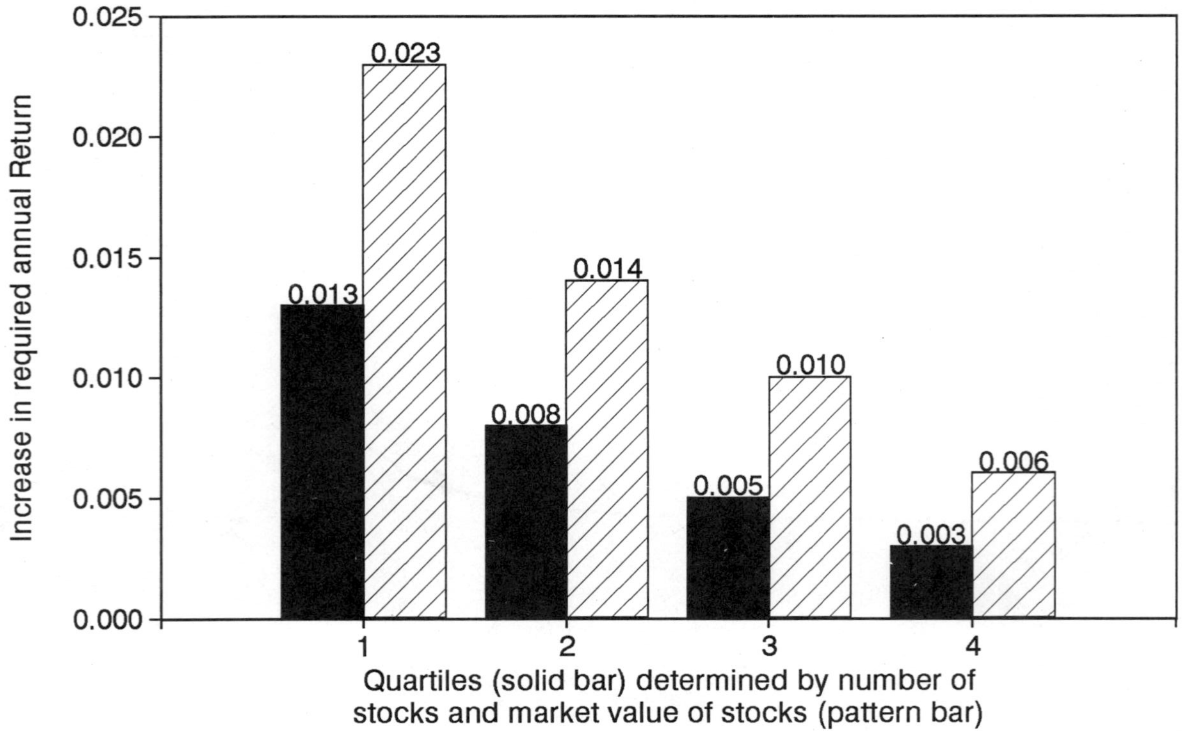

Figure 4
Effect of a 0.5% Transaction Tax on the Value of NYSE Liquidity-Base Portfolios

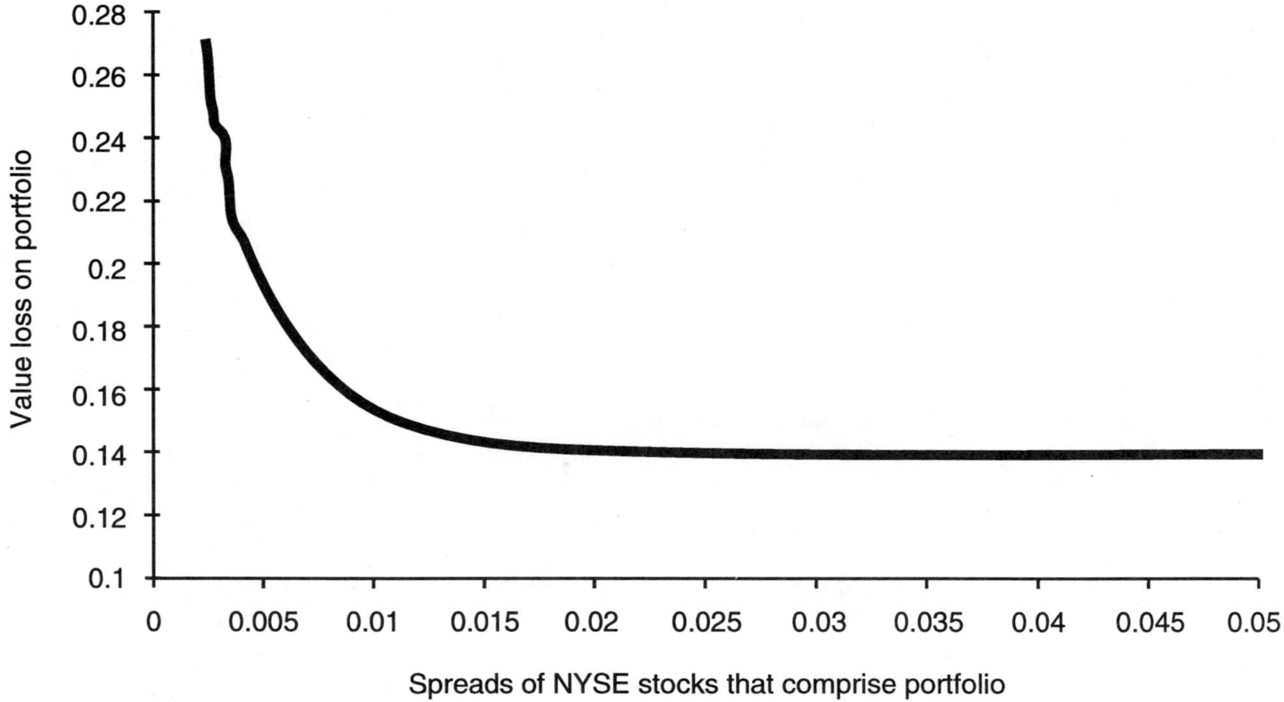

Figure 5
Cumulative Effect of a 0.5% Tax on NYSE Stocks

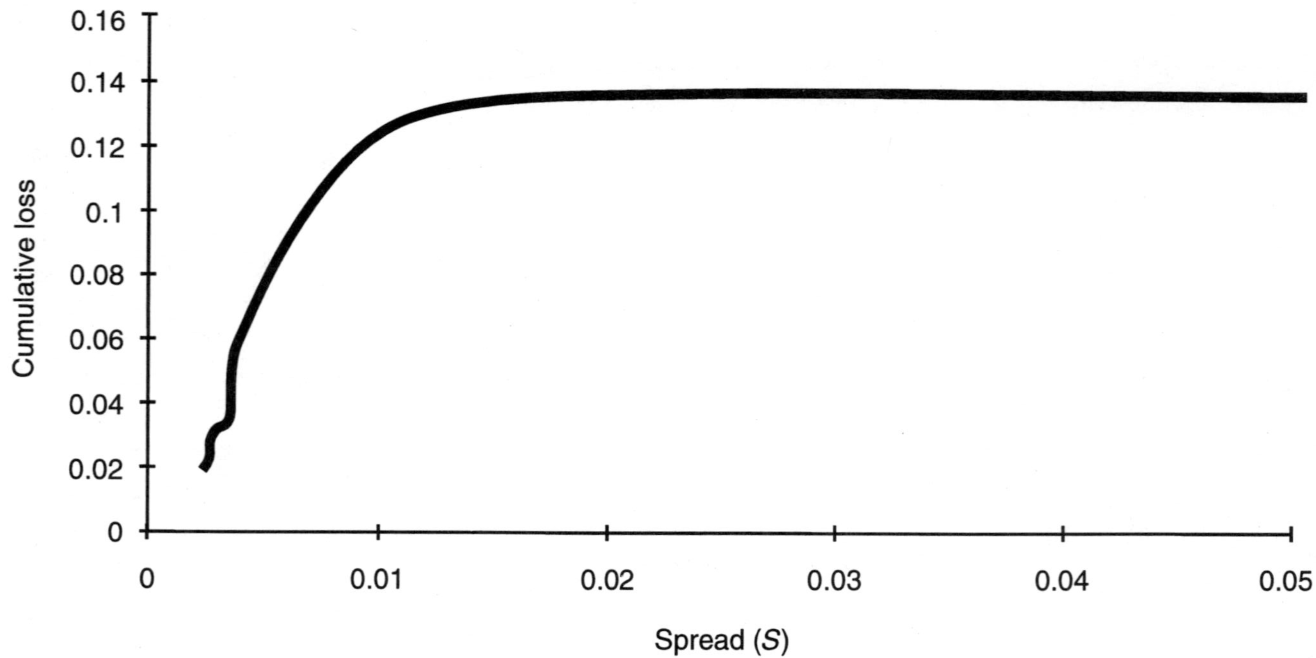

References and Suggested Readings

Amihud, Y., and H. Mendelson. 1986. "Asset Pricing and The Bid-Ask Spread." *Journal of Financial Economics* 17 (Dec.): 223–49.

——. 1988. "Liquidity and Asset Prices: Financial Management Implications." *Financial Management* 17 (Spring): 5–15.

——. 1989. "The Effects of Beta, Bid-Ask Spread, Residual Risk and Size on Stock Returns." *Journal of Finance* 44:479–86.

——. 1991a. "Volatility and Trading: Evidence from the Japanese Stock Market." *Journal of Finance* 46:1765–89.

——. 1991b. "Liquidity, Maturity and the Yields on U.S. Government Securities." *Journal of Finance* 46:1411–25.

——. 1991c. "Trading Mechanisms and Value Discovery: Cross-National Evidence and Policy Implications." *Carnegie-Rochester Conference Series on Public Policy* 34:105–30.

——. 1991d. "How (Not) to Integrate the European Capital Markets." In *European Financial Integration*, A. Giovannini and C. Mayer, eds. Cambridge: Cambridge University Press.

Amihud, Y., H. Mendelson, and R. A. Wood. 1990. "Liquidity and the 1987 Stock Market Crash." *Journal of Portfolio Management* (Spring): 65–69.

Benston, G., and R. Hagerman. 1974. "Determinants of Bid-Ask Spreads in the Over the Counter Market." *Journal of Financial Economics* 1:353–64.

Garbade, K. D. 1982. *Securities Markets*. New York: McGraw Hill.

Roll, R. 1984. "A Simple Implicit Measure of the Bid/Ask Spread in an Efficient Market." *Journal of Finance* 39:1127–39.

Stoll, H., and R. E. Whaley. 1983. "Transaction Costs and the Small Firm Effect." *Journal of Financial Economics* 12:57–79.

Voyanos, D., and J. Vila. 1992. "Equilibrium Interest Rate and Liquidity Premium under Proportional Transaction Costs." Working paper, Massachusetts Institute of Technology, Cambridge.

White, J. A. 1990. "Big Investors' Commission Rates Have Hit a Low." *The Wall Street Journal,* Apr. 24: C1, C9.

Regulation

of the

Government Securities Market

35

Regulation of the Auction Market for U.S. Treasury Securities

Dean Furbush[1]
Economists Incorporated

1. Background and Introduction

Like the funding of most governments around the world, the funding of the U.S. government includes a lot of debt. The debt is financed through auctions which are conducted by the Federal Reserve Banks on behalf of the U.S. Treasury Department. The debt is massive in absolute value (about $4 trillion at the end of fiscal year 1992) and is growing (the 1992 deficit of $290 billion is surpassed only by estimates for 1993). In order to finance each year's deficit and to refinance accrued debt as it comes due, the Treasury auctions must be large (about $10 billion each) and frequent (more than 150 per year).

Treasury auctions are one of several ways for investors to take market positions relative to risk-free debt. The other markets are, at once, substitutes for and complements to the Treasury auction, and their characteristics are, to varying degrees, dependent on the features of the Treasury auction, and hence on its underlying rules. These other markets include the secondary market for government securities, futures, options on futures, the repo market, and the when-issued (WI) market.

National attention was focused on the auction process in August 1991 when Salomon Inc. announced responsibility for "irregularities and rule violations" at three auctions earlier in the year; the press reported that Salomon had purchased up to 85 percent of the securities at the May two-

---

[1] I am grateful for input from Mark Fisher, who should not be associated with remaining errors.

year note auction.[2] Government investigations of Salomon's activities, which had preceded Salomon's admission, were followed by requests for further trading information from Salomon and other market participants and ultimately led to a settlement in May 1992 whereby Salomon paid a fine of $290 million.

The Salomon violations also produced more general repercussions. Calls for tougher market regulation led to new legislation including House Bill H.R. 3927.[3] If passed, it would have given the SEC authority to create an electronic trading audit trail and a large trader reporting system; to ensure the dissemination of market information; and to oversee new broker-dealer internal trading controls and sales practice rules. Like all the related legislation proffered in the 102nd Congress, H.R. 3927 would also have reinstated the Treasury Department's lapsed rulemaking authority.

Economists suggested that the auction market's contribution to squeezes could be mitigated by changing the auction process itself—switching from a multiprice auction to a single-price auction and allowing for an influx of securities in case of a squeeze—rather than by instituting new regulations. The ideas are not new. Milton Friedman described the single-price, sealed-bid auction before the Joint Economic Committee of Congress in 1959. It was tested briefly in the early 1970s and then discarded—until now.[4]

In January 1992, the Department of the Treasury, the Securities and Exchange Commission, and the Board of Governors of the Federal Reserve System issued a joint report (Dept. of Treasury et al. 1992; hereafter: Joint Report) that proposed reforms to the Treasury market, most of which were approved by all three agencies. The Joint Report provides an excellent

---

[2] Later it was determined that Salomon had controlled 94 percent of the May 22, 1991, two-year note auction.

[3] Public Securities Association (1992) provides a brief history of H.R. 3927 and related legislative and regulatory activities.

[4] The interchange began with Friedman (1959) and his testimony before the Joint Economic Committee (U.S. Congress 1959), and includes Brimmer (1962), Goldstein (1962), and Friedman (1963). The inconclusive results from the 1973 and 1974 experimental auctions are presented in Tsao and Vignola (1976). Recent publications in the popular press include Friedman (1991) and Furbush (1991). In a November 1991 meeting, the Shadow SEC, composed of eminent economists and lawyers, resolved that the Treasury should experiment with uniform price and tap auctions.

description of the Treasury markets and a summary of the regulatory issues, including a discussion of Friedman's single-price auction.[5]

In September 1992, Treasury announced that it would test the single-price auction at each two-year and five-year note auction from September 1992 through August 1993. Treasury has also committed to providing additional quantities of a particular issue in the case of an "acute, protracted" shortage. Other less important changes were also instituted following the revelation of the Salomon incident. For example, until recently, only primary dealers and depository institutions could bid at Treasury auctions without making a deposit and could bid on behalf of customers. Under new rules and using expanded autocharge facilities these bidding privileges now extend to all government securities brokers and dealers registered with the SEC. As discussed below, however, the concentration of bidding among a few institutions may have more to do with the multiprice auction system than with the previous bidding participation rules.

All this activity—a massive federal debt, auction rule violations, failed legislation, the need for a joint agency report, and a flurry of rule changes—suggests that there are serious problems in the U.S. auction process. But that is not the case. Essential to the discussion in this essay is the view expressed in the Joint Report (1992, 2): "The Agencies do not believe that the government securities market is flawed or broken in any fundamental sense."

Realizing that, this essay discusses minor improvements to a well-functioning system. First I establish the appropriate goals of Treasury auction regulation. In the context of those goals, I compare the current multiprice auction to the single-price auction that is being tested, and I examine the new commitment to provide further securities in case of an acute and protracted shortage, and the changing auction market role of primary dealers. Finally I consider the cumulative effect of the recent changes and suggest that the only additional legislation that is required is to reinstate Treasury's rulemaking authority.

[5] For more detailed descriptions of the Treasury auction and related markets see Fabozzi (1987, 1990) and Stigum (1990).

2. The Objectives of Treasury Auction Regulation

The Joint Report (1992, 2) states that the objectives of Treasury auction policy include

> preserving and enhancing the efficiency of the government's financing mechanism, ensuring the integrity and fairness of the marketplace, deterring and detecting fraud, and protecting investors. In particular, there is a strong consensus that, while change is necessary, that change should be managed with care to assure that the national debt is financed at the lowest possible cost.

With respect to new regulation, much of this list is of secondary importance. For example, "preserving and enhancing the efficiency of the government's financing mechanism" is mechanistic, is uncontroversial, and would almost certainly be advanced through more automation that is currently being planned; and "deterring and detecting fraud" is fully served under Section 10(b) of the 1934 Securities Exchange Act, as is "protecting investors" which must refer to their protection against fraud.[6] Direct investors in government securities are a highly sophisticated group.

Two objectives remain from the Joint Report: regulation should "ensur[e] . . . integrity and fairness," and it should "assure that the national debt is financed at the lowest possible cost." Low-cost financing takes precedence over fairness because a fair market is not necessarily a low-financing-cost market, but the reverse is not the case.[7] In fact a market with low financing costs is necessarily fair-using a particular definition of fairness—and fairness should be sought as a means to the end of low-cost financing.

While the definition of low-cost financing is plain, being determined over the long run so that it is not optimal to fool investors in one auction in a way that causes future adjustment or deters future participation, the

---

[6] In addressing fraud, Section 10(b) does not distinguish among types of securities and thus includes government securities.

[7] To see this, consider securities-distribution alternatives that are fair but lead to arbitrarily expensive financing outcomes: securities could be distributed equally among all citizens, or they could be apportioned by lottery with any number of payment possibilities.

definition of a fair auction is more problematic. For example, under the usual egalitarian notion of fairness, the current multiprice auction is unfair on its face in that bidders may pay different prices for the same product.

Consider then, the following definition of fairness: a fair system is one in which the rules are obeyed, regardless of what those rules are. Underlying a market are contracts in which participants have rights and obligations. In a perfectly fair market, contract rights and obligations are certain, regardless of whether they are appropriate by other standards. This notion of fairness turns out to provide appropriate guidance for auction policy.

Consider an auction, for example, that is designed to raise funds inexpensively and is fair in the sense of establishing certain rights but is unfair in the egalitarian sense. In this auction, only men named Ernie may participate. Perhaps at the first auction two Ernies will form a cartel enabling them to buy all the securities below the market price. Their demand for securities is based on the expected demand of natural holders of the securities. If some natural holders have entered into agreements under which they are bound to deliver the Ernie-bonds specific to that auction, the Ernies can squeeze them, selling them bonds at above-market prices; if there are no such agreements, the natural holders will pay the general market rate for the bonds. Either way the Ernies will make a killing.

But consider the next auction. Other Ernies will enter the auction in numbers sufficient to break the cartel, the auction price will be bid up to the level reflecting the demand of natural holders, and the natural holders, who will have learned not to enter derivative contracts that open them to a squeeze, will pay the market price for their Ernie-bonds. The excess funding cost in this system is not more than the competitive rate paid to transfer government securities to their natural holders. And even this amount is attenuated insofar as (1) the dispensation granted to Ernies is less than exclusive, (2) Ernies turn out to be natural holders of government securities, and (3) Ernies compete to add value as securities distributors.[8]

Even Ernie-auctions can finance debt cheaply if market rights and obligations are certain. Assets will reach owners who value them the most

---

[8] The natural holders' demand for bonds is highly elastic because of the many substitutes in the secondary market, and the supply of bonds at the auction is inelastic. Therefore the (relatively minor) burden of the egalitarian unfairness is borne by the Treasury which must accept a lower price at auction.

because transactions costs are low relative to the gains available through asset reallocation, and because of the recurring nature of the auctions.[9]

Egalitarian fairness at the outset of the auction will not affect the ultimate allocation, only the distribution of wealth on the way there. And because the ultimate allocation determines the revenue from the auction, egalitarian fairness is not an important input to financing costs.

Improvements in auction design should be made with an eye to their effect on certainty-fairness. This means choosing rules that are likely to be obeyed. An auction system that has as its primary goal financing the debt at minimum cost and is certain-fair will be close to optimal without further regulations. Additional regulations are likely to be either harmful because they reduce certainty-fairness or ineffective because nonbinding.

3. Recent Adjustments to the Auction System

A report by the Public Securities Association (1992) details the evolution of the Treasury auction rules and legislative proposals since the Salomon incident became public in August 1991. The 1992 Joint Report adds to that the legislative recommendations of the Treasury, the SEC, and the Federal Reserve Board, most of which did not receive unanimous agreement among the agencies. This is not the place to analyze the proposals in detail but to indicate that, even in the absence of legislation, significant changes were made to the Treasury auction system, and that most of the proposed legislative changes are unnecessary. Further improvements can be accomplished under the Treasury's rulemaking authority, which has lapsed and should be extended.

Recent changes to the auction administration and regulation include but are not limited to the following:

- The participation of all SEC-registered government securities brokers and dealers has been facilitated.

- The requirement that primary dealers must account for at least one percent of secondary market trades has been eliminated.

- An autocharge agreement may be used in lieu of deposit by any bidder.

---

[9] These results follow from Coase (1960) and Klein and Leffler (1981).

- Over time, as further automation allows, the system will be opened further.

- Noncompetitive bidders may be awarded as much as $5 million worth of securities, up from $1 million; this aspect of the market is being enforced more tightly against fraud such as combined bidding.

- The Federal Reserve checks customer bids for authenticity when they exceed $500 million, and spot-checks others. The agencies have formed a working group to improve surveillance of the market.

- The schedule for automating the market has been accelerated. Treasury has committed to providing additional securities in the case of an "acute, protracted shortage."

- Treasury has committed to running each two-year and five-year auction from September 1992 through August 1993 as a single price auction

The changes to date and the planned future changes such as automation and further broadening of the bidder base, if accompanied by adoption of the single-price auction design, will leave the U.S. with an auction system strengthened against squeezes and serving a broad range of sophisticated participants. The three important features of these changes from an economic standpoint are the single-price auction, the commitment to issue new securities in the face of a shortage, and the fading importance of the primary dealer concept. The single-price auction, which if established, will be partially responsible for the diminished importance of the primary dealer system, is discussed first, followed by the Treasury's commitment to issue new securities to alleviate a shortage and the role of primary dealers.

A. MultiPrice and Single-Price Auction Systems

Under the current system, participants submit a sealed bid and pay the price they bid. The government accepts the bids at descending prices until the price at which the auction is fully subscribed—the stop-out price. At the stop-out price, the remaining securities are rationed to bidders proportional to the size of their bids, which, for each bidder, cannot exceed 35 percent of the auction size at any price.[10]

Because investors pay what they bid in a multiprice auction and because it is immensely expensive to bid even one or two basis points above the stop-out price, bidders must take into account the expected bids of other participants as well as their own reservation price. Obtaining this information is costly, and, because the market for bidder services is competitive, the costs are borne by taxpayers through reduced proceeds at Treasury auctions, counteracting any increased proceeds from bids above the stop-out price. Investors search for this information in various ways.

The most obvious approach to obtaining the necessary auction price information is to conduct research directly, employing traders whose full-time job it is to stay abreast of the market. Because this is costly, potential bidders may hire a company to do their bidding leading to fewer bidders at the auction. It is likely that the use of bidding services has some basis in real market economies, but insofar as the degree of intermediation is artificially augmented because of the auction structure, there are additional costs. The level of concentration in the auction market may be a direct effect of this artificially augmented intermediation. Antitrust fears, which were heightened following the Salomon incident, none of which have been confirmed, could have been avoided if the market were less concentrated. The rule that prevents any bidder from bidding for more than 35 percent of the securities at any one price is a response to the perceived antitrust problems. Finally, the WI market provides a mechanism for learning about market-wide prices and for obtaining auctioned securities without submitting bids. Its importance is augmented by the importance of such marketwide data. All of these features of the Treasury system constitute expenditures undertaken to obtain marketwide Treasury auction price information, expenditures that are artificially increased as a result of the use of multiprice auctions.

A multiprice auction also affects the distribution of bids at auction, making them more homogeneous and undercutting the only source of advantage to the government from employing such an auction. The more successful is the information search, the less the bid distribution reflects the true demand schedule for securities, and the less advantage the government obtains from the multiprice auction.

Switching to a single-price auction would eliminate the cost to bidders of bidding their true reservation price. In a single-price auction each

---

[10] "Noncompetitive" bidders may be awarded up to $5 million in Treasury securities and pay the mean price, across all awarded securities.

bidder pays the stop-out price so there is no penalty for bidding a price above what others are bidding and there is no benefit to be obtained by knowing what others are bidding. Both the distribution of prices bid and the number of participants will be greater; and both effects will work to prevent squeezes.

The trade-off is clear. Switching to a single-price auction would eliminate the additional revenue from bids above the stop-out price, but the increase in apparent demand due to more aggressive bidding will work in the other direction. The magnitude of the two effects is less clear. Economic theory does not provide the exact answer, but the experiments announced by Treasury will provide the data to make a determination. The immediate revenue results from the experiment should be considered as a floor, because changes in the bidders' market structure that would increase demand may take time and may be more pronounced in the context of a permanent change.

B. Security Shortages

If a bidder or group of bidders is able to control a substantial majority of the auctioned securities, it can withhold the securities from the market, create an artificial shortage, and squeeze participants who hold short positions. Although a short squeeze can occur in any market in which participants hold short positions, a key concern with the 1991 Salomon incident involved the WI market in which traders had committed to delivering securities specific to that particular auction.[11] The effect of the WI market shortage is likely to be manifested in the repo market, the financing market for Treasury security transactions. Holders of the scarce securities could initiate repo contracts at a "special" repo rate with those who had contracted to deliver the security in the WI market. When an issue is "special," which occurs regularly for reasons unrelated to auction market squeezes, holders of the issue can borrow funds using that particular issue as collateral, at a rate below the market rate.

---

[11] About one week before each auction, the government announces the size of the auction and a market springs up for the securities "when, as, and if issued." When-issued deliveries coincide with the auction settlement day. This short-lived forward market, specific to each auction, has the effect of extending the effective open time of the auction. The WI price provides information about the expected auction price and can be used to lock in positions relative to the auction.

The squeeze problem, which can also occur in the secondary market and can occur for reasons having nothing to do with single-minded market manipulation, is due to a shortage of government securities in a particular issue. There are several methods for addressing the shortage. The solutions are of three types. First, the government can put more securities in the hands of participants, (a) by reopening the auction, (b) by selling more securities "on tap" through the Open Market Desk of the Federal Reserve Bank of New York (FRBNY), (c) by precommitting to issue more of a security should its price rise above the market by a specified amount, or (d) by lending securities through the Open Market Desk.

Government-induced supply augmentation is not without countervailing costs. Insofar as the government stands ready to increase supply in case of acute and protracted shortages, a bias is introduced to the market. The price of an issue includes both issue-specific and marketwide components. The possibility for supply augmentation insures shorts against acute and protracted issue-specific price increases, taking away one of the reasons for being long in the market—for wanting to buy government debt, keeping its price high, and lowering overall financing costs.

Second, the Treasury could allow market participants to STRIP securities in order to create synthetically a security with the features of the security that is in short supply. Although there are tax, legal, and accounting barriers to this solution, it has considerable economic appeal. The current STRIP program already allows separation of principal from the semiannual interest payments. These building blocks can be rebuilt just as easily, as a market response, to create a Treasury security that will substitute for the security in short supply.

The third solution also allows for a market response to the shortage, should there be a perceived persistent problem. With respect to the WI market, participants could make appropriate adjustments to the WI contract in order to alleviate the problem. There is precedent for such market solutions. The U.S. Treasury Note contracts traded at the Chicago Board of Trade have a contract specification that could be applied to the WI market. Notes maturing within a certain range can be delivered in fulfillment of the contracts. If there is a squeeze in one of the issues, any of the others may be delivered in its stead. In the two-year note futures contract relevant to the May 1991 auction, for example, seven issues could have been delivered, accounting for almost $70 billion, including longer term notes and bonds that became two-year notes on their way to maturity.

The presence of the 35 percent rule, which was broken by Salomon Inc., may have provided participants with a false sense of security with respect to the lack of market concentration at auction. Because of this lack of certainty-fairness, the market may be better off without a 35 percent rule, thus encouraging participants to take care of themselves through market responses such as contract amendment.

3. Primary Dealers

The primary role of primary dealers is to facilitate the Federal Reserve Board's Open Market Operations. Primary dealers have historically also played a central part in Treasury auctions. The most frequently articulated reason for the presence of primary dealers in Treasury auctions is that they are needed, particularly in times of slack demand, so that the Treasury can be sure there will be buyers at the auction. This argument, which was repeated in the Joint Report, is extraordinary. The market for U.S. Treasury securities is the largest and arguably the most liquid in the world. Arbitrage between the auction market and the vast and sophisticated secondary market makes it unthinkable that the auction price for any particular issue would move more than one or two basis points away from its normal relation with the secondary market.

Further, it is unreasonable to believe that primary dealers are currently buying billions of dollars worth of securities, solely because of the very general agreement associated with their role as primary dealers.[12] More likely their purchases are in their direct business interest. If, however, government involvement does play a role, the benefit received by the primary dealer may either (1) constitute government largesse, or (2) be due to a useful role the primary dealer is playing in another way (such as the primary dealers' open market involvement). Insofar as the participation is a gift from the government, it should stop; insofar as there is some ulterior, useful relationship, that relationship can be considered independently.

Primary dealers are currently required to make "reasonably good" markets with the FRBNY desk, to "participate meaningfully" in auctions, and to provide the FRBNY desk with information and commentary. What they receive for fulfilling these vague requirements is not clear. The right to trade at auction has been opened to all SEC-registered government-securities traders, and even the primary dealer moniker will be broadened when the system has been automated further. The value of the current agreement lies entirely in the extent to which it supports an orderly (and speedy) transition

---

[12] Some primary dealers do, however, submit out-of-the-money bids at auctions. These bids amount to giving the government insurance against the possibility that the market will move dramatically away from it during the auction process.

to a completely open Treasury auction system; one in which no such "unfair" agreements are necessary.

4. Conclusion

The attention focused on the government securities market as a result of the 1991 Salomon trading irregularities has yielded outcomes indicative of good government. First, market participants have received a clear signal that trading practices such as Salomon admitted to will not be tolerated and will constitute a massive business error—despite genuine reform and competent damage control, Salomon's punishment in lost customers, lost talent, lost credit rating, and lost focus far exceeded the $290 million fine they paid. Second, the responsible government agencies have shown sophistication in their economic responses to the issue, as indicated in the text and appendixes of the Joint Report and as manifested by their proposals allowing for expanded supply in the face of shortage and experimentation with single-price auctions. And third, the decision to experiment with the auction mechanism is a wise one; there is no need to rely on rhetoric here. Although the issues are complex, the policy objectives of the U.S. Treasury auction are not, and the market process contains within it the evidence for resolving the genuine cost minimization questions.

The effect of government action has been salutary in three key areas examined here. In each case, reforms are being considered or have been instituted, that increase the certainty-fairness of the system. Moving from a multiprice to a single-price auction removes from relevance, an entire area of uncertainty—the prices that other participants will bid. Though not perhaps without countervailing costs, Treasury's commitment to alleviating acute and protracted securities shortages removes uncertainty regarding the potential for market squeezes. Finally the transition away from reliance on primary dealers signals greater reliance on market forces. The current, tenuous situation with primary dealers maintaining broad and vague Treasury market obligations should be terminated as soon as possible. Such obligations are unfair—should the insurance provided by primary dealers become necessary it is likely to be shirked because of freerider problems or will be borne by some primary dealers at expense that puts them at a disadvantage to those who did not fulfill their obligations.

The government securities market is not broken and does not require further regulation. The Treasury's lapsed rulemaking authority should, however, be reinstated. Other than following through on projects such as automation and auction experimentation, further tinkering should be avoided, bearing in mind the predominant goal for auction administration and regulation: to minimize the cost of funding the debt. The size and breadth of the U.S. Treasury market and the sophistication of its participants make it unlikely that bidders can profit by treating their customers other than fairly and with integrity. Regulated customer protection, through sales practice rules, through forced information dissemination, and through trade and position reporting requirements would at best be redundant with the level of service already provided through market processes. Even the 1992 Joint Report, which is otherwise careful in analyzing the key auction issues, recommends such further regulations without justification or discussion of how they would have prevented past irregularities or will prevent future ones.

Economic theory does not predict that the costs of regulation always exceed the benefits. Economists do not deny the benefit of well-placed traffic signals. But the U.S. Treasury market is a super highway in need of few traffic signals. We are already very close to an auction process that takes advantage of this fact—one that minimizes the cost of financing the debt and is fair because it is in the business interests of the participants to obey the rules.

References and Suggested Readings

Brimmer, Andrew F. 1962. "Price Determination in the United States Treasury Bill Market." *Review of Economics and Statistics* 44:178–83.

Coase, Ronald. 1960. "The Problem of Social Cost." *Journal of Law & Economics* (Oct.).

Department of the Treasury, Securities and Exchange Commission, and Board of Governors of the Federal Reserve System. 1992. *Joint Report on the Government Securities Market.* Washington D.C.: U. S. Government Printing Office (Jan.).

Fabozzi, Frank J., ed. 1987. *The Handbook of Treasury Securities: Trading and Portfolio Strategies.* Ill.: Probus Publishing Co.

———., ed. 1990. *U.S. Treasury & Government Agency Securities.* Ill.: Probus Publishing Co.

Friedman, Milton. 1959. "Debt Management and Banking Reform." In *A Program for Monetary Stability.* New York: Fordham University Press: 52–76.

———. 1963. "Price Determination in the United States Treasury Bill Market: A Comment." *Review of Economics and Statistics*:318–20.

———. 1964. "Comment on 'Collusion in the Auction Market for Treasury Bills.'" *Journal of Political Economy* 72:513–14.

———. 1991. "How to Sell Government Securities." *Wall Street Journal*, Aug. 28.

Furbush, Dean. 1991. "Better Rules for More Ethical Finance." *Wall Street Journal*, Nov. 8.

Goldstein, Henry. 1962. "The Friedman Proposal for Auctioning Treasury Bills." *Journal of Political Economy* 70 (Oct.): 386–92.

Klein, Benjamin and Keith Leffler. 1981. "The Role of Market Forces in Assuring Contractual Performance." *Journal of Political Economy* 89.

Public Securities Association. 1992. *Special Report: Public Securities Legislation in the 102nd Congress.* Washington, D.C.

Rieber, Michael. 1964. "Collusion in the Auction Market for Treasury Bills." *Journal of Political Economy* 72 (Oct.): 509–12.

Stigum, Marcia. 1990. *The Money Market*, 3rd ed. Homewood, Ill.: Business One Irwin.

Tsao, Che S. and Anthony J. Vignola. 1976. *Price Discrimination and the Demand for Treasury's Long Term Securities.* Working paper, Treasury Department, Washington, D.C.

U.S. Congress Joint Committee. 1959. 86th Congress, 1st Session. Testimony by Milton Friedman. *Hearings on Employment, Growth, and Price Levels.*

VI

MUTUAL FUNDS

36

The Regulation of Mutual Funds: An Agenda for the Future

Burton G. Malkiel[1]
Princeton University

The Investment Company Act of 1940 represents one of the most successful endeavors of government regulation. The Act has provided important protections for individual investors such as full disclosure, market-value accounting, and prohibitions against self-dealing by investment company managers. At the time the legislation was enacted, total mutual fund industry assets were slightly more than $2 billion. Today, total assets held in the form of investment company shares amount to approximately $1.5 trillion. Mutual funds represent a major vehicle for individual savings, and nearly one in every four U.S. households owns mutual fund shares. This paper analyzes some suggestions for a reexamination of mutual fund regulation. While the core provisions of the Investment Company Act have protected investors for over 50 years, it is timely to ask if there are changes either in the administration of the act or in legislation that seem warranted in view of recent financial market developments.

The Securities and Exchange Commission staff itself has recently published a thoughtful report containing a number of recommendations for the future.[2] I will first assess those recommendations and then review some disclosure issues that were not emphasized in the SEC staff report and that might serve, in part, as an agenda for the Commission over the coming years.

---

[1] I am indebted to Yexiao Xu for extremely helpful research assistance.

[2] Division of Investment Management, U.S. SEC, *Protecting Investors: A Half Century of Investment Company Regulation,* Washington, D.C., U. S. Government Printing Office (May 1992).

1. The SEC Staff Report: *Protecting Investors: A Half-Century of Investment Company Regulation*

The staff report recognizes that while investor protection is vital to public confidence, regulation may not have kept pace with the vast changes in financial markets over the past half-century and may even have interfered with the ability of the financial industry to offer "flexible, efficient, and competitive" investment vehicles to the public. Thus, the focus of the report is to recommend changes in regulatory practice that may at once promote investment protection while encouraging competition, flexibility, and innovation. For the most part the staff report is on target and makes useful recommendations. As will be indicated below, however, most of the recommendations are relatively tame and unlikely to be of major consequence. The more controversial of the recommendations, which do promise significant change in the way funds are marketed, may need to be accompanied by even stronger guidelines regarding disclosure.

I will discuss the recommendations of the SEC staff report in three categories. The first are those sensible recommendations that are relatively uncontroversial but also unlikely to produce significant change. Next, I will discuss the more major and often more controversial recommendations. Finally, I will cover separately one of the major marketing recommendations—permitting funds to sell their shares "off the page."

A. Sensible Recommendations Unlikely to Promote Major Controversy or Significant Change

A number of the SEC staff recommendations seem to me to be entirely sensible and uncontroversial. For example, adopting a rule to expedite the treatment of routine applications is certainly desirable, although it is unlikely to shorten the time frame or cost for more complex, more innovative requests. Staff recommendations to exempt funds sold to institutional or professional purchasers from the definition of an "investment company" are quite reasonable and could increase the number of private placements and facilitate the creation of new fund products. The staff also makes the sensible recommendation that foreign investment companies be allowed to sell shares in the United States if they can demonstrate compliance with investor protection requirements. In addition, U.S.-based investment advisers would be given greater flexibility in structuring fee arrangements with professional investors. The study also recommends that directors of investment companies be given broader authorization to initiate transactions with affiliates. The staff further recommends that shareholders no longer be required to approve changes in routine investment policies and favors increasing the percentage of independent directors for all funds from 40 percent to over 50 percent.

The staff recommendations listed above are typical of a large number of what in many cases might be considered housekeeping amendments to current procedures. They are generally well argued, remove unnecessary burdens on fund directors, and allow expedited treatment of at least some applications. These kinds of reforms can mostly be accomplished through SEC rulemaking, and it would appear reasonable for the Commission to move swiftly to adopt those changes that do not require congressional action. While they are unlikely to engender significant change in the industry, the emphasis on increasing the proportion of independent directors could be very helpful to mutual fund shareholders, especially if such directors were charged with a statutory fiduciary standard.

B. More Controversial Recommendations of the Staff Study

Structured Finance

The SEC staff recommends that certain very high quality and low-risk financings be exempted from the definition of an investment company under the Investment Company Act. The rule is meant to address an anomalous situation in which certain asset-backed arrangements are exempt from a registration requirement and others are not and cannot be offered to the public because they cannot meet some of the act's core requirements. While this proposal is opposed by the industry trade association, it represents no compromise with the principle of investor protection and it would reduce unnecessary barriers to securitization.

Retail Price Maintenance

Currently broker-sold funds have a fixed set of commissions (load charges) described in the prospectus at which the funds can be sold to the public. The staff proposes repeal of retail price maintenance in the hope that greater competition will be fostered in the distribution of mutual fund shares. The industry has complained that the staff proposal would permit "insidious price discrimination among investors" and opposes the proposal strongly. Since there is already considerable price competition in load charges among broker distributed funds and since there are many directly marketed funds available with no loads and with low expenses, the Commission may not see much benefit from the staff's proposal and may not believe it is worth a fight with the industry. It is difficult, however, to justify a fixed commission schedule for selling mutual funds now that laws against discounting stock-trading commissions have been eliminated. A battle with the broker-distributed funds that may be more worth a fight is to require that at least a one-page prospectus, with all loads and fees clearly indicated, be given to every prospective investor *before* a sale is consumated. This issue will be discussed in further detail below.

Hybrid Funds

Traditionally, investment companies have either been open-end funds, which agree to offer and redeem shares based on daily closing prices or closed-end funds, which do not (and in most cases cannot) repurchase their shares from investors. The staff proposes that open-end funds be allowed to be offered with more limited redemption provisions and that closed-end companies be permitted to make regular repurchases of shares directly from shareowners at net asset value. It is hard to argue against giving funds added flexibility, but the proposal is unlikely to make a major change in the industry. Closed-end fund advisers whose shares sell at discounts are unlikely to find the possibility of shrinkage of the asset pool advantageous. Investors staying in the funds would also be disadvantaged since expense ratios would increase as the funds' fixed expenses were spread over a smaller shareholder base.

Pooled Investment Vehicles for Employee Benefit Plan Assets

The staff recommends that the Securities Act of 1933 be amended to remove the exemption from registration for bank and insurance company pooled funds used in participant-directed defined contribution plans. Investors in these pooled funds would then receive prospectuses and periodic shareholder reports. The proposal will entail additional costs but there is no reason why these investors should be given less information than investors in regular mutual funds. The staff wisely stopped short of recommending that bank and insurance pooled vehicles be required to register under the Investment Company Act. ERISA already imposes a number of obligations on these vehicles, and there is no evidence of abuses under the current system that would be eliminated by requiring registration.

C. Off-the-Page Sales of Mutual Fund Shares

Potentially the most significant and controversial change recommended in the SEC staff report would permit investors to purchase mutual fund shares directly in response to certain off-the-page advertisements. The advertisements would include a cut-out application form, which an investor could fill out and mail without further delay. The ability to sell shares directly in response to a written advertisement, rather than having to wait for a prospectus to be mailed, would reduce delays and distribution costs. It would also level the playing field between directly marketed funds and broker-distributed funds, which now can be sold *prior* to the distribution of a prospectus.

Under the staff proposal, mutual fund advertisements that include purchase applications would themselves be prospectuses, and the SEC would require that they contain key information regarding risk, fund objective, expenses, and so forth. Moreover, these advertisements would be subject to stringent liability standards with respect to prospectus disclosure. A full prospectus would be sent to the fund investor along with the confirmation of the transaction.

The SEC staff's recommendation to allow off-the-page sales is potentially a good one. A well-designed, clearly worded, one-page prospectus could actually give investors more information about their propsective investment than a longer and more complicated prospectus. Prospectuses today are often written in a particularly dull and opaque syntax—designed more to protect the fund from subsequent legal liability rather than to inform potential investors. A shorter and more readable document would provide more usable information to investors than they now get. The key to whether the proposal is a good one is, therefore, whether the disclosure required will be adequate and whether, in fact, the advertising prospectus provides the investor with the information he or she needs. I will return to this question in the final section of this paper.

2. Broadening the Areas of Future Emphasis

The SEC staff report outlines a very useful agenda of issues with respect to mutual funds that should be considered by the SEC over the coming years. My own view is that disclosure issues could have been given even more emphasis in the staff report. In this section, I will indicate some of the disclosure problems I view as important, from a public policy perspective, and where I think additional recommendations might be developed. In particular, if the staff's recommendation for off-the-page sales of fund shares is to be adopted, disclosure issues will become especially important in the future.

Before indicating where I see some unresolved disclosure problems with respect to mutual funds, it is important to note that the mutual fund industry is a wonderful example of a competitive, innovative, responsible industry, which offers a variety of useful products to investors. The enormous success of the industry is well deserved. Moreover, the SEC has generally done an excellent job of ensuring that investors receive adequate and complete information necessary for them to make informed judgments. The Commission has also kept a watchful eye on the sales practices of the industry and has generally succeeded in ensuring that investors have been protected from excessive claims. Nevertheless, there are, I believe, three areas in which even more needs to be done: (1) information about the expenses paid by investors needs to be made even clearer and more transparent; (2) information about the risks assumed by investors needs even more emphasis; and (3) as some advertising and sales practices border on being misleading, these practices need to be better curbed.

A. Expense Ratios

A mutual fund's expense ratio is one of the best indicators of the value the investor receives from his or her investment. In general, investors receive a larger net rate of return from funds with lower expense ratios. The situation is clearest with a commodity product such as a money market fund investing exclusively in U.S. Treasury securities. Here, investment management is likely to produce equivalent gross returns for all funds, whereas net returns will be largest for the funds with the lowest expense ratios. The situation is similar for general money market funds, and it is not surprising that the funds showing the highest *net* returns have been those funds that have temporarily waived all expenses charges. It is also the case that general bond market funds with the lowest expense ratios tend to produce the highest net rates of return for fund shareholders.

What is perhaps more surprising is that even general equity funds with lower expense ratios show a tendency to produce larger net returns. Since some equity funds pay advisory fees that have incentive features and rise as a proportion of assets managed if the fund outperforms some benchmark, one ought to find a positive relationship between net returns and expense ratios. In fact, the relationship is negative. For example, one study published by Morningstar[3] compared the 10-year net average returns of approximately 700 mutual funds relative to portfolio turnover and expense ratios. The data are shown in Table 1.

---

[3] Morningstar Mutual Funds, August 7, 1992.

Table 1
Morningstar Analysis of Turnover and Expense Ratios

Annual Turnover	Return	Expense Ratio
Low (<50%)	15.4%	1.19%
Moderate (50–100%)	15.0%	1.44%
High (>100%)	14.5%	1.64%

Low turnover (implying low trading costs) and low expense ratios are associated with better performance. Regression studies I have also performed, comparing net rates of return and expense ratios, have also found a statistically significant negative relationship over the period 1982–1991.[4]

All equity funds with a ten-year history of performance continuously followed by Lipper Analytic Services were included in the sample. The 10-year after-expense total return (including dividends and capital changes) for each fund was regressed against the average 10-year expense ratio (total expenses expressed as a percentage of fund assets). The results are shown in Table 2 and are pictured in Figure 1. The first row of the table, which analyzes the entire sample, shows that a fund's expense ratio is negatively related to its total return. While the coefficient of determination is low, the analysis does show that the coefficient of the expense ratio is statistically significant with a t-statistic of about four.[5] The regression coefficient implies that increasing expenses has a multiplier effect on returns after expenses. A one–basis-point increase in the expense ratio appears to produce a little more than a two–basis-point reduction in net return. This may result from a positive correlation between measured expenses and other nonmeasured expense factors such as turnover. Greater turnover also involves larger trading-cost expenses, which are not captured in the measured expense ratio. The same pattern appears to be found in the Morningstar data in Table 1. For example, moving from the moderate to the high turnover category, expense ratios go up by 20 basis points whereas returns fall two and a half times as much, by 50 basis points.

---

[4] I am indebted to Lipper Analytic Services for their help in providing the data.

[5] A few outlying funds with extremely high expense ratios and particularly poor net rate of return were eliminated from the analysis because their inclusion made the negative relationship we found appear unrealistically strong.

Table 2
Bivariate Regression Results
10-year Performance as a Function of Total Expense Ratio (1982–91)

	No. of Observations	Estimated Coefficient Expense Ratio	Standard Error of Coefficient	R^2
Total Sample	233	-2.16	0.56	.06
Captial Appreciation Funds	30	-1.59	1.32	.05
Equity Income Funds	17	-4.68	2.15	.24
Growth Funds	94	-3.23	1.05	.09
Growth and Income Funds	74	-2.34	0.76	.12
Small Company Growth Funds	18	1.57	1.97	.04

The remaining rows of the table present separate analyses by categories of funds. The pattern of higher expenses tend to reduce net returns holds for all categories of funds with the exception of small company growth funds. Here the coefficient of expenses is positive, implying that after paying these expenses the investor is actually better off. This would be consistent with a view that the stock market is less efficient for smaller companies and the expenditure of additional investment management expenses may indeed have a positive payoff. The coefficient is not statistically significant, however, and probably the safest statement one can make is simply that the typical negative relationship between expenses and net returns fails to hold for the smaller growth company mutual funds.

One might argue that a negative relationship between nonadvisory expenses and net performance is to be expected. After all, there is no reason to expect 12b-1 distribution expenses or other administrative expenses to enhance performance. Investment advisory expenses, however, ought to improve performance. Indeed, to the extent that these expenses vary with performance because of incentive features, a higher expense ratio should be associated with higher net returns. In Table 3, the expense ratio is broken down into two components and separate coefficients are estimated for each. Advisory expenses include only expenses paid for investment advice. Nonadvisory expenses include all other expenditures including administrative expenses, 12b-1 fees, and so forth. As expected, nonadvisory expenses tend to have a strong negative correlation with net returns. The pattern for advisory expenses is less clear. While the correlation is positive for the whole sample, the positive coefficient is never significant and is (significantly) negative for one of the fund categories. The data do not support the contention that investors get their money's worth even from investment advisory expenditures.

Table 3
Multivariate Regression Results
10-year Performance as a Function of Advisory and Non-advisory Expenses
(1982–91)

	No. of Observations	Estimated Coefficient of Advisory Expense Ratio (Standard Error)	Estimated Coefficient of Non-Advisory Expense Ratio (Standard Error)	R^2
Total Sample	233	0.79 (1.12)	-3.29 (0.67)	.10
Captial Appreciation Funds	30	2.84 (2.81)	-2.14 (1.34)	.15
Equity Income Funds	17	1.23 (4.52)	-1.46 (0.68)	.33
Growth Funds	94	0.70 (2.14)	-5.02 (1.17)	.18
Growth and Income Funds	74	-4.30 (1.78)	-1.85 (1.02)	.13
Small Company Growth Funds	18	3.28 (3.85)	2.52 (2.79)	.11

It would appear that investors do not gain from higher expense ratios. Moreover, the general level of expense ratios has approximately doubled since the early 1950s despite the existence of considerable economies of scale in the money management business. What has been happening is that mutual fund managers have been extracting substantial fee increases from the funds they manage; in addition, new 12b-1 distribution charges have been imposed that greatly exceed any potential gain from the economies of scale that could come from an expanded asset base. The industry has become extraordinarily profitable, but it is hard to find the customers' yachts.

As a matter of principle, I do not believe in price fixing and do not favor having the SEC promulgate expense rate ceilings, despite my belief that many mutual funds impose unconscionable fees on their investors. But I do believe it is essential that investors be made aware, as clearly as possible, of the price they are paying for the privilege of investing in a mutual fund, especially since expenses do not seem to enhance performance. The SEC has made significant strides in this regard and now requires a fee table showing the annual expense ratio for holding periods of different length. But this information needs to be simplified, and summary statistics should appear on page one of the prospectus, not buried within the document. Moreover, total expense information should be displayed prominently in any advertising prospectus that the Commission may allow in connection with the staff study recommendations for off-the-page sales of mutual funds. In addition, customers of broker-sold funds should be entitled to the same page of information prior to confirming their purchase of shares. Clearer and more transparent disclosure of fees should be among the highest priority goals for the Commission over the coming years.

B. Disclosure of Significant Risk Factors

Investors cannot be protected from assuming substantial investment risk even if that risk is not a suitable one for the financial circumstances of the individual. But individuals should not be encouraged to buy mutual fund shares without being informed about the significant risk factors involved in the investment. Too often, mutual fund investors have been induced, either by advertisements or by sales personnel, to purchase fund shares without full appreciation of the risks involved. The SEC can and should help insure that investors receive clear and readable written information about the major risk factors involved in any prospective fund purchase.

Recently, many individuals have been induced to cash in their domestic money market funds or maturing certificates of deposit and purchase so-called global short-term funds in the mistaken belief that by so doing they could increase their rate of return without incurring substantial additional risk. Unfortunately, many of these investors had not understood that such funds carried substantial foreign currency risks and could fall substantially in price if the dollar were to strengthen against foreign currencies. Today, some money market funds have lengthened the average maturity of their portfolios in an attempt to increase current yield. It is not clear to most investors that longer portfolios carry significant risk of principal loss (and therefore lower future returns) should interest rates rise in the future.

My point is not to suggest that short-term global funds or money funds with longer average maturities are inappropriate investments. But I do believe that investors are entitled to know the significant risk factors involved in their investments, and I do not believe that they receive that information in concise and readable form today. What is needed in any one-page advertising prospectus is a small box, not unlike those on packs of cigarettes, outlining in highly readable prose the general degree of uncertainty regarding future returns and highlighting the significant risk elements (which should be analyzed in greater detail in the actual prospectus).

C. Advertising and Sales Practices

As indicated above, mutual funds are often sold without full disclosure of either the expenses paid by investors or the risks involved in the investment. Short-term global funds have been heavily marketed by stressing short-term local currency return and ignoring risk. In addition, there have been instances where some funds have been sold with highly misleading sales pitches. "Government Plus" funds were marketed as if the total payouts of the funds (which included *both* interest and return of principal) could continue indefinitely.

Common stock funds with excellent performance over some specific period of time and with respect to some particular group of funds have sometimes run "We're number one" advertisements only to have investors find that there is no consistency to such superior performance. In one example, a growth fund advertised itself as the "best performing fund." In small print the fund indicated that it was best only among 12 funds of a particular asset size and for a specific chosen period. Over the next 12-month period the fund ranked in the bottom quartile of similar growth funds. While there is nothing wrong with presenting performance data over certain standardized intervals and relative to clearly defined benchmarks, the SEC can do a great deal to restrain fund advertising so that it fairly represents the product being offered and the major risks involved. Investors may still wish to buy, but they should know clearly that some investments may be hazardous to their wealth.

3. Concluding Comments

The investment company industry has in general performed extremely well over the past 50 years. It has grown to its present size because it has offered consumers a variety of serviceable products that have greatly simplified individual portfolio decisions. Moreover, the Investment Company Act of 1940 has done an excellent job in protecting investors while leaving the industry enough leeway to innovate and spawn healthy competition. One might reasonably then ask, "If it ain't broke, why fix it?" Why should the SEC tinker with a system that is working well?

The answer is that in some cases the regulatory system has been overtaken by events and by innovations within the financial services industry. The regulatory structure does need to be amended from time to time to adjust to the growth of securitization, to the proliferation of new products available for employee benefit plan assets, to the internationalization of markets, and so on. Many of the suggestions in the SEC staff report are designed simply to permit the regulatory structure to adjust to changes in the financial landscape. Other changes recommended by the SEC would simplify the regulatory structure. Certainly suggestions for simplifying the approval process for routine exemptive orders are consistent with healthy deregulation and are unambiguously desirable.

Probably the most controversial of the SEC recommendations would be to permit off-the-page sales of mutual funds where investors could buy funds from a newspaper advertisement without being given a full prospectus first. Were this recommendation to imply less disclosure and less information available to investors, it would not be advantageous. However, the prospectus today is written in a manner to avoid legal liability rather than to inform investors. It is quite possible that a well designed one-page advertisement, which itself would be a prospectus, could give investors more information and not less. The key is whether important items such as the objectives of the fund, the risks to which investors are subject, and, above all, the costs imposed by the fund on the shareholders are clearly and understandably presented. If so, investors will actually be better off and better informed rather than worse off under the SEC's proposal. Moreover, by making costs more transparent the SEC can perform a service by fostering healthy competition in the pricing of mutual funds.

Figure 1
Mutual Fund Performance versus Average Expense Ratio over Ten Years 1982–1991

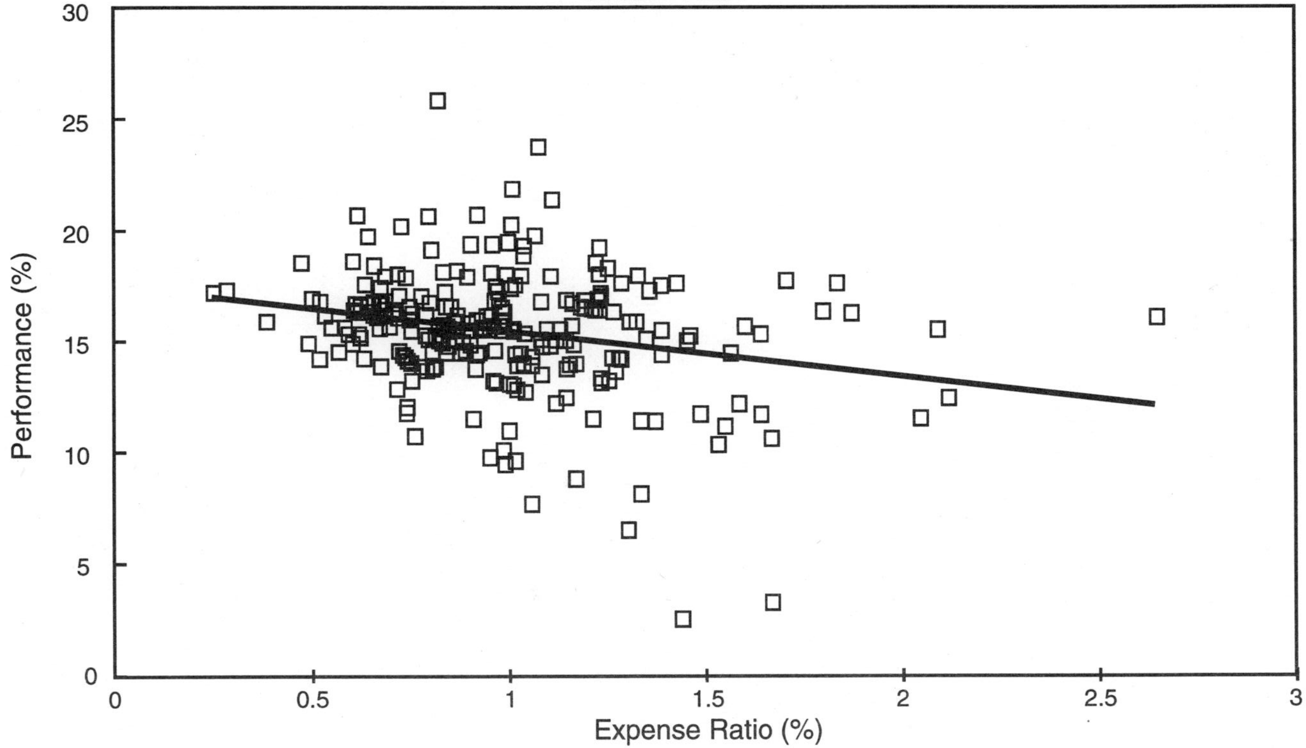

37

Market Structure and the Regulation of the Mutual Fund Industry

Lawrence J. White
New York University

1. Introduction

The mutual fund industry is subject to a considerable amount of regulation by the Securities and Exchange Commission. Much of this regulation involves the amounts and types of information that existing shareholders and prospective shareholders (i.e., potential purchasers) should receive; some of this regulation entails safety considerations (e.g., limitations on the types and maturities that money market funds can hold). The justification for these types of regulation usually rests on perception and/or belief that the marketplace, by itself, will not provide an adequate amount of information (or in adequately standardized form) to allow investors to make suitably informed choices.

The mutual fund industry is relatively free of the type of *economic* regulation (e.g., limitations on prices, profits, and/or entry) that characterizes state regulation of electric utilities or city regulation of taxicabs and that formerly characterized federal regulation of airlines, railroads, buses, and trucking. Though there are some limitations on fees (e.g., load [sales charge] funds are permitted to charge a maximum up-front sales fee of 8.5 percent, and fund managers and advisers are limited in the fees that they can charge) these limitations appear to be motivated by the same concerns about the adequacy of information that drive the bulk of SEC regulation rather than by the concerns about the adequacy of competition that traditionally have been used to justify economic regulation.

Nevertheless, proposals for specific forms of economic regulation, based on concerns about competitive adequacy, do occasionally surface. A recent example is the proposal by the staff of the SEC that would eliminate the ability of load funds to specify the size of the load that would accompany the distribution of their shares.[1]

Since the logical foundation for economic regulation must be a concern that competitive forces are not adequate to achieve socially desirable outcomes, an examination of the structural characteristics of the mutual fund industry—to indicate the likelihood that structural features of the industry might impede competition—seems worthwhile. The remainder of this paper will provide the details of these structural characteristics and indicate their implications for the adequacy of competition.

2. A Brief Overview

It is useful to begin with a brief overview of the mutual fund industry. Mutual funds provide an excellent way for investors,— especially small investors,—to obtain the advantages of portfolio diversification and specialized financial markets expertise at relatively small costs. By pooling their relatively small amounts of funds into the much larger aggregate pools of mutual funds, groups of investors can effectively diversify their portfolios and obtain the services of financial market experts. The transactions costs per dollar invested are generally quite small as compared with what investors would face if they tried to achieve these advantages individually.

These features have been recognized by the investing public, and, aided by favorable changes in restrictive regulations and laws (including tax laws), the mutual fund industry has enjoyed substantial growth over the past fifty years. Table 1 illustrates this growth. Since 1940, the net assets of long-term funds have increased by more than 2000-fold; even since 1980 the extent of the increase has been fourteen-fold. Money market funds did not exist prior to 1972; since 1980 their net assets have increased by a factor of seven.

Table 2 indicates the array of choices that have been available to investors in the major categories of funds. The 2,603 funds in the equity and bond and income categories in 1991 were offered by 295 separate mutual fund companies ("complexes"). Table 3 provides yet greater detail on the categories (by investment objective) of long-term mutual funds and their relative shares of the total in 1991.

In sum, the mutual funds industry is a growing, vibrant part of the financial services sector of the U.S. economy. The industry has been

---

[1] *See* U.S. SEC (1992, 291-315).

offering a steadily widening array of investment vehicles to the public, and the public continues to respond favorably.

3. Market Structure

The competitive behavior and performance of an industry is likely to be determined by a few important structural characteristics of that industry: the number and size-distribution of the firms in the industry, the ease with which new firms can enter the industry; and the ease with which smaller firms can expand their sales.[2] If the number of firms is comparatively small and a few account for a large fraction of the industry's sales *and* if entry by new firms is difficult *and* if expansion by smaller firms is difficult, then the handful of relatively large firms may be able to reach an explicit or implicit understanding among themselves to restrict competition, and the smaller firms will go along. On the other hand, if the number of firms is large and none have large market shares *or* entry by new firms is easy *or* expansion by smaller firms is easy, the attainment and enforcement of any kind of understanding among these firms will be difficult—especially if explicit communication among them as to the understanding is prohibited. In this case the temptations for each firm to "cheat" on the understanding at the expense of the others (and the fears that the others may be surreptitiously cheating) become too great.

For the mutual fund industry, the structural data indicate a relatively unconcentrated industry, with relatively easy entry. Table 4 shows two frequently used measures of industry concentration—the four-firm concentration ratio and the Herfindahl-Hirschman Index[3] (HHI)—for the overall mutual fund industry (including money market funds) during the 1980s. As can be seen, the leading four firms accounted for only 35.3 percent of net assets in 1982, and by early 1987 this figure had declined to

---

[2] Two other important structural characteristics are the nature of the product and the size distribution and expertise of the industry's customers. For a general discussion of this approach to industry competitive analysis *see* Scherer and Ross (1990).

[3] The Herfindahl-Hirschman Index is constructed by squaring the market share of each firm in the marketplace and summing all of those squared market shares.

24.9 percent. The HHI for the industry was similarly low by antitrust standards.[4]

Similar data are available for a narrower segment of the industry for which concerns about competitive adequacy (including the specific proposal mentioned in the Introduction) are sometimes raised: the group of long-term funds. As can be seen in Table 5, the leading four firms have accounted for only 24%-31% of net assets and of sales during the 1985–1991 period, and the number of complexes in this segment of the mutual fund industry has risen to approximately 300. Though the combined net assets share of the leading four firms' net assets has been rising (at a rate of about 1% per year), the 1991 level (30.8%) is still well below the levels (50%–60%) that have been linked empirically to the likely exercise of market power.[5] It seems unlikely that an industry with this large a number of firms and this low a combined market share for its leading four firms could achieve any common understanding as to anticompetitive pricing.

Further, entry into the mutual fund industry and expansion by firms within it appear to be quite easy. Table 2 showed the sharp increases in the number of funds offered to the public since 1940. Table 6 shows the increase in the number of mutual fund advisers (roughly comparable to the number of companies) during the 1982–1987 period. Again, it seems unlikely that this industry could succeed in reaching and maintaining any common understanding as to anticompetitive pricing.

The structural characteristics of mutual fund *distributors* point to a similar conclusion. Long-term mutual funds are distributed through a number of different channels, as is seen in Table 7. Load funds tend to be distributed primarily through affiliated and unaffiliated broker-dealers; other significant distribution channels include insurance agents, captive sales forces, independent financial planners, other sales forces, and deposit institutions. No-load funds tend to be distributed primarily through direct mail and telephone responses to advertising and through in-house personnel. If we focus on the set of distribution channels for load funds, they appear to

---

[4] The Department of Justice's Antitrust Division *Merger Guidelines* describe a market with a HHI below 1,000 as "unconcentrated" and one with a HHI between 1,000 and 1,800 as "moderately concentrated."

[5] The *Merger Guidelines'* HHI dividing point of 1,000 is empirically equivalent to a four-firm concentration ratio of 50%; see Kwoka (1985). For some empirical evidence on a "critical" four-firm concentration ratio in the 50%–60% range *see* White (1976) and the discussion in Scherer and Ross (1990, 422–23).

be far too diverse to be able to achieve any understanding among themselves about noncompetitive pricing. Even if we examine the largest segment of the distribution of load funds—affiliated and unaffiliated broker-dealers—this group is relatively unconcentrated. Table 8 shows the combined shares of the leading four firms (among the 371 members of the Securities Industry Association) in 1991 for each major category of *capacity* in the securities industry; none of these measures of four-firm concentration is above 50 percent. Extrapolation from SIA data concerning the 1991 *revenues* of securities industry firms yields an estimate of well under 40 percent for the combined shares of the largest four firms.[6] Further, there do not appear to be substantial entry barriers in any of the major channels of distribution.

One other structural characteristic is worth noting: the array of product varieties available to investors. Tables 1 through 3 provided an indication of the broad array of products available. Further, the method of distribution and the sales charges that attach to those methods are another important dimension of variety. Long-term funds are available with various sizes of loads and various combinations of load payment mechanisms, including up-front fees, annual (12b-1) fees, and redemption fees. A number of mutual fund advisory services publish thick reference guides that provide investors with extensive information on the characteristics, fee structures, and performance records of all funds. Long-term investors can avoid some load fees by choosing funds that emphasize "contingent deferred sales loads" (redemption fees) that decline with the time that the investor holds the fund's shares. Equally important, no-load funds are a prominent part of the mutual fund industry. Table 9 shows the net assets and sales for no-load funds for the years 1985–1991. As can be seen, these funds have accounted for 17–25% of net assets and 19–32% of sales since 1985; as of 1991 they represented slightly more than a quarter of mutual fund net assets and almost one-third of mutual fund sales. Further, as Table 10 indicates, direct market funds (which are overwhelmingly no-load) are available to investors in 18 of the 19 "investment objective" categories listed for mutual funds.[7]

---

[6] The combined revenue share for the leading *10* firms was 56 percent of all NYSE firms' revenues, and NYSE firms were 77 percent of the securities industry's total revenues. Thus, the combined share of these *10* leading firms was only 43 percent of total industry revenues.

[7] The category "option/income," in which there were no direct-market funds, has been a declining segment of the mutual fund industry. In 1991 the total net assets for this segment were only $1.4 billion; in 1986 they had been $6.8 billion.

In sum, a wide array of types of mutual funds and methods of distribution are available to investors. Extensive information is available to investors about those funds. The opportunity for choice does not appear to be a problem.

4. Conclusion

The structural characteristics of the mutual fund industry are strongly indicative of a competitive industry. It seems unlikely that anticompetitive understandings among mutual funds could be maintained or could have any significant marketplace effects. Accordingly, though informational and safety regulation may still be warranted for this industry, any case for economic regulation that would involve limitations on prices or pricing practices in this industry—based on concerns about the adequacy of competition—would have little foundation.

Table 1: Net Assets of Mutual Funds, 1940-1991
(billions of dollars)

	Equity, Bond, and Income Funds	Money Market Funds	Total
1940	$ 0.4	--	$ 0.4
1945	1.3	--	1.3
1950	2.5	--	2.5
1955	7.8	--	7.8
1960	17.0	--	17.0
1965	35.2	--	35.2
1970	47.6	--	47.6
1975	42.2	$ 3.7	45.9
1980	58.4	76.4	134.8
1985	251.7	243.8	495.5
1990	568.5	498.3	1066.8
1991	807.1	539.6	1346.7

Source: Investment Company Institute, *Mutual Fund Fact Book*, various years.

Table 2: Numbers of Mutual Funds, Major Categories, 1940-1991

	Equity	Bond and Income	Taxable Money Market	Tax-Exempt Money Market	Total
1940	68	[a]	-	-	68
1945	73	[a]	-	-	98
1950	98	[a]	-	-	98
1955	125	[a]	-	-	125
1960	161	[a]	-	-	161
1965	170	[a]	-	-	170
1970	361	[a]	-	-	361
1975	286	104	36	-	426
1980	267	191	96	10	564
1985	579	492	346	111	1,528
1990	1,127	1,235	508	236	3,106
1991	1,216	1,387	553	267	3,423

[a] Included with equity funds

Source: Investment Company Institute, *Mutual Fund Fact Book*, various years.

Table 3: Numbers and Net Assets of Long-Term Mutual Funds, by Investment Objective, 1991

	Number	% of Total	Net Assets[a]	% of Total
Aggressive growth	209	8.0%	$ 63.3	7.8%
Growth	395	15.2	105.0	13.0
Growth and income	308	11.8	129.5	16.0
Precious metals	35	1.3	2.9	0.4
International	128	4.9	19.1	2.4
Global-equity	65	2.5	17.3	2.1
Income-equity	72	2.8	29.3	3.6
Option/income	4	0.2	1.4	0.1
Flexible portfolio	60	2.3	10.0	1.2
Balanced	77	3.0	20.2	2.5
Income-mixed	95	3.6	25.6	3.2
Income-bond	139	5.3	27.5	3.4
U.S. Government income	223	8.6	96.9	12.0
Ginnie Mae	54	2.1	36.6	4.5
Global bond	59	2.3	26.8	3.3
Corporate bond	61	2.3	15.5	1.9
High-yield bond	95	3.6	26.1	3.2
Long-term municipal	193	7.4	88.3	10.9
Single-state municipal bond,	331	12.7	65.9	8.2
Total	2603	100.0%	$807.1	100.0%

[a] Billions of dollars

Source: Investment Company Institute, *1992 Mutual Fund Fact Book.*

Table 4: Structural Measures of Concentration in the Overall Mutual Fund Industry, 1982-1987[a] (measured by net assets)

Ratio	Four-Firm Concentration Index (HHI)	Herfindall-Hirschman
1982	35.3%	475
1983	32.1	393
1984	29.9	350
1985	27.8	327
1986	26.0	307
1987	24.9	301

[a]Data for each year are for March 31, except for 1987 (which is measured as of December 31, 1986)

Source: Baumol, Goldfeld, Gordon, and Koehn (1990)

Table 5: Structural Characteristics, Long-Term Mutual Funds, 1985-1991

	Number of Complexes	Four-Firm Concentration Ratio, Net Assets	Four-Firm Concentration Ratio, Sales
1985	164	24.3%	30.7%
1986	199	27.4	29.2
1987	244	27.0	27.3
1988	263	27.1	24.3
1989	290	27.6	28.0
1990	301	28.4	28.4
1991	295	30.8	28.8

Source: Data supplied by ICI.

Table 6: Numbers of Mutual Fund Advisers, 1982-1987

	Total Number of Advisers
1982	174
1983	202
1984	222
1985	254
1986	291
1987	315

Source: Baumol, Goldfeld, Gordon, and Koehn (1990)

Table 7: Distribution Channels for Long-Term Mutual Funds, 1990

	Load funds	No-load funds[a]
Affiliated broker-dealers	26.4%	1.4%
Unaffiliated broker-dealers	35.9	2.9
Insurance agents	7.4	0.3
Discount brokerage firms	0.6	0.3
Captive sales force	6.1	1.4
Independent financial planners	5.6	0.5
In-house personnel	1.6	23.0
Other sales force	7.1	3.3
Deposit institutions	6.6	0.7
Mail and telephone	2.1	65.7
Other direct marketing	0.5	0.6
Total	100.0%	100.0%

[a] Includes load funds with sales charges of less than 3%.

Source: Investment Company Institute, "Source of Mutual Fund New Sales, 1991"

Table 8: Combined Share of the Leading Four Securities Firms, Major Categories of Capacity, 1991

	Combined Share of Leading Four Firms
Capital	48.2%
Offices	42.8
Employees	41.0
Registered representatives	41.8

Source: Securities Industry Association, *Securities Industry_Yearbook, 1991*.

Table 9: Net Assets and Sales of No-Load Mutual Funds, 1986-1992

	Net Assets[a]	% of All Long-Term Fund Assets	Sales	% of All Long-Term Fund Sales
1985	$ 50.8	20.2%	$21.9	19.2%
1986	82.2	19.4	45.5	21.2
1987	77.1	17.0	42.7	22.4
1988	106.1	22.5	26.5	27.8
1989	134.6	24.3	39.2	31.2
1990	140.3	24.7	46.1	30.8
1991	207.2	25.7	75.2	32.1

[a]Billions of dollars

Source: Investment Company Institute

Table 10: Mutual Funds That Rely on Direct Marketing, by Investment Objective, 1991

	Number of Funds	Net Assets[a]
Aggressive growth	100	
Growth	109	$45.5
Growth and income	73	34.3
Precious metals	24	36.7
International	18	1.4
Global-equity	10	8.5
Income-equity	54	0.6
Option/income	0	14.4
Flexible portfolio	54	0.0
Balanced	11	2.4
Income-mixed	13	9.0
Income-bond	38	4.5
U.S. government income	71	10.9
Ginnie Mal	9	13.4
Global bond	19	11.2
Corporate bond	36	2.3
High-yield bond	11	5.5
Long-term municipal bond	10	4.0
Single-state municipal bond	9	29.9
		17.3

[a] Billions of dollars

Source: Investment Company Institute, 1992 Mutual Fund Fact Book

References and Suggested Readings

Baumol, William J., Stephen M. Goldfeld, Lilli A. Gordon, and Michael F. Koehn. 1990. *The Economics of Mutual Fund Markets: Competition versus Regulation*. Boston: Kluwer.

Kwoka, John E., Jr. 1985. "The Herfindahl Index in Theory and Practice." *Antitrust Bulletin* 30 (Winter): 915–47.

Scherer, F. M. and David Ross. 1990. *Industrial Market Structure and Economic Performance*, 3rd edition. Boston: Houghton Mifflin.

U.S. Securities and Exchange Commission, Division of Investment Management. 1992. *Protecting Investors: A Half Century of Investment Company Regulation*. Washington, D. C.: U.S. Government Printing Office, (May).

White, Lawrence J. 1976. "Searching for the Critical Concentration Ratio: An Application of the `Switching of Regimes' Technique." In *Studies in Non-Linear Estimation*, Stephen M. Goldfeld and Richard E. Quandt, eds. Cambridge: Ballinger: 61-76.

Securitizing Open-End Funds

38

The Regulatory Impediments to Viable Cash Index Securitization

Lawrence Harris
University of Southern California

Introduction

The Securities and Exchange Commission is currently considering changes to the Investment Company Act of 1940 that would affect how mutual funds are distributed. In particular, the SEC is considering whether to recommend to Congress a partial or complete repeal of Section 22(d) of the act.

Section 22(d) prohibits dealers from trading mutual funds at prices different from the net asset values determined by the funds. In effect, this restriction requires that all transactions in mutual funds be made as deposits or redemptions with the funds themselves at prices determined by the funds. This section effectively enforces retail price maintenance of fund sales loads. Dealers cannot discount a loaded fund by rebating a portion of their share of the load. It also effectively eliminates a secondary market in funds in which shares owned by one investor could be directly transferred to another investor.

Most of the interest in repealing Section 22(d) is related to the retail price maintenance issue. Many investors feel that it unfairly supports high loads by preventing dealer discounting and by effectively preventing secondary trades among investors. The loaded fund industry, of course, is strongly opposed to changing this law. They claim that the loads support legitimate sales practices in the public interest that would not be sustainable without Section 22(d).

Although the retail price maintenance issue is important, the effective prohibition on secondary trading in any mutual fund–loaded or unloaded–has had an unseen and largely unappreciated effect that is probably more important. Section 22(d) prevents the creation and trading of an economically viable security that represents the risk inherent in an underlying index like the S&P 500 Index. Such a cash index alternative would be of great benefit to the public if it were available.

This paper examines why a viable cash index alternative would be attractive. It then explains how it might be obtained even if retail price maintenance of loaded funds is to be preserved.

Indexation

Indexation represents the single most important innovation in the U.S. equity markets over the last twenty years. Investors now commonly hold index funds, and traders now commonly employ index trading strategies.

Hugh amounts of institutional (and increasingly, individual investor) capital are now invested in index funds whose investment strategies are solely designed to replicate the returns to broad market indices like the S&P 500 Index. In practice, these funds simply buy and hold the stocks in the underlying index. The strategy is attractive to investors because it effectively guarantees that they will obtain an average return on their investment. Index investors do not risk systematically choosing poorly performing stocks, and they do not lose much through transaction costs because the index replication strategy does not require many stock trades. Index funds are now estimated to hold about 35 percent of all outstanding U.S. equity.

Index trading strategies have grown with the growth of index funds. These strategies include program trading, portfolio trading and stock index futures trading.

An index program trade is the simultaneous trade of all (or a representative sample of all) stocks in an index. Each stock is traded separately in its own market.

Index portfolio trading (also called package trading) is the simultaneous trade of all stocks in an index at a single negotiated price for the entire list.

Index program and portfolio trades are often done when investors want to invest in or disinvest from index funds. Program trading tends to be more expensive because each stock must be traded separately. It is easier, however, because portfolio trades must be negotiated.

Stock index futures contracts allow traders to trade the risk inherent in an underlying index without trading the underlying securities. These derivative contracts, however, do not represent any net investment. They are simply agreements between buyer and seller (guaranteed by an exchange clearing house) to deliver or receive cash based on changes in the value of the underlying index. Traders who use stock index futures are exposed to the risk in the underlying index and to the risk that the exchange clearing house will not be able to meet its commitments if traders default. Although the default risk is generally considered to be very small, it would grow substantially during a crash.

Stock index futures contracts are often used to create synthetic index funds. These funds replicate the returns to a true cash index fund (and to the underlying index) by holding long positions in the futures contract and in treasury bills. The synthetic index fund is attractive to investors because it is very liquid. Money can be invested or disinvested from synthetic index funds at low cost because the stock index futures market and the Treasury-bill markets are both very liquid. Many institutions, however, cannot take advantage of this strategy because their investment policies do not allow them to trade futures contracts. Institutions may impose these restrictions because futures contracts are not investment contracts and because futures contracts expose them to default risk.

The SEC through its report by the Division of Market Regulation on the market break of 1987, through its approval of index participations,[1] and through numerous comments has expressed its interest in new cash index instruments that would allow the public to trade the value of broad market indices in orderly and well-regulated markets. The Commission's interest appears to be grounded in the belief that more liquid and less volatile markets would result if a cash index product were widely and continuously traded. This view has also received substantial support in the academic literature.[2]

---

[1] Index participation is the generic name for a class of index instruments first proposed for trade by the Philadelphia Stock Exchange. These instruments are perpetual, zero net supply contracts that entitles long-holders to receive quarterly from short-holders dividends equal in amount to those paid to an underlying index portfolio. In addition, once a quarter, long-holders have the right to cash-out at a price equal to the value of the underlying portfolio.

Index participations traded briefly in 1989 at the Philadelphia Stock Exchange and at the American Stock Exchange after they were approved by the SEC. Trade was halted when the Seventh Circuit Court of Appeals determined that index participations are essentially futures contracts and therefore fall under the regulatory jurisdiction of the Commodity Futures Trading Commission. The CFTC offered to negotiate some arrangement that would allow the index participations to continue to trade, but no agreement was reached.

[2] *See*, for example, Harris (1990), Rubinstein (1989), Stoll (1988), or Gehr (1988).

A fully collaterized cash index instrument would allow traders to trade an instrument that represents investment in the underlying stocks. When secondary trading in such an instrument becomes well established, the instrument would be as liquid as the current stock index futures market. Many, perhaps most, tax-exempt index funds would probably convert their portfolios to this instrument.[3] The securitization of their portfolios would decrease their management costs and would decrease their costs of investing and disinvesting.

The Regulatory Problem

Section 22(d) of the Investment Company Act of 1940 effectively prevents active secondary market trading in redeemable cash index instruments. Such redeemable cash index instruments include open-end index funds, warehouse receipts,[4] and certain unit trusts such as proposed by SuperShare Services, Inc.[5] and by the AMEX.[6]

---

[3] Taxable funds would lose tax timing options if they securitized their portfolios. When these funds need to disinvest, they sell stocks that have dropped in value since they were purchased. This strategy minimizes their taxes. Taxable funds, however, do not hold the largest fraction of indexed equity assets. The bulk of index funds are held by tax exempt pension funds.

[4] Warehouse receipts, or depository index receipts, would be receipts for a basket of stocks left on deposit with a depository trust company (the warehouse). Investors would create or redeem receipts by tendering or receiving the actual basket of stocks. Receiptholders would have the right to receive the dividends paid on the stocks, less a storage fee. A warehouse, in effect, would be an open-end index fund for which deposit and redemption transactions are conducted only in-kind. Receipts would be registered securities and traded like stocks.

[5] SuperShare Services, Inc. (Leland O'Brien Rubinstein, Inc.) proposes to offer for trade a unit trust, to be called a SuperUnit, which would hold the shares of an open-end mutual index fund. The proposal is part of their more general proposal to trade SuperShares. SuperShares are fully collateralized option-like instruments that will provide returns similar to index options. The SEC recently approved trading in these instruments and trading is expected to begin once the instruments are funded. The SuperUnits will trade at the AMEX and the SuperShares will trade at the Chicago Board Options Exchange.

[6] The AMEX has proposed trading Spiders, which would be a unit trust that would hold an S&P 500 index fund.

Specifically, Section 22(d) prohibits funds, principal underwriters, and dealers from selling redeemable securities at prices different from net asset value. As a result, no secondary dealer market in open-end mutual fund shares exists. Although a brokered market legally could exist,[7] in practice, the exclusion of dealers makes the organization of such a market difficult and unlikely.

The remainder of this paper explains why a redeemable security is desirable as a cash index alternative, why continuous trading is important, why Section 22(d) was incorporated into the Investment Company Act, why the intended protections are no longer necessary, and how an exemption or repeal should be crafted.

Cash Index Alternatives and Redeemable Securities

A cash index instrument will be successful only if it closely replicates the returns to its underlying index. Close replication requires easy and inexpensive arbitrage between the instrument and the underlying index stocks. If arbitrage is difficult or near impossible, as it is with closed-end funds, the instrument may trade at a discount or premium to the underlying index. This discount or premium will be uncertain. As a result, individuals and institutions will be reluctant to trade the instrument. If arbitrage is easy, arbitragers will ensure that the value of the instrument always closely tracks the value of the underlying index stocks.

Note that arbitrage does not increase the total volatility in the two related instruments. Rather, it decreases volatility by exposing order-flow imbalances in one market to liquidity in the other market.

Arbitrage in redeemable securities is easy and cheap. Arbitragers in such securities do not have to construct and hold hedge portfolios for long and/or indefinite periods of time. They need only buy or sell the underlying index stocks and offset the transaction by redeeming or depositing the cash index instrument. Among the redeemable securities, arbitrage is least costly for those that allow deposits and redemptions in-kind. Those

---

[7] The U.S. Supreme Court in *United States v. National Association of Securities Dealers, Inc., et al.* (422 U.S. 694 (June 26, 1975)) held, however, that this prohibition does not apply to a distributing broker-dealer acting in a brokerage capacity. The secondary brokerage market apparently does not currently exist because provisions contained in uniform sales agreements between underwriters and broker-dealers effectively prohibit brokerage activity. (*See* SEC Investment Company Act Release No. 8570, November 4, 1974.) The Supreme Court case cited above was an unsuccessful effort by the Justice Department to use antitrust law to open a limited secondary market.

securities that only allow cash deposits and redemptions must invest and/or disinvest whenever there is net imbalance of deposit and redemption orders.[8] Arbitrage in these funds would therefore cause stock sales and or purchases that are exactly equal and opposite those made by the arbitrager. A facility for in-kind deposits and redemptions would eliminate some of this duplication and thereby make arbitrage less expensive.

Continuous Trading

Practitioners clearly value the immediacy provided in continuous markets. Evidence of their preferences can be found in the high intraday volumes observed for index futures and in the fact that the total assets in existing public open-end mutual index funds (such as the Vanguard Index Trust) that can only be bought or sold at day-end net asset values are not particularly large (about $9 billion) considering the great interest in index products. If a new cash index instrument is to be successful, it must be possible to trade it continuously while the equity markets are open.

Any reduction in index price volatility that may be associated with the introduction of a new cash index alternative will depend on whether dealers are willing to make a continuous market in the product and on whether other traders are willing to supply liquidity to the market when they feel prices do not reflect fundamental values. If the product cannot be traded continuously when markets are open, it is hard to imagine how it could reduce intraday index volatility.

The History of Section 22(d) of the Investment Company Act of 1940

Section 22(d) of the Investment Company Act of 1940 prohibits dealers from making a secondary market in redeemable securities at prices different from net asset value.[9] It was enacted to correct an abusive practice

---

[8] Open-end mutual funds try to lower stock transaction costs by satisfying some deposit and redemption orders from a cash buffer. If net order imbalances are negatively serially correlated, some imbalances cross over time so that transitory changes in the size of the fund can be made without trading the portfolio. Doing so, however, reduces replication efficiency since the cash does not earn a return equal to the index return.

[9] In relevant part, Section 22(d) states:

> No registered investment company shall sell any redeemable security issued by it to any person except either to or through a principal

observed prior to 1940 that involved secondary trading in those mutual funds that filled deposit and redemption orders (primary trading orders) at the net asset value of the fund that was last determined (based on previous day closing prices). This primary pricing practice is known as backward-pricing.

When funds were permitted to backward-price their shares, well informed traders diluted fund values by timing their transactions so that they deposited to the funds (bought shares from the funds) only on days when the posted last net asset values were lower than the current net asset values and redeemed shares when the opposite was true. For pre-1940, backward-priced open-end funds, the difference in current fund values and last computed net asset values rarely exceeded their sales loads. This strategy, therefore, was not generally profitable for individual investors. Dealers, however, could exploit the strategy to the extent that they could attract order flow by offering secondary market prices to the public that were better than the last net asset value prices offered by the funds. On days when fund values rose, they would bid higher prices than the previously determined net asset value prices offered by the funds to those who wanted to redeem their shares. The dealers would then redeem their newly acquired inventory on the next day at the new higher net asset values. On days when fund values fell, the dealers would offer lower prices to purchasers. They would then replenish their inventory on the next day at the new, lower net asset values.

Strategic trade timing in the secondary dealer market therefore diluted fund values for existing shareholders as dealers and their clients shared in the profits. Section 22(d) of the Investment Company Act of 1940 eliminated this practice by preventing dealers from selling at prices different from the net asset value of the fund.

A Better Remedy

In 1975, the SEC adopted Rule 22c-1 under Section 22(d) of the Investment Company Act of 1940. This rule requires that all deposits and redemptions of redeemable securities take place at the net asset value of the

---

underwriter for distribution or at a current public offering price described in the prospectus, and, if such class of security is being currently offered to the public by or through an underwriter, no principal underwriter of such security and no dealer shall sell any such security to any person except a dealer, a principal underwriter, or the issuer, except at a current public offering price described in the prospectus.

fund that is next determined after the receipt of such orders.[10] This practice is called forward-pricing.

The elimination of backward-pricing is a sufficient remedy to eliminate the abuses that Section 22(d) of the Investment Company Act of 1940 was designed to correct. Unfortunately, in an attempt to eliminate this abuse, the 1940 drafters of the Investment Company Act inadvertently eliminated certain dealer markets that would be in the public interest.

The Industry Remedy

The industry response to the regulatory problems associated with dealer market-making in redeemable securities has been to request exemptive relief for the trading of unit trusts. Relief along these lines has been granted for American Depository Receipts, for the Americus Trusts, and for the SuperUnits proposed by SuperShare Services, Inc.

This approach is costly because the resulting products must be constructed with an additional and otherwise unnecessary level of organization (the trust) and since each request for an exemption must be separately processed by the SEC.

A Complete Repeal

In November 1972, the SEC released an extensive staff study entitled, *On the Potential Economic Impact of a Repeal of Section 22(d) of the Investment Company Act of 1940.* Nothing at the time came of the issue, most probably because of the substantial impact such a repeal would have on the sales practices of loaded mutual funds. In particular, such a repeal would allow dealers in a secondary market to cross deposit and redemption orders for loaded funds so that the load could be avoided. The buyer, the seller, and the dealer could all benefit under such an arrangement, but current

---

[10] Rule 22c-1 states in relevant part:

> No registered investment company issuing any redeemable security, no person designated in such issuer's prospectus as authorized to consummate transactions in any such security, and no principal underwriter of, or dealer in, any such security shall sell, redeem, or repurchase any such security except at a price based on the current net asset value of such security which is next computed after receipt of a tender of such security for redemption or of an order to purchase or sell such security; . . .

fund distribution systems would suffer a loss. Although well accepted economic theory suggests the aggregate loss would be less than the aggregate gain, it is unlikely that any market-based arrangement could compensate the funds for their losses. A complete repeal of Section 22(d) apparently was not politically feasible then and may not be now.

A carefully crafted exemption, however might be feasible. In particular, the following exemption should meet the reasonable objections of all parties.

A Proposed Specific Exemption to Enable Secondary Trading of Index Funds

Section 6(c) of the Investment Company Act of 1940 permits the SEC upon its own motion to exempt any class of persons from any provisions of the Act if and to the extent that such exemption is necessary or appropriate in the public interest and consistent with the protection of investors and the purposes fairly intended by the policy and provisions of the act.[11]

Accordingly, the following narrow exemption should meet the requirements of the Investment Company Act without unduly threatening the existing loaded mutual fund industry while still providing for securitized index funds:

> Dealers may sell the redeemable securities of qualified open-end investment companies at prices that may differ from net asset value.

---

[11] Section 2(d) in its entirety states:

> The Commission, by rules and regulations upon its own motion, or by order upon application, may conditionally or unconditionally exempt any person, security, or transaction, or any class or classes of persons, securities, or transactions, from any provision or provisions of this title or of any rule or regulation thereunder, if and to the extent that such exemption is necessary or appropriate in the public interest and consistent with the protection of investors and the purposes fairly intended by the policy and provisions of this title.

A qualified open-end investment company is one

(a) whose stated investment objectives and practices are to hold a stock portfolio designed to replicate as closely as is reasonably possible the returns to a value-weighted or price-weighted index that is defined, maintained, and publicly disseminated by unrelated persons,

(b) that charges a total sales load of no more than one-half of the corresponding value- or price-weighted average bid/ask spread of the stocks in its portfolio,

(c) that fills deposit and redemption orders at the net asset value next computed after their receipt, and

(d) that elects to allow its shares to be traded in a secondary market pursuant to this exemption.

If deemed necessary, additional protections may be added by limiting the access of such secondary market dealers to the primary market, by further regulating the timing of deposit and redemption orders, and/or by requiring the index funds to have some procedure for in-kind redemptions.

Potential Objectors

The most likely opponents to this exemption would be existing loaded mutual funds. They may fear that this narrow exemption is a step toward a more general blanket exemption.

Existing open-end public index funds should embrace this exemption since the liquidity in an active secondary market would make their funds more attractive investments and therefore lead to significant potential growth. Secondary trading would also absorb some of the order imbalances for redemptions and deposits that occur from day to day. These funds would therefore be able to reduce the size of the cash balances that they carry in order to meet redemption and deposit order imbalances.

Other opponents to this exemption might include the non-index equity mutual funds. They rightly may fear that the increased liquidity that this exemption would bring to the index funds would cause investors to shift out of their funds and into index funds. This objection could be met by granting all open-end mutual funds the same exemption. Doing so, however, would be to the disadvantage of the heavily loaded funds, most of which probably would not elect to allow secondary trading in their funds.

Conclusion

Without the simple regulatory change proposed here, successful cash index instruments that represent ownership in the underlying index stocks are unlikely. Such securities, if properly constructed and traded, would be in the public interest and would be consistent with the protections sought by the original drafters of the Investment Company Act of 1940. It therefore would serve the public interest and the stated desires of the Commission to seek the repeal of Section 22(d), or at a minimum, grant the proposed narrow exemption using the authority given to the Commission under the act.

References and Suggested Readings

Gehr, Adam K., Jr. 1988. "Undated Futures Markets." *Journal of Futures Markets* 8, no. 1: 89–97.

Harris, Lawrence. 1990. "The Economics of Cash Index Alternatives." *Journal of Futures Markets* 10, no. 2 (Apr.): 189–94.

Rubinstein, Mark. 1989. "Market Basket Alternatives." *Financial Analysts Journal* (Sept./Oct.).

Stoll, Hans. 1988. "Portfolio Trading." *Journal of Portfolio Management* 14, no. 4 (Summer): 20–24.

U.S. Securities and Exchange Commission. Division of Market Regulation. 1988. *The October 1987 Market Break: A Report by the Division of Market Regulation U.S. Securities and Exchange Commission.* Washington, D. C.: U.S. Government Printing Office.

Soft Dollars

39

The Incentive Effects of Soft Dollar Brokerage

D. Bruce Johnsen
University of Pennsylvania

This paper examines the incentive effects of soft-dollar brokerage. Soft dollars are a form of *in-kind* rebate on brokerage commissions received by mutual fund, pension fund, and other professional portfolio managers. The beneficiaries of these funds hire managers as their agents to research, identify, and execute profitable portfolio trades. Having once identified a likely trade, a manager must hire a broker to execute it, paying the broker a commission out of fund assets. In a typical soft dollar arrangement, a broker normally prepays the manager's research expenses in proportion to the future brokerage commissions the manager promises to pay the broker. The manager receives research inputs up front from third-party research originators,[1] whom the broker pays in cash. If all goes as planned, the manager then directs future portfolio trades to the broker as necessary to generate the promised commissions to pay off the balance of his or her soft-dollar account.

Perhaps the best way to understand this arcane practice is historically. Until minimum brokerage commissions were eliminated on the New York Stock Exchange (NYSE) in May, 1975, securities brokers competed for the lucrative business of institutional portfolios by providing fund managers with research bundled into the commission charges on portfolio trades. With the unfixing of commissions pursuant to the *Securities*

[1] The following types of research products can be purchased with soft dollars: performance measurement services, third-party research, fundamental data bases, technical analysis software, portfolio modeling software, stock quote systems, political or economic analyses, computers and terminals, fundamental research, data on expected earnings, macroeconomic services, portfolio consulting services, educational services, and office support activities. For documentation of these and other facts and detailed citations to sources contained in this paper, *see* Johnsen (1992).

Acts Amendments (1975), nominal brokerage commissions declined considerably, from perhaps 40 cents per share to between five and 10 cents per share.[2] Yet, even under competition, brokers continued to bundle research and execution together into a single commission. In fact, Congress apparently foresaw this turn of events when it included § 28(e) in the 1975 amendments. This section, known as the "paying up" amendment, provides an institutional manager with a safe harbor from fiduciary suits by fund beneficiaries when he or she pays more than the lowest available brokerage commission in exchange for "research services." The question that comes to everyone's mind is why, in a competitive market, research continues to be bundled together with execution rather than being priced and transacted separately in the market exclusively for cash.

Unjust Enrichment

Soft dollars have been met with widespread hostility from financial-market commentators, established Wall Street brokerage firms, and securities market regulators, largely because they are thought to allow managers to unjustly enrich themselves at the expense of fund beneficiaries. To understand this argument, it is important to recognize that soft dollars are used almost exclusively in the principal-agent context of professional portfolio management. Since no single fund beneficiary has sufficient incentive to investigate and report his or her manager's brokerage practices, soft dollars are nearly invisible. And since brokerage commissions go into the price basis of a portfolio security, they are indirectly paid by fund beneficiaries. By bundling the costs of research and portfolio trades into a single brokerage commission, soft dollars are thus said to compromise the manager's fiduciary duty to fund beneficiaries; they encourage managers to engage in excessive portfolio trading—so-called churning—and to concede to excessively high commissions to pay the research bill they should properly pay out of their own pocket. What is more, having received research in advance, the manager may develop a misplaced sense of obligation to continue using a broker whose execution quality falls below an acceptable level. Being unwilling to terminate the broker, there is little reason for the manager to devote much time and attention to monitoring the quality of his or her executions.

Whether the result of churning, payment of excessively high commissions, or indifferent monitoring, soft dollars allow managers to

---

[2] Jarrell (1984).

unjustly enrich themselves at the expense of fund beneficiaries. To the alarm of its critics, soft-dollar use has grown considerably during the past decade, amounting by some estimates to over $1 billion annually in the U.S. alone. This growth has been met with repeated calls for further regulation and even outright prohibition. Most important, the SEC has recently identified soft dollars as one of the subjects it will investigate in its Market 2000 study.

Agency Costs

The widespread criticism of soft dollars relies implicitly on what is known in the law and economics literature as a standard transaction cost problem and in the finance literature more narrowly as an agency-cost problem. In general, the problem arises because an agent, such as a mutual or pension fund manager, has only a partial stake in the profitability of the principal's enterprise, while the cost to the principal of monitoring the agent to completely prevent "misbehavior" is prohibitive. As a result, the principal will tolerate deviations in the agent's behavior from that which is in the principal's best interest. The agent may shirk or consume too many of the principal's resources for his or her own benefit, and the parties' joint wealth will be less than it otherwise would be. The problem is especially acute where the principal is in fact a large number of dispersed, rationally disinterested fund beneficiaries.

As with all agency arrangements, there is little doubt that agency costs limit the advantages of professional portfolio management or that, in their absence, fund beneficiaries would be somewhat wealthier than they are today. But there is also little doubt that every agency-cost problem presents the parties with the opportunity to increase their joint wealth if they can organize their arrangement in a way that efficiently avoids or reduces the problem. This says nothing more than that there are gains from trade when inefficiencies can be corrected. Moreover, excessive or careless trading by a fund manager is only one source of agency costs. In truth, virtually all agency arrangements create value on a variety of interrelated dimensions; price, quality, and timeliness are just a few of the dimensions that are normally subject to an agent's discretion. Competition between brokers is likely to ensure that an agent who, for example, pays a higher-than-average price on behalf of his or her principal may also receive higher quality or more timely performance. A given agent action may therefore increase the agency problem on one dimension while simultaneously reducing it on another. And conduct that appears to be a source of agency costs when evaluated on one dimension might actually reduce aggregate agency costs when its effects are summed across all dimensions. Indeed, this essay makes out a strong *prima facie* case that soft dollars constitute just such a solution to the agency-cost problem in professional portfolio management.

Incentive Alignment

According to their advisory contracts, most managers receive just a small share of any wealth increase they generate for the fund. Consequently, if they were required to pay the entire research bill out of their own pocket in cash they would have too little incentive to perform well-researched trades. Here we see a second source of agency costs. One way for fund beneficiaries to reduce the attendant losses is to subsidize the manager's use of research. By bundling the costs of research and execution into a single trading commission paid by fund beneficiaries, soft dollars may provide the ideal solution. They not only increase the manager's incentive to trade, they also provide him or her with the research necessary to identify *profitable* trades.

Of course, profitable trading requires the manager to monitor his or her brokers to ensure that they receive best execution and that their search activity has a minimum adverse impact on the price of the security. But execution quality, and especially price impact, are notoriously difficult to assess in the short run. An inept, indolent, or opportunistic broker could cheat the manager (and fund beneficiaries) by doing a careless job of execution, thereby saving the added costs of properly working the trade or, in the limit, by front-running the trade, thereby transferring wealth from his principal. Here we see yet a third source of agency costs. And here again soft dollars may provide the ideal solution. Having already received research at the soft dollar broker's expense, the commissions a manager owes the broker serve to bond the quality of the broker's executions. Since the manager's promise to use the broker's services is legally unenforceable, the broker risks being terminated with the account balance unpaid if he or she cheats the manager. Rather than diluting execution quality, soft dollars may therefore guarantee it, much to the advantage of fund beneficiaries.

It does not necessarily follow that soft-dollar brokers provide the highest quality executions available in the market, only that the quality of their executions is *higher than it would otherwise would be.* Neither the repeated claims by full-service brokers that they provide better execution than soft dollar brokers nor the limited empirical evidence in support of these claims are inconsistent with the notion that soft dollars bond execution quality. It may be true that for extremely large, difficult trades in noisy or illiquid securities, where price impact is potentially large, managers prefer to use full-service brokers. Not only do these brokers have established business reputations to bond the quality of their performance, but the cost to the manager of monitoring execution quality relative to the benefits is fairly low simply because of the large dollar value of the transaction. For smaller, less difficult trades that cannot, however, be classified as "no-brainers," the cost to the manager of closely monitoring every trade is likely to be too high. It may be in the interest of the fund for the manager to pay a lower commission, net of the advanced research rebate, and to rely instead on the quality assurance the advanced rebate provides. Unlike the established full-service firms, who have long-standing business reputations, soft dollar brokers must rely on a more immediate method of bonding execution quality.

Specialization and Vertical Dis-integration

The incentive alignment hypothesis explains why the bundling engendered by soft dollars serves to align the incentives of fund managers and their executing brokers with the interests of fund beneficiaries. In a very important sense, however, these arguments beg the decisive question. Virtually all institutional brokers bundle research and execution into a single commission. This is true of soft-dollar brokers, who act as conduits in providing investment managers with research produced by third parties. But it is also true of the few remaining full-service firms that produce investment research in-house and make it available to fund managers on an informal basis. Indeed, the available evidence shows that there is little difference between the gross commissions charged by full-service and soft-dollar brokers.[3] Any criticism of bundling, per se, therefore applies to both types of brokers. The relevant question, then, is why use soft dollars to formally account for this bundling?

The answer to this question follows directly from Ronald Coase's famous essay *The Nature of the Firm*.[4] There, Coase asserted that the extent of the firm will be determined by an equality between the cost of performing transactions within the firm and the cost of performing transactions in the market between separate firms. When the transaction costs of market exchange fall relative to the transaction costs of internal organization, some activities previously performed by a single firm will come to be performed by separate firms and exchanged in the market. This hypothesis appears to fit rather closely the evolution of soft-dollar brokerage, which can be seen

---

[3] Blume (1992).

[4] Coase (1937).

as an organizational innovation that reduces the transaction costs of market exchange.

Full-service brokers produce research in-house and bundle it together with portfolio executions on an informal basis; the broker's research obligations are only loosely tied to the trading commissions expected from the manager. This is perfectly reasonable, since over time the parties can be presumed to know whether their expectations are being met. With soft dollars, however, the broker's research obligations are explicitly tied to the cash value of future trading commissions. By precisely metering these obligations, soft dollars allow them to be separately priced and transacted in the market between distinct firms. With specialty research originators producing the manager's research inputs, the soft dollar broker is free to specialize in performing portfolio executions, while the manager specializes in using his or her research inputs to identify profitable trades. In industries as competitive as investment management and institutional brokerage, many of the benefits of this functional specialization have no doubt been passed on to fund beneficiaries.

Policy Implications

With few exceptions over the years, the SEC has narrowed its interpretation of Section 28(e)'s safe harbor. Most recently, in July 1990, the SEC's Division of Market Regulation ruled that the protection afforded soft dollars by the safe harbor applies exclusively to "broker" trades (those performed on an agency basis) and not to "dealer" trades (those performed on a principal basis), in spite of the provision's language specifically applying to "brokers *or* dealers." With this single feat of interpretational legerdemain, the SEC staff caused the growing soft-dollar trade in fixed income and OTC securities, which are uniformly traded on a principal basis, to virtually disappear. The SEC is now entertaining suggestions that soft-dollar brokers, but not traditional brokers, be subject to onerous disclosure requirements that could easily bury the soft dollar industry under a mountain of paperwork.

Given the SEC's declaration to investigate soft dollars in its upcoming Market 2000 study, a few policy implications of the incentive alignment hypothesis are in order. First, dealer trades should once again be covered by Section 28(e). Bundling research into the dealer's mark-up or mark-down provides the same benefits to the fund from subsidizing the manager's research as on broker trades, but the benefits from quality assurance may be even greater; there is ample evidence to suggest that the problems associated with assessing the quality of dealer trades are as bad or worse than those associated with broker trades. Unlike brokers, however, dealers have no general common law and statutory fiduciary duties to either the fund or the manager to deter misdealing. And dealers generally are not required to disclose their mark-ups or mark-downs, making it far more difficult for fund managers to evaluate their performance. For all of these reasons, the role of soft dollars in providing up-front research to bond the quality of the broker-dealer's performance is much more compelling in the context of dealer trades. Bringing dealer trades back within Section 28(e)'s safe harbor is therefore likely to serve the interests of fund beneficiaries.

A second policy implication concerns the disclosure by investment managers of their soft-dollar–brokerage practices. The NASD recently urged the SEC staff to require managers to completely disclose their soft-dollar–allocation practices, while retaining the current, substantially less complete disclosure rules for full-service brokerage. What this proposal makes clear is that few soft-dollar critics have inquired into the practice vigorously enough even to recognize that the arguments against soft dollars apply with equal force to *all bundled research.* This fact has been entirely lost on those who criticize soft dollars for hiding from view the costs of fund management. It is incredible that soft dollars should be condemned because they only partially reveal what is entirely hidden from view with other forms of bundled research. Any proposal to require more detailed disclosure should therefore apply equally to all bundled research, including that provided on an in-house basis by traditional full-service firms. The discriminatory application of disclosure rules is ill-advised on equity grounds as well and will invariably work against the interests of fund beneficiaries.

Concluding Remarks

Where property rights are problematic, market participants often develop innovative ways to reduce any residual wealth loss associated with their socially productive activities. Precisely because these methods of enforcing property rights are innovative, and therefore often unusual, the tendency is to condemn the innovators as either anticompetitive or downright dishonest. Like the renowned "man on the spot" in F. A. Hayek's Nobel prize–winning essay, *The Use of Knowledge in Society,*[5] they may neither know nor care about the broader social benefits of their actions, and they are therefore likely to be at a disadvantage when called upon to defend themselves in the public policy arena. In analyzing the SEC's failure to

[5] Hayek (1945).

pursue Congress's vision of a "national market system" following passage of the Securities Acts Amendments, Macey and Haddock perceptively describe the tendency of regulators to condemn organizational innovation:

> The economic theory of regulation predicts that the owners of investments [specific] to an industry—in the present case, the investments consist of the infrastructure and human expertise of the exchanges and their members—will *seek* regulation whenever innovations make potential new forms of competition threatening. The legislative body usually gives a regulatory agency powers that enable the agency, allegedly in the "public interest," to require [uniform] behavior that before regulation only the "most reputable" members of the regulated industries practiced. This policy has the political advantage of appearing to retard "unethical" practices. But, in a way not nearly so apparent, the policy hampers the innovation of techniques that new entrants otherwise may have introduced. Indeed, these new techniques may have been the principal attraction of the entrants from the consumer's viewpoint.[6]

It is important to reiterate that none of the popular criticisms of soft dollars focus specifically on what is really novel about them, the formality with which they account for bundled research and the specialization of functions they engender. This report has provided both theory and evidence in favor of the hypothesis that soft-dollar brokerage has generated considerable benefits for fund beneficiaries and therefore raises a *prima facie* case that it is a legitimate form of business organization. Further evidence of the effects of soft-dollar brokerage awaits extensive empirical work. In the meantime, the presumption of legitimacy Congress intended for all bundled research when it passed Section 28(e) should gain renewed support from the benefits of soft dollar brokerage identified in this essay.

---

[6] Macey & Haddock (1985).

References and Suggested Readings

Blume, Marshal E. 1992. "Soft Dollars and the Brokerage Industry." Working paper, Rodney L. White Center for Financial Research, The Wharton School of the University of Pennsylvania, Philadelhia.

Coase, R. H. 1937. "The Nature of the Firm." *Economica* 4:386–405.

Hayek, F. A. 1945. "The Use of Knowledge in Society." *American Economic Review* 35:519.

Jarrell, Gregg A. 1984. "Change at the Exchange: The Causes and Effects of Deregulation." *Journal of Law and Economics* 27:273.

Johnsen, D. Bruce. 1992. "Property Rights to Investment Research." Working paper, the Wharton School of the University of Pennsylvania, Philadelphia.

Macey, Jonathan R., and David D. Haddock. 1985. "Shirking at the SEC: The Failure of the National Market System." *University of Illinois Law Review* 315.

INDEX